AF580935

Memphians

LIMITED EDITION

Editor, Richard Murff • *Creative Director & Publisher*, Neil White

THE NAUTILUS PUBLISHING COMPANY

Creative Director & Publisher
Neil White

Editor
Richard Murff

Associate Editor
Genie Leslie

Contributing Editors
Richard Alley
Dan Conaway
Kate Hooper
Dennis Phillippi
David Tankersley

Contributing Photographers
Maude Schuyler Clay
Michael Ochs Archive

To order bulk copies for educational or corporate use, contact:

Richard Murff, *Editor & Associate Publisher,* ***Memphians***
P.O. Box 111517, Memphis, TN 38111
Tel: 901.412.7362 • Fax: 662-234-9266 • richard@memphians.com
or
Neil White, *Creative Director & Publisher*
The Nautilus Publishing Company
P.O. Box 40, Taylor, MS 38673 • Phone: 662-513-0159
Fax: 662-234-9266 • Email: neilwhite@nautiluspublishing.com • memphians.com

PRINTED IN CHINA BY EVERBEST PRINTING THROUGH AN ARRANGEMENT WITH FOUR COLOUR PRINT GROUP, LOUISVILE, KENTUCKY

FROM THE EDITOR

Shelby Foote very nearly ran me over at the Prescott Street post office. Walking to the car with my first, dramatically un-publishable, novel in hand, I wanted to believe he was taking out a rival. But I have my doubts.

Memphis can be a maddening, infuriating place — vibrant communities generally are. It took less than a generation for Memphis to recast itself from the throne of King Cotton to the largest financial center you've never heard of. We are a distribution center for decades boasting the busiest airport in the world by freight. Memphians pioneered the self-service grocery store, the modern hotel and unisex hair salon.

But it isn't all about money; the medical center in Memphis — anchored by the best pediatric research hospital in the country — is nothing short of a miracle in progress. A Memphian brought color to artistic photography.

Memphis, literally, is music for the soul. From two small record labels downtown, bluesy guitar riffs and horn blasts blew apart cultural and racial barriers in a country badly in need of a wake-up. Rock n' roll would become the anthem for restless youth around the world. It still is. There is a reason why Memphis is mentioned in song more than any other city on the planet.

If we try, we can envision a world without the innovations in finance, logistics, medicine, music, art, and social reform that have sprung from this little bend in a big river, but what fun would that be?

What Makes a Memphian?

For the purposes of this book, a Memphian is defined as someone who was born in the city, went to school here, has made the city home, or has spent a significant portion of their life here. Significant being the key word: neither B.B. King nor John Lee Hooker lived in Memphis for very long, but it was on Beale Street their careers were launched. Danny Thomas never lived in Memphis, but St. Jude has left an indelible mark on each of us, as well as on the many families who find hope here. It wouldn't be the same city without them.

Just the Beginning

This book is about Memphians, by Memphians: the stories are penned and, where possible, the photographs taken by our hometown writers and photographers. It is a celebration of the best, the brightest and the most colorful — but this is just the tip of the iceberg. Coming editions will feature new and expanded categories. As such, we want to hear from you. You may nominate Memphians at www.memphians.com or email at info@memphians.com.

The process of putting this book together was hectic, surprising, at times infuriating, but mostly it was great fun. Just like Memphis. We are very proud of this book and hope that you will be as well.

Richard Murff, *Editor*

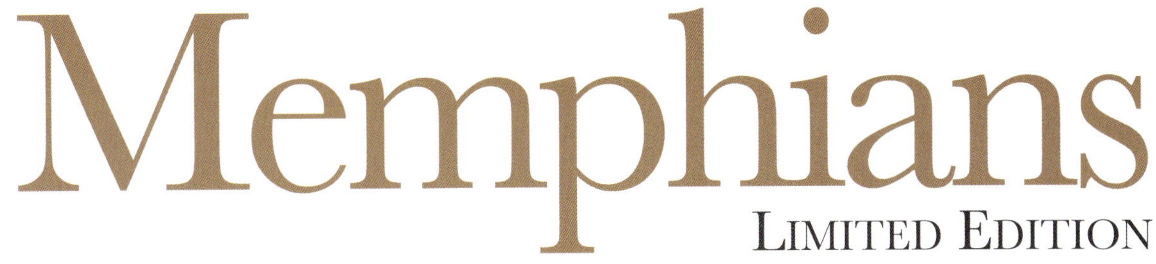
Memphians
LIMITED EDITION

Memphis Icons

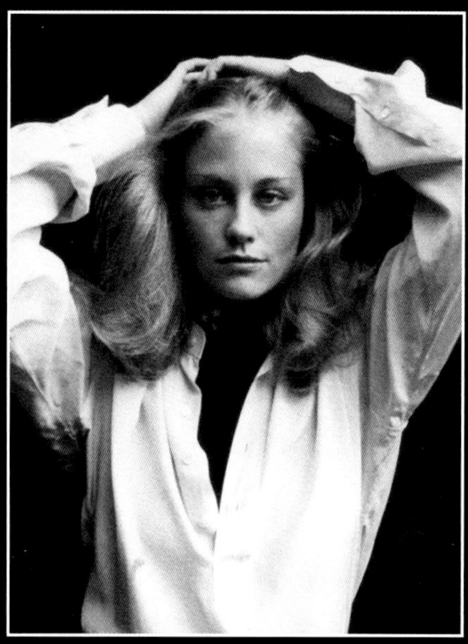

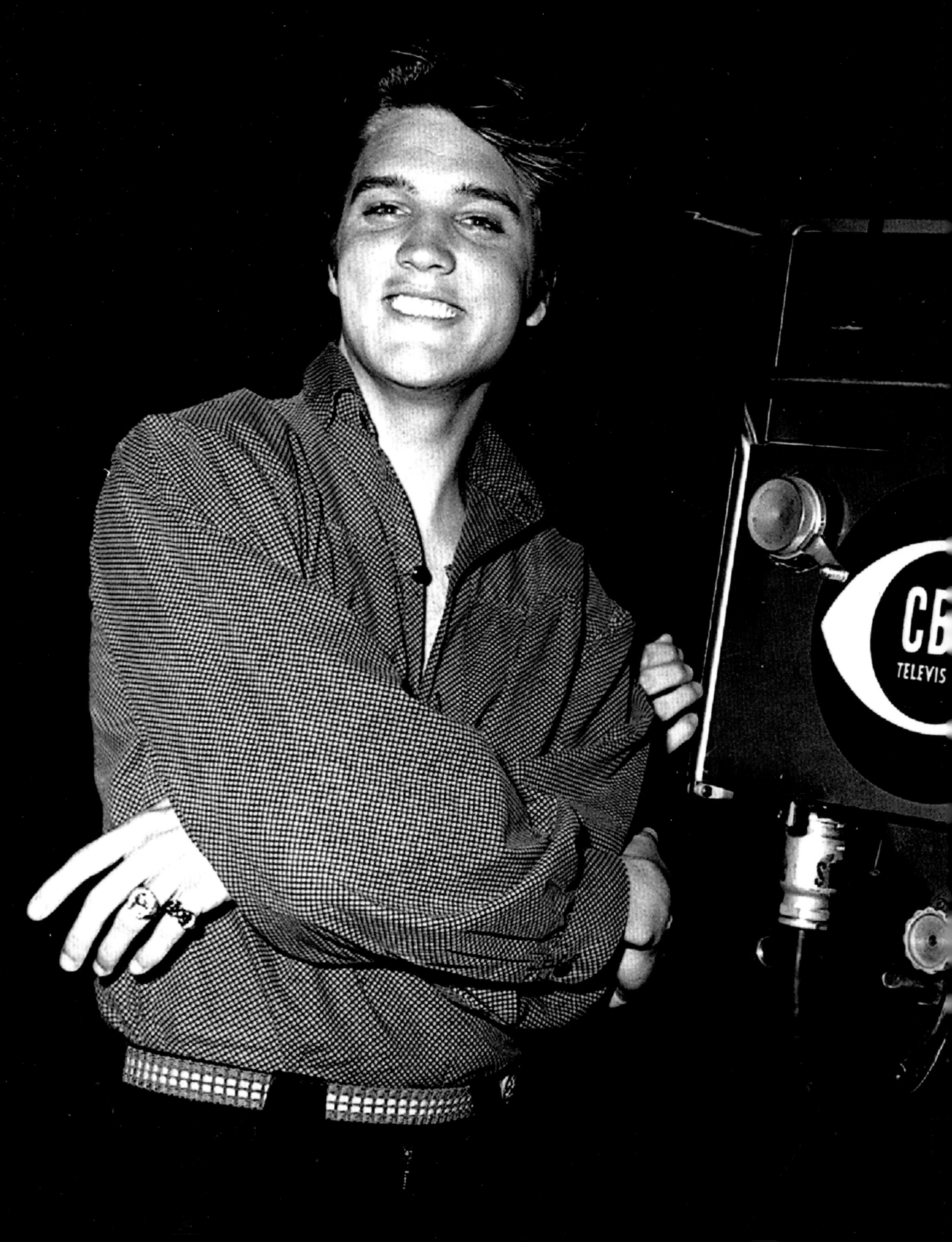
CB
TELEVIS

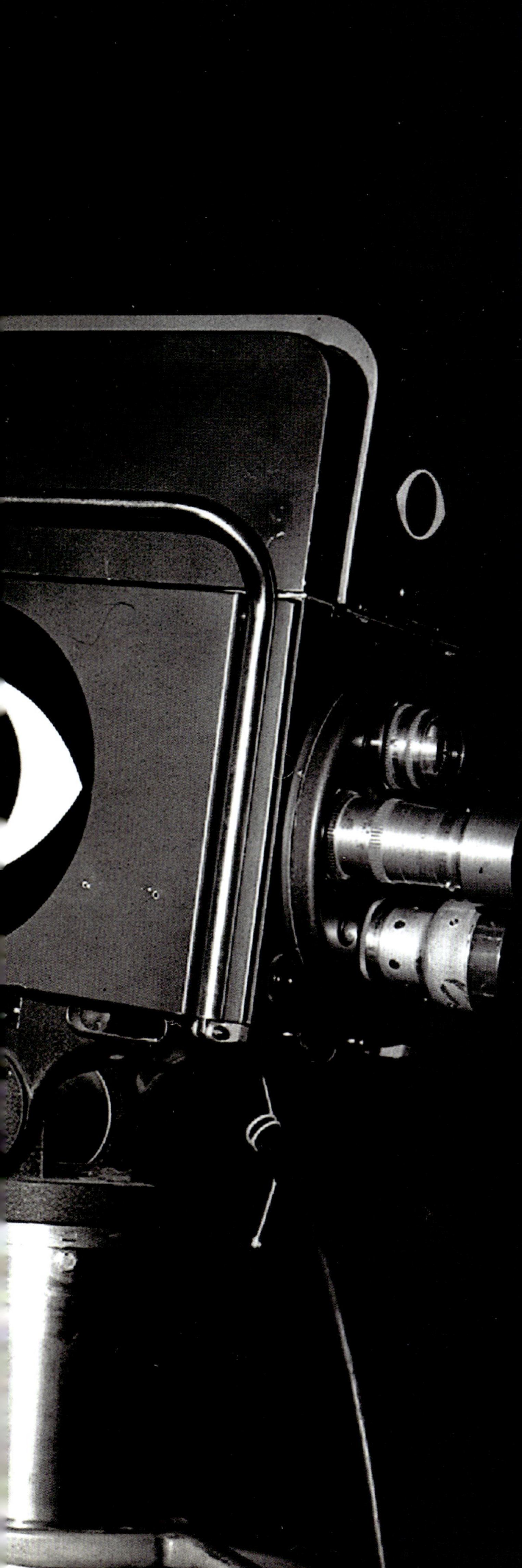

ELVIS PRESLEY

SINGER, MOVIE STAR, KING

"Rhythm is something you either have or don't have, but when you have it, you have it all over."

Elvis

Though his first radio performance as a young boy ended in stage-fright disaster, Elvis Presley managed to calm his nerves enough to audition for Sam Phillips and Sun Records. After a third audition, Phillips finally agreed to a recording session. Three days later, DJ Dewey Phillips played "That's All Right" on the air, and listeners began calling in to ask about the singer. Influenced heavily by R&B and gospel, Elvis was often mistaken for a black man. It wasn't long, though, before Elvis' face and leg-shakin' dance movements were just as famous as his voice.

Inducted into four music halls of fame, with 33 films, 14 Grammy nominations (and three wins), and countless songs and hits, Elvis "permanently changed the face of American popular culture," as Jimmy Carter said. He was a major symbol for the changing times in the 50s and 60s.

Photograph courtesy CBS Archive • **Story** by Genie Leslie

EDWARD H. CRUMP

POLITICIAN, BOSS, ICON

"The man in charge of . . . well . . . everything."
Dan Conaway

From the flaming red hair of his youth he brought to Memphis from Holly Springs in 1892 to the flowing white mane he sported at the pinnacle of his power, not much that mattered much happened in these parts that E.H. "Boss" Crump wasn't responsible for one way or the other, directly or indirectly. For the first half of the 20th century, one political machine with one man firmly at the controls ran Memphis. Not only did Mr. Crump decide who got elected, appointed, fired and indicted around Memphis, he pretty much did that for the whole state of Tennessee, and wielded considerable influence in the national Democratic Party. Memphis Mayor for six years and Congressman for four, he was the power behind everything for almost 50. He seemed to think of himself as a benevolent uncle, rewarding nieces and nephews for good behavior and punishing them for bad. The rules were his determination. His statewide power began to wane in the late forties with opponent victories, rare indeed, in both the governor and U.S. Senate races in 1948, and again in the senate race of 1952. He died in 1954. He even had a hand in inventing the blues. W.C. Handy wrote a campaign tune for Crump's first mayoral run in 1909 called "Mr. Crump," and later rewrote it and changed the name to "Memphis Blues."

Photography Time/Life Archive • **Story** by Dan Conaway

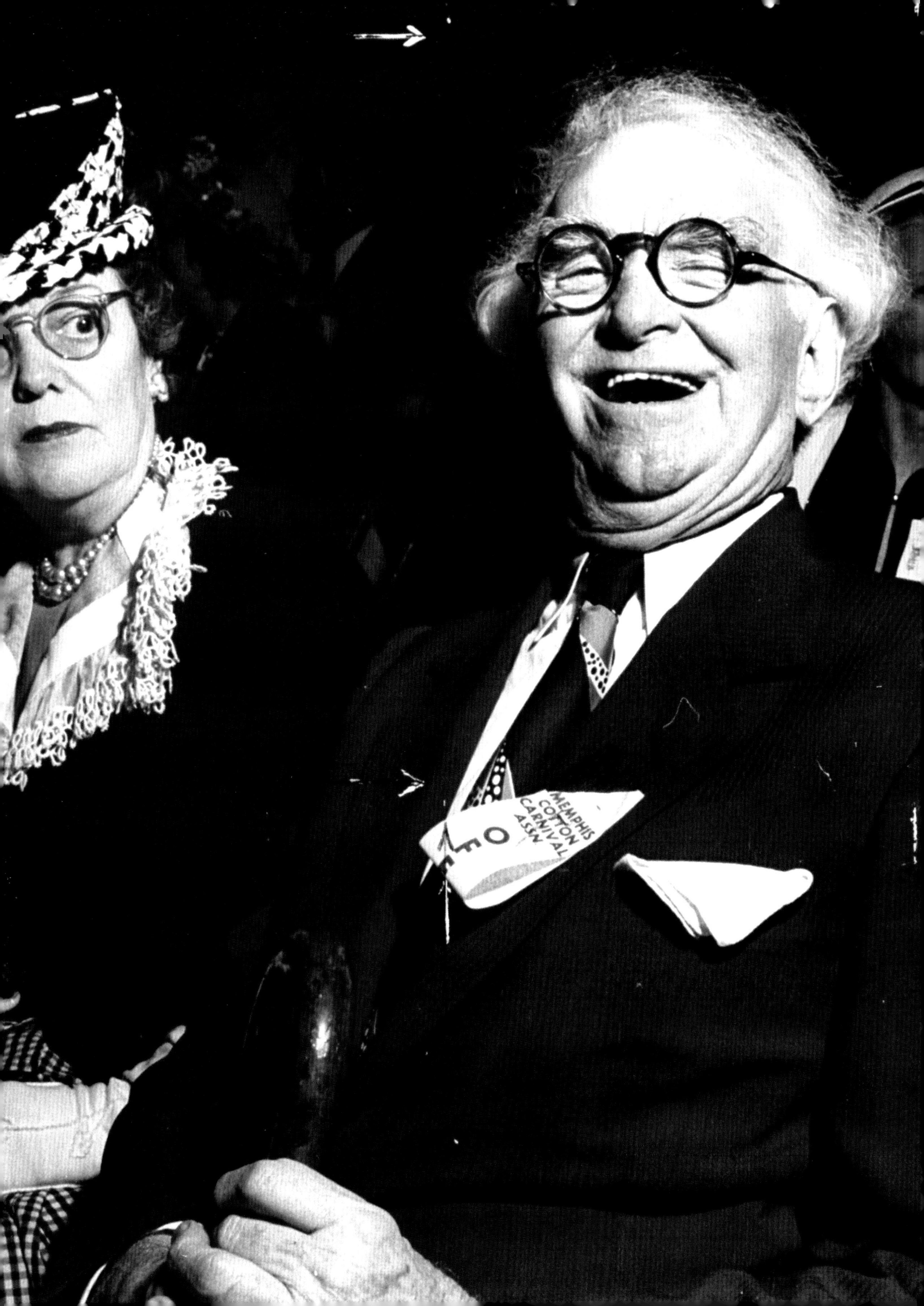
MEMPHIS
COTTON
CARNIVAL
ASS'N

DANNY THOMAS

ACTOR, PHILANTHROPIST

"Success has nothing to do with what you gain in life or accomplish for yourself. It's what you do for others."
Danny Thomas

It wasn't so much a promise as it was a Hail Mary, in the most literal sense. A desperate young comedian with a wife and a baby on the way, kneeling before a statue of St. Jude Thaddeus – the patron saint of hopeless causes. He promised to build a shrine in return for guidance. He was Amos Alphonsus Muzyad Yakhood, the son of Lebanese immigrants, and he took the names of his two brothers, Danny and Thomas, as his stage name. He was the star of *Make Room For Daddy*, one of the most popular sitcoms of all time, and his production company would create such iconic hits as *The Dick Van Dyke Show*, *The Andy Griffith Show* and *The Mod Squad*.

He never forgot his promise. With his friends in show business, Thomas raised the money to build St. Jude's Children's Research Hospital and established American Lebanese Syrian Associated Charities through a network of Arab-American businessmen to fund its daily operations. At the urging of spiritual mentor, Cardinal Samuel Stritch, Thomas located the shrine in Memphis. It opened in 1962.

St. Jude never turns away patients for an inability to pay. Donations come in from across the world – the average is only about $30 – but those donations cover the roughly $2.2 million in operating costs per day not covered by insurance.

He would be awarded a Papal Knighthood and the Congressional Gold Medal, but it is the shrine he built, not the awards he received, for which he is remembered. Danny Thomas was a part of a miracle — and it wasn't in show business.

Photography Hulton Archive/Handout • **Story** by Richard Murff

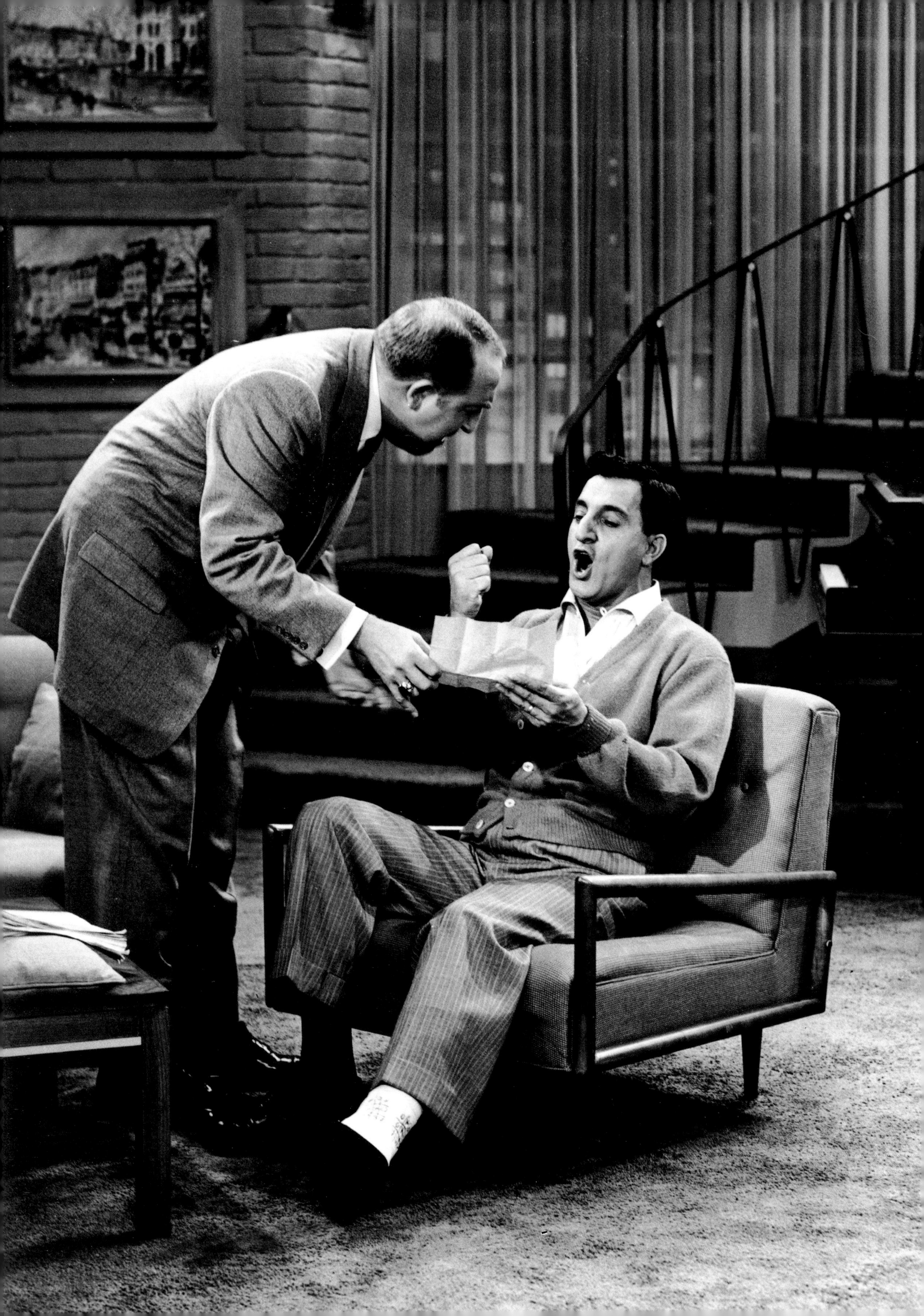

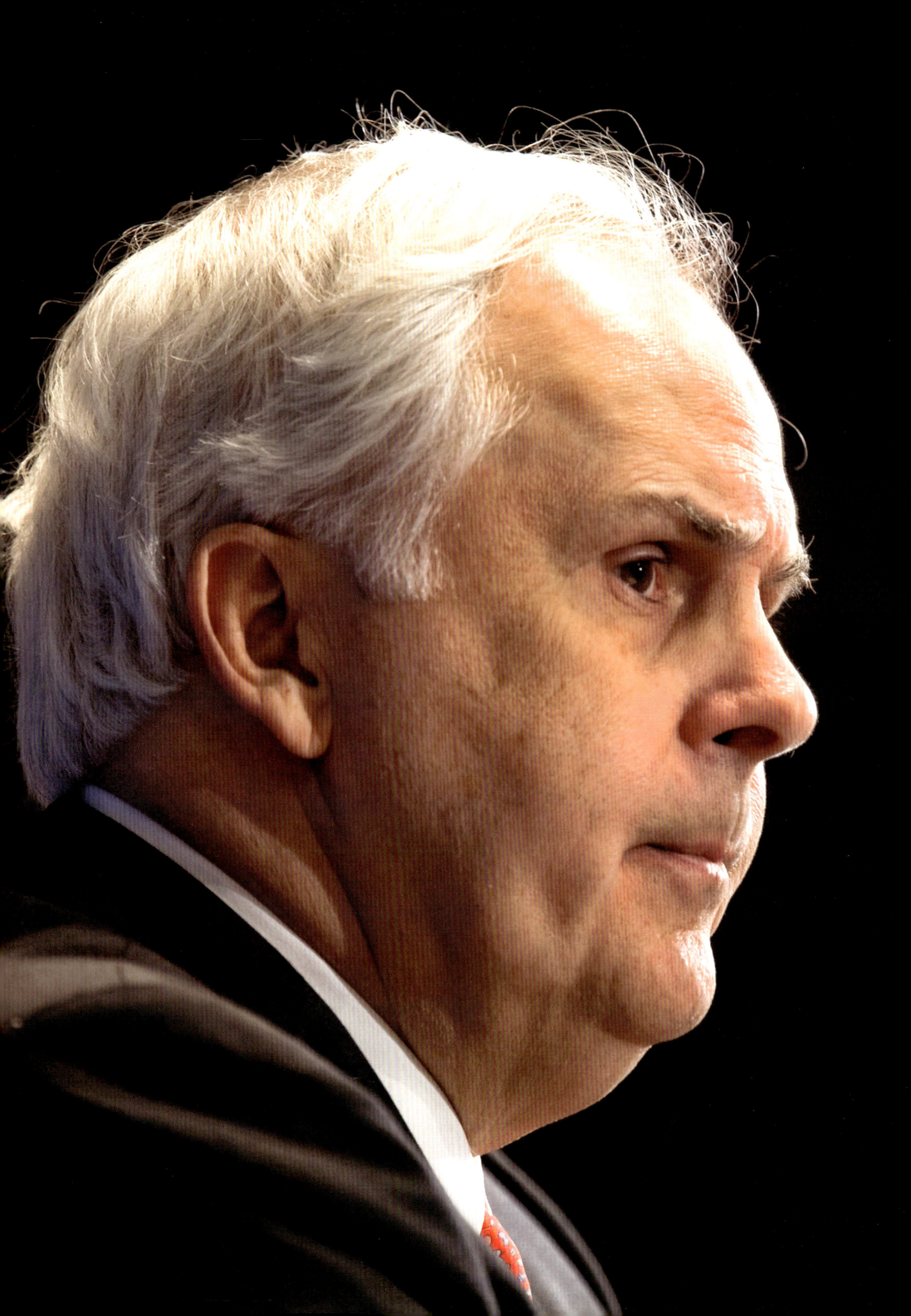

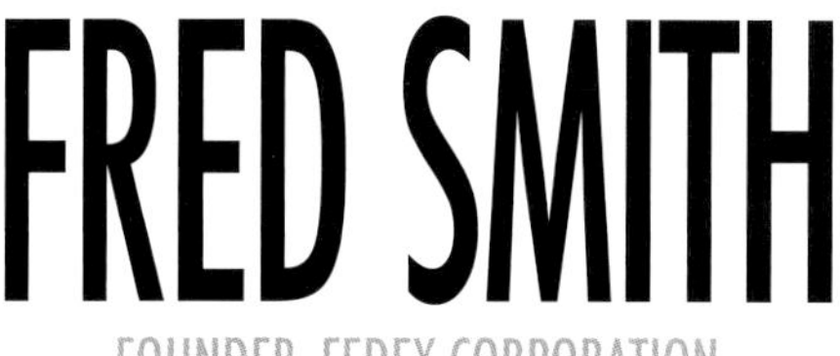

FRED SMITH

FOUNDER, FEDEX CORPORATION

"The concept is interesting and well-formed, but in order to earn better than a 'C', the idea must be feasible."

Yale University Management Professor

It is impossible to calculate the impact Fred Smith has had on Memphis. Smith, the son of another entrepreneur who founded the Toddle House restaurant chain and for a time had controlling interest in Dixie Greyhound Lines, nurtured the idea of an overnight delivery company from his early days in college. In fact, Smith wrote a paper while at Yale outlining his concept — for which he received a C because the idea was impractical.

Smith served in Vietnam with the Marines to great distinction, serving on over 200 combat missions, and earning the Silver Star, the Bronze Star, and two Purple Hearts. During his service with the Marines he observed the logistics involved in moving so much material efficiently, and further honed his concept for what would be come FedEx. In 1970, after being honorably discharged from the Marines, Smith took his $4 million inheritance, raised another $91 million in venture capital, and founded Federal Express.

In 1973 the company was offering service to 25 cities. It was the first company of its kind, and is the largest of its kind in the world. Economically, the impact of FedEx on Memphis is arguably the single most important of any business in the city's history. Employing more than 30,000 people the company is far and away the largest employer in the city. FedEx has been crucial to the city's economic stability and growth.

Smith's various investments include part ownership of both the Washington Redskins and Joe Gibb's NASCAR racing team. Having known George W. Bush at Yale, Smith was twice offered the position of Secretary of Defense in the Bush administration, declining each time.

Photography by Bloomberg • **Story** by Dennis Phillippi

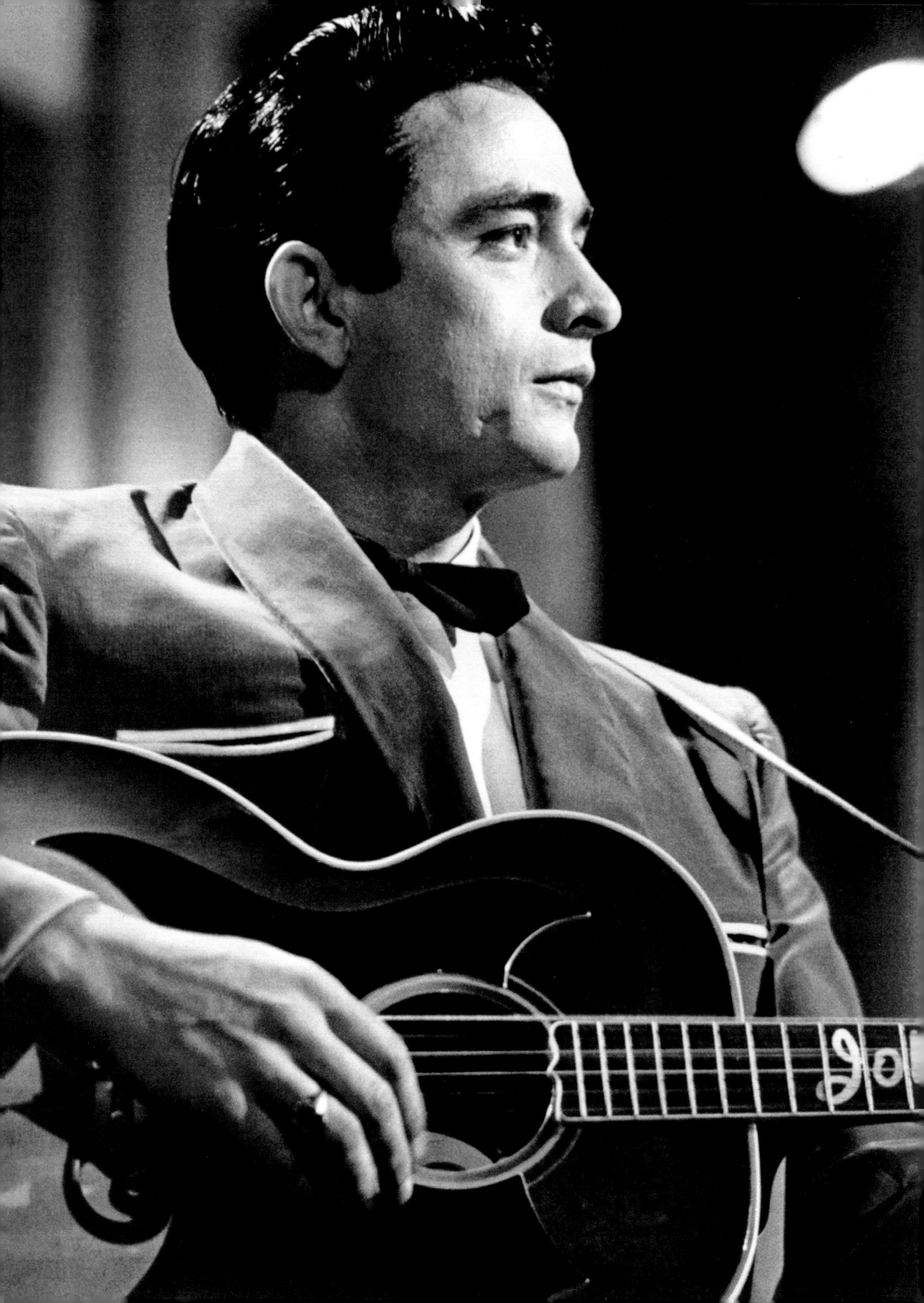

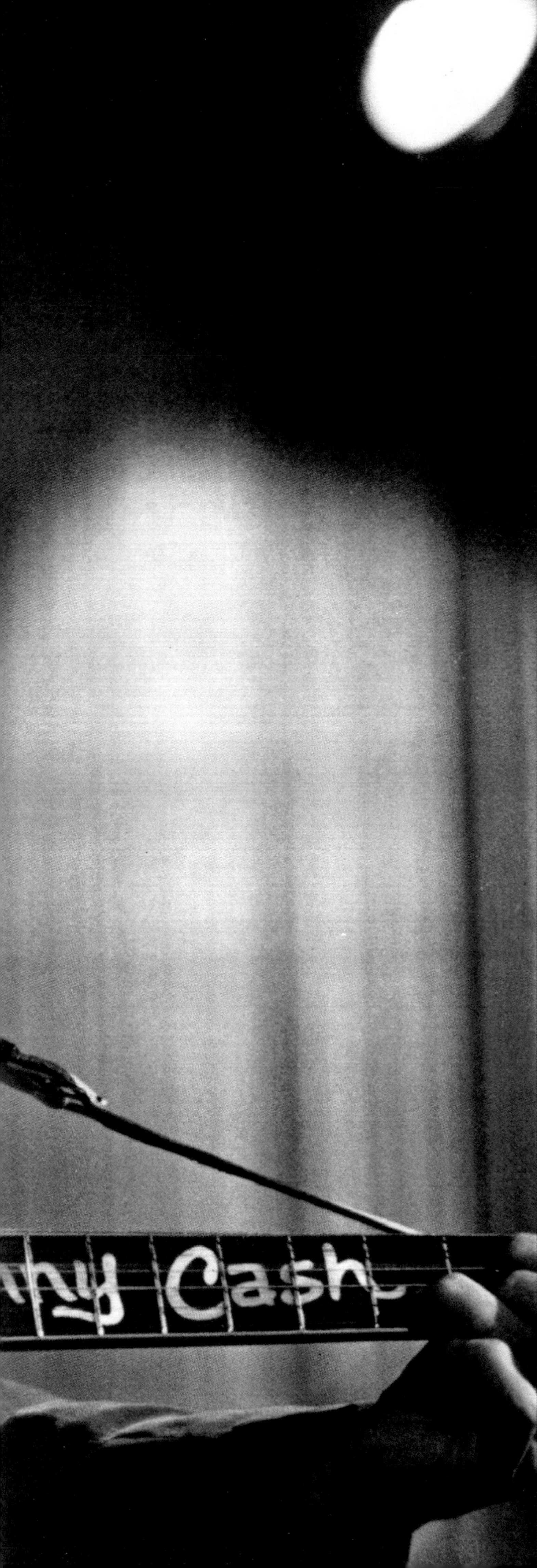

JOHNNY CASH

SINGER, SONGWRITER, ICON

"I wore black because I liked it."
Johnny Cash

Forever known as "The Man in Black," Johnny Cash will be remembered, not only for his dark fashion choices, but also for his driving, steady musical sound, his tough persona, and his standard introduction: "Hello, I'm Johnny Cash." Experiencing music first through gospel church music and singing with his family while working in the cotton fields, Cash began playing with Luther Perkins and Marshall Grant (later known as the Tennessee Two).

When Cash and the Tennessee Two auditioned for Sam Phillips, they were told that gospel music was not marketable. Cash responded by playing "Cry! Cry! Cry!" He won over Phillips, and began recording with Sun Records.

Johnny Cash's music was loved all over the country and his songs ended up on both country and pop music charts. He was inducted into both the Country Music Hall of Fame and the Rock and Roll Hall of Fame. His music continues to be popular, and "The Man in Black" lives on, especially in the Navy: Sailors often refer to their winter uniforms (which have solid black shirts, ties, and trousers) as 'Johnny Cashes.'

Photograph Michael Ochs Archives • **Story** by Genie Leslie

CYBILL SHEPHERD

ACTOR

"I never wanted to be Jane. I always wanted to be Tarzan."
Cybill Sheperd

Proof that Cybill Shepherd is more than just a Memphian in name is the fact that in 1978, when she was miserable about the direction of her Hollywood career and recent box office failures, Shepherd fled the West Coast, returning to Memphis and leaving show business behind for four years, during which she married a Memphian and had her first child. Shepherd had early success in Memphis, winning "Miss Teenage Memphis" at 16, and a 1968 "Model of the Year" contest, which led to modeling work throughout high school and beyond. Director Peter Bogdonovich spotted her on the cover of a magazine and cast her as Jacy in his film *The Last Picture Show*. The film was well received but Shepherd was somewhat traumatized by her semi-nude appearance in the film, which earned her a kind of notoriety she had not anticipated. Praised for her performance in *Taxi Driver*, she was also in a number of unsuccessful films, several of which were directed by Bogdonovich, her boyfriend.

After her hiatus, Shepherd returned to Hollywood to star in the television series *The Yellow Rose* with Sam Elliott. Then she was cast as former model turned private detective Maddie Hayes on *Moonlighting*. Her electric chemistry with then unknown costar Bruce Willis became her most famous role, earning her two Golden Globes, an Emmy, and a reputation as being occasionally difficult, mostly due to the mercurial relationship with Willis. Her star had risen anew, and she had roles in *Chances Are* with Robert Downey Jr., *Texasville*, the sequel to *The Last Picture Show*, and went on to star in her own sitcom, *Cybill* — for which she also won Emmys and Golden Globes. She has been seen most recently on *The L Word*.

Photograph by Getty Archive/Jack Robinson • **Story** by Dennis Phillippi

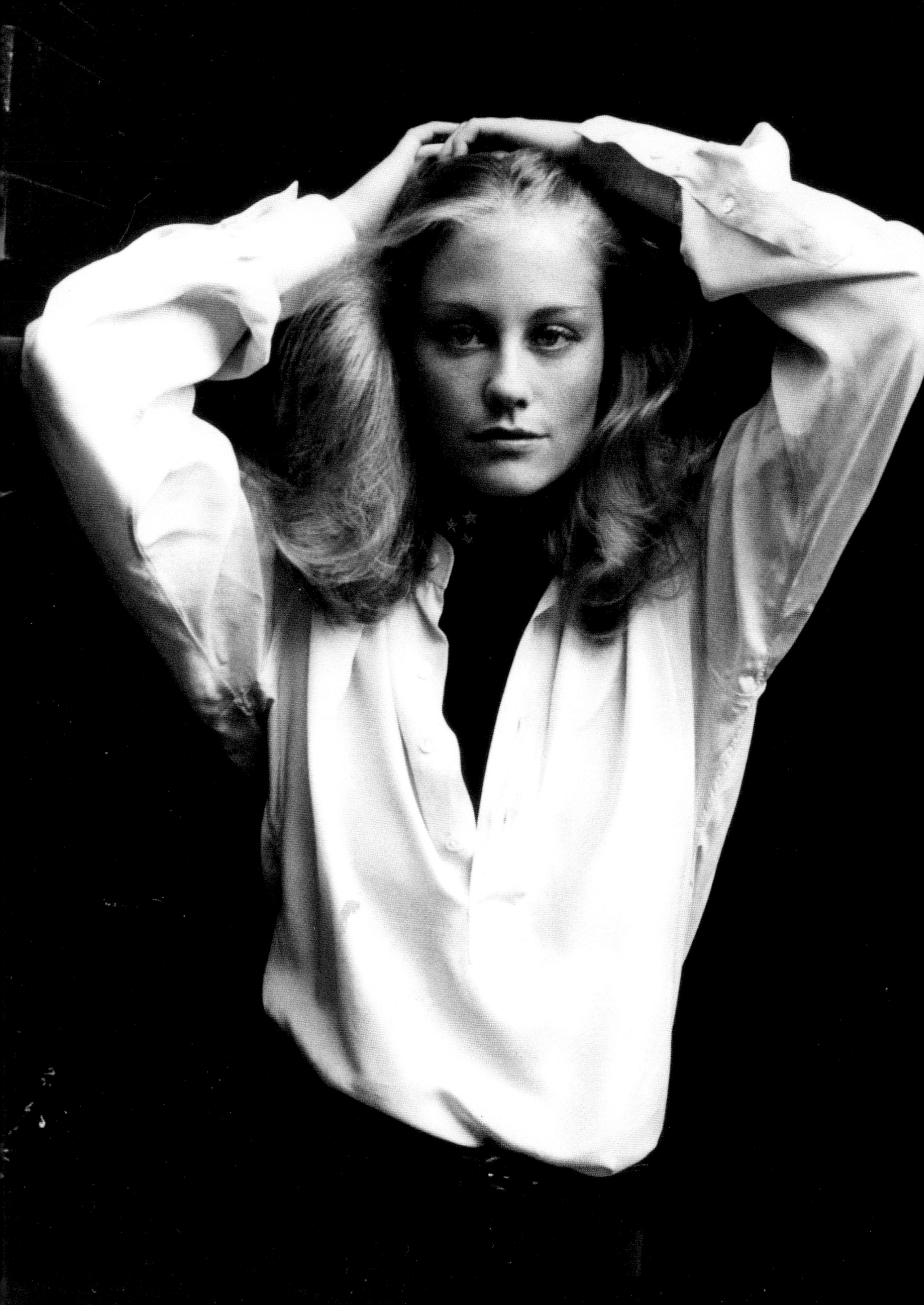

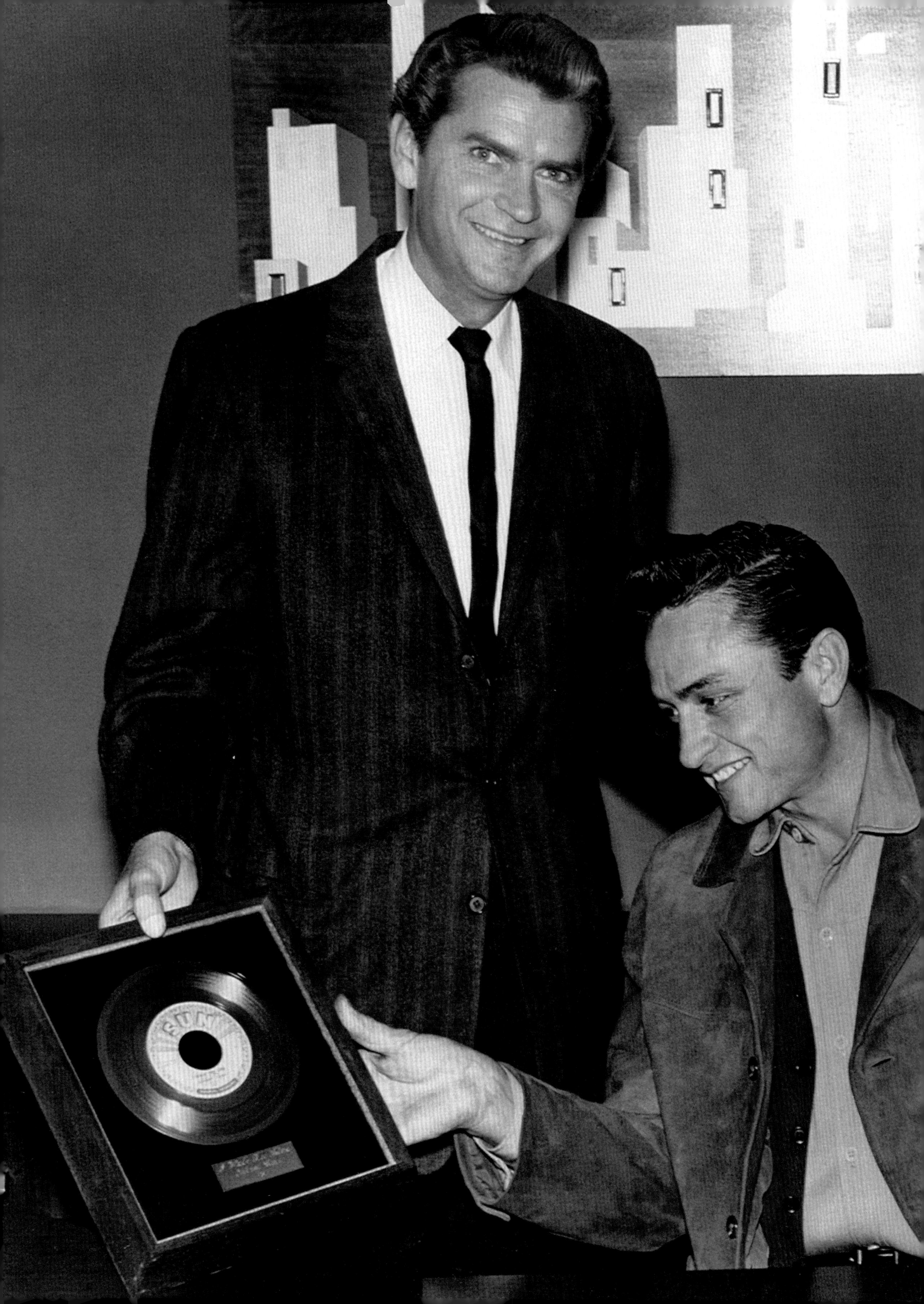
SUN

SAM PHILLIPS

MUSIC VISIONARY

"The blues, it got people – black and white – to think about life, how difficult, yet also how good it can be."

Sam Phillips

Sam Phillips didn't want to discover Elvis or Johnny Cash or Howlin' Wolf, or rock n' roll for that matter. He didn't want to make Carl Perkins, B. B. King, Jerry Lee Lewis, Charlie Rich and Roy Orbison famous. He never intended to unleash a sound on a restless America that would create a new art form, shatter race barriers, be the conduit of rebellious youth the world over for generations to come. He wanted to be a lawyer – but some prayers weren't meant to be answered.

Lacking the money for law school Phillips got a job as a DJ in Muscle Shoals, Alabama. The station's "open format" – playing both white and black music – would inspire his Memphis Recording Service and his own label, Sun Records. It was in Memphis that he recorded what many believe to be the first rock n' roll record: "Rocket 88" by Jackie Brenston and his Delta Cats, a band fronted by Ike Turner.

Phillips famously sold Elvis's contract for $35,000 — which gave him the ability to launch Carl Perkins' career on a national scale and invest in a local hotel chain started by fellow Memphian Kemmons Wilson. He has been portrayed in countless films and television series. He died in Memphis, the day before his original Sun Studio was declared a National Historic Landmark.

Photograph: Sam Phillips with Johnny Cash/Getty Archive • **Story** by Richard Murff

MORGAN FREEMAN

ACTOR, NARRATOR, ACTIVIST

"Acting means living, it's all I do and all I'm good at."

Morgan Freeman

We all know his voice. We know his face as that of a chauffeur, a prisoner, the U.S. President, and God. We know his critically acclaimed — and commercially successful — body of work.

But Morgan Freeman is much more than the familiar face and voice. He's an activist trying to raise awareness about the environment, as well as racial issues. He's also a businessman. He co-owns a blues club, Ground Zero, which opened in Memphis in 2008.

Before all that, before the films and the clubs, Morgan Freeman was just a Memphis-born 12-year-old who won a state drama competition. He was an Air Force mechanic, and he was a clerk typist. Getting his acting start on a children's show, *The Electric Company*, he worked his way into other shows and films, eventually becoming an Oscar winner and one of the most highly sought after actors in Hollywood.

Photograph by Getty Images/Munawar Hosain

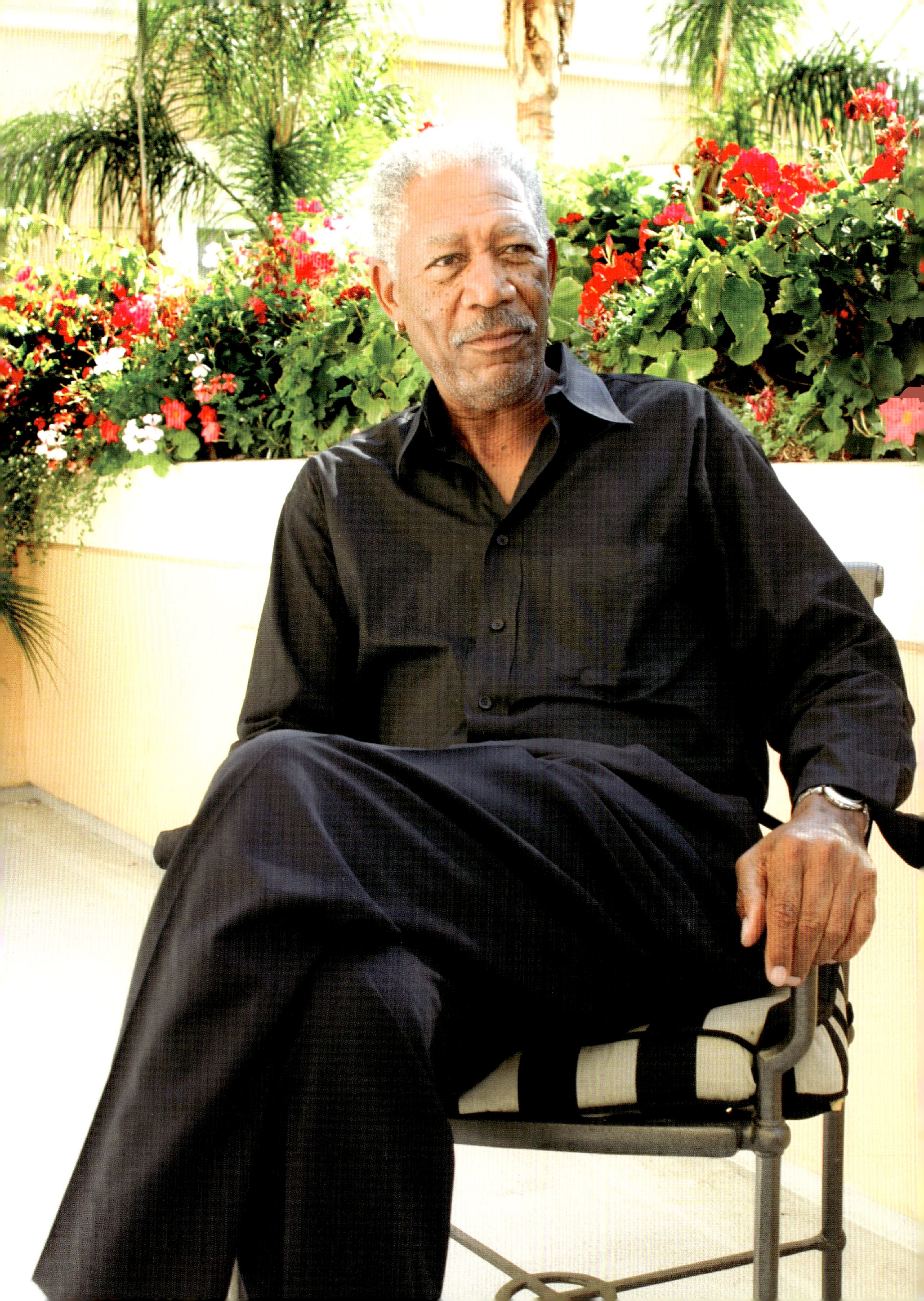

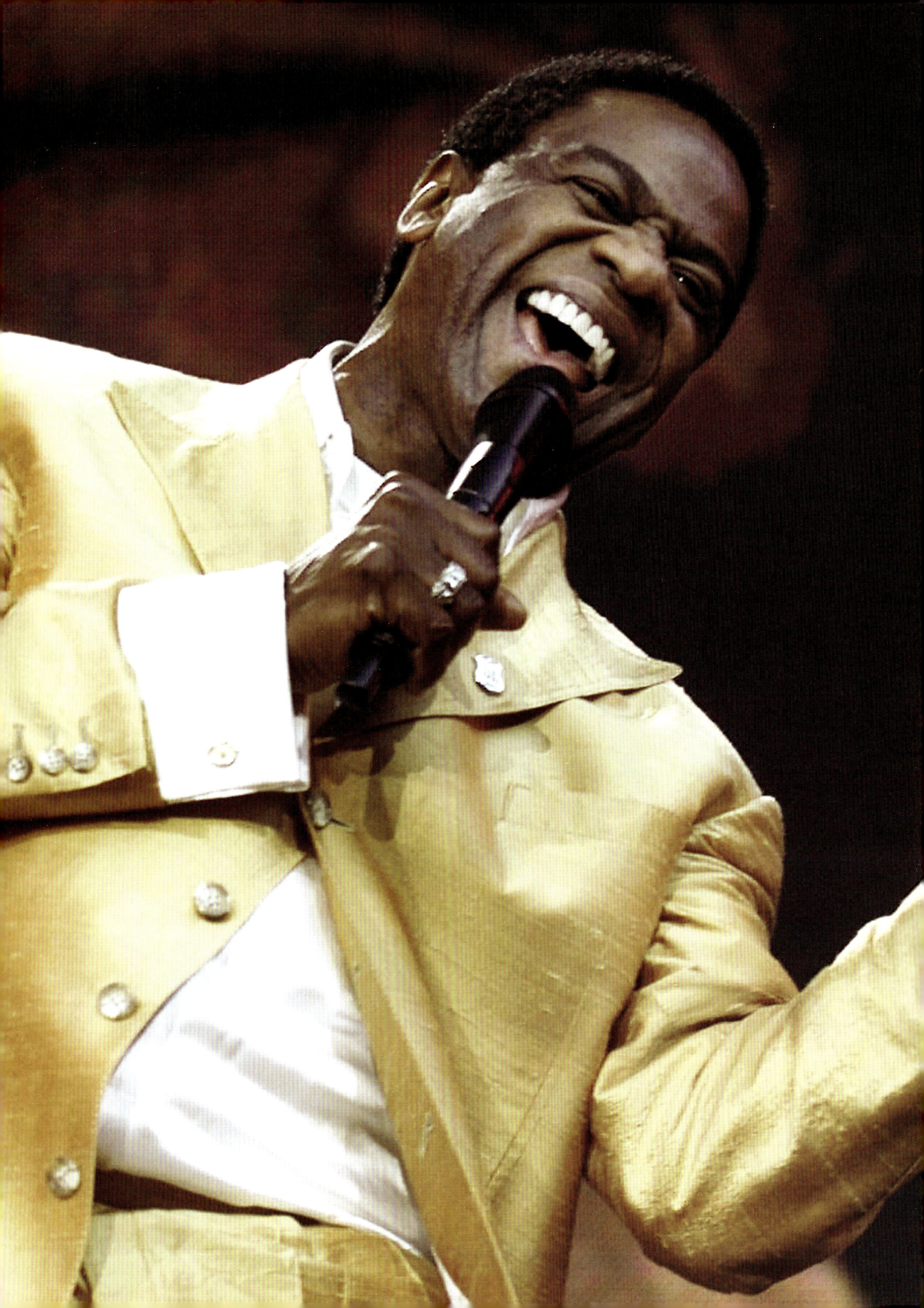

AL GREEN

SINGER, MINISTER

"To me, the ultimate is to be of some value, some use to someone else. I like people who are able to serve the people, bearing a positive message."

Rev. Al Green

Albert Greene began performing at age ten with a quartet called The Greene Brothers. They toured in the 50s but Al's dad kicked Al out of the group for listening to Jackie Wilson. When he began a solo career he dropped the final "e" in his name. In 1969 Al came into contact with Willie Mitchell, of Memphis, and Mitchell signed him to his Hi Records. His second album with Green produced "Tired of Being Alone," the first of Al Green's seven straight gold records. Willie Mitchell, who died January 5, 2010, aged 81, produced dozens of classic soul music records, and created the so-called Memphis Sound, while launching the career of Al Green. In 1974 a girlfriend of Green's scalded him with boiling grits and then committed suicide. Green credits this tragic episode with an astonishing change in his life. In 1976 Green was ordained as a Pastor in the Full Gospel Tabernacle church. He spent many years recording only gospel music but returned to R&B in 1988. In 2000, Green published a memoir, *Take Me to the River*, and in 2002 he received a Grammy Lifetime Achievement Award. To this day, Reverend Al Green still serves as the pastor of his church, holding services just down the street from Graceland.

Photograph by AFP/Getty Images/Paul J. Richards

SHELBY FOOTE

WRITER, HISTORIAN

"It's the damndest book I have ever read and one of the best. Twice the book that *The Red Badge of Courage* is."
William Faulkner on Shiloh

Long before documentary filmmaker Ken Burns sat author Shelby Foote down in front of the camera as the guru of his *The Civil War*, Foote sat down to put pen, nib and ink to paper and write of a single battle in that war told from several points of view. The ensuing novel was called *Shiloh*, and the writing of it would cast Foote as a novelist long before the world knew him as a historian.

Foote was born in Greenville, MS, in 1916 and briefly attended the University of North Carolina at Chapel Hill, where he contributed to the literary magazine *Carolina*. His career began at the Associated Press in New York. After moving back to Greenville, he wrote four novels in as many years: *Tournament* (1949), *Follow Me Down* (1950), *Love in a Dry Season* (1951) and *Shiloh* (1952).

Foote moved to Memphis in 1952. "The capital of the Mississippi Delta" is where he would write every word of his masterpiece, *The Civil War: A Narrative*. He also set his 1977 novel *September September* on Beale Street and the banks of the river in his adopted hometown.

When Foote wanted to meet his idol, William Faulkner, the story goes, he simply drove with his best friend, Walker Percy, over to the Southern icon's house in Oxford and knocked.

It was with this same straight-ahead bulldoggedness that Foote would approach his craft as well, whether sitting down with a plan in mind to write a 100,000-word novel or a 1.5 million-word narrative history of the Civil War.

Foote died in 2005, leaving behind his wife Gwyn and their son, Huger. He is interred in historic Elmwood Cemetery beside the family plot of General Nathan Bedford Forrest. His collection of more than 2,500 pieces of handwritten manuscripts, first edition books of his, as well as those of Faulkner, Eudora Welty and Percy, hand-drawn maps, copious notes and collections was acquired by Rhodes College in 2011.

Photograph by Washington Post/Getty Images
Story by Richard Alley

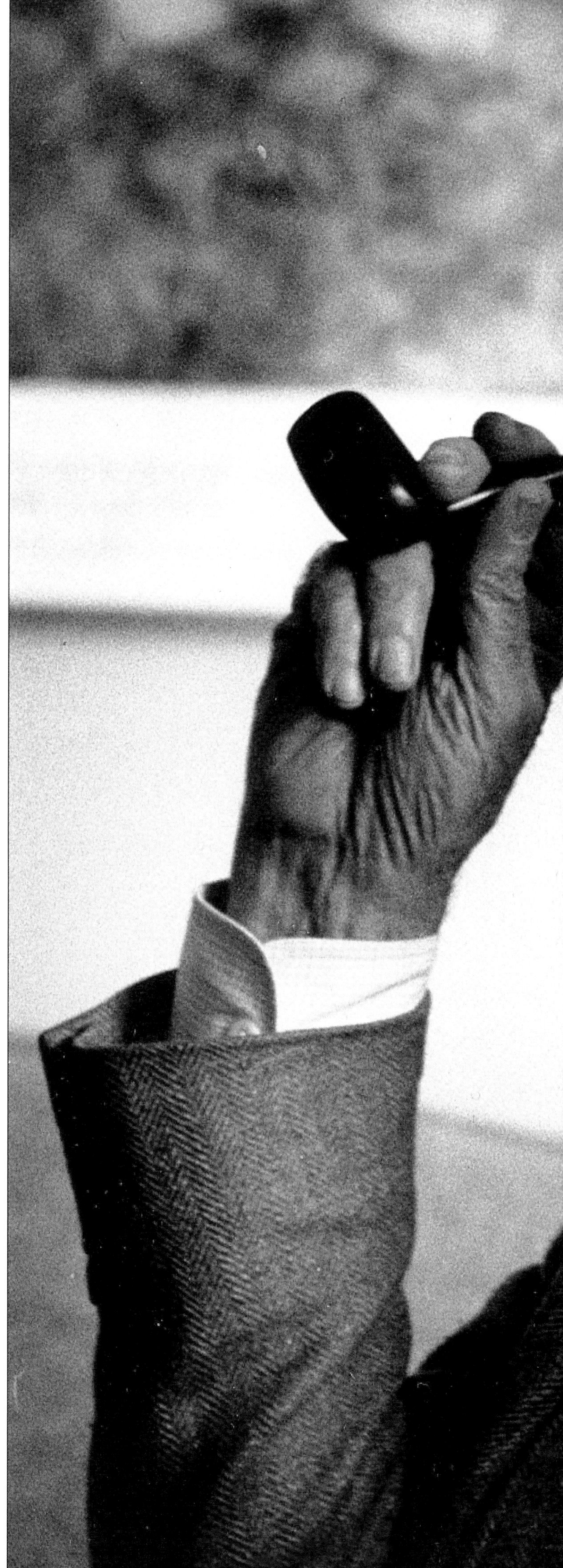

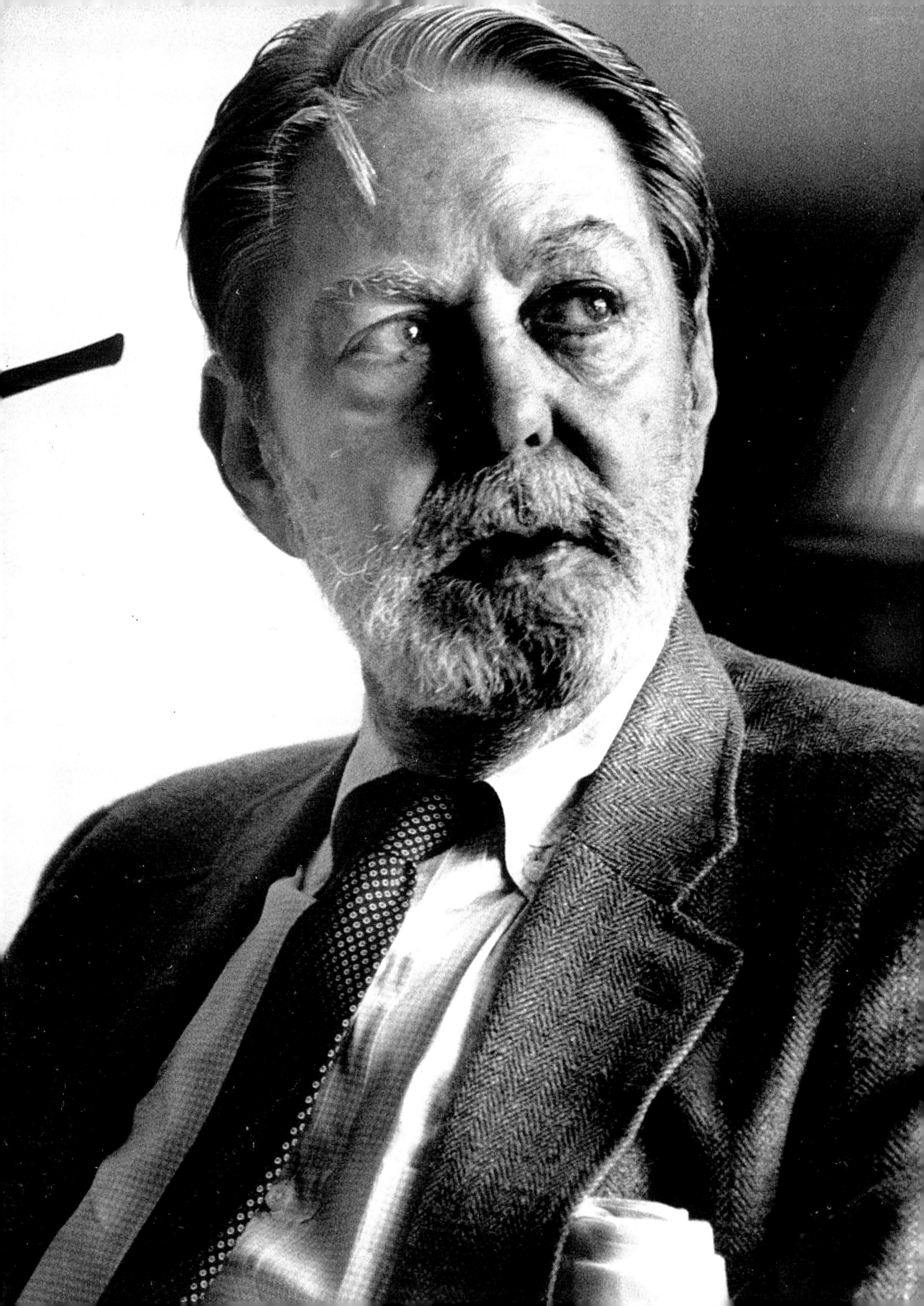

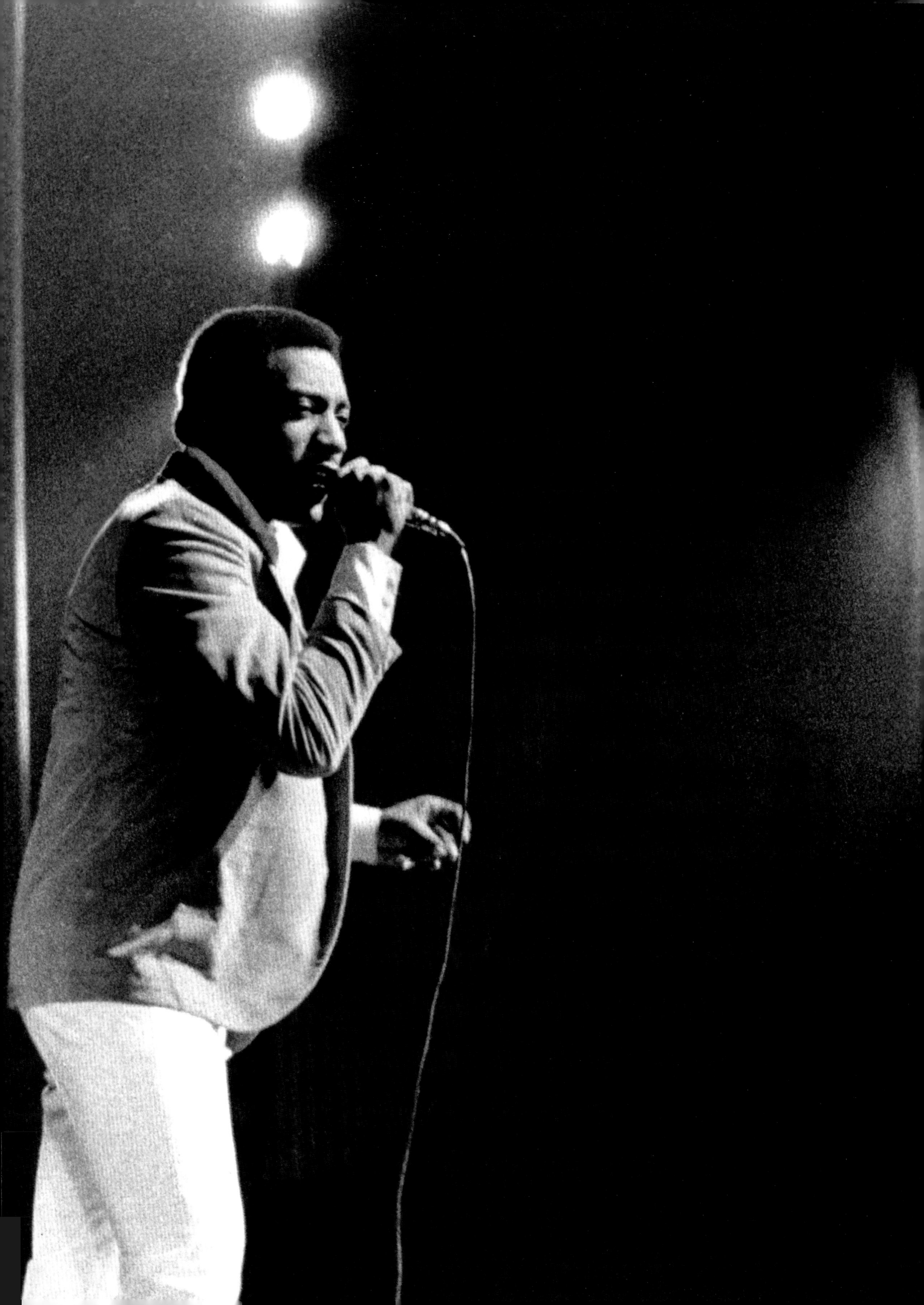

OTIS REDDING

SINGER, SONGWRITER

"I've got a sweeter song than the birds in the trees."
Otis Redding

The whistling at the end of his song "(Sittin' On) The Dock of the Bay" has become famous, but it was originally intended as a filler until Otis Redding could write and record a final verse. Unfortunately, a plane crash ended his life before he could ever return to the studio. In the short span of about seven years, he made a huge impression on the music world. Many of his hit songs are still popular today, such as "These Arms of Mine" and "Try A Little Tenderness." Recording with Stax Records, Redding toured with Sam & Dave and played with the Bar-Kays. Even with a career (and life) that was far too short, Redding is known as the "King of Soul," and one of the best singers in history.

Photograph by Getty Entertainment • **Story** by Genie Leslie

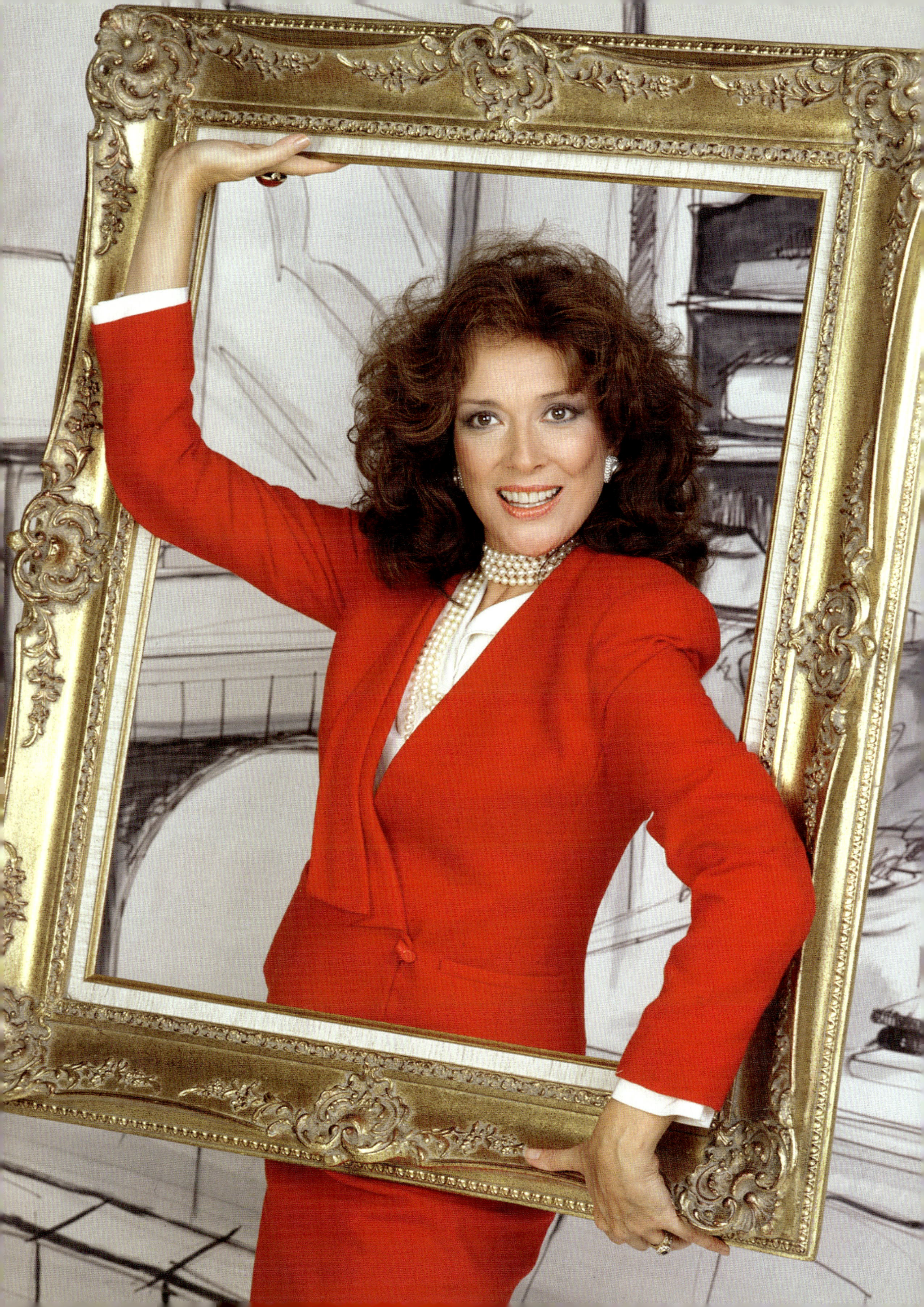

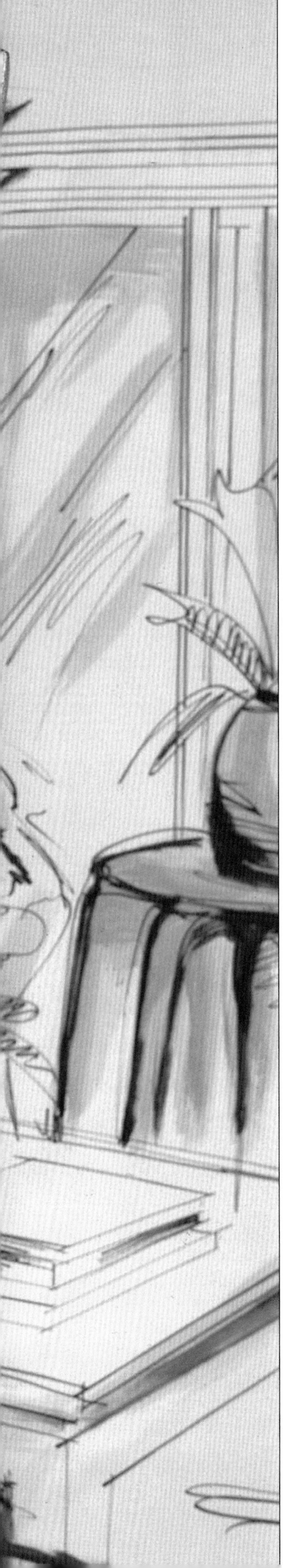

DIXIE CARTER

ACTOR

"The plane never touches down in Memphis that I don't say, spontaneously, I'm home again, so that's how I feel, I'm home again."

Dixie Carter

Valedictorian of her high school graduating class, Dixie Carter could have done anything she put her mind to, and she put her mind to performing. As a young child, she wanted to perform as an opera singer; however, effects from a tonsillectomy kept her from pursuing that dream. Even so, she kept singing and studying music, learning to play the piano, trumpet and harmonica. Carter attended Southwestern at Memphis and graduated from Memphis State.

Her debut on the stage was a Memphis production of *Carousel*, in which she played Julie. She moved to New York and worked in many plays, musicals, and TV shows. Her most popular role, however, was as interior decorator Julia Sugarbaker on *Designing Women*. Since the opinionated character's political views were so different from Carter's own, she made a deal with the producers: for every speech she gave with which she disagreed, Julia Sugarbaker would get to sing a song in a future episode.

In 1996 she published her memoir, *Trying to Get to Heaven: Opinions of a Tennessee Talker*. She saw renewed popularity in 2007 when she played the recurring character of Gloria Hodge on the popular show *Desperate Housewives*; her performance earned her an Emmy nomination. In the summer of 2008, she and long-time husband Hal Holbrook filmed *The Evening Sun in East Tennessee*; it was to be her final film. Her legacy lives on in Tennessee with the Dixie Carter Performing Arts Center (often referred to as "The Dixie") in the town of Huntingdon.

Photograph CBS Photo Archive • **Story** by Genie Leslie

KATHY BATES

ACTOR

"The Oscar changed everything. Better salary, working with better people, better projects, more exposure, less privacy."

Kathy Bates

Kathy Bates has been nominated for — and often received — every award offered to actors. Born in Memphis in 1948, Bates graduated from White Station High School before attending SMU, studying, not surprisingly, acting. After moving to New York, she began her acclaimed theater career, getting nominations for several Tonys. By the seventies, she was respected within the industry but didn't become part of the national consciousness until her menacing turn as the demented "fan" Annie Wilkes in *Misery*. As Wilkes, Bates turned in a performance of such chilling psychosis that she received not only her first Academy Award nomination, but also her first win. Annie Wilkes remains one of the screen's most unforgettable lunatics.

Her other remarkable portrayal of an unhinged madwoman was as Jay Leno's manager Helen Kushnik in the television movie *Late Shift* about the Late Night War between Leno and David Letterman. Bates has since been nominated twice more, for *Primary Colors* and *About Schmidt*, which featured another memorable turn by Bates, this time in the nude. She portrayed the unsinkable Molly Brown in *Titanic*. She has been nominated for Emmys eight times, for work in television movies, miniseries, and even sitcoms.

Bates is a private person, despite her life as a public figure, and only revealed her battle with ovarian cancer after having been in full remission for over five years.

Photograph: Kathy Bates with Rob Reiner at the Academy Awards. Time Life Pictures/Getty Images • **Story** by Dennis Phillippi

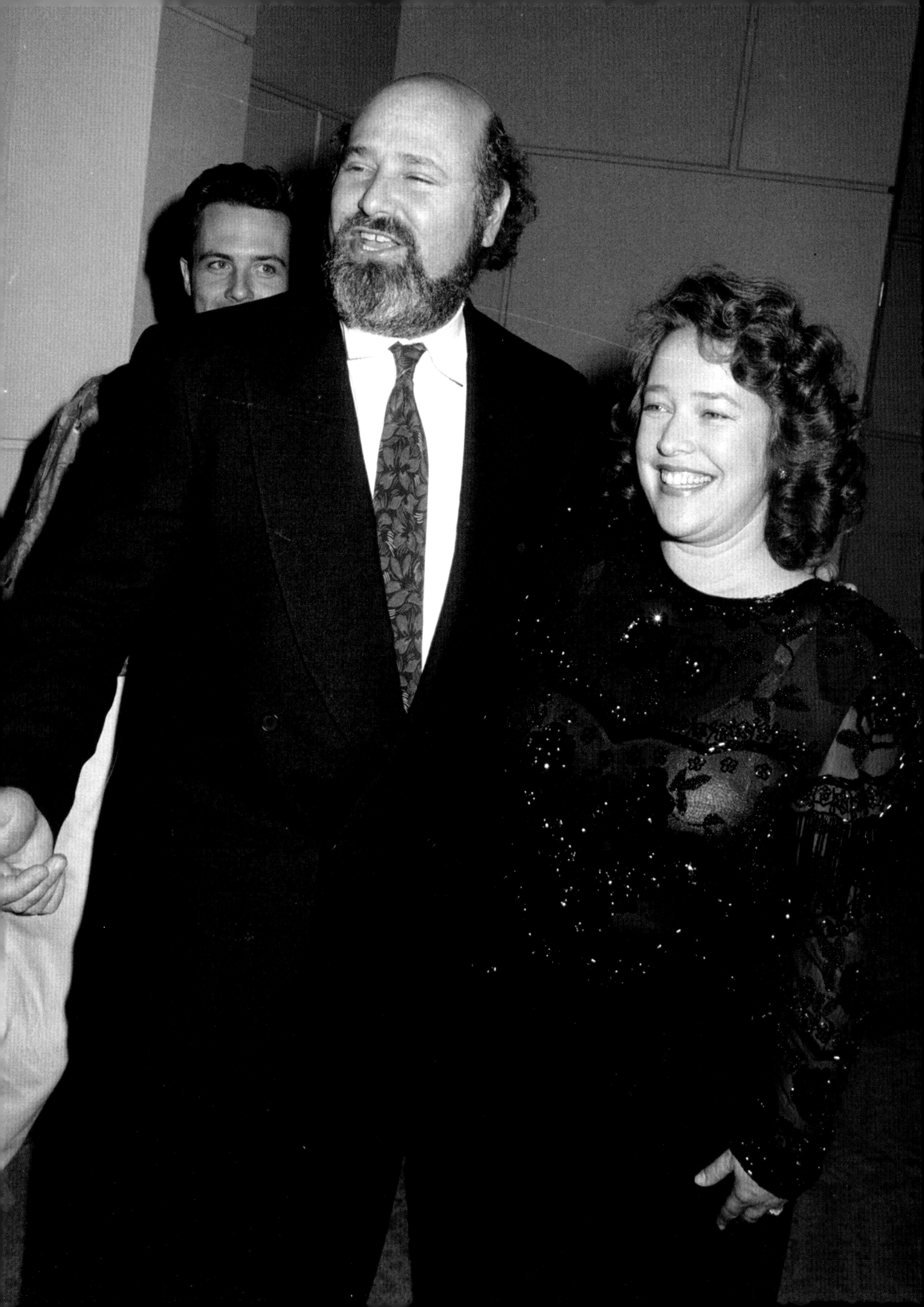

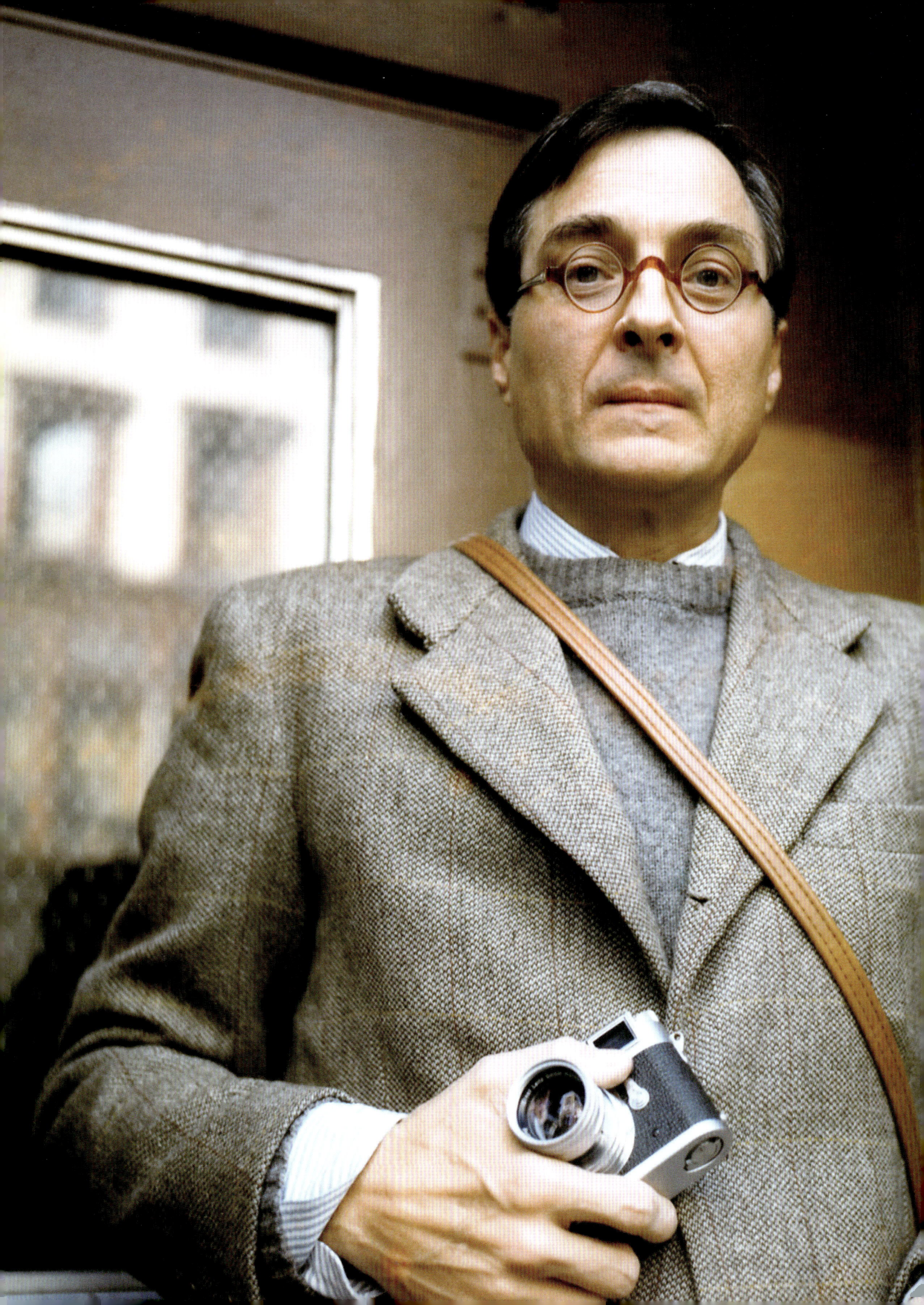

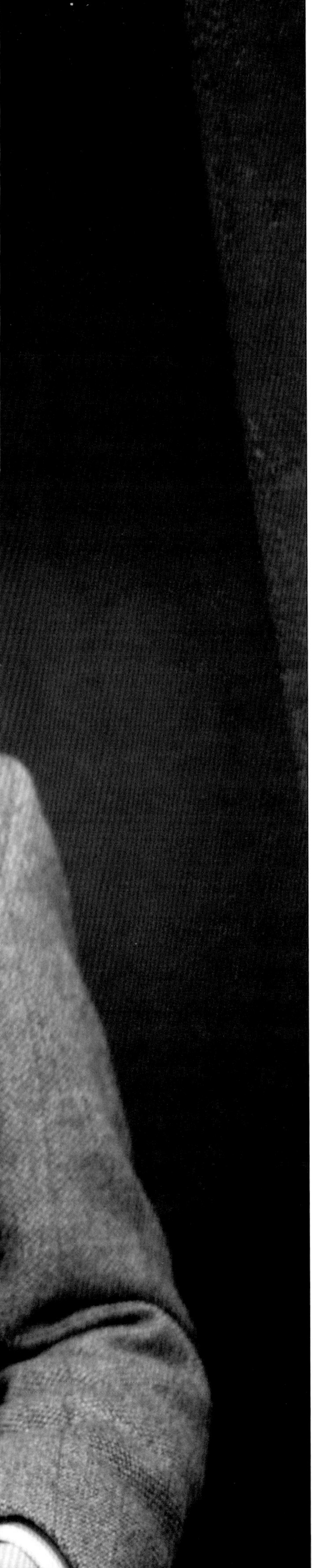

WILLIAM EGGLESTON

PHOTOGRAPHER

"When celebrated US photographer William Eggleston turned his lens on Paris, he uncovered a world of graffiti and garbage. How refreshing."

The London Telegraph

As a child he was an introvert with a good eye. That remarkable eye waged a one-man "war on the obvious" through his Lieca camera. William Eggleston was introduced to color photography by friend and Memphis College of Art professor William Christenberry; the dye-transfer method of printing his haunting photographs makes commonplace images come alive, saturated, almost sinister. His *14 Portraits* was the first one-man show of color photography in the history of the Museum of Modern Art. He is credited with validating color photography as a legitimate art form, yet his images grace album covers. Eggleston has traveled widely to document seemingly everyday images. Both famously Southern and world famous, he always returns to Memphis, the city of his birth.

Photo by Maude Schuyler Clay

MICHAEL OHER

PROFESSIONAL FOOTBALL PLAYER, AUTHOR

When Michael Oher — who dreamed of being a professional basketball player — joined the football team at Briarcrest Christian School his junior year, he couldn't imagine how his life would change.

In 2003, he was named the Division II Lineman of the Year. Scout.com listed him as the #5 offensive lineman prospect in the country. And after offers from several colleges, he chose to play football for the Ole Miss Rebels.

When Michael Lewis' *The Blind Side* was published, Michael Oher became a sensation. And in 2010, his stardom skyrocketed with the release of the Sandra Bullock film.

Oher, in stunningly mature fashion, never fell into the trappings of celebrity. In fact, he didn't bother reading the book until he graduated from Ole Miss. His reaction: "It was OK," he said, "but it made me look pretty stupid."

Oher focused on classroom work and football. And it paid off. He was added to the Rebels' starting lineup in the second game of his freshman season (2005) and in 2007 was rated the 3rd best offensive tackle in college football by *Lindy's* magazine. He considered leaving school after his junior year, applying for inclusion in the 2008 NFL draft, but decided he wanted to stay on to support his team. He graduated in 2009, and was signed by the Baltimore Ravens in the first round of the 2009 NFL Draft.

Photograph Sports Illustrated/Getty Images

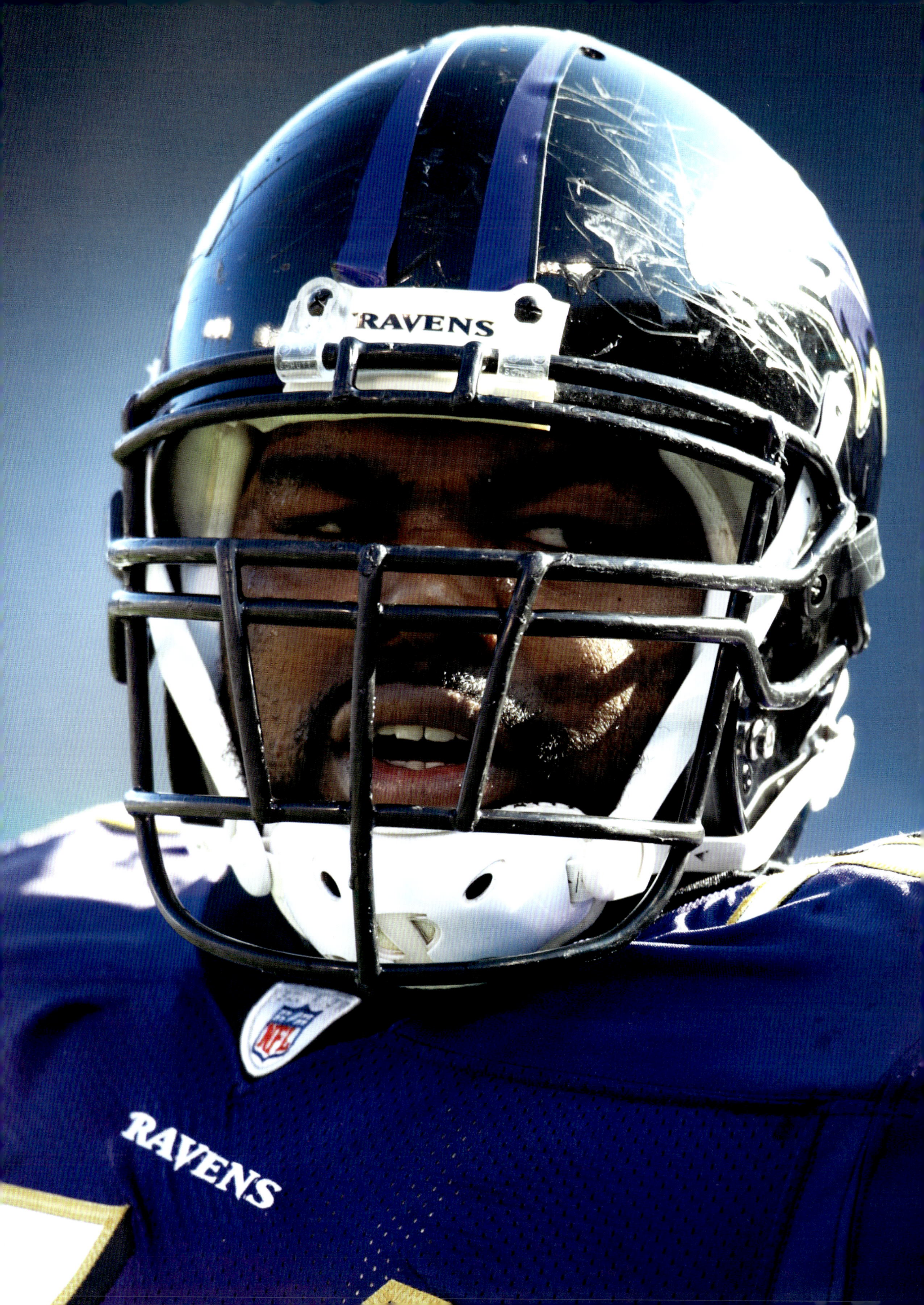
RAVENS
RAVENS

Movies, Television & Stage

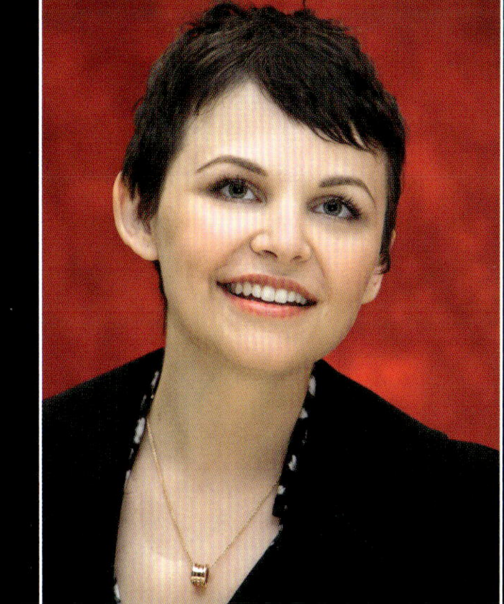

GINNIFER GOODWIN

ACTOR

Jennifer (later Ginnifer) Michelle Goodwin was born on the 22nd of May 1978, in Memphis. She graduated from Lausanne Collegiate School in 1996 and spent a year at Hanover before going to Boston University where she received her BFA in Acting. She lived in New York City for a time doing stage work. Then, she moved to Los Angeles. Her first recurring role on a TV series was in the underrated *Ed* (2001); her first big break in film came in the Julia Roberts film *Mona Lisa Smile*. She also played Johnny Cash's first wife in the acclaimed biopic, *Walk the Line*, and landed a plum role in the HBO series, *Big Love*, about a modern Mormon family, playing Bill Paxton's third wife. Ginnifer's sister, Melissa, is a stop-motion animator for such shows as the Emmy-winning Robot Chicken, where Ginnifer has guest-starred as a voice actor. In 2008, MaxMara honored Goodwin with a "Face of the Future" award, an award recognizing promising young women in film. Also, Goodwin was one of the celebrities featured in Gap's Fall 2008 ad campaign. About returning to Memphis and shopping here, in particular at the local hipster music emporium, Goner Records, Ginnifer said, "My fiancé and I actually listen to vinyl—plus this place is next to my favorite coffee shop (Java Cabana)." Ginnifer's dad, Tim Goodwin, used to own a recording studio in Memphis. She says, "It's a Hard Rock Café now, but before they began remodeling, my grandfather ran in and signed the names of everyone in the family, so Melissa and I are on the wall."

Photograph by Getty Images/Stephen Lovekin

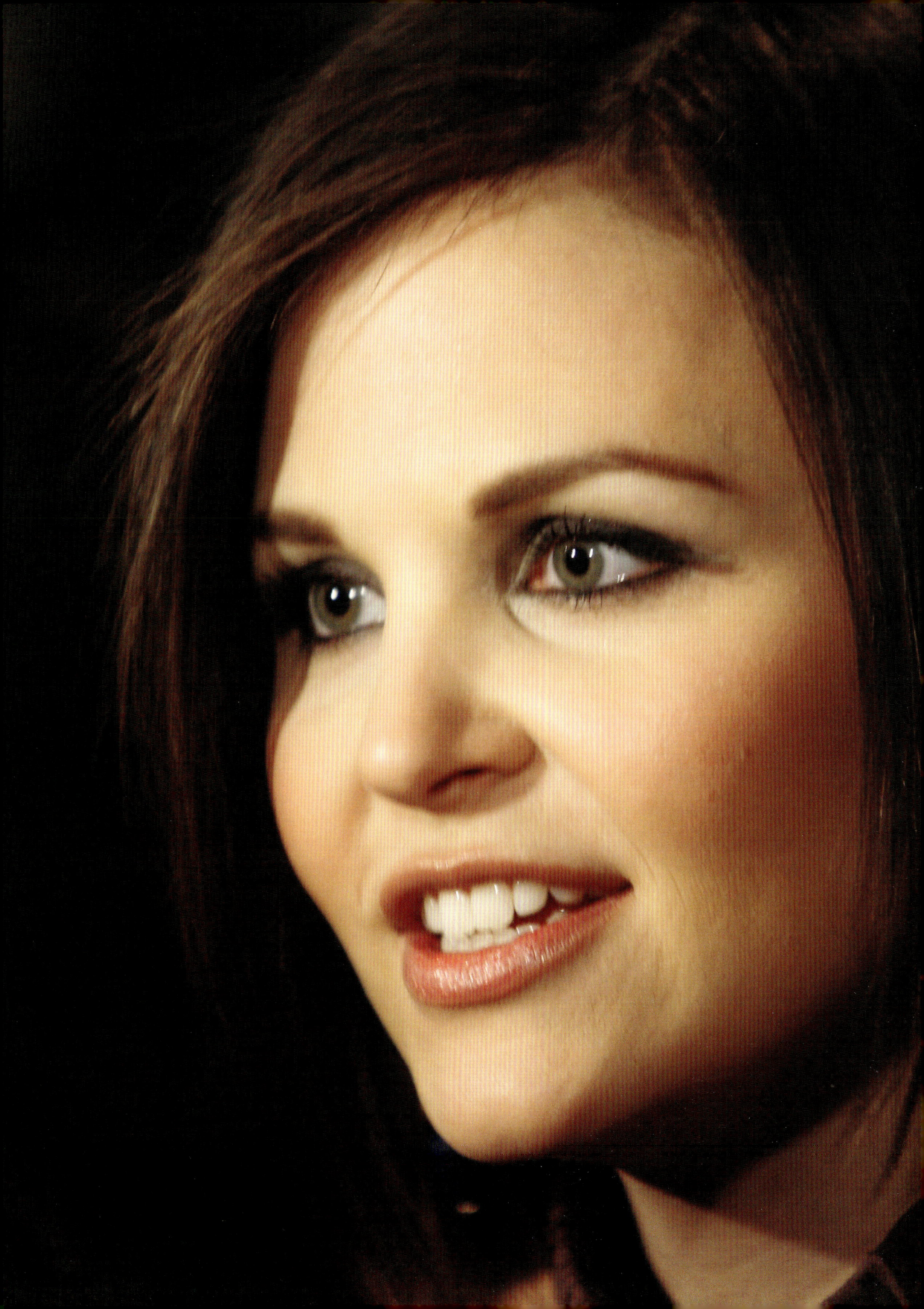

PAT & GINA NEELY

TV CHEFS

Pat Neely began cooking at the age of 15, learning the tricks of Southern barbecue from his uncle. In 1988, he and his three brothers opened their first restaurant in Memphis. At his 10-year high school reunion, Pat reunited with his high school sweetheart, Gina, and both a marriage and a working team were born. Gina manages the catering division of Neely's Bar-B-Que, as well as all the merchandise (seasonings, aprons, sauces, etc.). The co-hosts of the Food Network's *Down Home with the Neelys* (which is filmed in their Memphis home), the Neelys are big supporters of Memphis youth, sponsoring children to attend Memphis Grizzlies home games, and supporting other athletic events.

Photograph FilmMagic/Tom Briglia

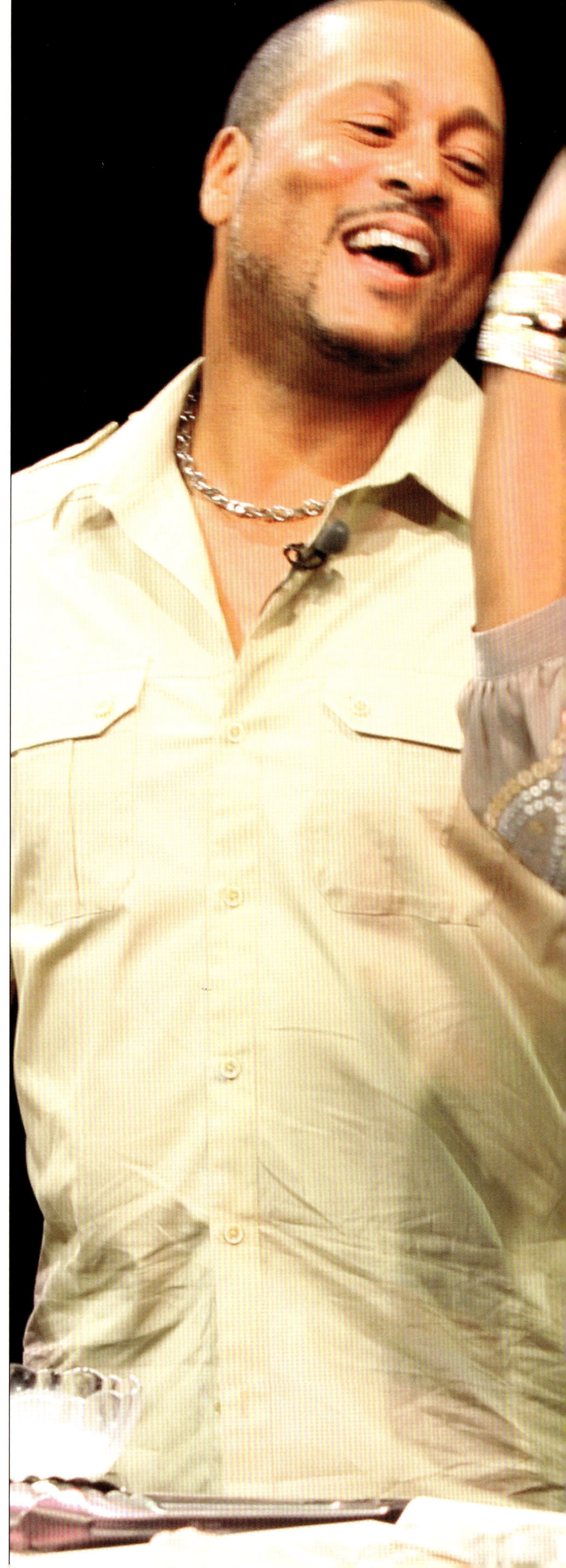

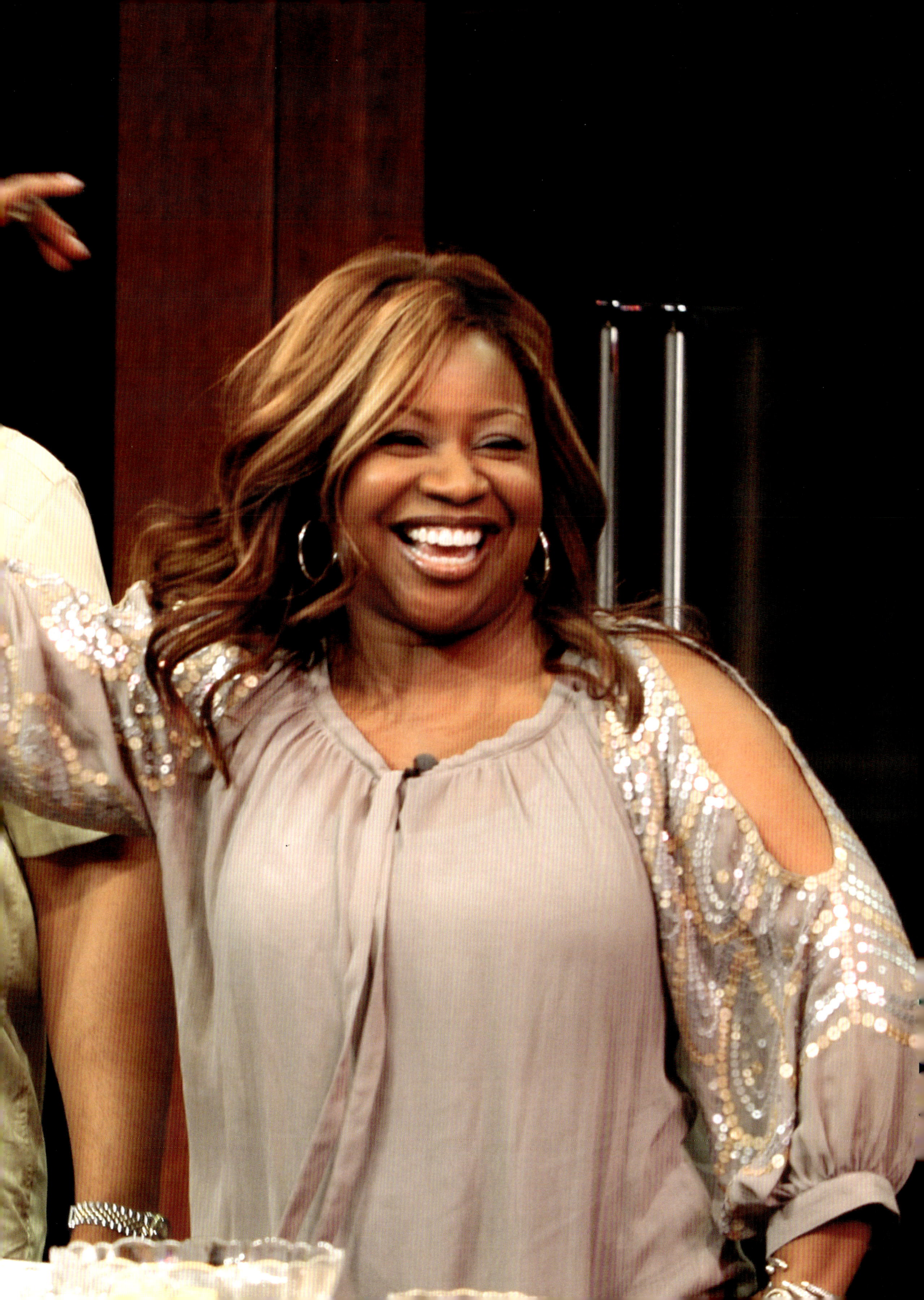

CHRIS PARNELL

COMEDIAN

"The main thing is to be funny."
Chris Parnell

His voice is unmistakable, yet Chris Parnell is a master of impersonation. The son of Jack Parnell – the "image voice" of companies like Kroger and FedEx – Chris was voted "most talented" his senior year at Germantown High School, where he returned to teach drama and film after college. Best known for his years on *Saturday Night Live* he remains the only cast member hired and fired twice. Over the years his impersonations have ranged from Emeril Lagasse, George W. Bush, Joe Leiberman, Moe Howard and Eric Bloom of Blue Öyster Cult suffering from far too much cowbell. A devoted supporter of his high school alma mater, Parnell recently chaperoned a theater trip to London.

Photograph by Getty Entertainment/Chad Buchanan

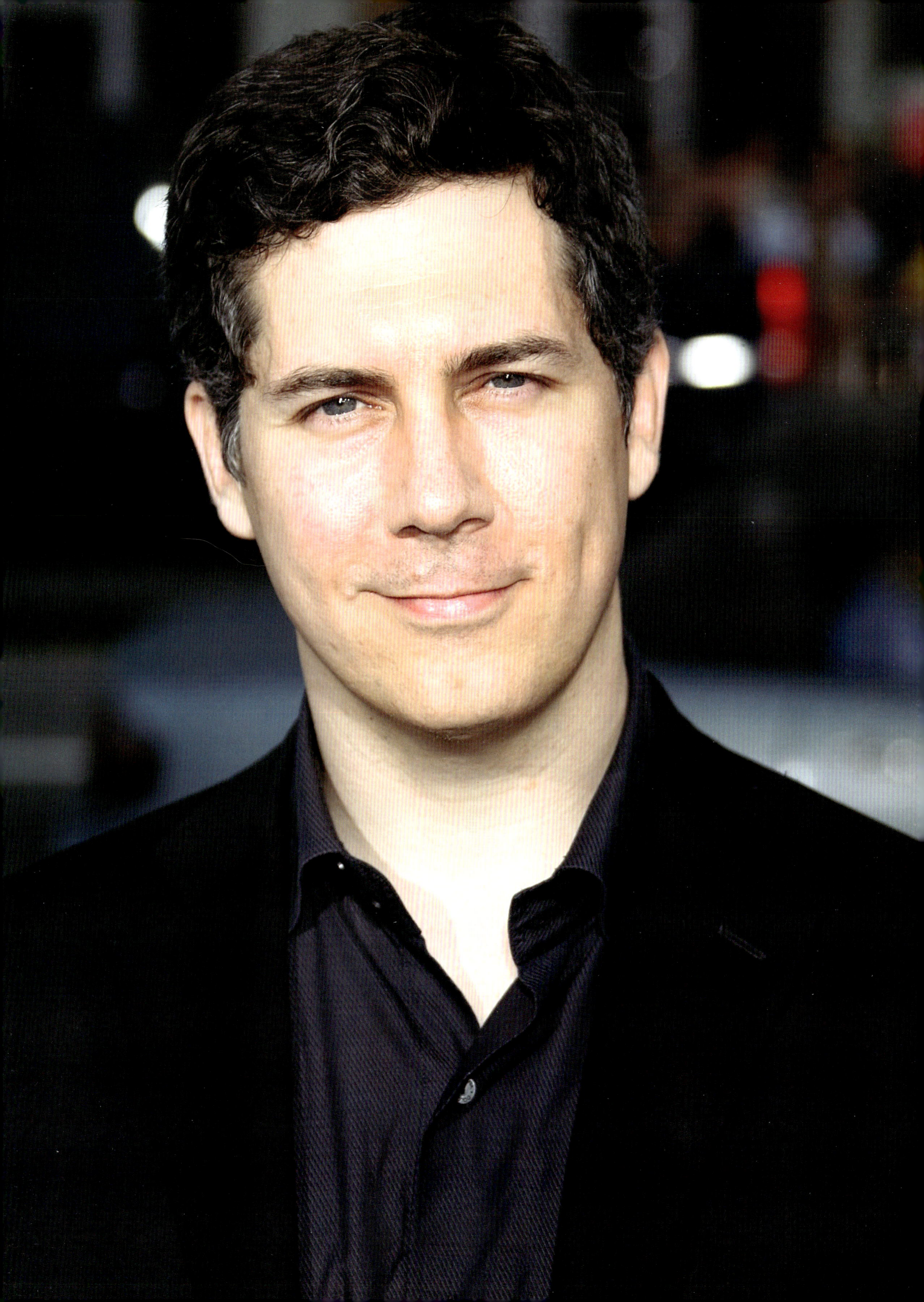

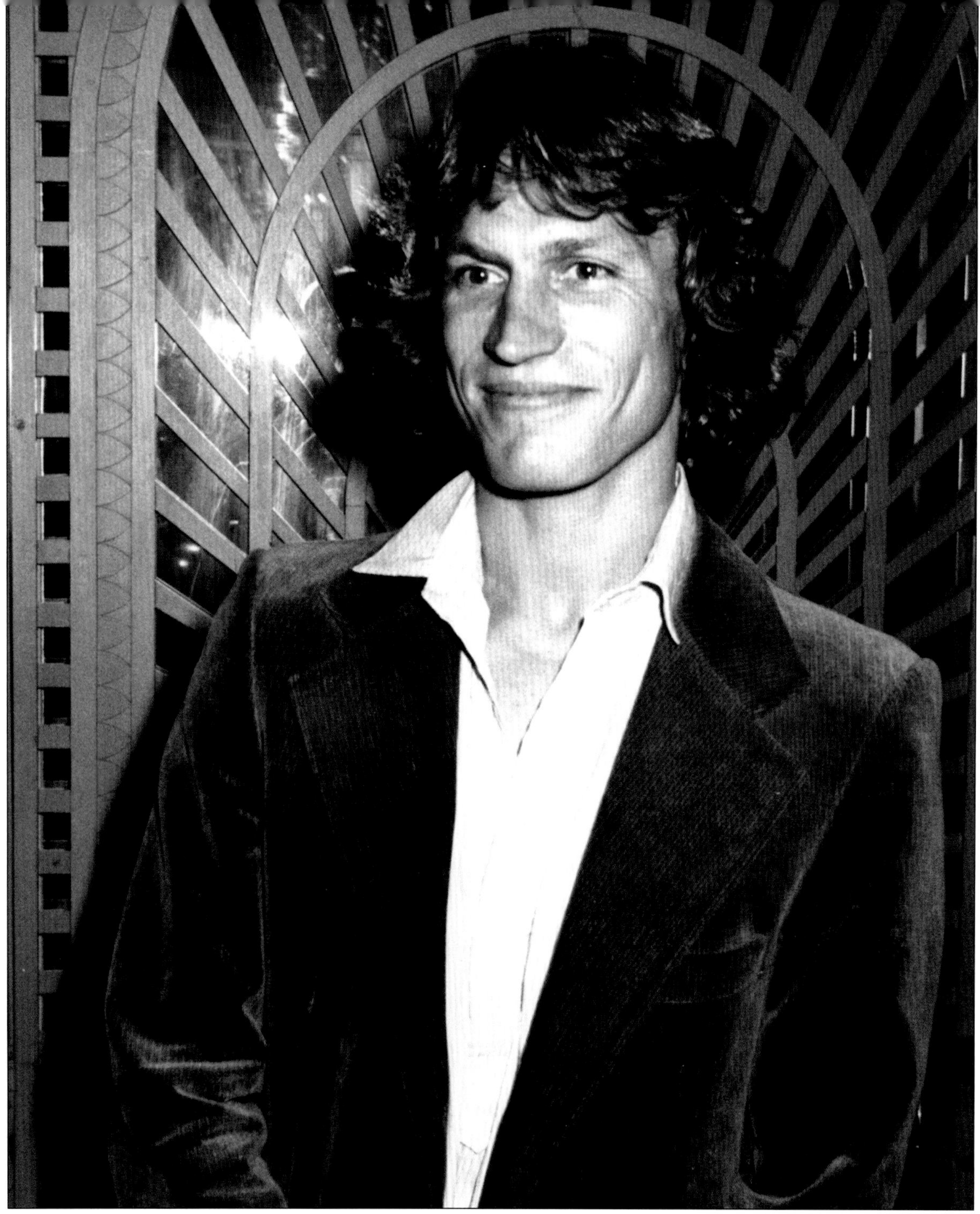

MICHAEL BECK

ACTOR

After graduating from MUS, Michael Beck went to Millsaps on a football scholarship. He first hit the stage in *Camelot* and *Cat on a Hot Tin Roof.* His big Hollywood break came with a starring role in the 1979 action classic *The Warriors* and was followed by 1980's *Xanadu* with Olivia Newton-John. Of his career Beck has said, "*The Warriors* opened a lot of doors in film for me, which *Xanadu* then closed." He has appeared in supporting roles in movies and television, and has lent his voice to audiobooks by John Grisham and other bestselling writers. He currently lives in California with his wife of 30 years.

Photograph by WireImage/Ron Galella

CRAIG BREWER

FILMMAKER

Equipped with an early generation digital video camera and little else, Craig Brewer crafted his first feature film, *The Poor and Hungry* on a shoestring budget that didn't allow for buying more shoelaces. With hardly any resources he created a gritty, human film, somehow combining car thieves and classical music. That was enough to garner him the budget to make his next film, *Hustle & Flow*. That film won the first ever Academy Award for a rap group, Three 6 Mafia for the theme song "Hard Out Here For a Pimp," and a Best Actor nomination for leading man Terrence Howard. Brewer's follow-up, *Black Snake Moan* featuring Samuel L. Jackson and a barely clad Christina Ricci, was Brewer's tribute to the Blues. Currently Brewer is finishing post-production on his first big budget studio film, a re-imagining of the classic *Footloose*. While budgetary constraints mandated that film being shot in Atlanta, Brewer has vowed that he will remain a Memphis filmmaker whenever possible. The bedrock of Brewer's filmmaking has been his love of music, and his affection for his damaged characters. When asked to give advice to young people who want to make movies, Brewer's advice has always been the same he followed himself – "Make movies."

Photograph by Getty Entertainment/Paul Hawthorne • **Story** by Dennis Phillippi

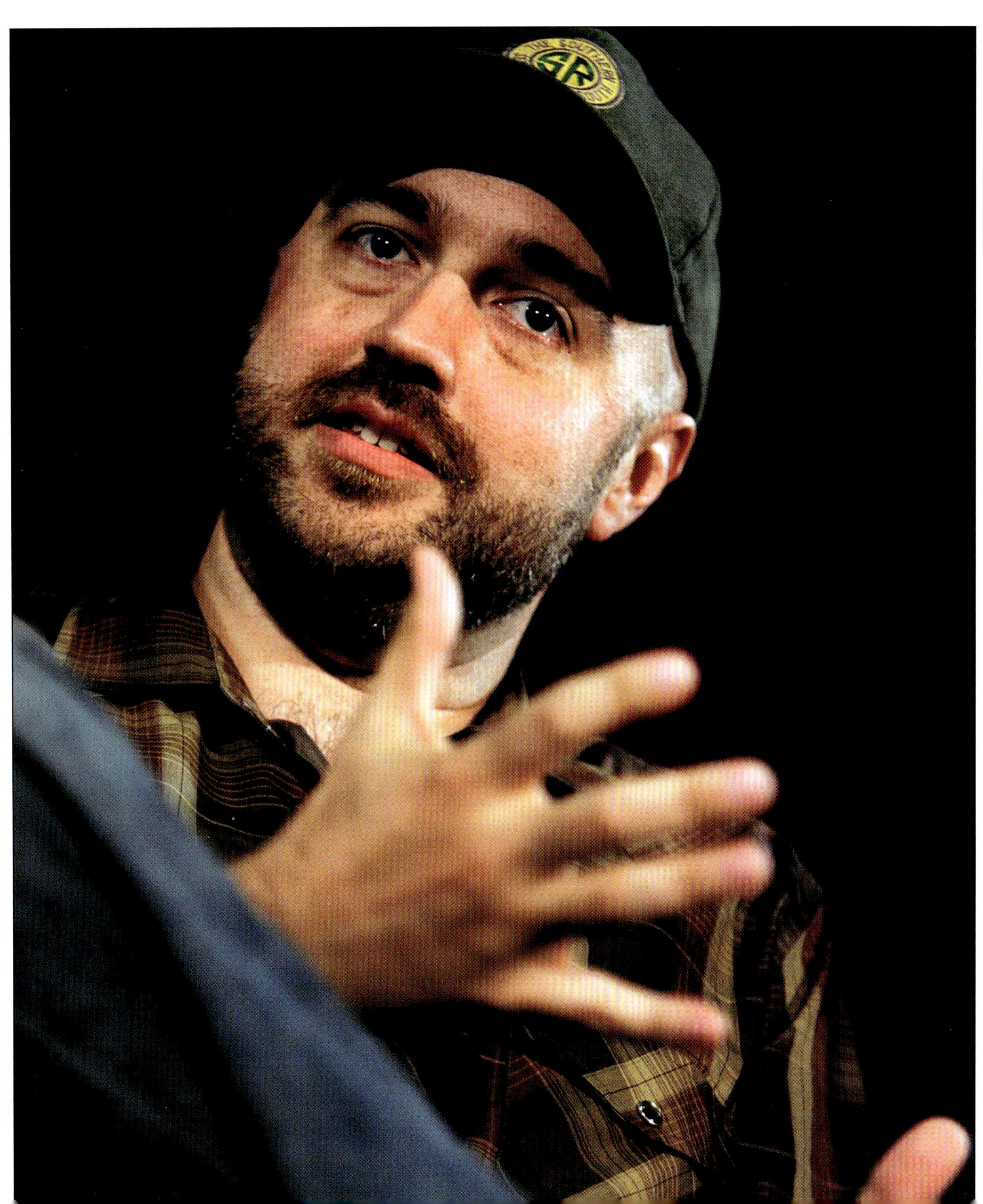

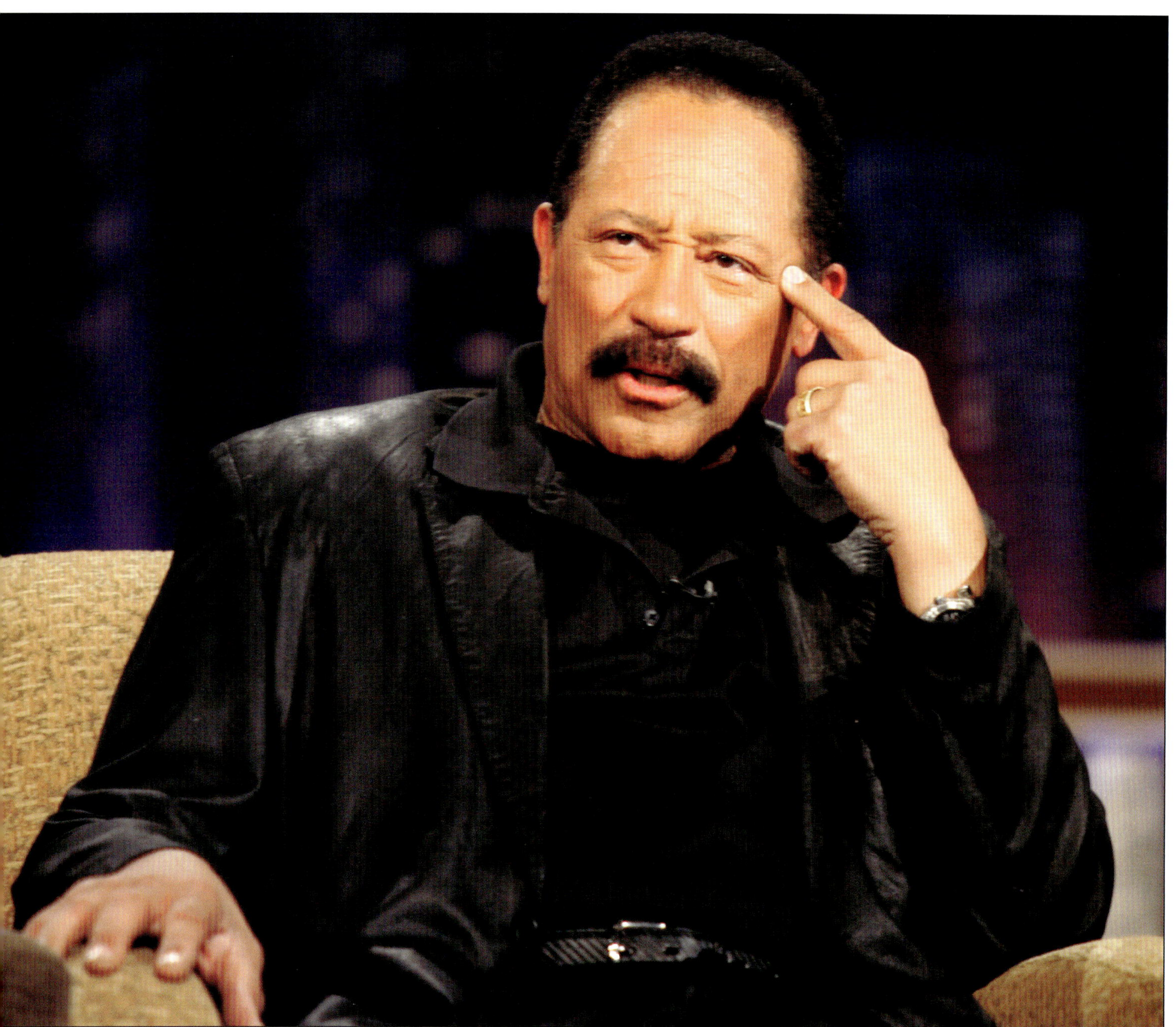

JUDGE JOE BROWN

TELEVISION JUDGE

Joe Brown was the first African-American prosecutor for the City of Memphis. It was his role as a judge on the State Criminal Court of Shelby County, presiding over James Earl Ray's last appeal from his conviction for the assassination of Martin Luther King, Jr., that first brought Judge Brown to the national stage. Ironically, it was his being removed from the case for alleged bias (he believed Ray was framed) that caught the attention of television producers. *Judge Joe Brown* first aired in 1998, and since then, Brown has become a regular for talk shows and the game show Hollywood Squares.

Photograph by WireImage/Jesse Grant

DANIEL BRUNT

FILM PRODUCER

Literally working his way up from the mail room, Memphis-born Daniel Brunt has tried his hand at just about everything. Since graduating from the University of Denver, Brunt worked as an agent's assistant, a marketing director for a Tennessee music production company, and finally made his way into film producing. Now a co-president of Room 9 Entertainment, Brunt was a co-producer for the popular film *Thank You For Smoking*.

Photograph by WireImage/Contributor

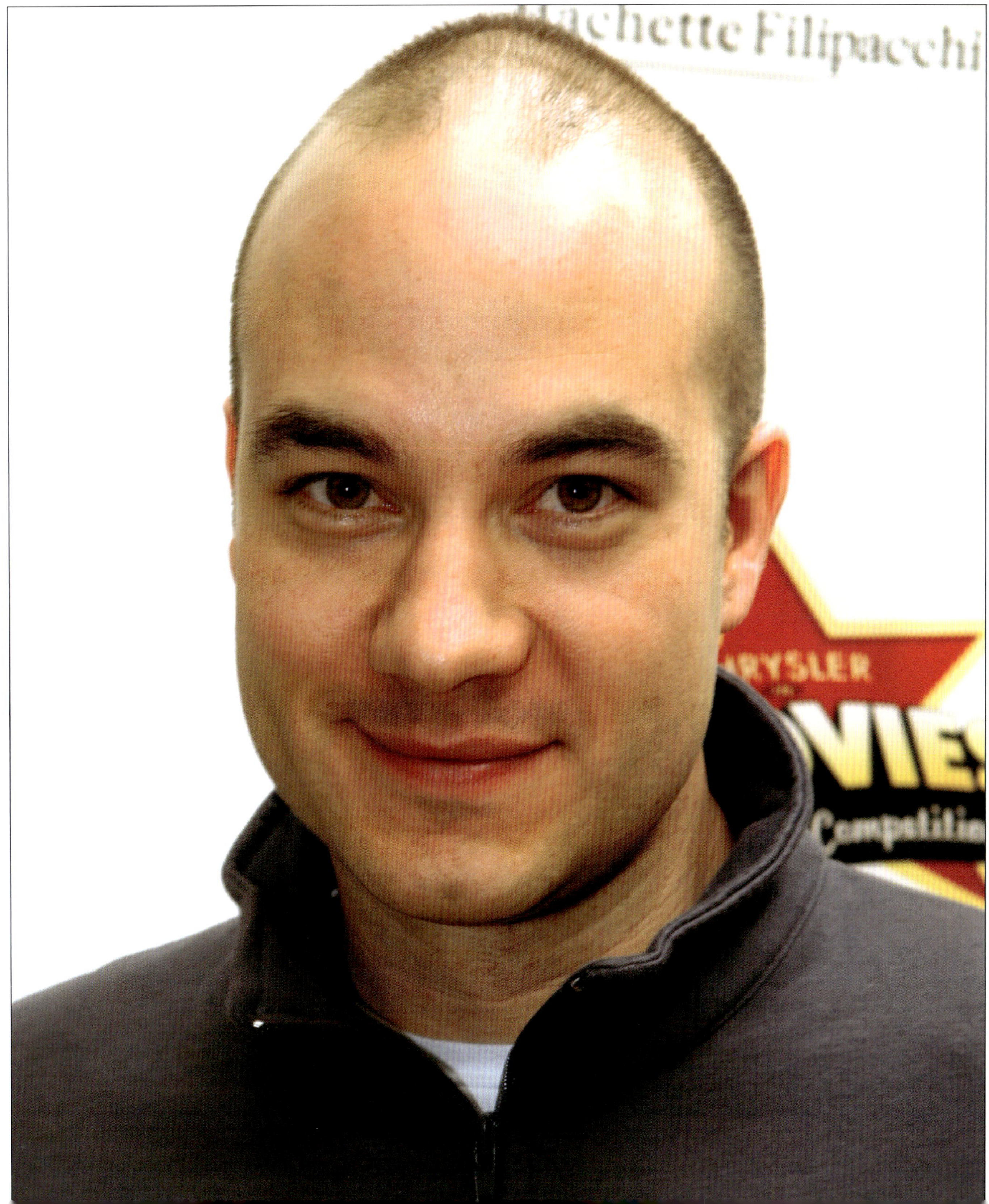

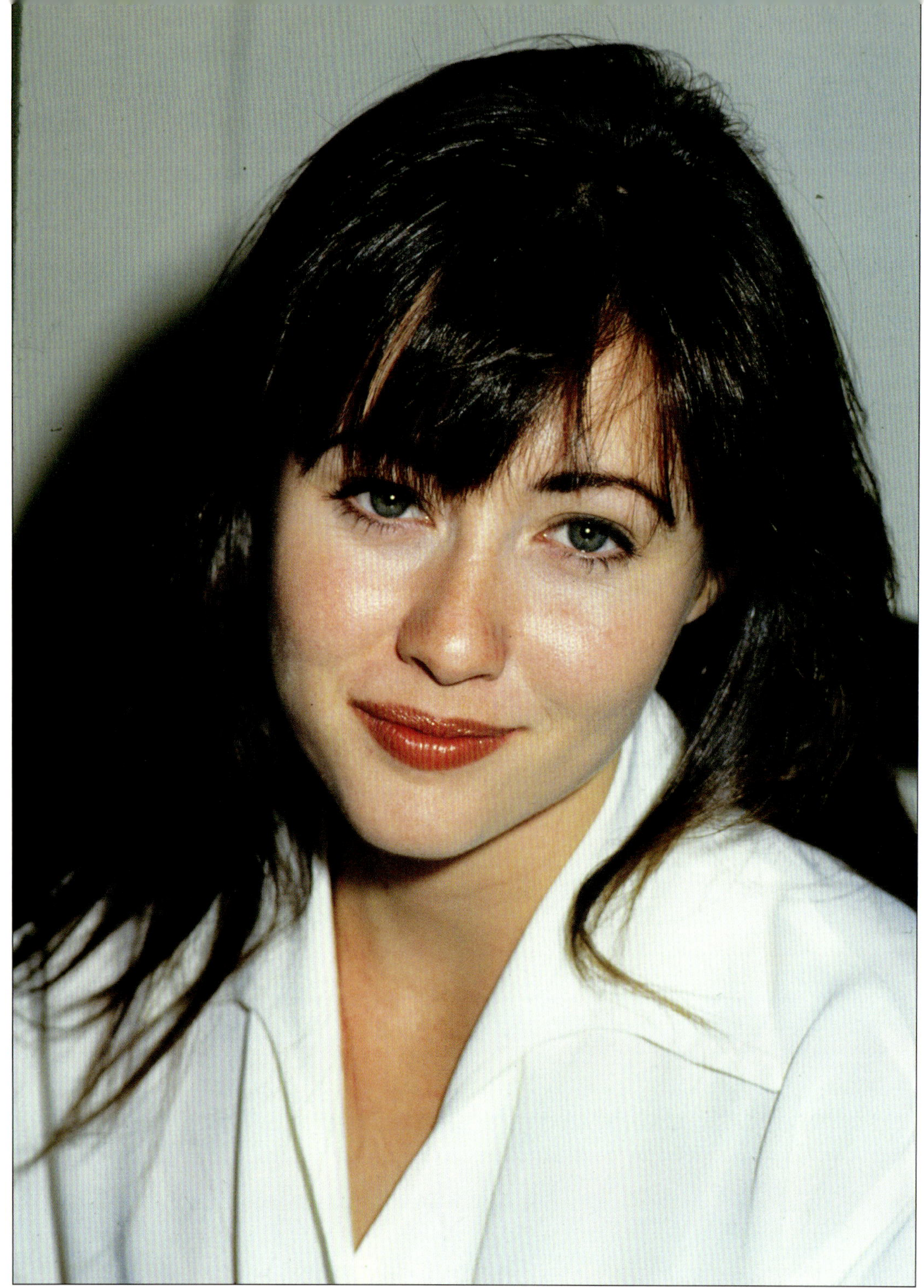

SHANNEN DOHERTY

ACTOR

When Shannen Doherty's family moved from Memphis to Los Angeles, she knew immediately that she wanted to be an actor. Beginning with roles in *Girls Just Want to Have Fun* and the cult classic *Heathers*, she became well known for her roles on *Beverly Hills 90210* and *Charmed*. In 2010, she released her first book, *Badass: A Hard-Earned Guide to Living Life with Style and (the Right) Attitude*.

Photograph by Time Life Pictures/Getty Images

GEORGE HAMILTON

ACTOR

Yes, that George Hamilton. Born the youngest son of bandleader "Spike" Hamilton in Memphis, he is as well known for his suave manner, natty style, and perpetual tan as he is for his 55 feature films, many television appearances, and star on the Hollywood Walk of Fame. He has played such far flung roles as Hank Williams, Evel Knievel, Dracula and Zorro. With himself as spokesman and customer, Hamilton has launched a line of cigars and skin care products. The 2009 film *My One and Only* was loosely based on his life on the road. This year he will star in the national tour of the Tony-winning *La Cage aux Folles*.

Photograph CBS Photo Archive

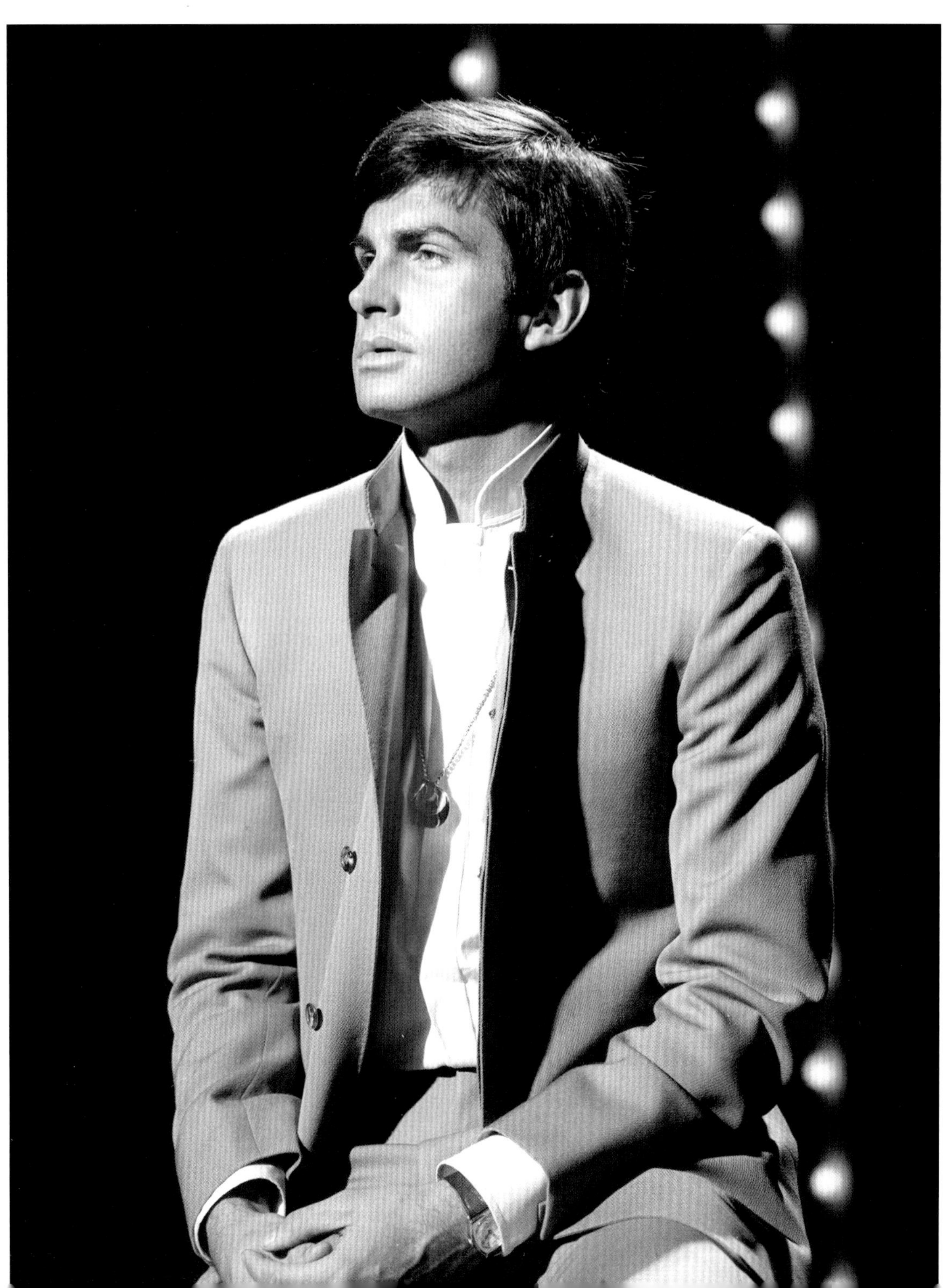

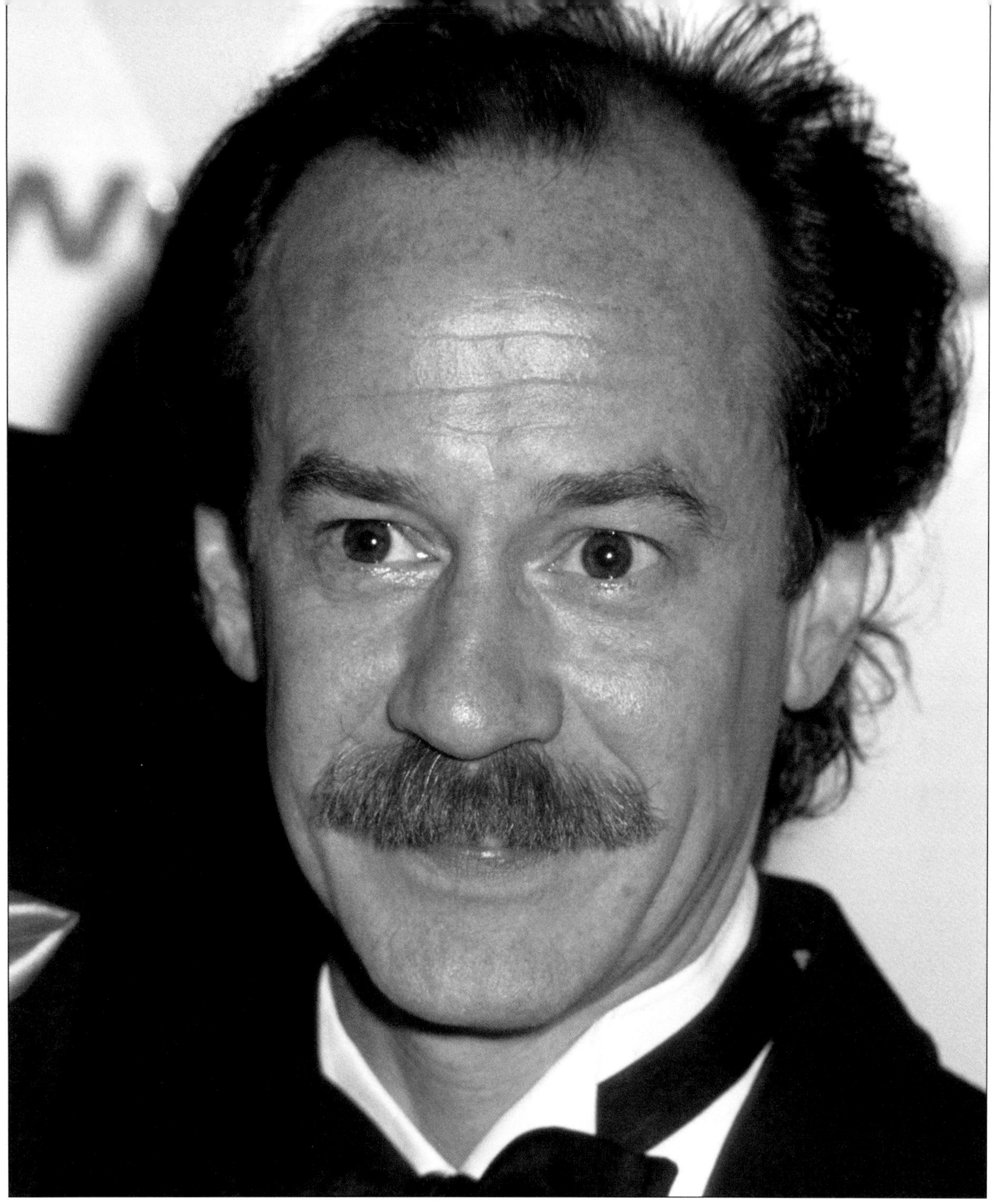

MICHAEL JETER

ACTOR

"I often see myself in my private life as being a pinched and confined person. When I get on the stage I can open up."

Michael Jeter

Originally attending Memphis State University as a pre-med student, Michael Jeter discovered his love for acting and soon changed his major. He got his start performing in plays and musicals at Memphis's Circuit Theatre and Playhouse on the Square. In 1990, Jeter won a Tony Award for his performance in the musical *Grand Hotel*, and has appeared in such films as *Fear and Loathing in Las Vegas*, *Jurassic Park III*, and *The Green Mile*. He passed away at home in 2003.

Photograph by WireImage/Jim Smeal

ASHLEY JONES

ACTOR

"From a very young age my mind was opened up to different possibilities than the norm, especially growing up in Tennessee . . ."

Ashley Jones

Born in Memphis, 3-year-old Ashley Jones's dream was to become a violinist. She later moved into acting, appearing in her first commercial at age 5, and working in theater as she grew up. In 2004, she joined the cast of *The Bold and the Beautiful* as medical student Bridget Forrester, and appeared in 2009 as Daphne on the popular drama *True Blood.*

Photograph by Getty Entertainment/Frederick M. Brown

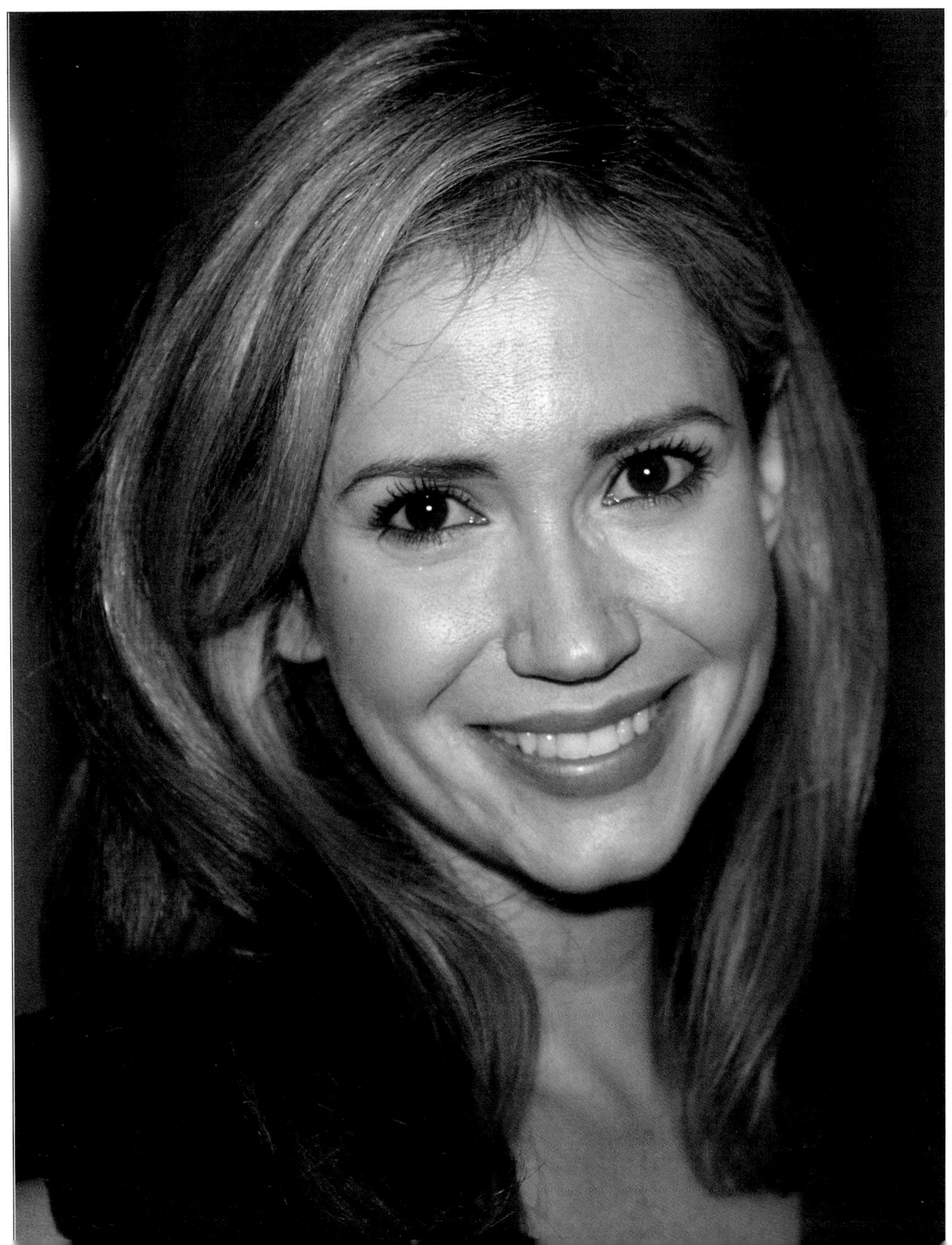

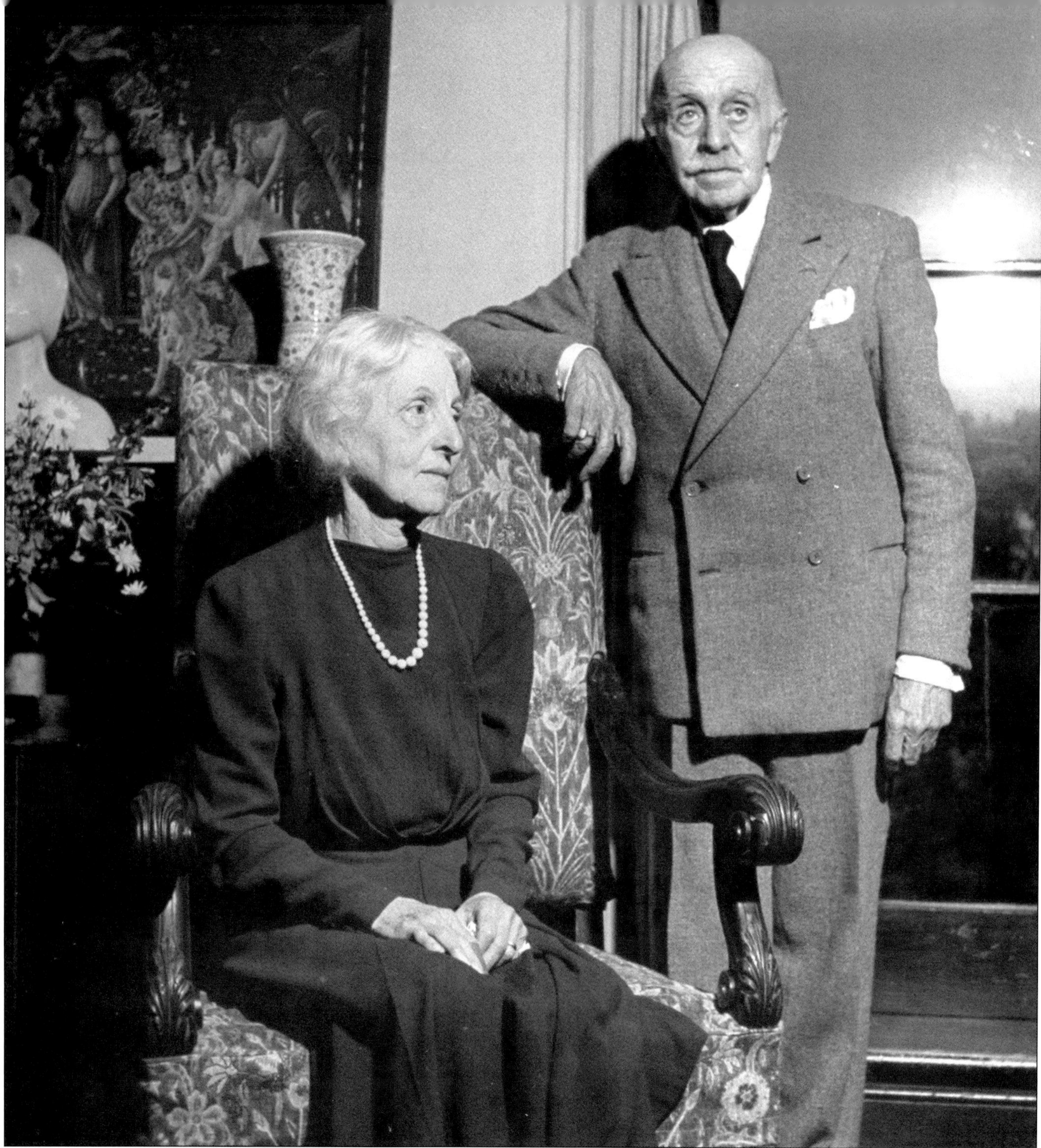

FLORENCE KAHN

ACTOR

Her father owned the dry goods store Kahn & Freiberg, her brother became the editor of the *Commercial Appeal*, but Florence Kahn's ambitions took her across the world. She studied at Miss Grace Llewllyn's studio in Memphis before heading to the American Academy of Dramatic Arts in New York. Soon she was a fixture on Broadway, noted for her many leading roles in the plays of Norwegian writer Henrik Ibsen. While performing in London, she caught the eye of famed English writer and caricaturist Max Beerbohm. Alfred Hitchcock's 1936 film *Secret Agent* was the first movie she'd ever been in or even seen, for that matter. When Max was knighted in 1939, this world-famous actress and Memphis girl became Lady Beerbohm.

Photo of Florence Kahn and her husband, Max Beerbohm, Time & Life Pictures

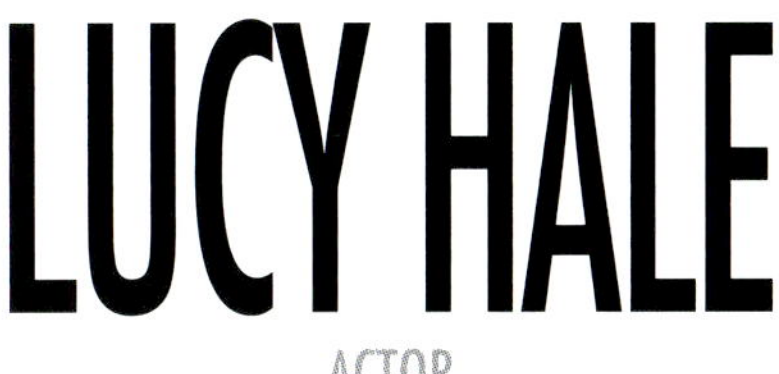

LUCY HALE

ACTOR

Born and raised in Memphis, Lucy Hale made her TV debut on the reality show *American Juniors*, showcasing her musical talent. Since then, she has made many guest appearances on popular TV shows such as *Wizards of Waverly Place*, *The O.C.*, and *How I Met Your Mother*. She played Rose Baker on the show *Privileged* and Sherrie in Wes Craven's latest horror installment, *Scream 4*.

Photograph by Getty Entertainment/David Livingston

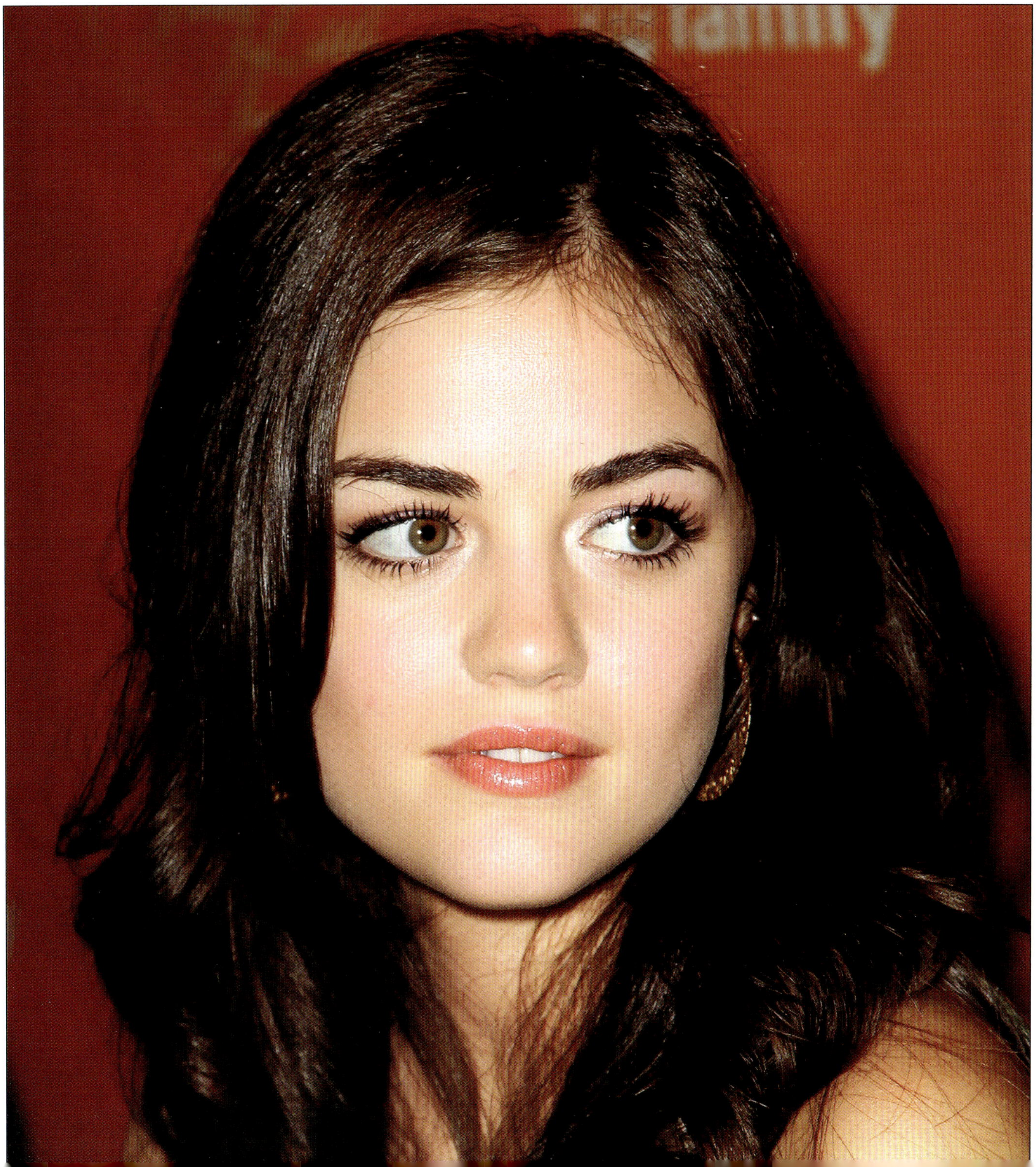

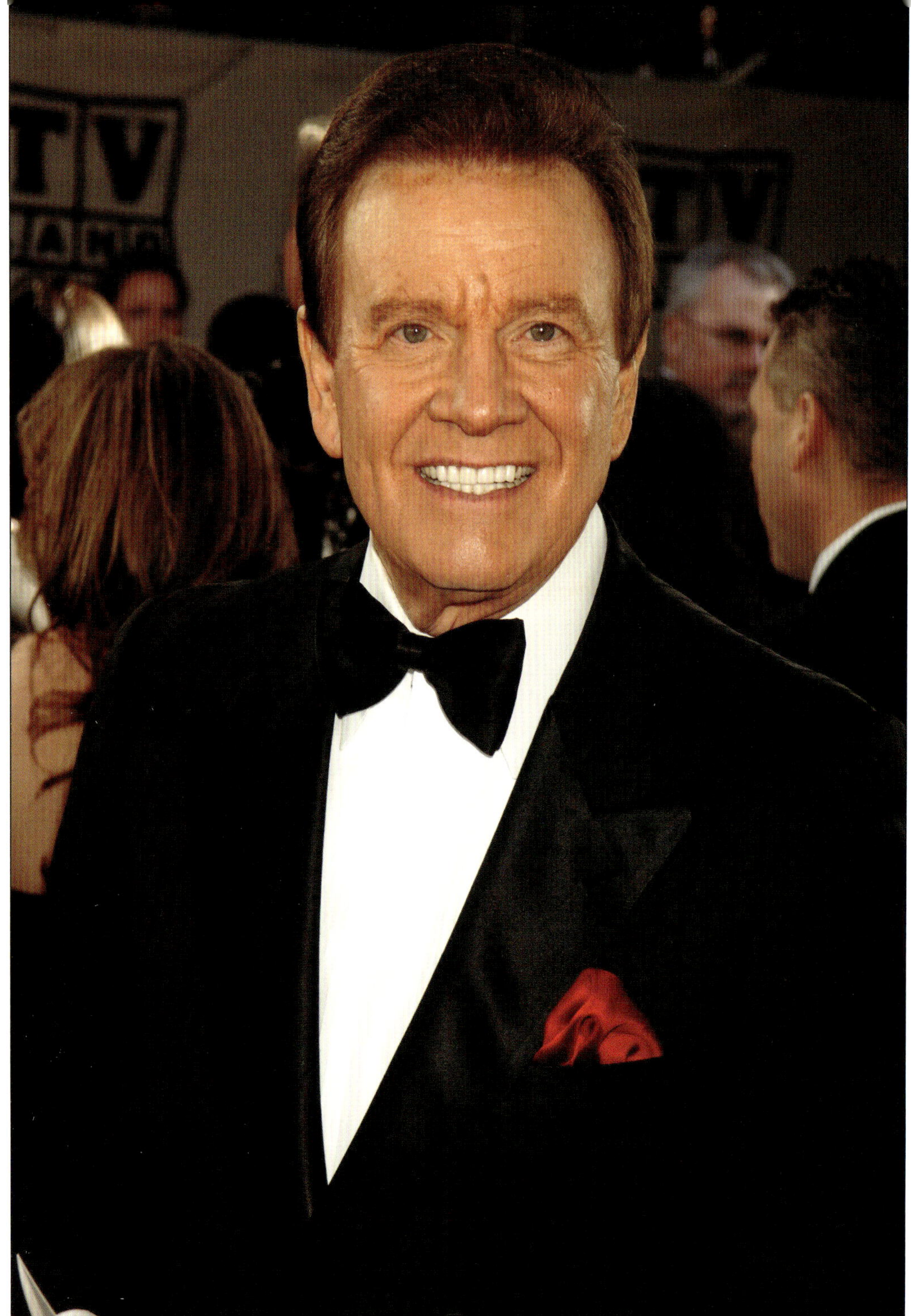

WINK MARTINDALE

GAME SHOW HOST

"I always thought I'd want to have a restaurant."
Wink Martindale

His mother wanted him to be a preacher. He wanted to be a restaurateur. He did neither. As a student at Memphis State University, Winston "Wink" Martindale hosted mornings on WHBQ, and broke into the fledgling medium of TV as the host of *Mars Patrol*, a children's show, and *Teenage Dance Party* where his friend Elvis Presley would make the odd appearance. Wink even had a hit record of his own with the spoken-word country song "Deck of Cards." He would go on to host 15 different game shows over the years, including *Gambit*, *High Rollers*, and *Tic Tac Dough*. He is currently the host of *Instant Recall*.

Photograph by FilmMagic/Jeff Kravitz

ELISE NEAL

ACTOR

Elise Neal began her career as a dancer at the very young age of 6. Born in Memphis, she graduated from the Watkins Overton High School for the Creative and Performing Arts and quickly moved to New York City to pursue an acting career. Well known for her roles in *Scream 2*, *Malcolm X*, and the TV show *The Hughleys*, Neal returned to Memphis a few years ago to film the critically acclaimed and Oscar-winning film *Hustle & Flow*.

Photograph by Getty Entertainment/Frederick M. Brown

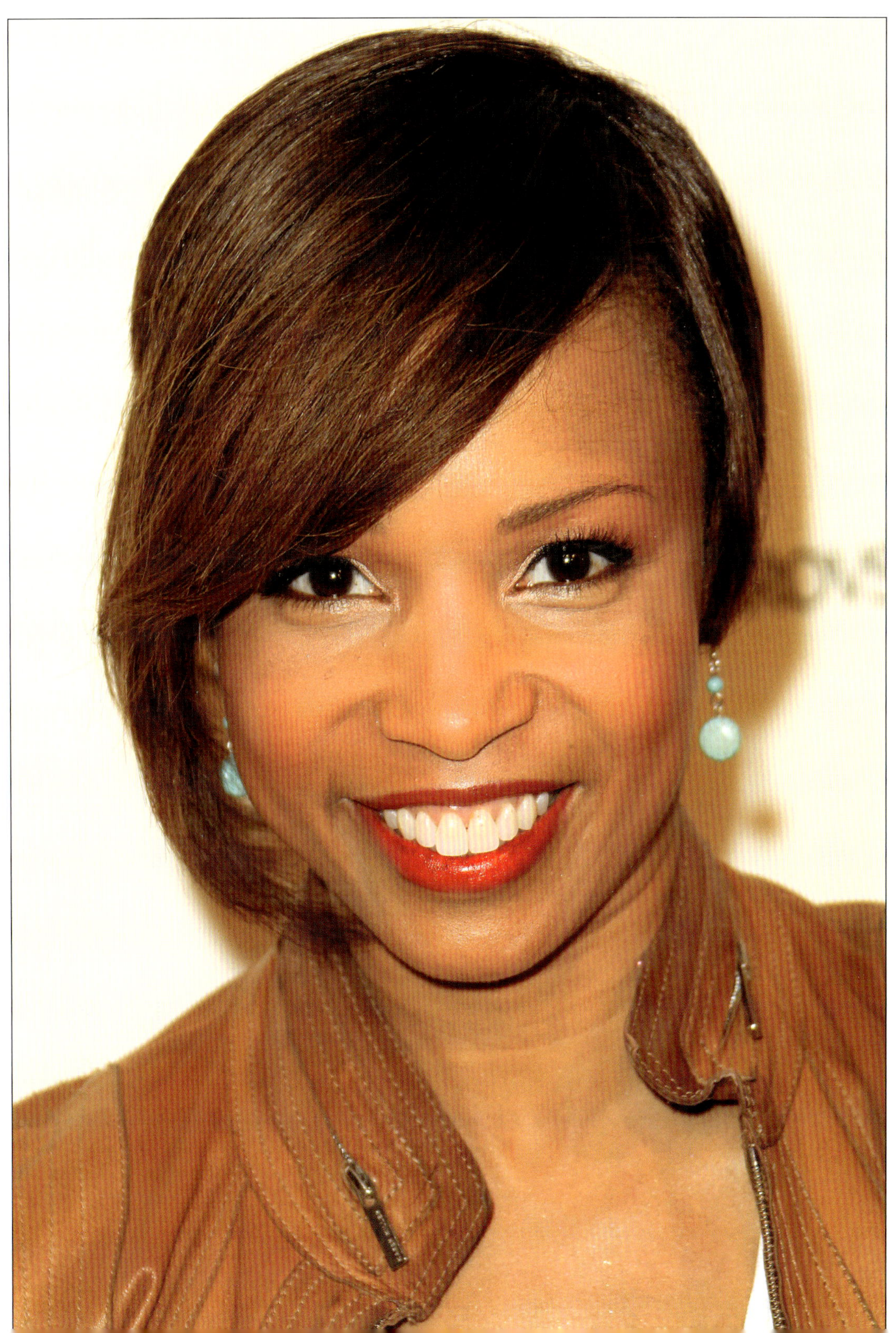

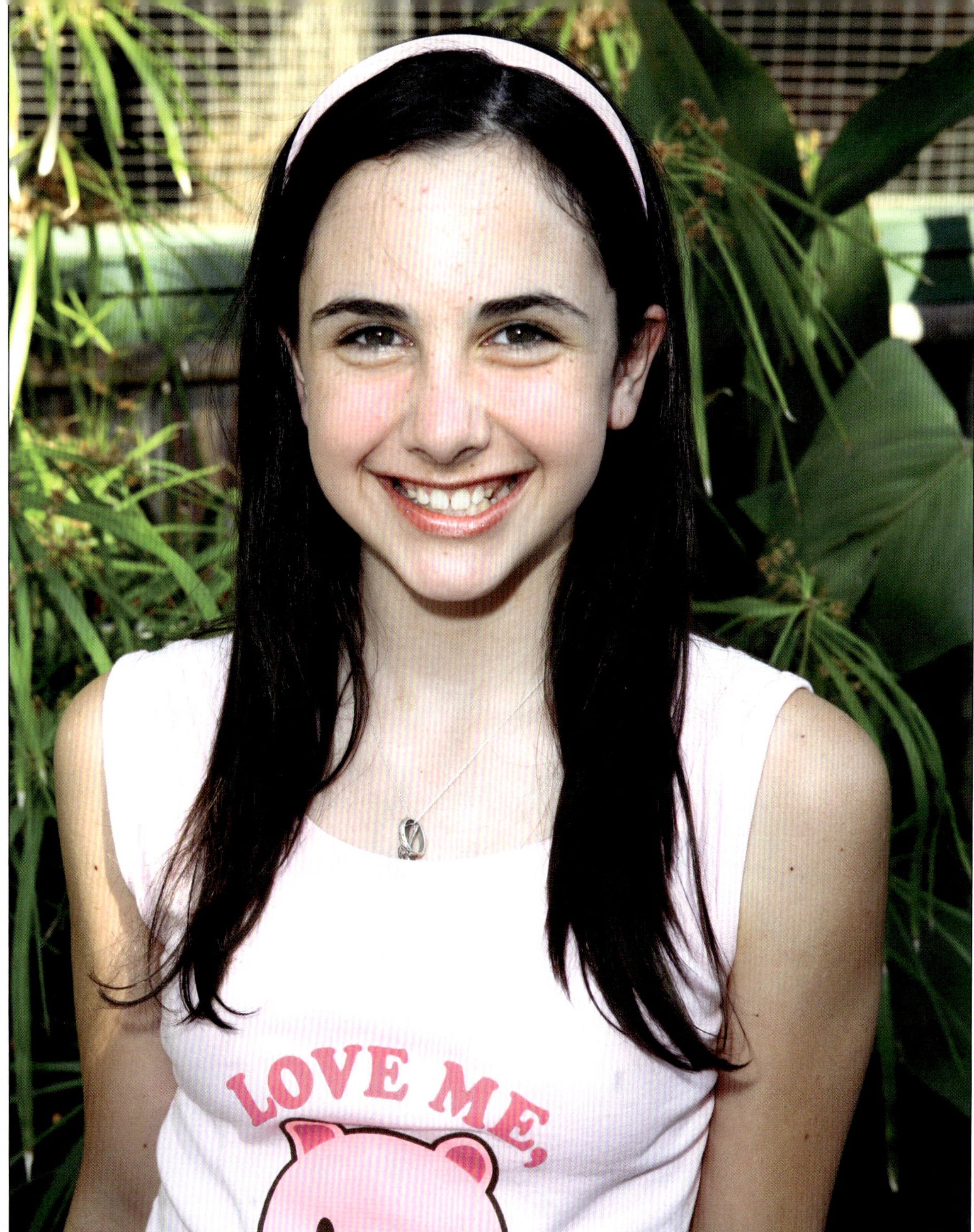

HAILEY ANNE NELSON

ACTOR

Hailey Anne Nelson must be the only serious actress to relocate to Memphis from Los Angeles. Starting on the stage at the age of five, her first film break came in 2003 as Jenny in Tim Burton's *Big Fish* and she's been working ever since. She played a young Rosanne Cash in *Walk the Line*, where she met fellow Memphian actress Ginnifer Goodwin, now both friend and mentor. In 2010's *A Disjointed Proposal*, she proved that she can do comedy as well. A full-time student at Lausanne Collegiate School, she is an avid animal rights activist and vegetarian.

Photograph by Getty Entertainment/Chad Buchanan

DENNIS PHILLIPPI

ACTOR, COMEDIAN, RADIO PERSONALITY

What began as a two-day trip to Memphis in 1985 turned into a lifelong stay when Dennis Phillippi met his future wife Janet. He performed as the house comedian at Sir Lafs-A-Lot and the Comedy Zone, resulting in over 6,000 shows. He has appeared in films such as *The Poor and Hungry*, *Hustle & Flow*, and *Daylight Fades*. Working in radio for many years, he has hosted many shows, most recently as one half of Dennis and Ric on Rock103.

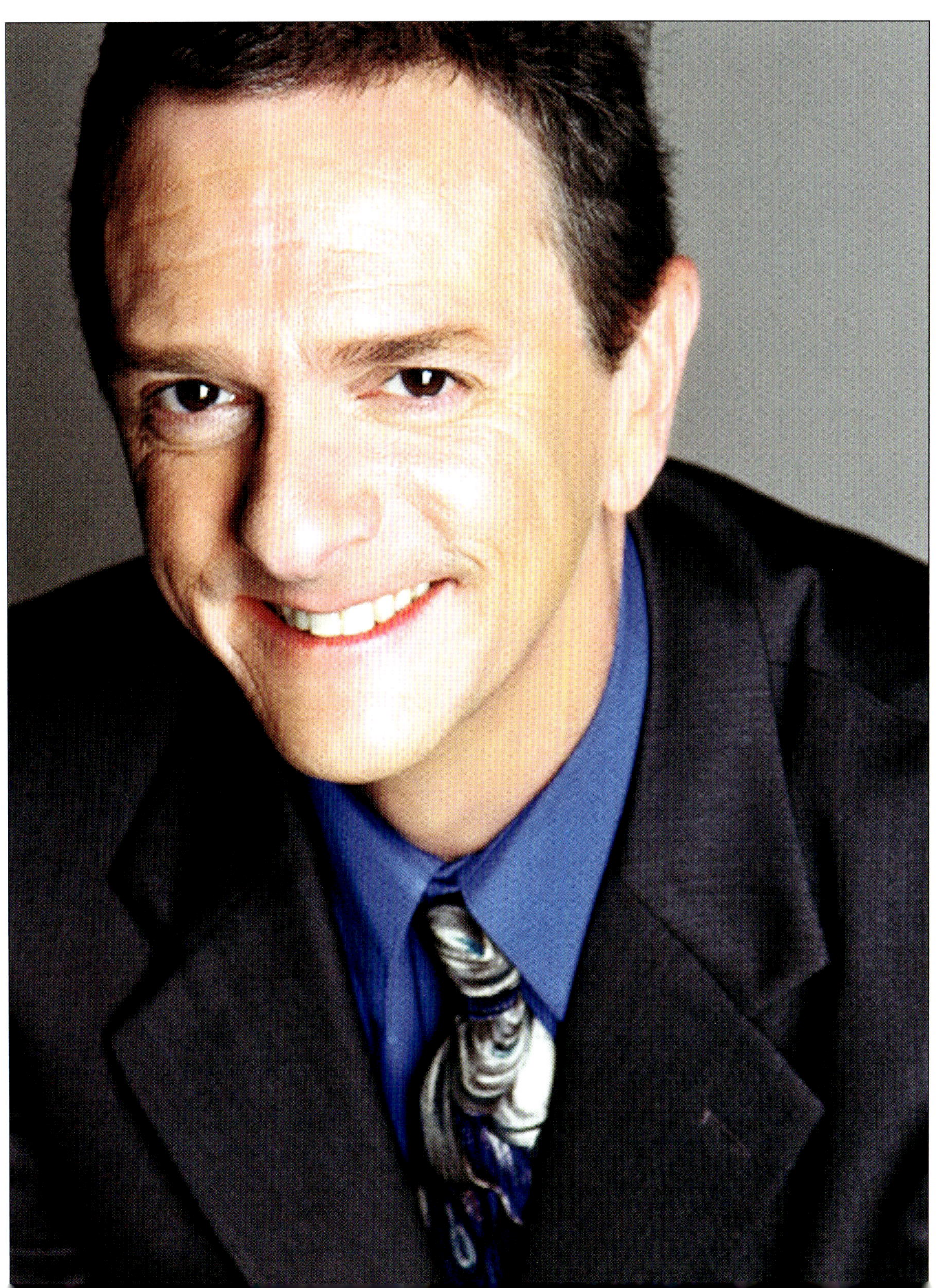

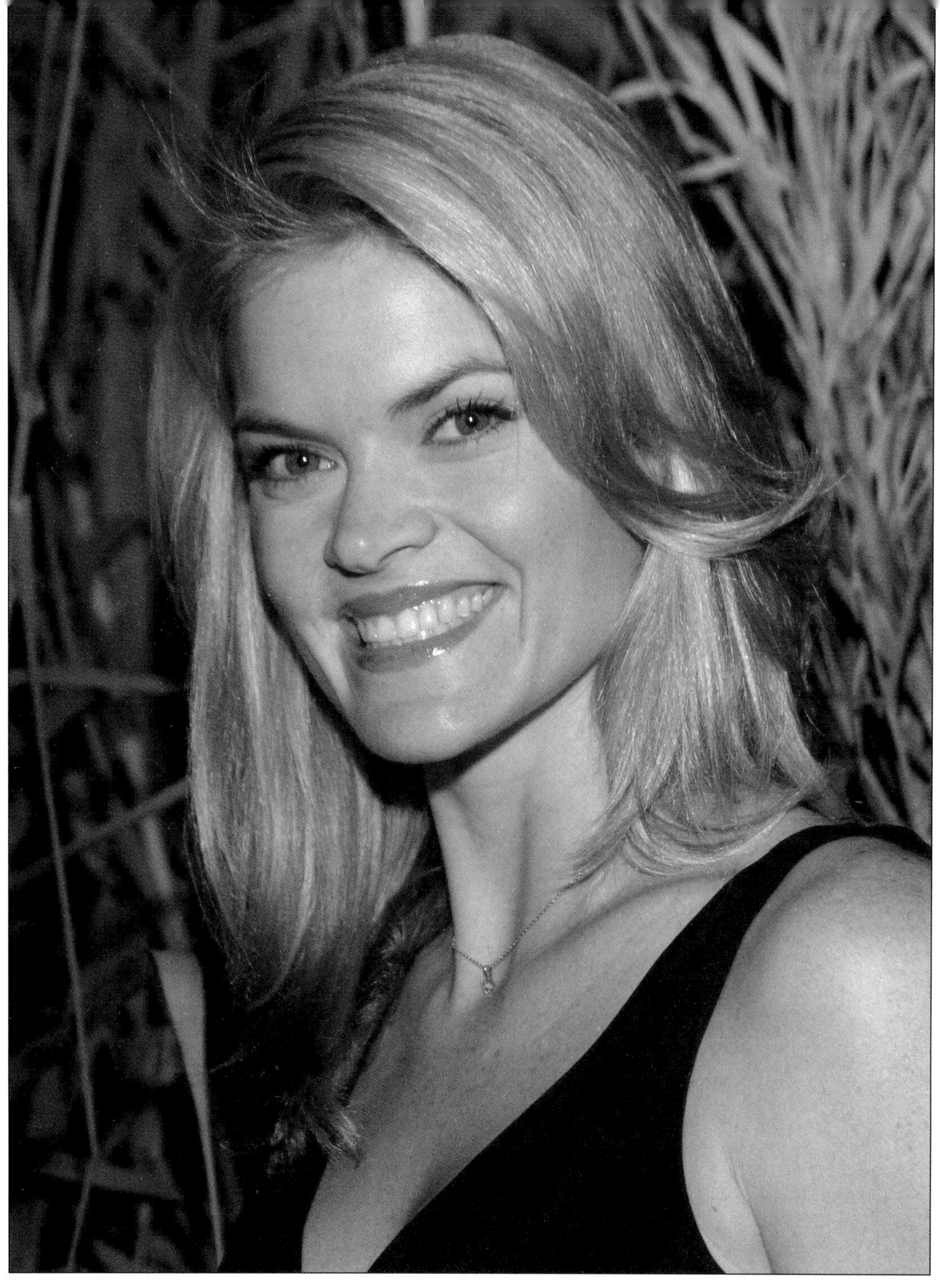

MISSI PYLE

ACTOR

Actor Missi Pyle was raised in Memphis, often performing at the Poplar Pike Playhouse as a teenager. Her first big role was as Laliari in *Galaxy Quest*, and she has appeared in many films, including *Big Fish* and Tim Burton's remake of *Charlie and the Chocolate Factory*. Staying true to her musical Memphis roots, Pyle is part of a country music group, with actress Shawnee Smith, called Smith & Pyle. They have also started a record label, Urban Prairie Records.

Photograph by FilmMagic/J. Merritt

LISA QUINN

DESIGNER, AUTHOR

Born in Memphis, Lisa Quinn first launched an interior design consultation business from her own home in 1997. She later moved to LA, expanding her business into a design entertainment firm, specializing in set dressings and commercial staging, among others. She has appeared on *Good Morning America* and *Oprah*, and has worked as a contributing writer for *Better Homes and Gardens*, *Redbook*, and *PARADE*. In 2010, she published her first book, *Life's Too Short to Fold Fitted Sheets*.

Photograph by Getty Image News/Martin Klimek

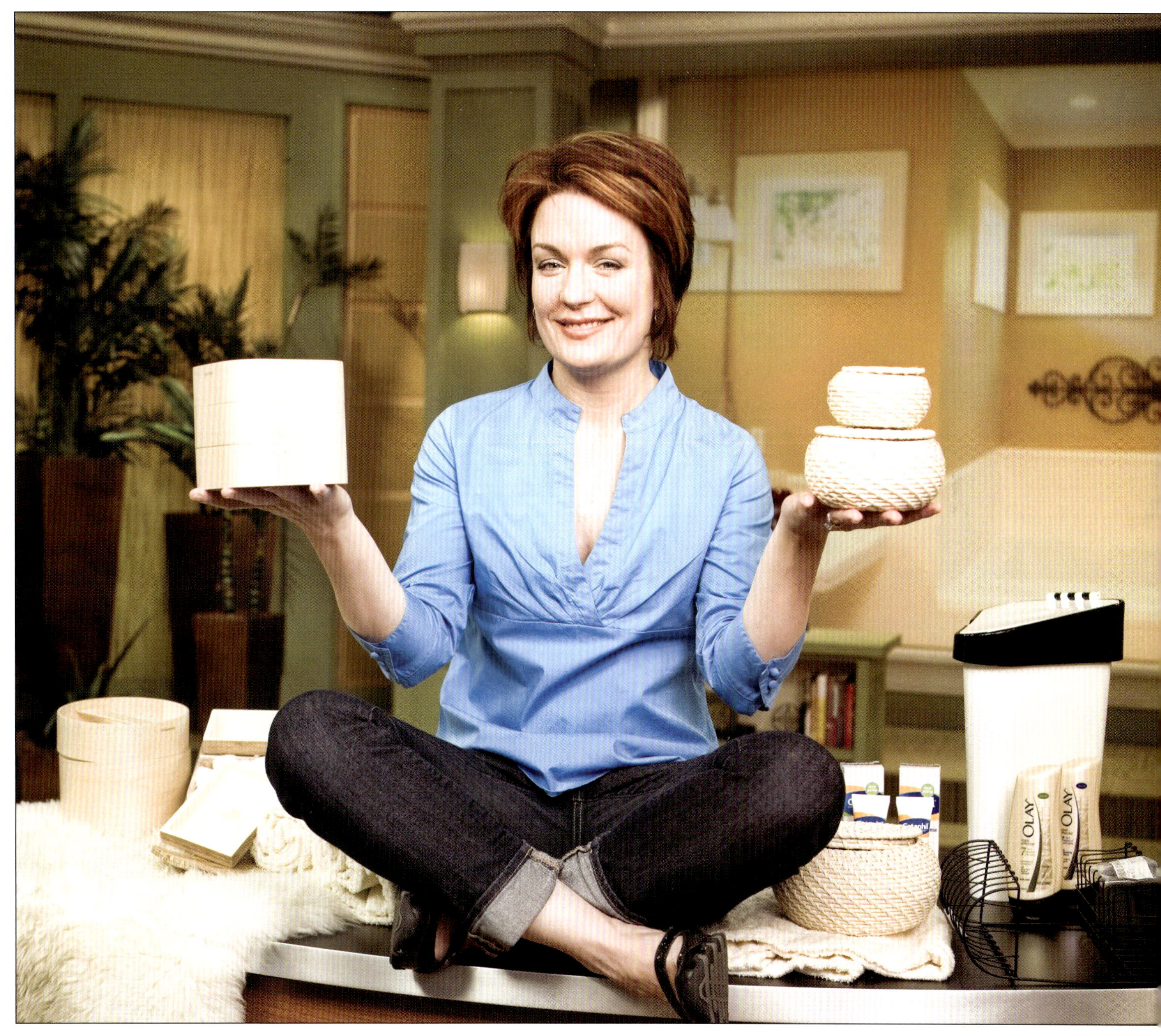

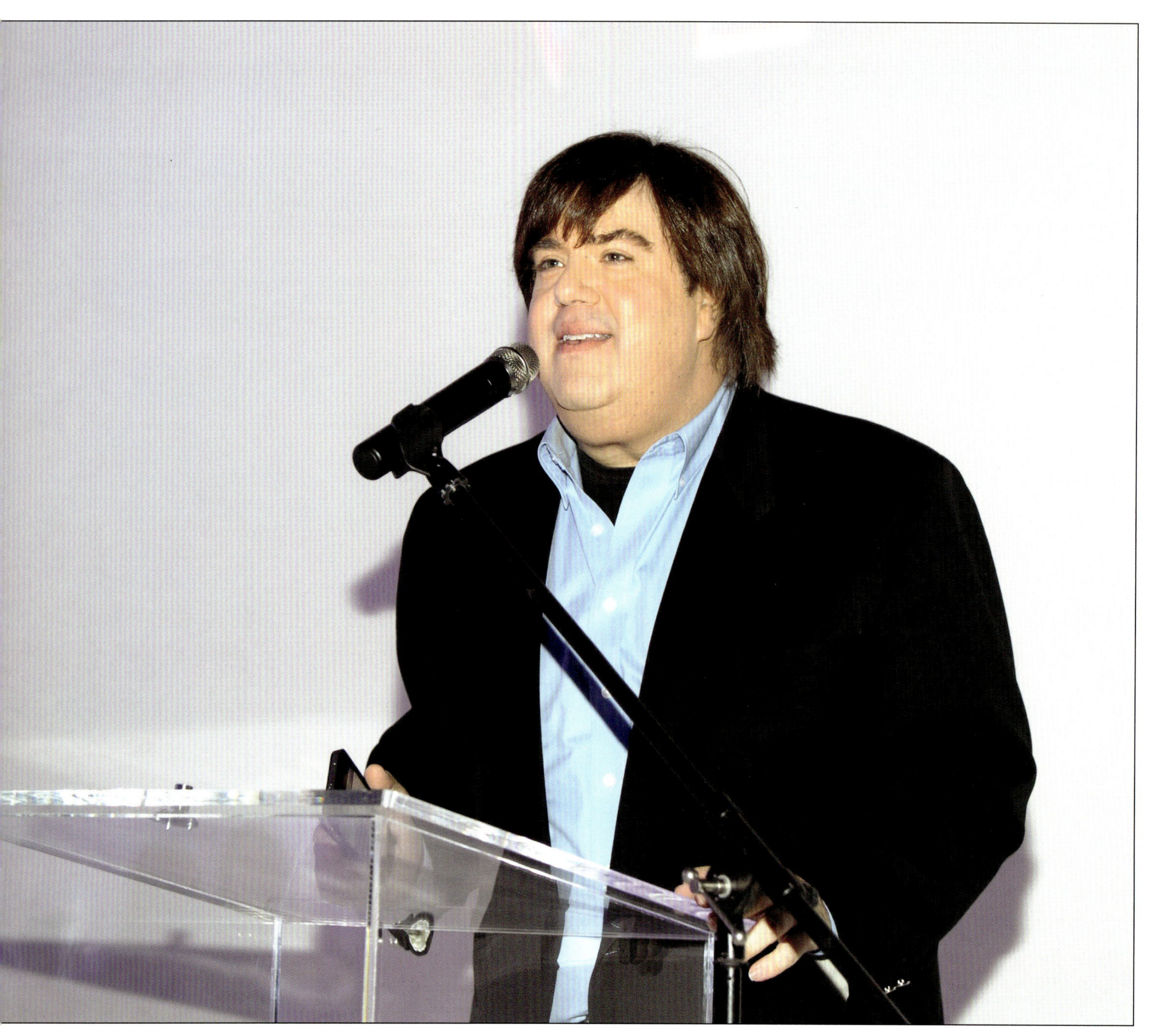

DAN SCHNEIDER

WRITER & PRODUCER

"My goal is to have the 10-year-olds and the 40-year-olds laughing together."
Dan Schneider

When he's not collecting Bakelite radios or restoring Chevy convertibles from the late 60s and early 70s, Dan Schneider has a full-time career as a writer and producer. He got his start when he was spotted by a movie producer while attending Memphis State University and asked to audition for a role. He appeared in the film *Better Off Dead* and then in the TV show *Head of the Class* before switching to the other side of the camera. As a writer and producer, he has helped to create popular television shows such as *All That*, *Kenan & Kel*, and *iCarly*. Born and raised in Memphis, he still visits his hometown a few times a year.

Photograph by Getty Entertainment/Michael Buckner

PAUL SHANKLIN

IMPERSONATOR

"He's a small army . . . make that a medium-sized army . . . of character voices."

Stan Freberg

Paul Shanklin's career as the "man of many voices" on the Rush Limbaugh show started, of all places, at the Oldies 98/Turner Dairy booth at the Mid-South Fair. His spot-on impersonations of Ross Perot got him invited as a regular on the Oldies 98 morning show. He reached a national audience when he called Limbaugh's producer in 1993 posing as President Bill Clinton and asked, "I don't feel Rush and I are as close as we used to be. Can you work things out between me and Rush?" It worked. He has since written and produced 1300 song parodies and spoofs and released 12 albums.

Photograph courtesy of Paul Shanklin

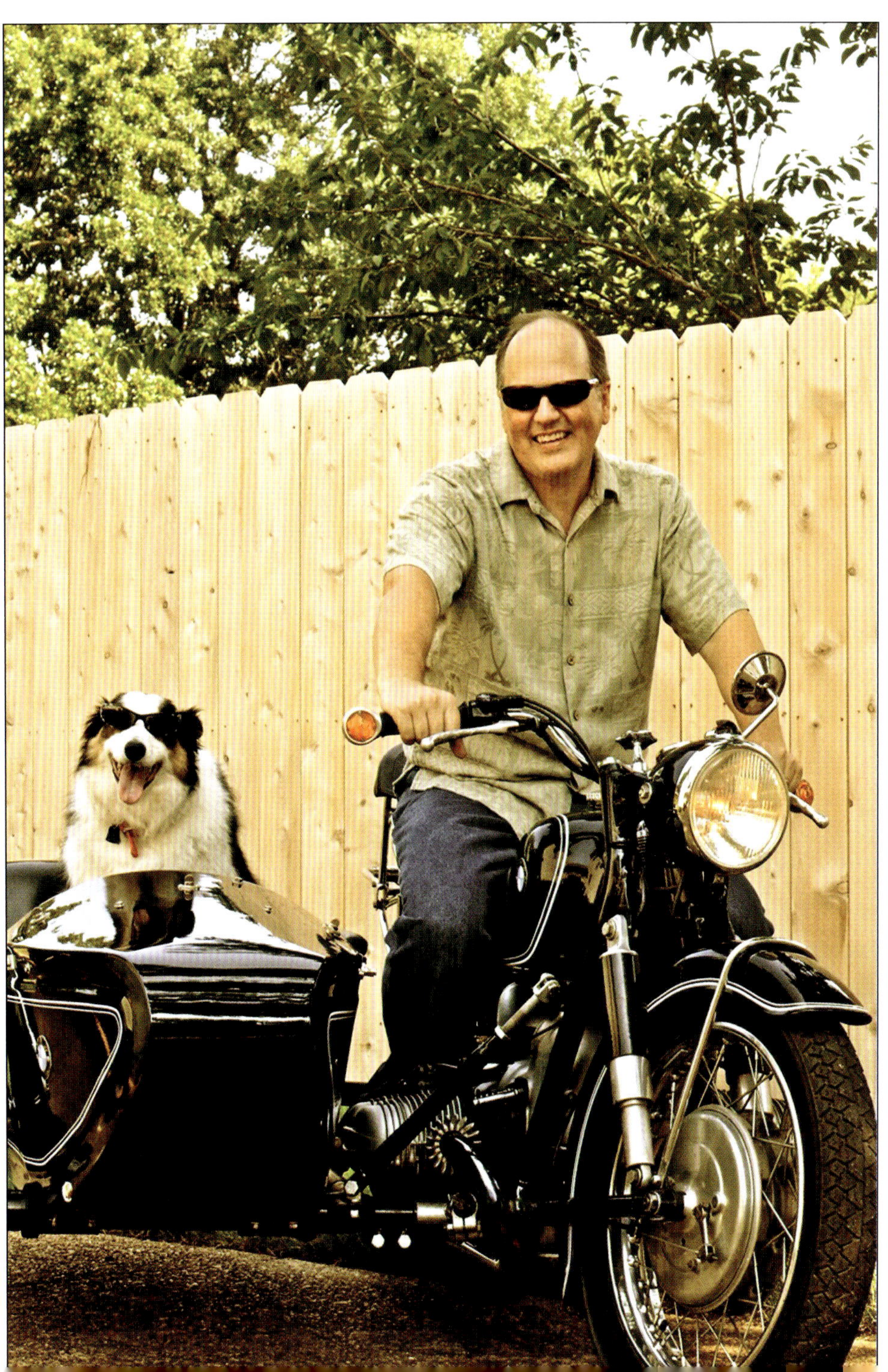

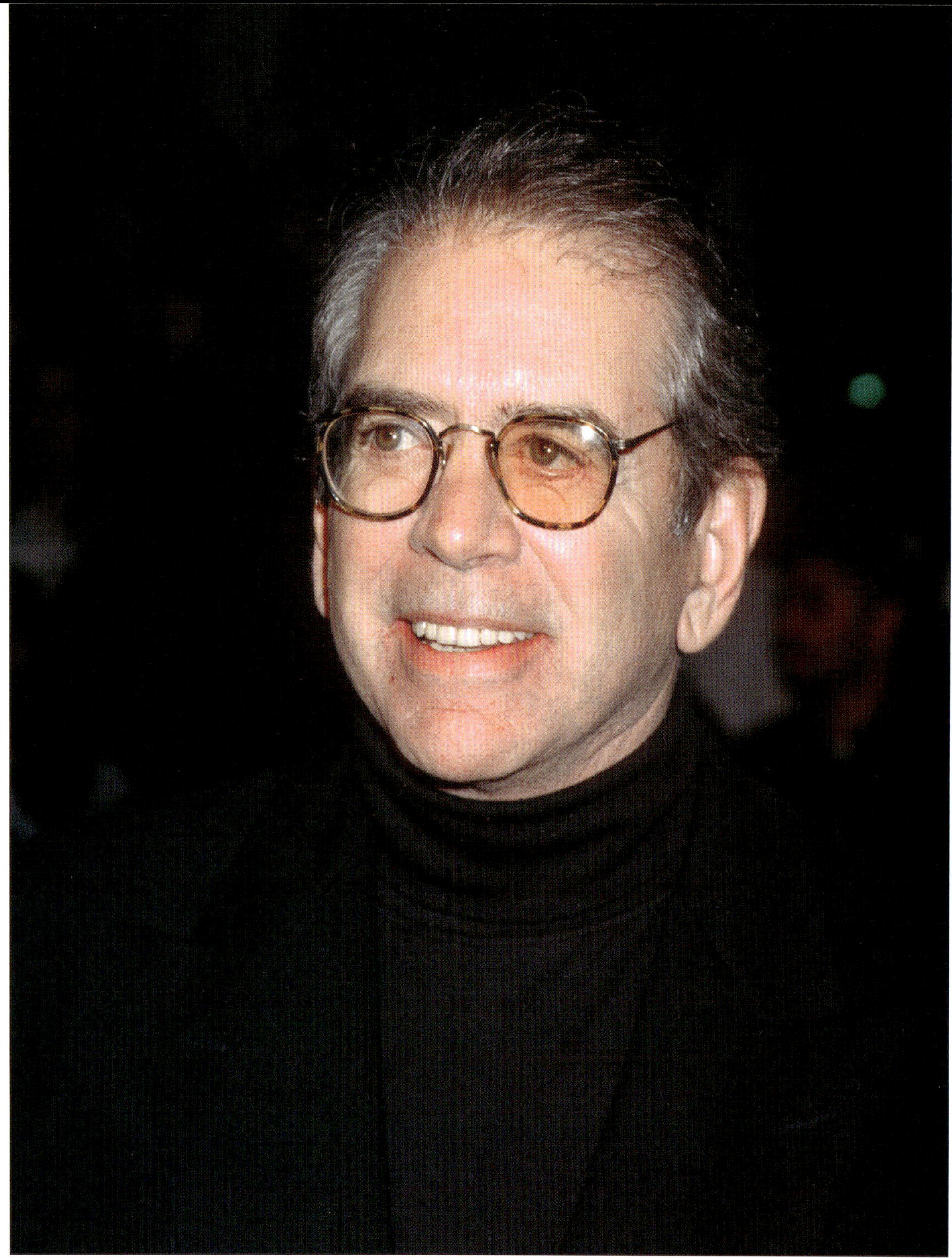

LANE SMITH

ACTOR

When he dropped out of Carnegie Mellon to join the Army, Lane Smith may not have planned on becoming a famous actor; however, he moved to New York to study at the Actors Studio after his stint in the military. Born in Memphis, Smith appeared in the original stage production of *Glengarry Glen Ross*, as well as the film *My Cousin Vinny* and the popular TV series *Lois & Clark: The New Adventures of Superman* (in which his character, Perry White, was obsessed with fellow Memphian, Elvis Presley). Smith was praised by critics and viewers for his portrayal of Richard Nixon in *The Final Days*.

Photograph by WireImage/Jim Smeal

STELLA STEVENS

ACTOR

Stella Stevens first became interested in acting while she was a student at Memphis State College. A press-agent spotted her working in a Memphis department store, and she headed to New York to start looking for work. Her first big role was with *Li'l Abner* and she went on to appear in *The Courtship of Eddie's Father* and *Girls! Girls! Girls!* with fellow Memphian, Elvis. In later years, she stepped behind the camera to film the documentary *The American Heroine*.

Photograph by Hulton Archive

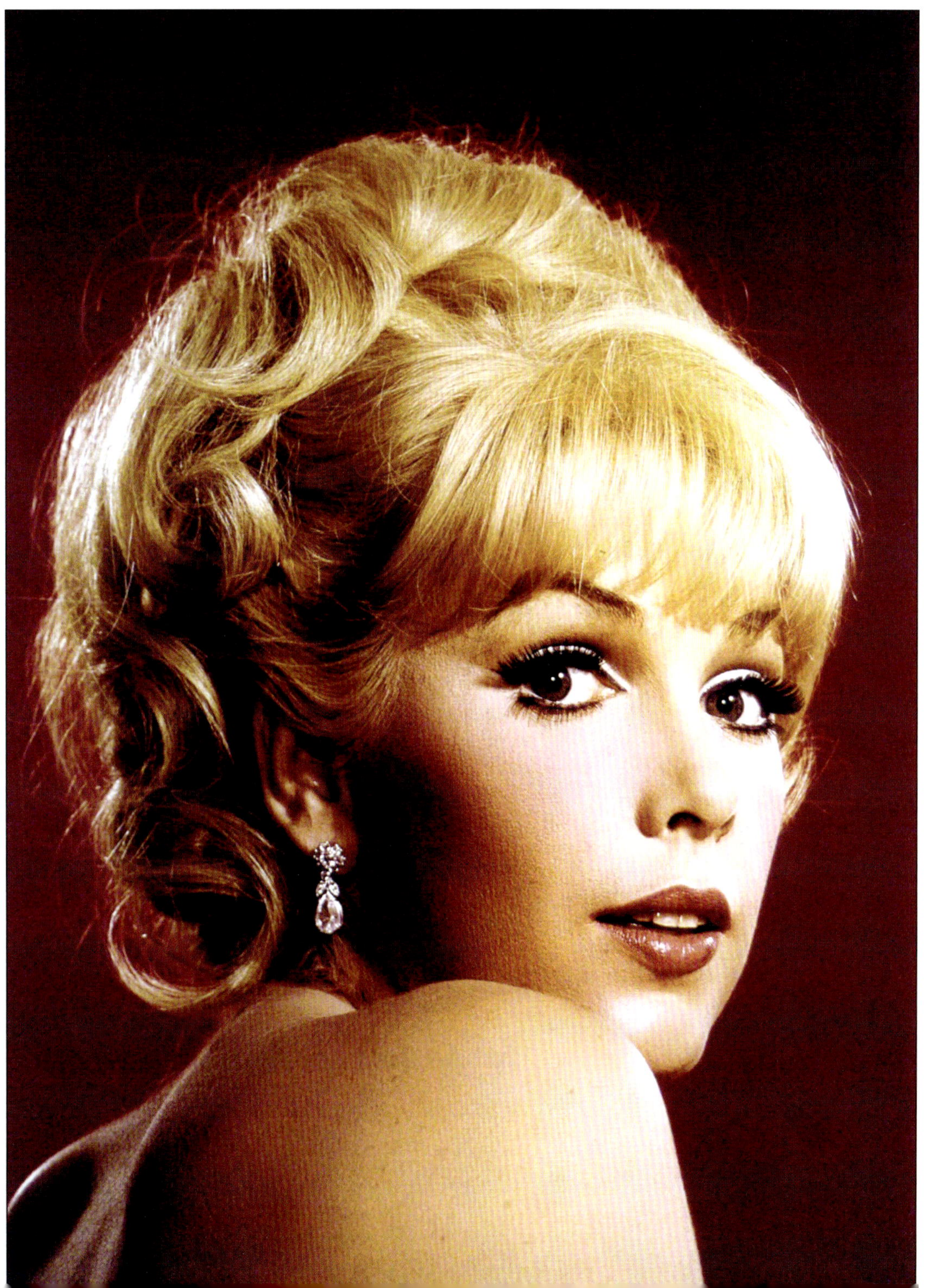

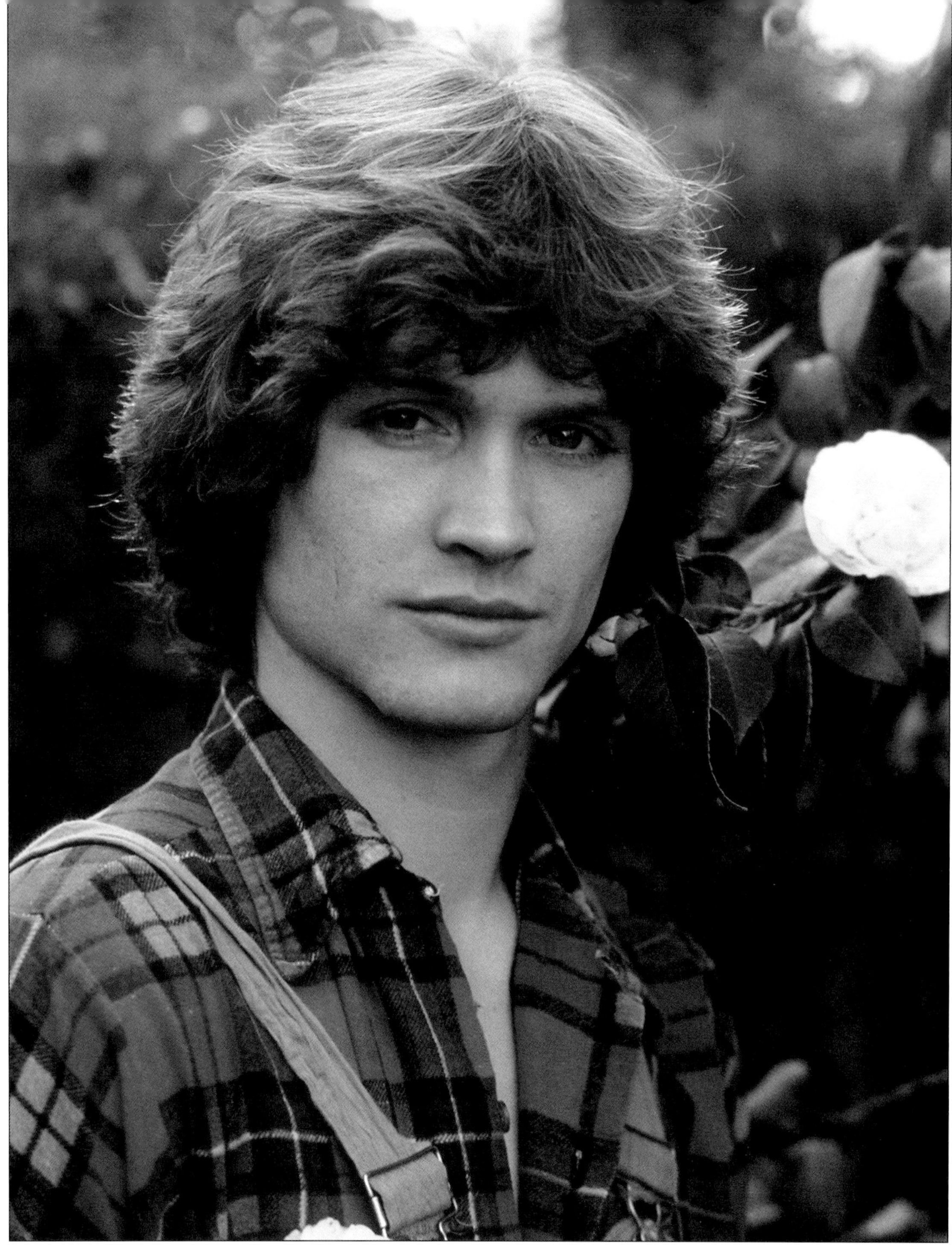

ANDREW STEVENS

ACTOR & PRODUCER

"...some of the most interesting and challenging roles are the most villainous. There's just so much more to work with when the character is the heavy."

Andrew Stevens

Son of actress Stella Stevens, Andrew first appeared alongside his mother as a child in *The Courtship of Eddie's Father* and then as an adult in *Las Vegas Lady*. He found early success as an eighties era "shirtless hunk" until he shifted his focus to making, rather than starring in, movies. Through various production companies, Stevens has produced some 170 films for television and the big screen.

Photograph by Michael Ochs Archive/Donaldson Collection

FRED THOMPSON

ACTOR & POLITICIAN

"When Hollywood directors need someone who can personify governmental power, they often turn to Fred Thompson."

New York Times

Fred Thompson's first movie role was playing himself as District Attorney of Tennessee. He served as minority counsel to the Senate Watergate Hearings, but it was his defense of Marie Ragghianti, a parole board chair who refused to go along with a cash-for-clemency scheme, that made his name a household item. Her story was made into a book, then a movie.

After that, the roles just kept coming for the tall, deep-voiced country boy. The first in his family to go to college, Thompson graduated from then Memphis State University with degrees in philosophy and political science. On joining the Tennessee Bar in 1967, he shortened his name to Fred from Freddie, but that short name would get very big. A popular character actor since the eighties, Thompson has balanced his political and acting careers famously. Serving two terms as a Tennessee Senator (1994-2003), he ran for the Republican presidential nomination in 2002 and again in 2007.

Photograph CQ-Roll Call Group/Scott J. Ferrell

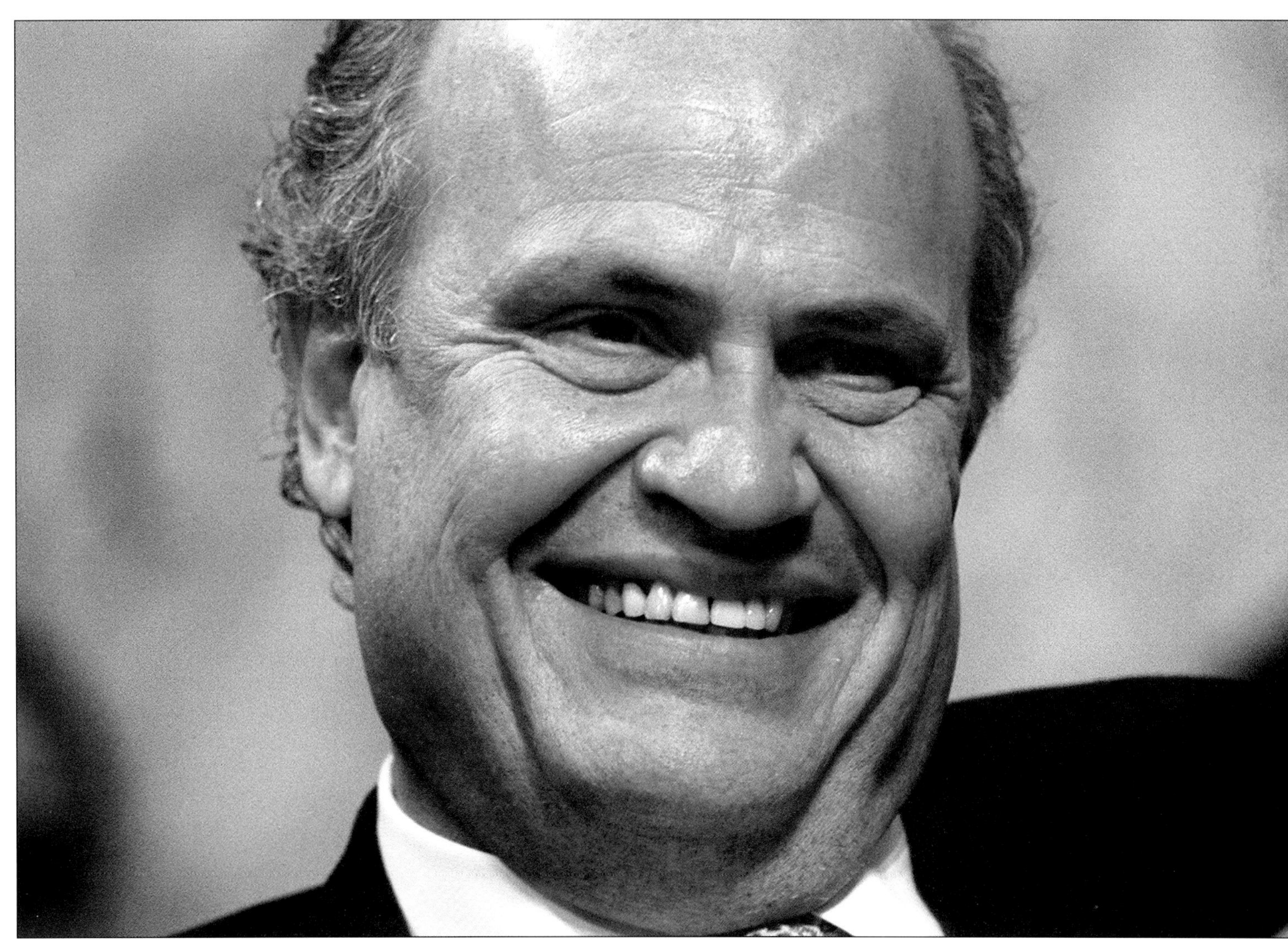

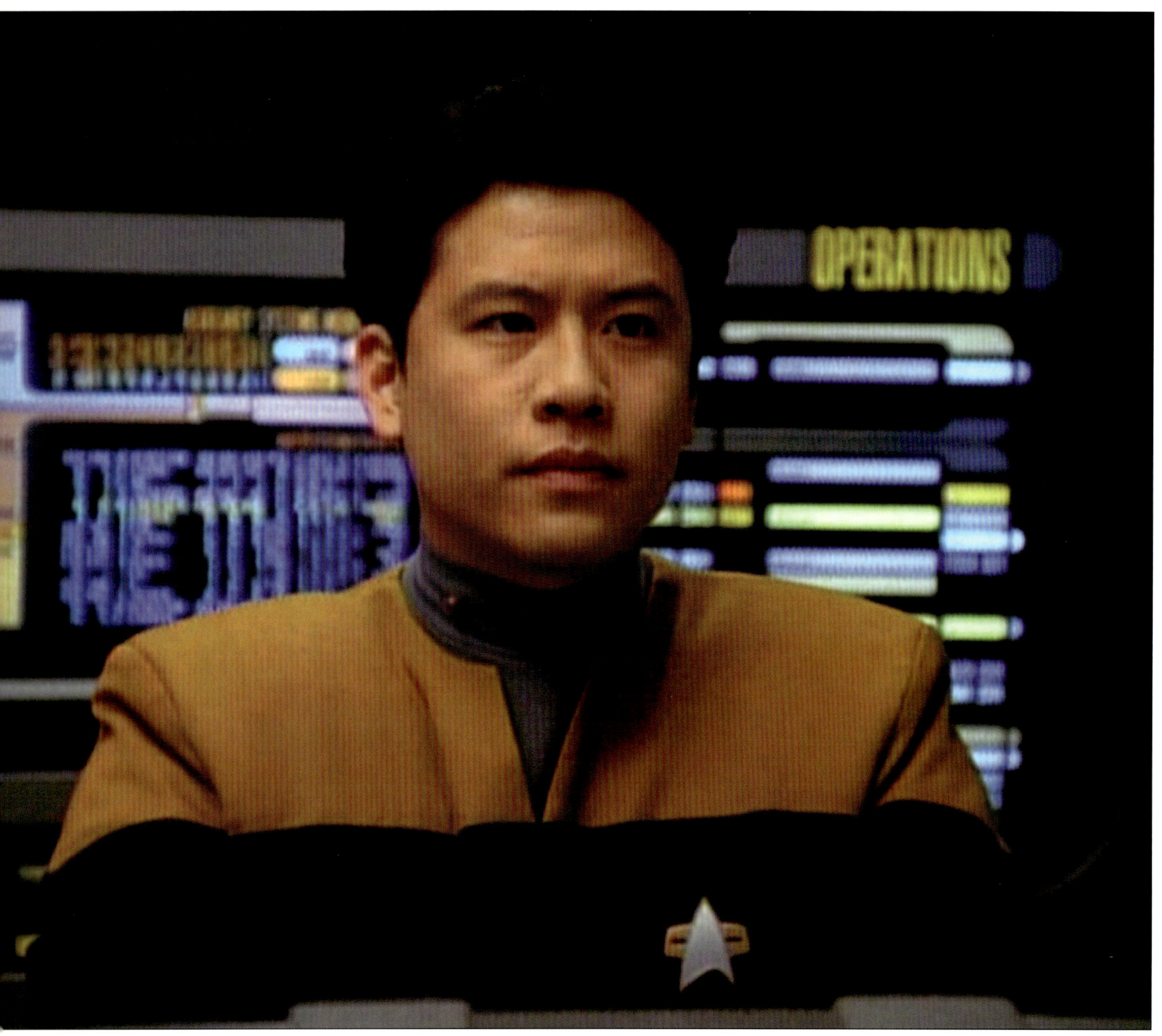

GARRETT WANG

STAR FLEET ENSIGN, ACTOR

A science fiction fan as a child, it should be no surprise to Garrett Wang that his best-known role came in the form of Ensign Harry Kim on *Star Trek: Voyager*. A graduate of Memphis's Harding Academy High School, Wang majored in Asian Studies at UCLA, where a professor encouraged him to pursue acting. He began work on *Voyager* in 1995. In 2010, he became the Director of the *Star Trek* track from Dragon*Con.

Photograph by Paramount

RED WEST

ACTOR, BODYGUARD

Red West began driving for Elvis Presley in 1955. A friendship developed and soon West was penning songs for Presley and other artists. Tagging along with Presley to Hollywood in the sixties, West befriended Nick Adams and Robert Conrad and appeared on both actors' television series, as both a stunt man and actor.

Most people today think of Red West as a member of Elvis' Memphis Mafia, and an occasional actor in television and film. Largely forgotten is the controversy surrounding West's contentious split with Presley. West had been a long time friend, driver, bodyguard, and even costar of Presley's, but in 1977, it was West's attempt to perform a very public intervention that led to his dismissal from the Presley camp. West, along with two other former bodyguards of Presley, West's cousin Sonny West, and Dave Hebler, collaborated on a book about Presley, *Elvis: What Happened,* that detailed the singer's heavy use of prescription drugs. Reportedly Presley was furious, and had his father Vernon, fire West. Presley was known for being forgiving, and may have ultimately reconciled with his old friend, but within weeks of the book's publishing, Presley died. West continued to work in television and film, even founding his own film acting school in Memphis. West was critically acclaimed for his performance in 2009's *Goodbye Solo.*

Photograph: Red West with Elvis, WireImage/Tom Wargacki • **Story** by Dennis Phillippi

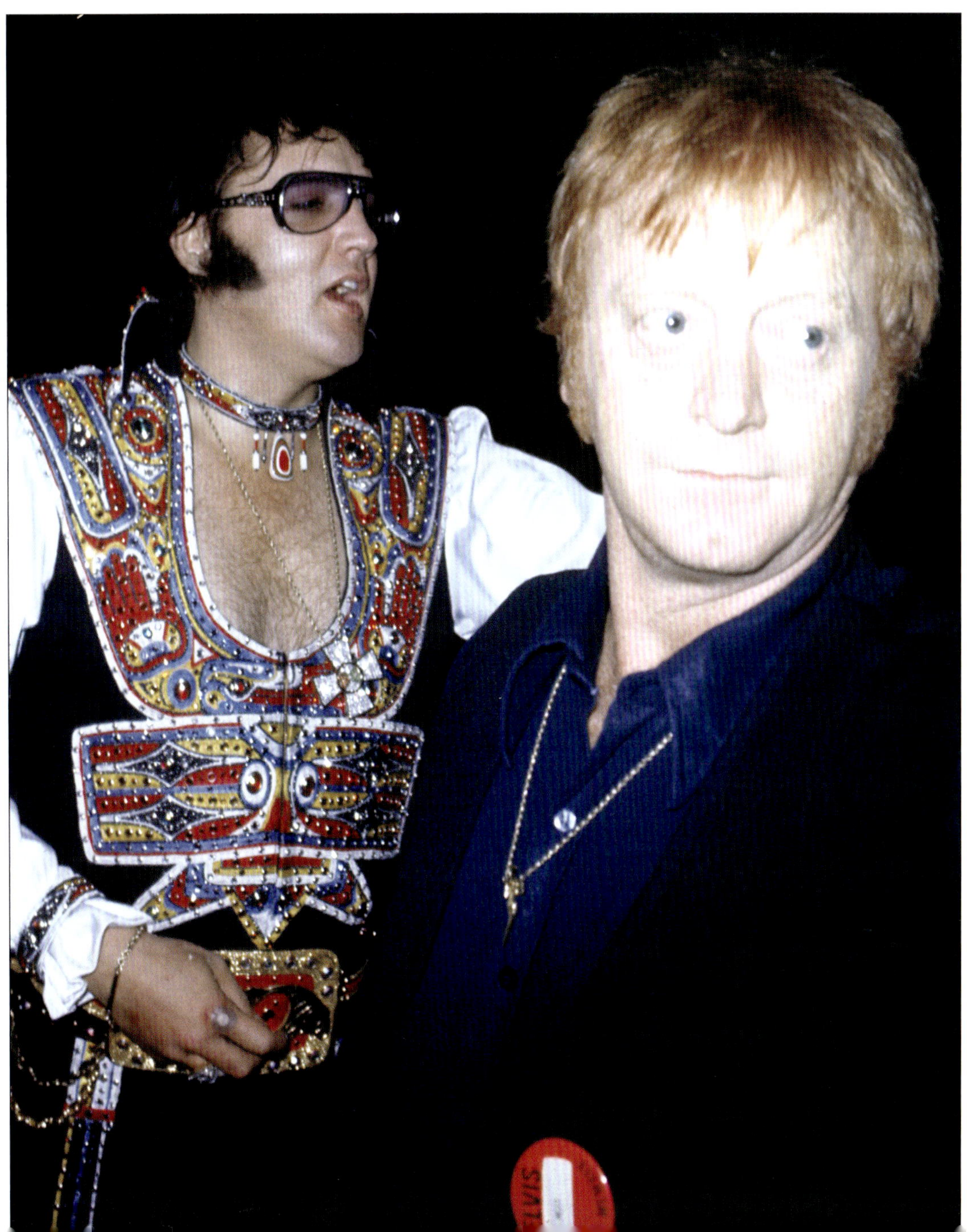

Music

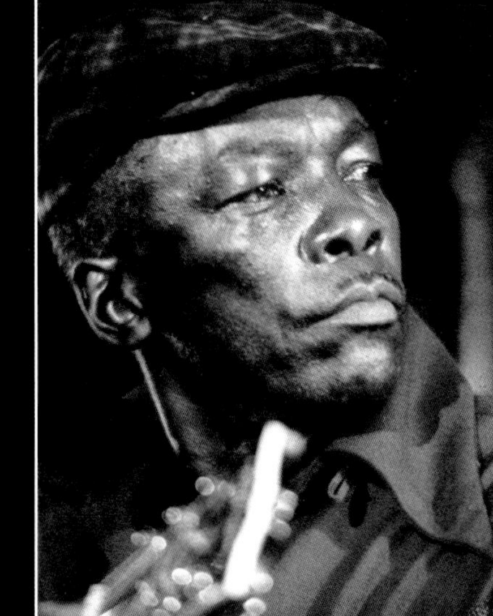

B.B. KING

KING OF THE BLUES

"All I did was copy B.B. King."
Eric Clapton

He ran into a burning building to save his guitar, and named it Lucille after the woman who started the fight that started the fire. *Rolling Stone* listed him as #3 of the "100 Greatest Guitar Players of All Time." Eric Clapton, Jeff Beck and George Harrison called him both friend and mentor. It was on Beale where B.B. King honed his craft and caught the attention of DJ Rufus Thomas. He got his first nickname "Beale Blues Boy" here, and his *King's Spot* on legendary radio station WDIA was wildly popular.

In 1956 he and Lucille played a jaw-dropping 342 shows. After 50 records and 15 Grammies, he still plays 250 shows a year. His blues clubs in Memphis and around the country keep promoting the music that he helped define for millions. He is B.B. King and the thrill is not gone.

Photograph courtesy Tom Davis • **Story** by Richard Murff

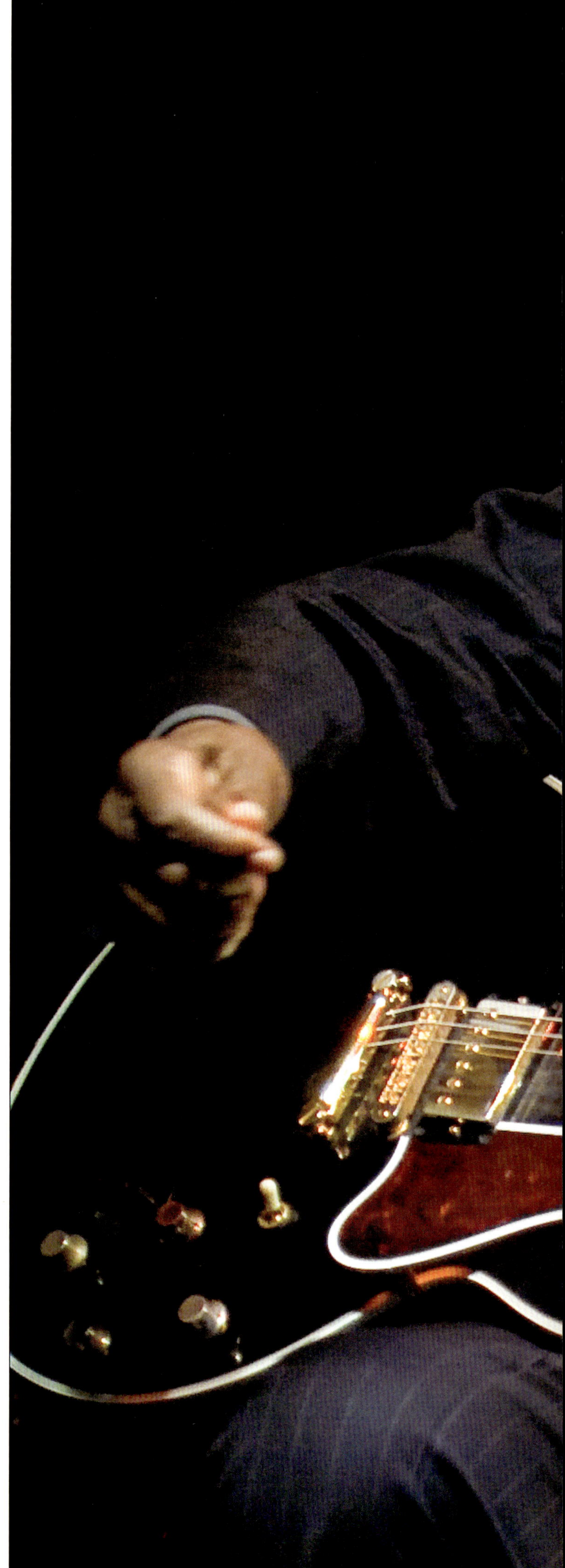

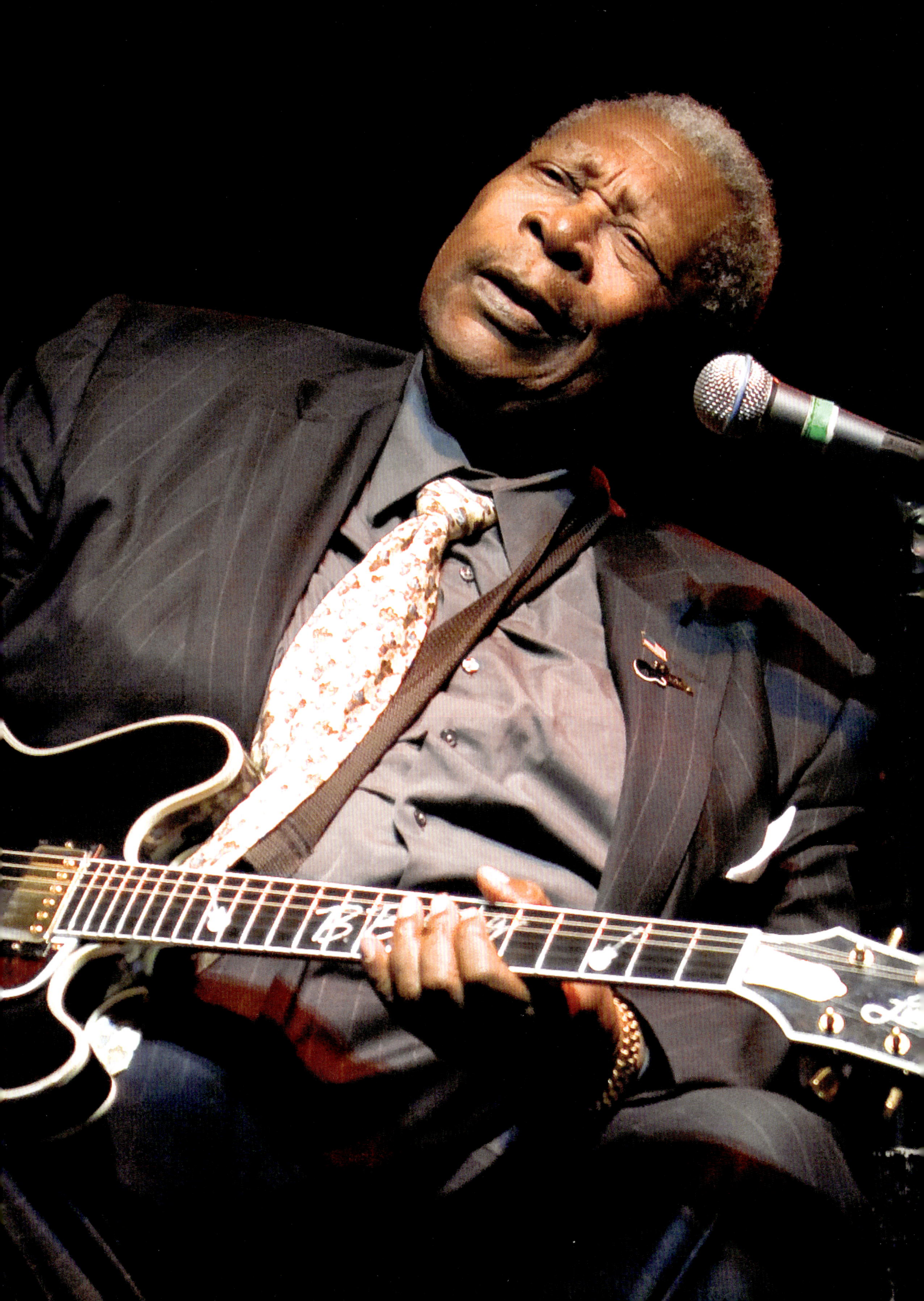

JUSTIN TIMBERLAKE

SINGER, SONGWRITER, ACTOR

"The many sounds of Memphis shaped my early musical career and continue to be an inspiration to this day."
Justin Timberlake

Growing up in Shelby Forest outside of Memphis, Justin Randall Timberlake had early ambitions to be a singer. At the age of 10, he sang at the Grand Ole Opry and, at 11, he appeared on *Star Search*, decked out in a cowboy hat and boots and singing country music. Only two years later, he joined the cast of *The Mickey Mouse Club*.

He shot to stardom with the formation of the boy band *NSYNC, which produced both the fastest (*No Strings Attached*) and second fastest (*Celebrity*) selling albums of all time. He moved on to a solo career, with albums debuting at #1 and #2 on the Billboard charts, as well as an acting career, appearing in flims such as *Alpha Dog*, *Black Snake Moan*, *Social Network*, and *Shrek the Third*. He has become a favorite guest on both *The Ellen Degeneres Show* and *Saturday Night Live*.

With all his success, Timberlake continues to give back to his Memphis community. He started the Justin Timberlake Foundation in order to fund music education programs in schools, the first donation going to his own school, E. E. Jeter Elementary, and has donated to both the Memphis Rock 'n' Soul Museum and the Memphis Music Foundation.

Photography WireImage/Kevin Mazur • **Story** by Genie Leslie

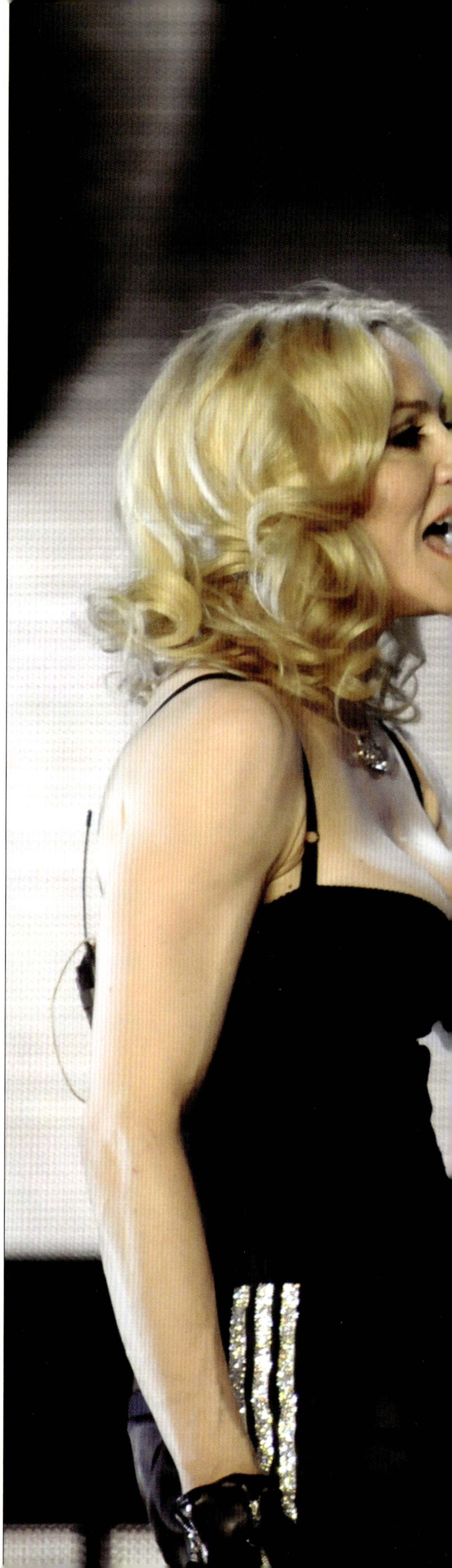

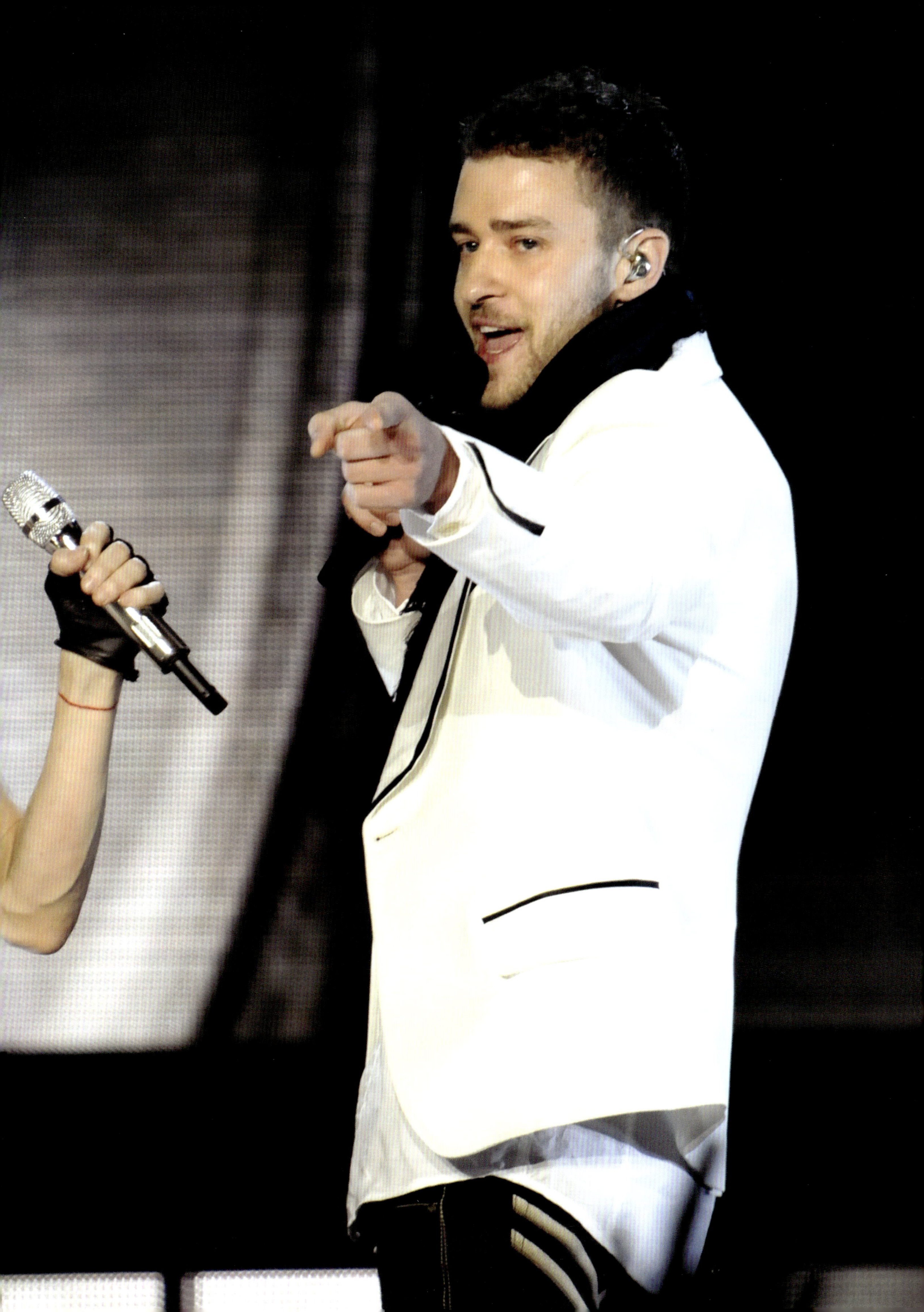

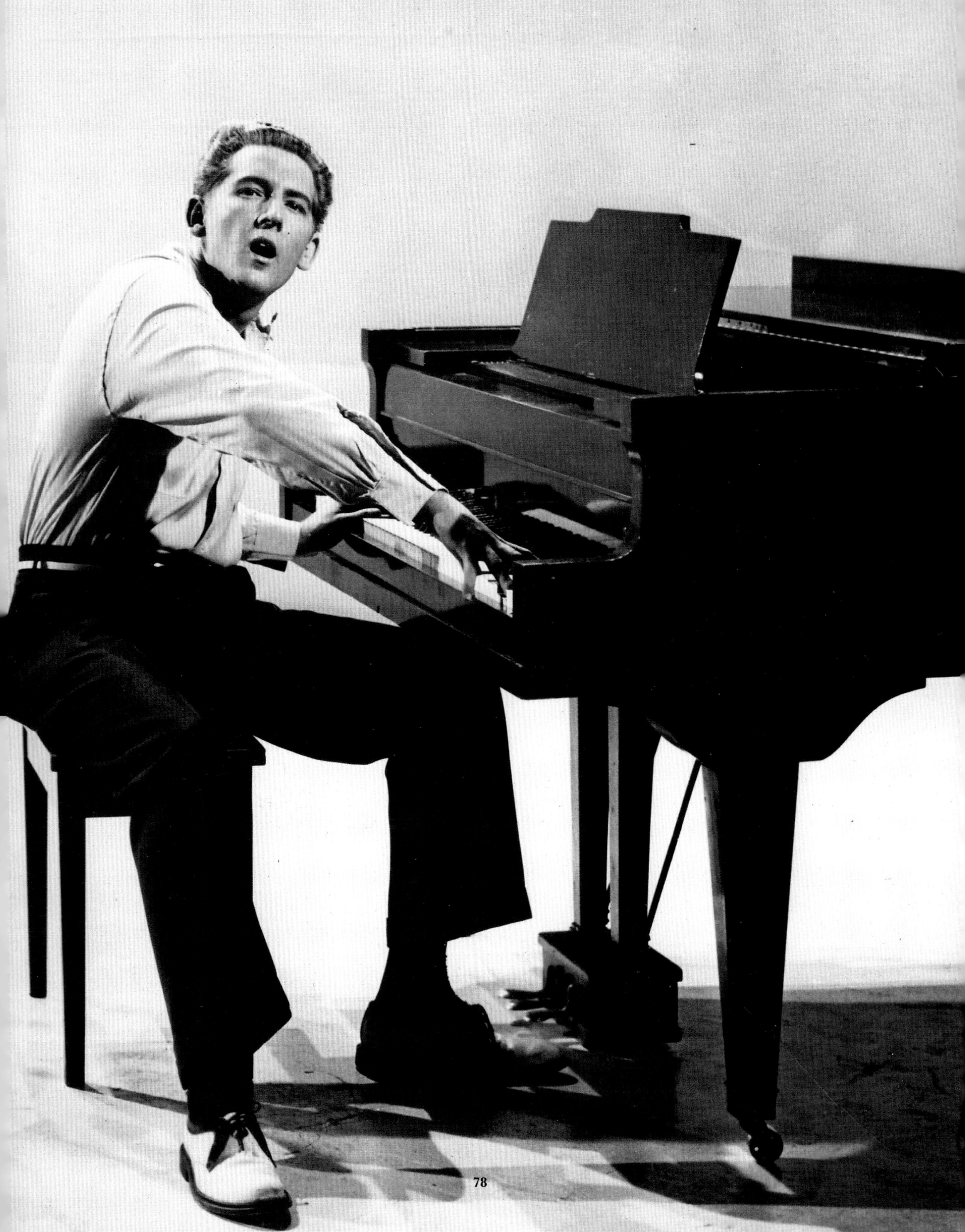

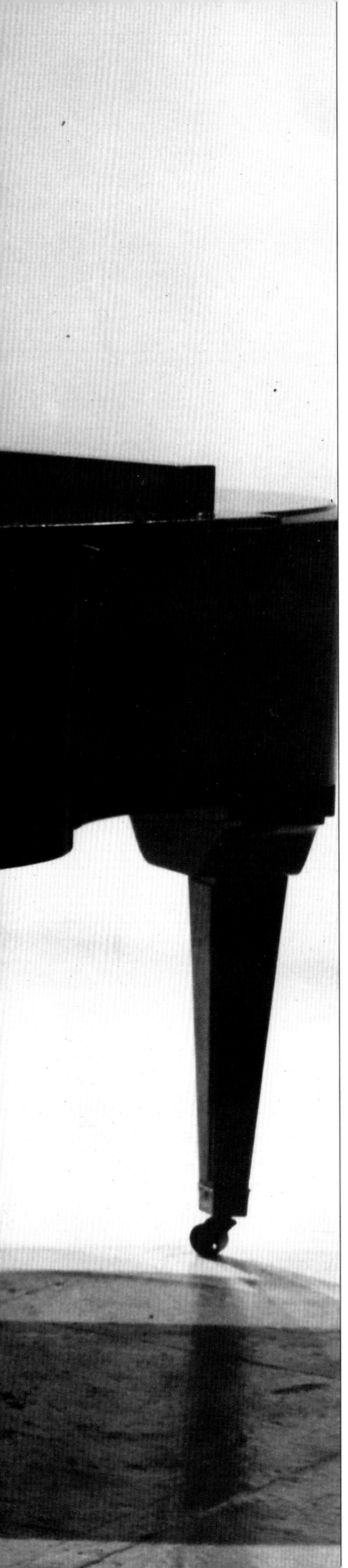

JERRY LEE LEWIS

THE KILLER

"Just gimme my money and show me where the piano is..."
Jerry Lee Lewis

Jerry Lee Lewis may have been expelled from his religious school for playing a boogie woogie version of "My God is Real" during church, but that didn't stop him from pursuing his passion for playing "sinful" rock n' roll piano music. He auditioned for Sam Phillips' Sun Records in 1956 and started working as an occasional session artist playing backup for Carl Perkins, Johnny Cash and Elvis Presley.

Well known for his raucous performance style, standing at the piano, kicking the bench away, and sliding his hands all over the keyboard, Lewis' life has been filled with fame, scandal, and rock n' roll history in the making.

Roy Orbison said Lewis was "the best raw performer in the history of rock and roll."

Photography Redferns/Gilles Petard

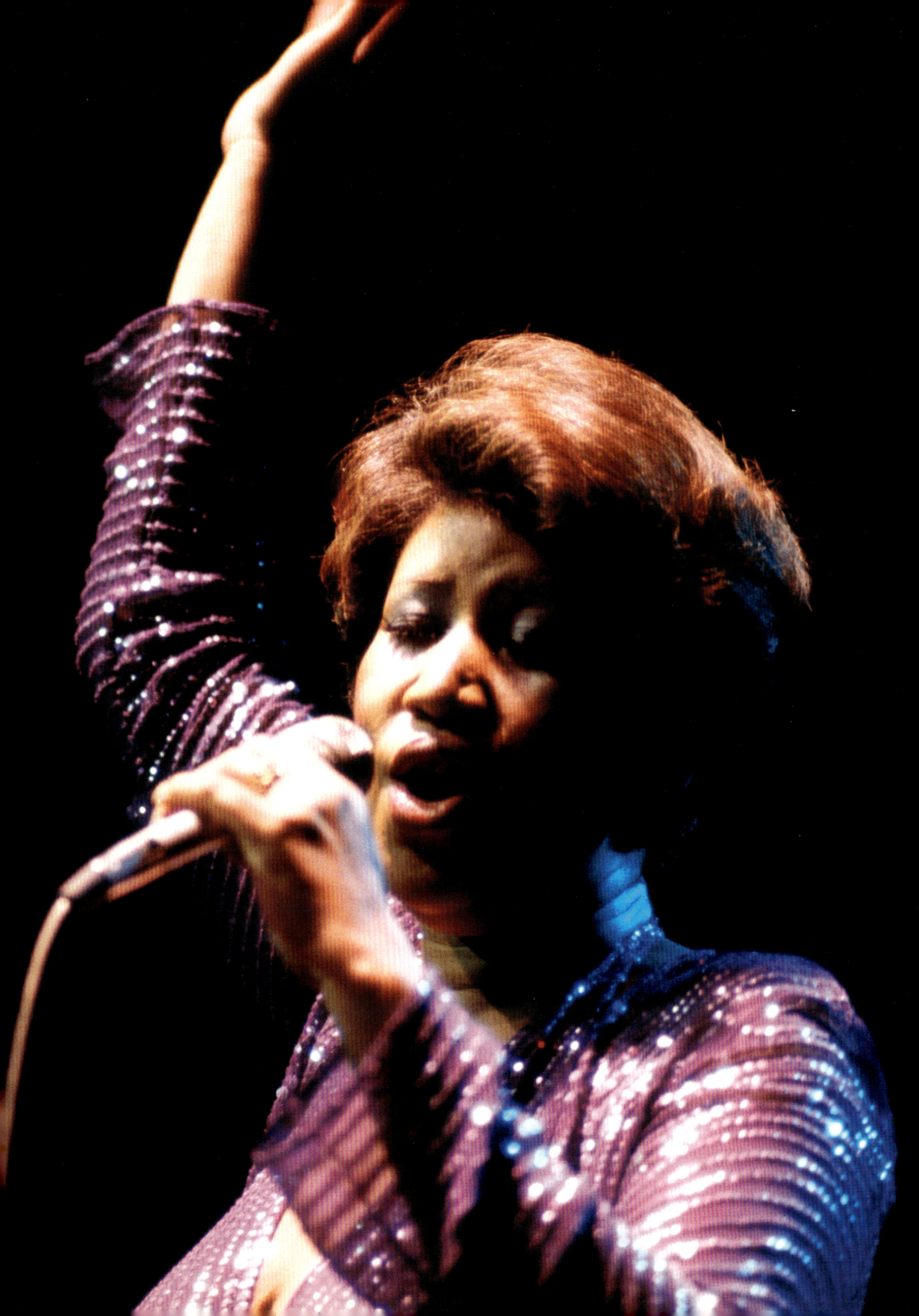

ARETHA FRANKLIN

THE QUEEN OF SOUL

"I want to sing like Aretha Franklin."
Lena Horne

Her voice declared a "natural resource" by the governor of Michigan, Aretha Franklin grew up singing in church. Born to a Baptist minister, she honed her vocal skills with frequent choir solos and she learned to play the piano by ear. She released her first single at age 18 and her first album a few months later, in 1961. She scored 10 Top Ten hits in about 18 months (early 1967-late 1968) and between 1967 and 1982, she had ten No. 1 R&B albums. Known as the Queen of Soul, many of her songs are still popular today, including "Respect," "Chain of Fools," and "I Say a Little Prayer."

Known worldwide for her big voice and bigger personality, Franklin has commented, "I'm a big woman. I need big hair." And when asked about her comeback, she quipped, "Don't say Aretha is making a comeback, because I've never been away!"

In 1987, she became the first woman inducted into the Rock and Roll Hall of Fame and, in 1999, she published her memoir, *Aretha: From These Roots*. In 2009, Franklin was personally asked by President Obama to sing at his inauguration. Franklin has never forgotten her beginning: born in a 2-room house in Memphis, Tenn., and crafting her voice in the church choir.

Photography Redferns/David Redfern

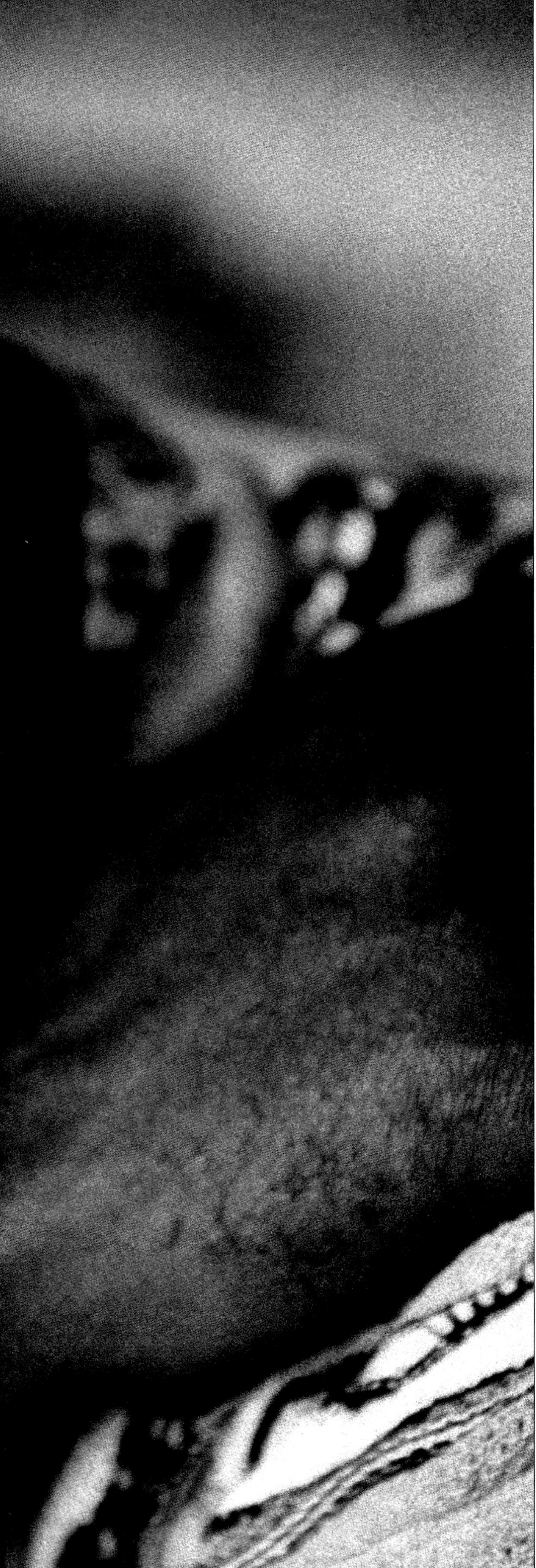

ISAAC HAYES

SINGER, SONGWRITER

"He was cool before it was cool to be cool. He left us a storehouse of classics, pure poetry that will live forever because they are, quite simply, among the greatest songs ever sung."

Susan Lacy, executive producer of American Masters

Possibly most famous for his Academy-award-winning theme song from the film *Shaft*, Isaac Hayes got his start at Memphis' Stax Records. Beginning as a studio session musician, he was soon writing songs for popular Stax acts such as Sam & Dave. "Hold On, I'm Comin'" and "Soul Man" are two songs Hayes and co-writer David Porter created, songs that are still popular today; "Soul Man" has been honored by both the Rock and Roll Hall of Fame and the Grammy Hall of Fame. Hayes also recorded his own albums and composed scores for films.

He later branched out from music, moving into acting with his role as "Chef" on *South Park* and appearing in the films *Hustle & Flow* and *Soul Men*. As a humanitarian, he was honored with the title of "honorary king" from Ada, Ghana in 1992.

In 2008, Hayes passed away at home.

Photograph by Redferns/Paul Bergen

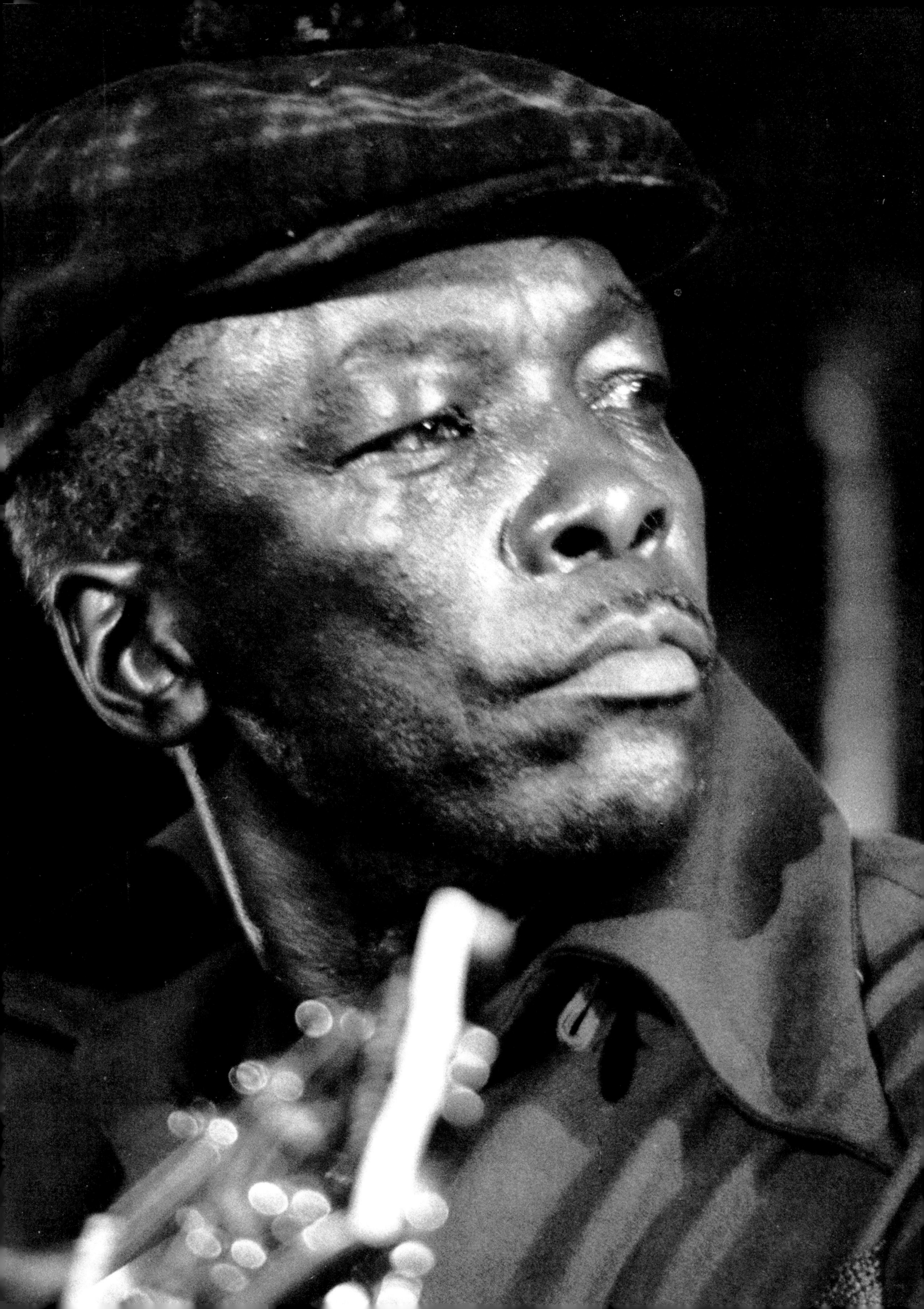

JOHN LEE HOOKER

BLUESMAN

"I don't think about time. You're here when you're here. I think about today, staying in tune."

John Lee Hooker

John Lee Hooker is the blues. Born near the fabled crossroads in Clarksdale, Hooker ran away from home at 15. During the 1930s he was a fixture on Beale Street and at the New Daisy Theater. Born out of the Delta, he adopted a droning Louisiana blues sound, and polished it in the heart of Memphis. Hooker's first single, "Boogie Chillun" was an instant hit in 1948. Along with "I'm In The Mood" and "Crawling Kingsnake," Hooker release over a hundred songs in the 50s and 60s. It was 1989's *The Healer* that projected him back to selling millions at the age of 72. The last ten years of his life were some of his most accomplished.

Photograph by Michael Ochs Archive/Tom Copi

ESTELLE AXTON & JIM STEWART

PRODUCERS

Jim Stewart and his sister, Estelle Axton, served up soul to the world; some of that hot, buttered soul that Isaac Hayes would come to sing about. And how could they not serve it up right with a kitchen staff that included a house band better known as Booker T. & the M.G.'s?

Jim and Estelle were raised on a farm in Middleton, Tennessee. They both worked as bank clerks in Memphis before Jim, an aspiring country musician, launched Satellite Records and convinced his sister to invest. Estelle, in turn, convinced her husband that they should remortgage their house to buy into the enterprise.

In 1959 they moved the operation into the former Capitol Theatre in a predominantly black South Memphis neighborhood. Two years later, Stewart took the first two letters of both his last name and Estelle's to create the new label's moniker, STAX.

Over the next 15 years, the duo would put out such hits as "Walking the Dog" by Rufus Thomas, "Soul Man" by Sam & Dave, "Crosscut Saw" by Albert King, "Soul Finger" by the Bar-Kays, "Green Onions" by Booker T. & the M.G.'s and "(Sittin' On) the Dock of the Bay" by Otis Redding, released posthumously.

Estelle sold her interest in STAX in 1970 and later began Fretone Records, whose biggest hit was "Disco Duck" by disc jockey Rick Dees, and she founded the Memphis Songwriters Association in 1973. The National Recording Academy honored her with the Trustee's Award at the 2007 Grammys. STAX Records went bankrupt in 1976 and Jim went into seclusion, sending his granddaughters to accept his award for induction in the Rock and Roll Hall of Fame in 2002.

Jim Stewart and Estelle Axton looked past the divisiveness of the times to feed a world hungry for some of the greatest soul music ever from their all-inclusive studio at STAX.

Photograph by Redferns/Charlie Gillett Collection • **Story** by Richard Alley

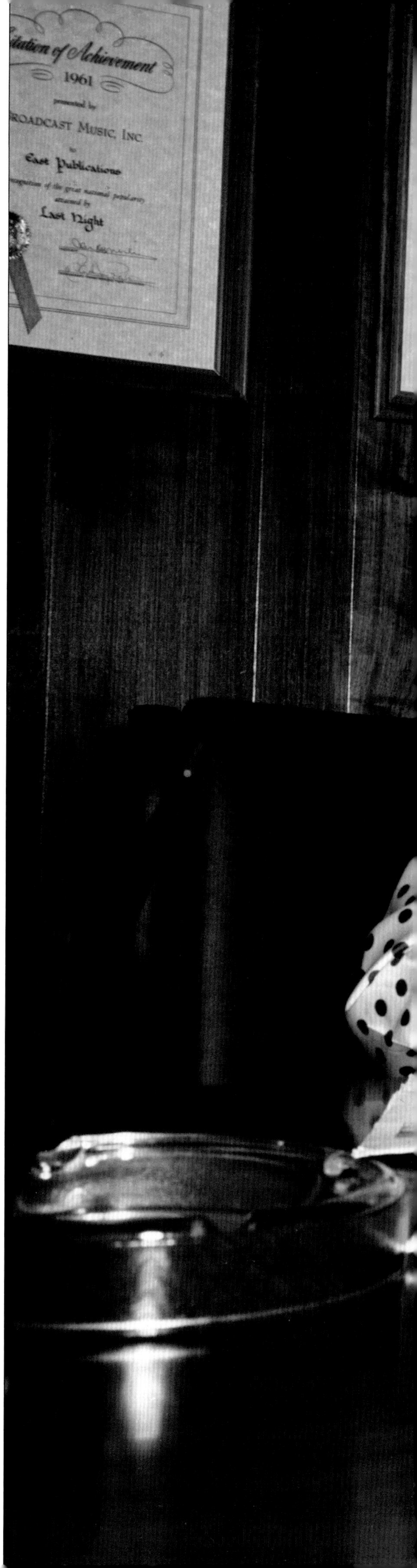

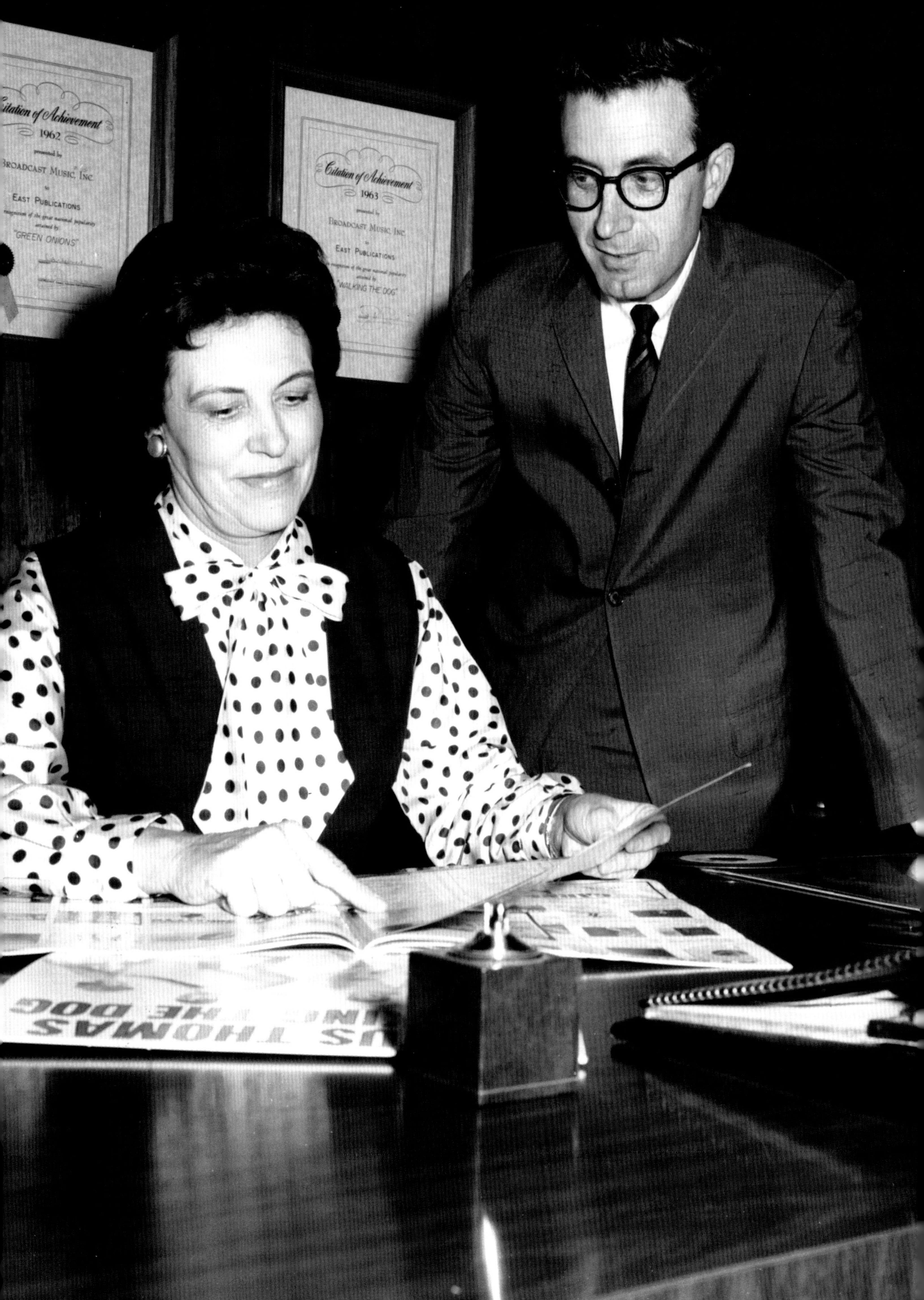

Citation of Achievement
1962
Broadcast Music, Inc.
East Publications
"GREEN ONIONS"
Citation of Achievement
1963
Broadcast Music, Inc.
East Publications
"WALKING THE DOG"

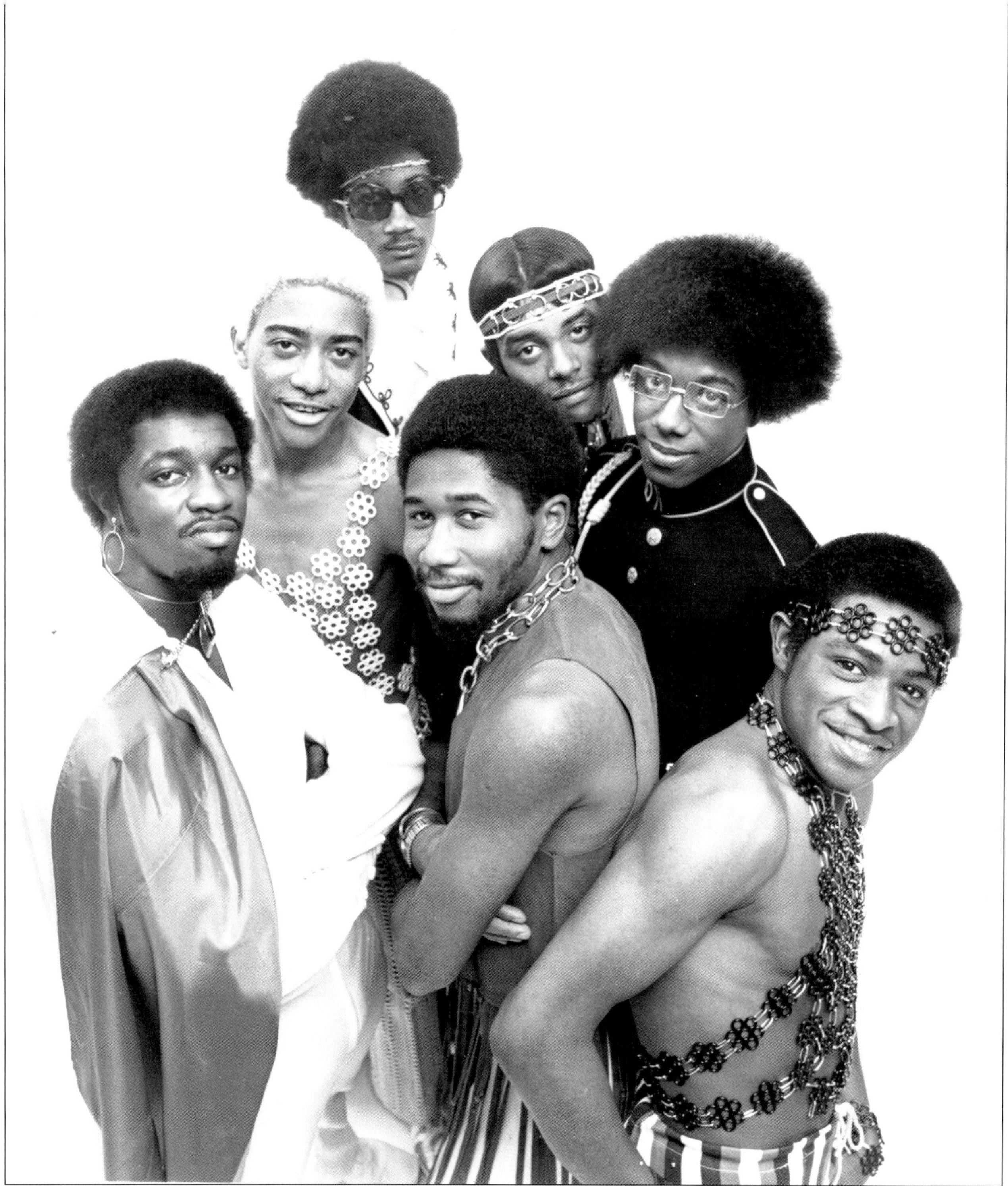

THE BAR-KAYS

STAX HOUSE BAND

Originally formed as a studio session back-up band for Stax Records, the Bar-Kays have been through a roller coaster of a career. Not long after the band formed in 1966, four of the original band members were killed in the plane crash that also claimed the life of Otis Redding. Trumpet player Ben Cauley and bass player James Alexander re-formed their band to continue making music. Working with many Stax artists, including Isaac Hayes, the Bar-Kays have continued to have R&B hits as a band in their own right.

Photograph Michael Ochs Archives

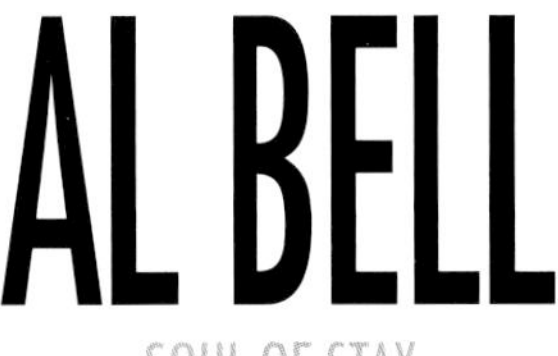

AL BELL

SOUL OF STAX

If founders and namesakes Jim Stewart and his sister, Estelle Axton, were the original heart of Stax Records, Al Bell was the soul. After the tragic death of Stax star Otis Redding in 1967, Bell (born Alvertis Isbell) took over and revived the dying label into the epitome of "the Memphis sound," signing groups like The Staple Singers and promoting the phenomenal success of Isaac Hayes. He famously scheduled the release of 29 albums in the middle of 1969 alone, and one of them was *Hot Buttered Soul*. Controversial disputes with CBS Records brought Stax down in 1975, but Al Bell would go on to be president of Motown Records and form his own label. He was recognized in 2011 with the Trustees Award Grammy – the Recording Academy's version of a lifetime achievement award for non-performers.

Photograph Michael Ochs Archives • **Story** by Dan Conaway

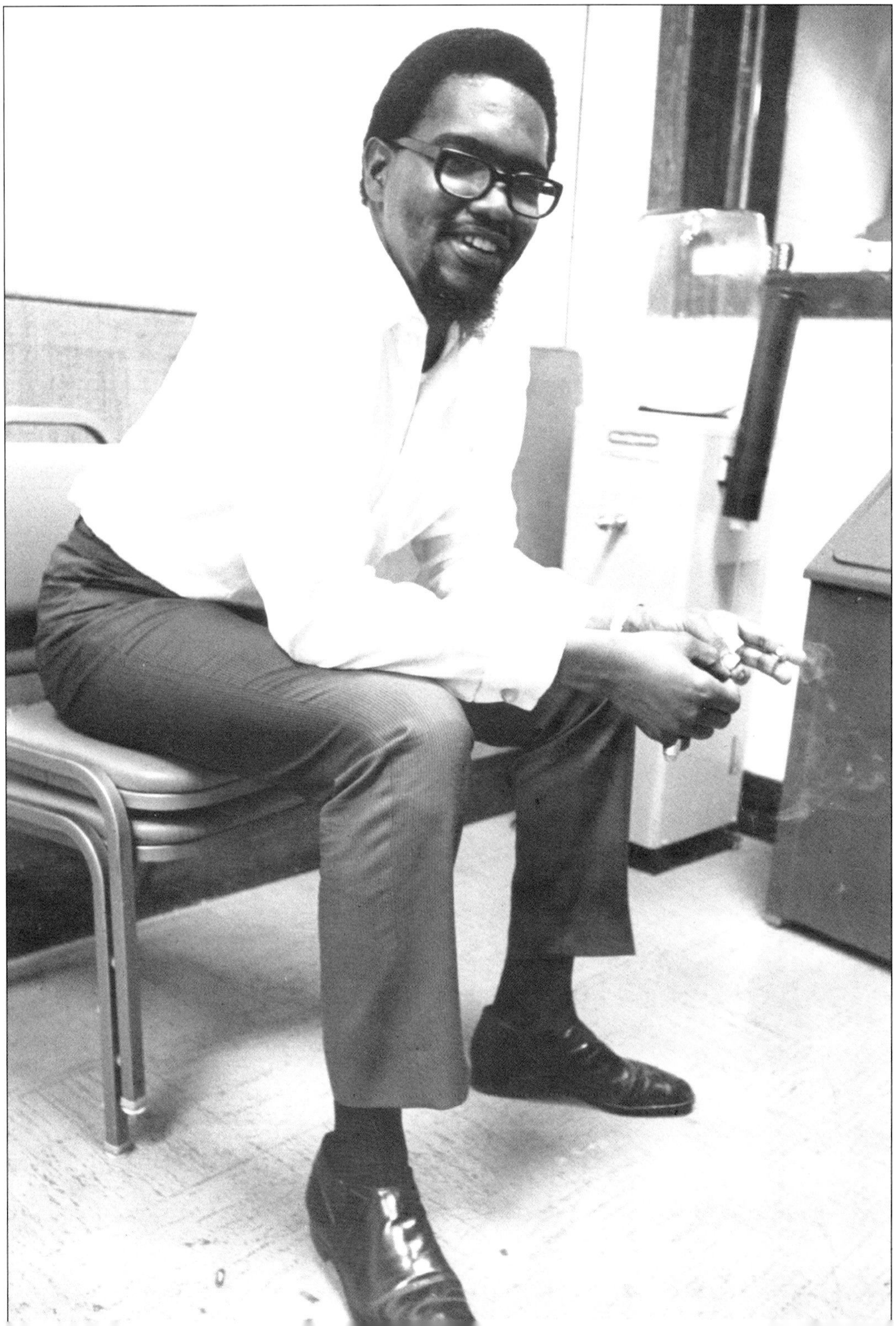

CHRIS BELL

SINGER, SONGWRITER

Before founding Big Star with Alex Chilton, Chris Bell was at the center of the Memphis garage band scene in the 1960s where he, Terry Manning, and many others combined the sounds of British invasion groups with the feel of Memphis Soul. Although he and Chilton found critical praise with Big Star, the band saw little commercial success. In 1978, at the age of 27, he died on his way home from his father's restaurant. Bell's influence is evident in bands like REM, the Replacements and the Flaming Lips.

Photograph by David Bell

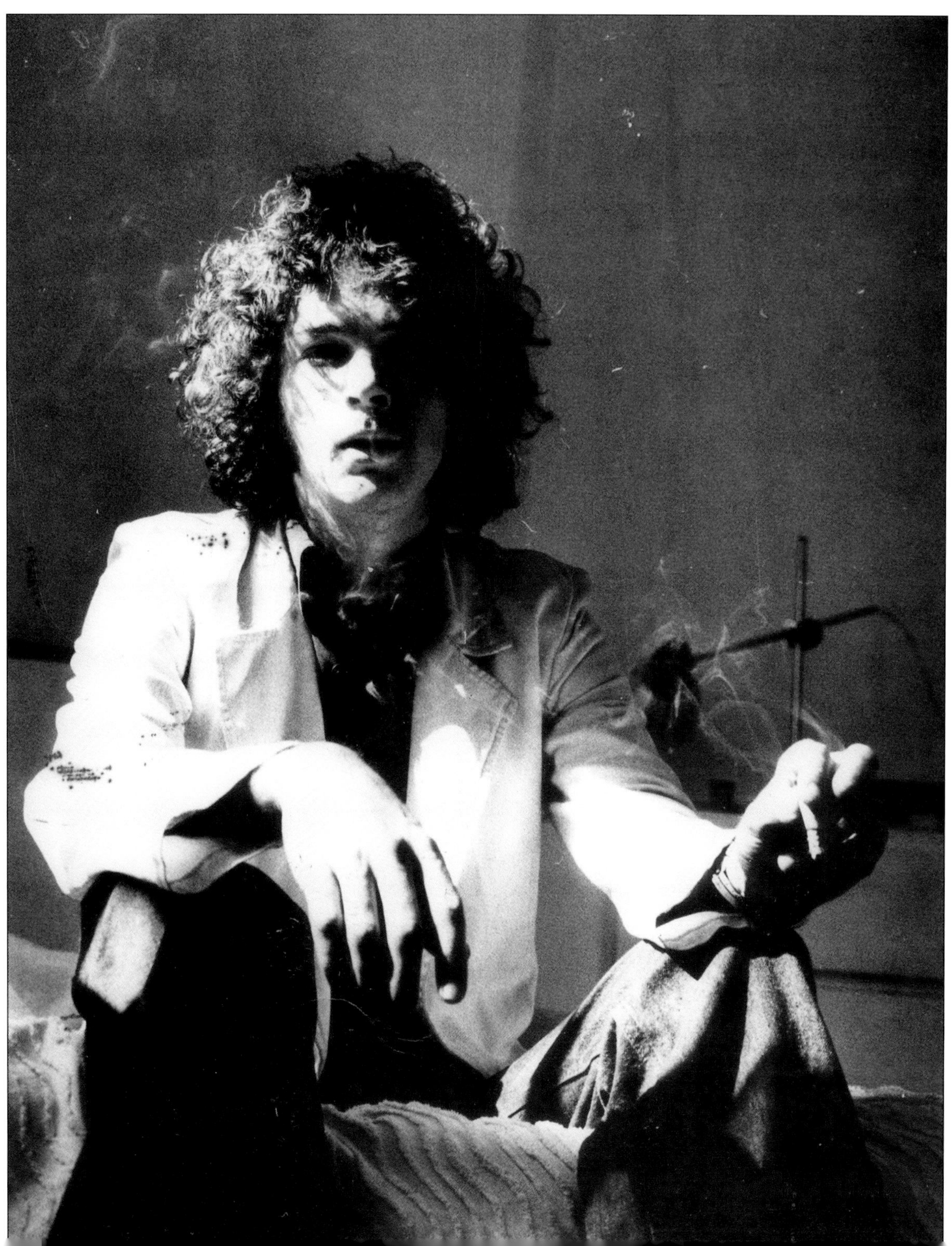

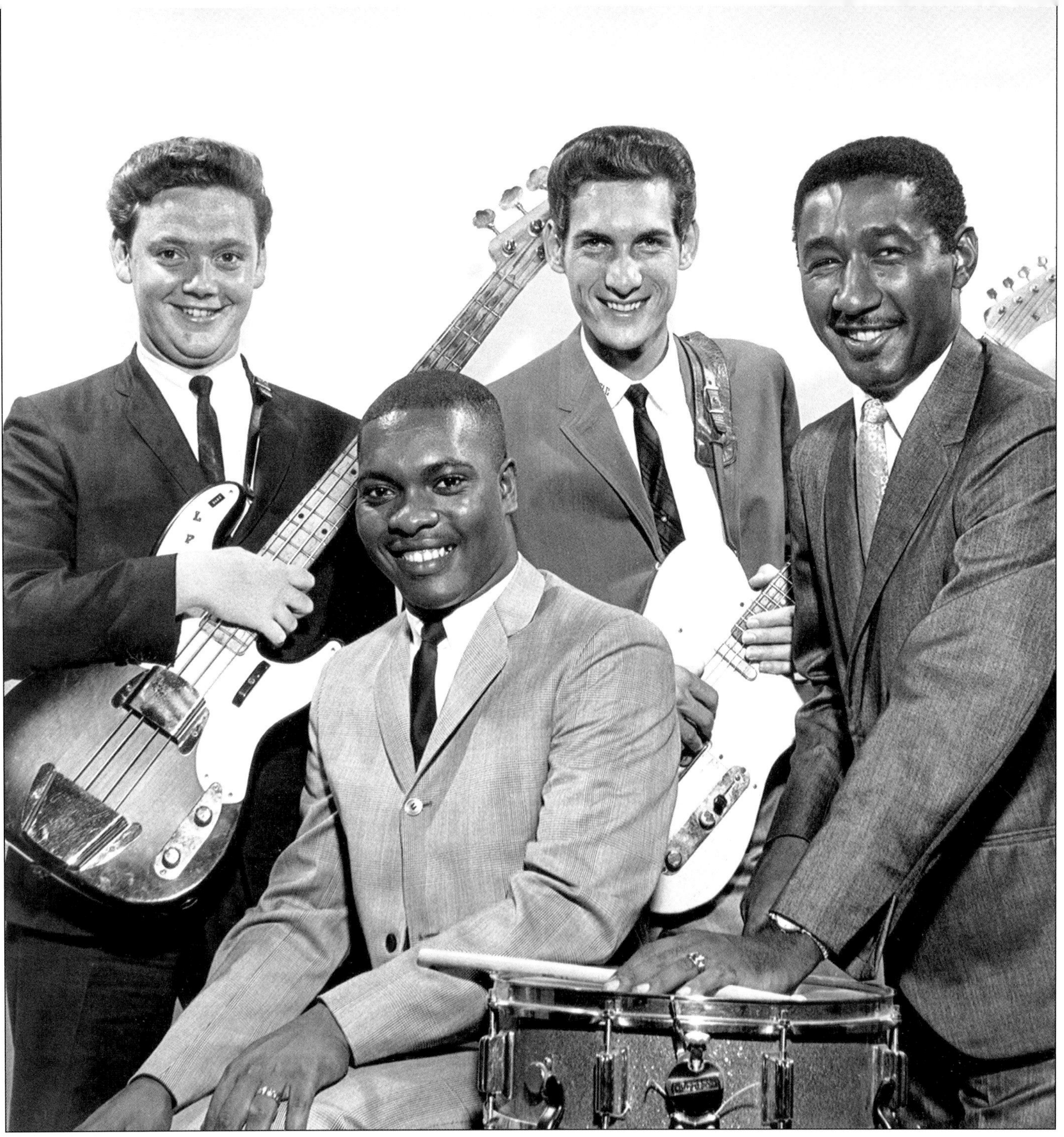

BOOKER T & THE MG's

HALL OF FAME HOUSE BAND

They were the sound behind hundreds of hits. They had their very own chart buster before they even had a name. When you were listening to Wilson Pickett, Otis Redding, Sam & Dave, Rufus and Carla Thomas — any of the original Stax stars of the sixties, and other legends to follow – you were listening to Booker T. Jones on organ, Steve Cropper on lead guitar, Donald "Duck" Dunn on bass, and Al Jackson, Jr. on drums. You were listening to the southern-soul-defining groove of Booker T. & The MG's, or, as fan John Lennon called them, "Book a Table and the Maitre D's." Setting styles and defying stereotypes, they were 50% black, 50% white, 100% soul, and 1,000% smooth. When you hear their monster instrumental hit "Green Onions," you're hearing something they just knocked out fooling around in the studio one day in 1962. The band they would call Booker T. & The MG's (for Memphis Group) after that day was inducted into the Rock and Roll Hall of Fame in 1992.

Photograph Michael Ochs Archives • **Story** by Dan Conaway

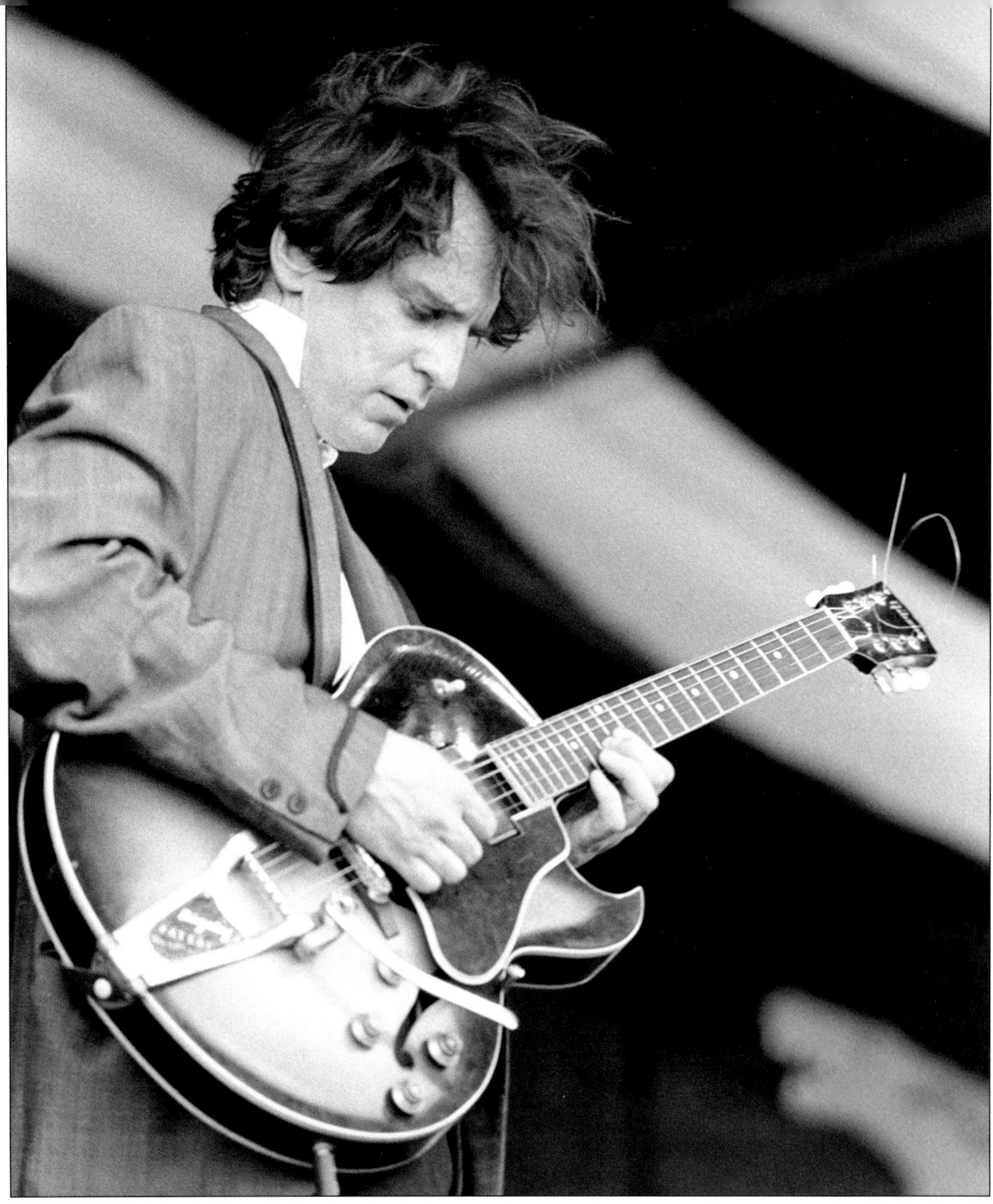

ALEX CHILTON

SINGER, SONGWRITER

Children by the million/ Sing for Alex Chilton
When he comes on/They sing I'm in love
What's that song?/ I'm in love with that song.
From Alex Chilton, The Replacements

The Box Tops had their first number one hit in 1967 with "The Letter," and at 16, front man and Central High student Alex Chilton was world famous. A string of hits followed, but the band broke up in 1970.

He taught himself guitar by watching Steve Cropper at Ardent Studios. That chewy rock n' roll style can be heard in his next band, Big Star. It turns out the title of their first album, *#1 Record*, was wishful thinking; the track "In The Street" can be heard as the theme for *That 70's Show*. The cover for their follow up *Radio City* featured a startling red ceiling and walls shot by legendary photographer William Eggleston, a friend of Chilton's parents.

While Chilton never recaptured the commercial success of those early years, his influence and reputation in the rock world continued — continues, rather — to expand. Big Star was the band for band people. It blazed the trail for the alternative rock sound that dominated the late 80s and 90s.

Although written in the eighties, the question posed by The Replacements in "Alex Chilton" seemed to foreshadow the cult legend's death in 2010.

Photograph by Redferns/Ebit Roberts • **Story** by Richard Murff

RICK DEES

DJ, SONGWRITER

Many people only think of Rick Dees as a one-hit wonder for his late 70s novelty single, "Disco Duck," which sold over six million copies. But he also has had a long and distinguished career in broadcasting. He worked at a number of radio stations throughout the southeastern United States, but it was at WMPS-AM (the Great 68) in Memphis that he conceived the record that would propel him to international fame. The song appeared in the movie, *Saturday Night Fever*, and earned Dees a People's Choice Award and a BMI Award. Ironically, WMPS forbade Dees from playing the song and later fired him for mentioning it. At the time it had almost reached the #1 spot in the nation. He then moved to WHBQ in Memphis, before eventually landing in Los Angeles where he hosted the top-rated morning show and received many more accolades.

Photograph Michael Ochs Archives

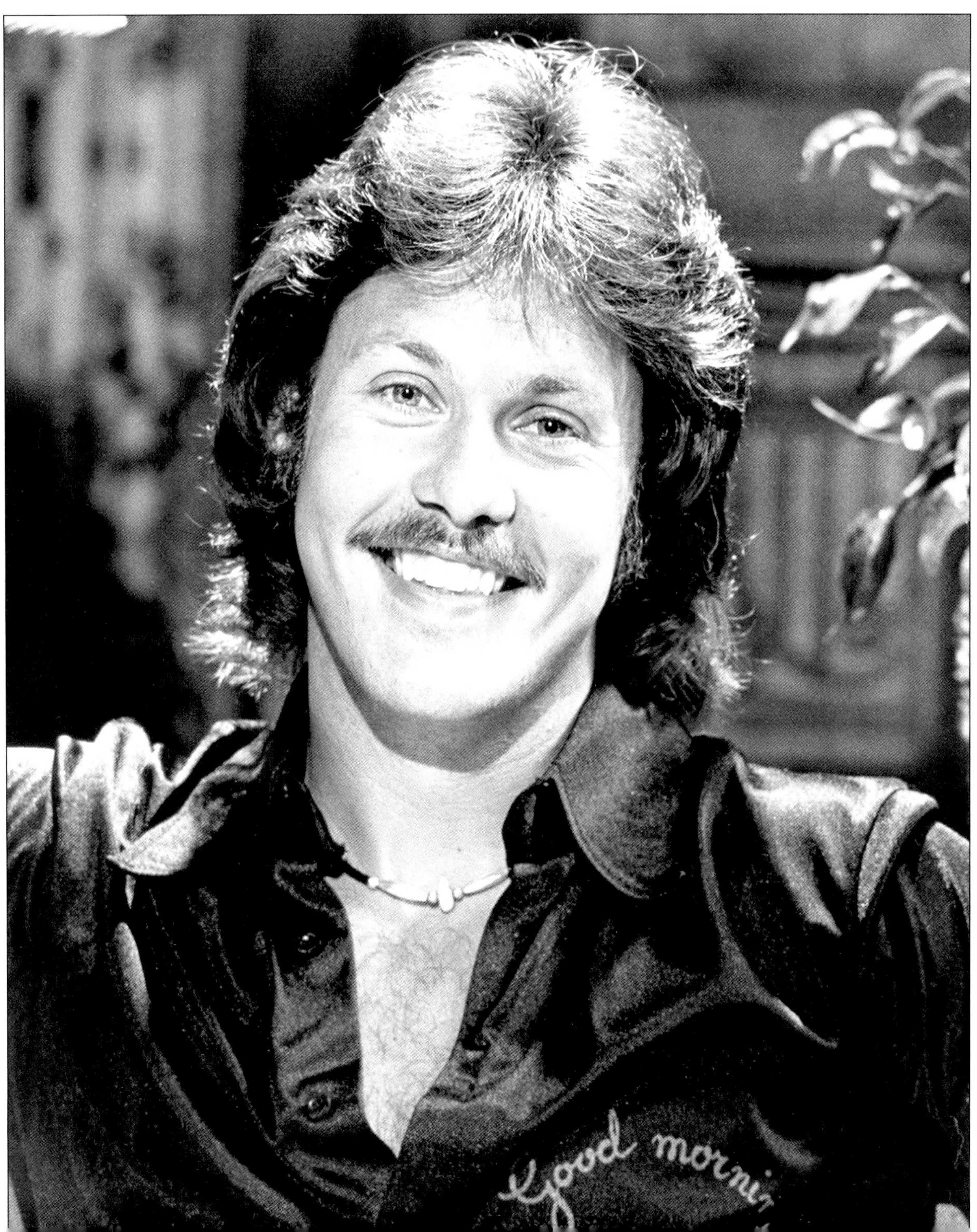

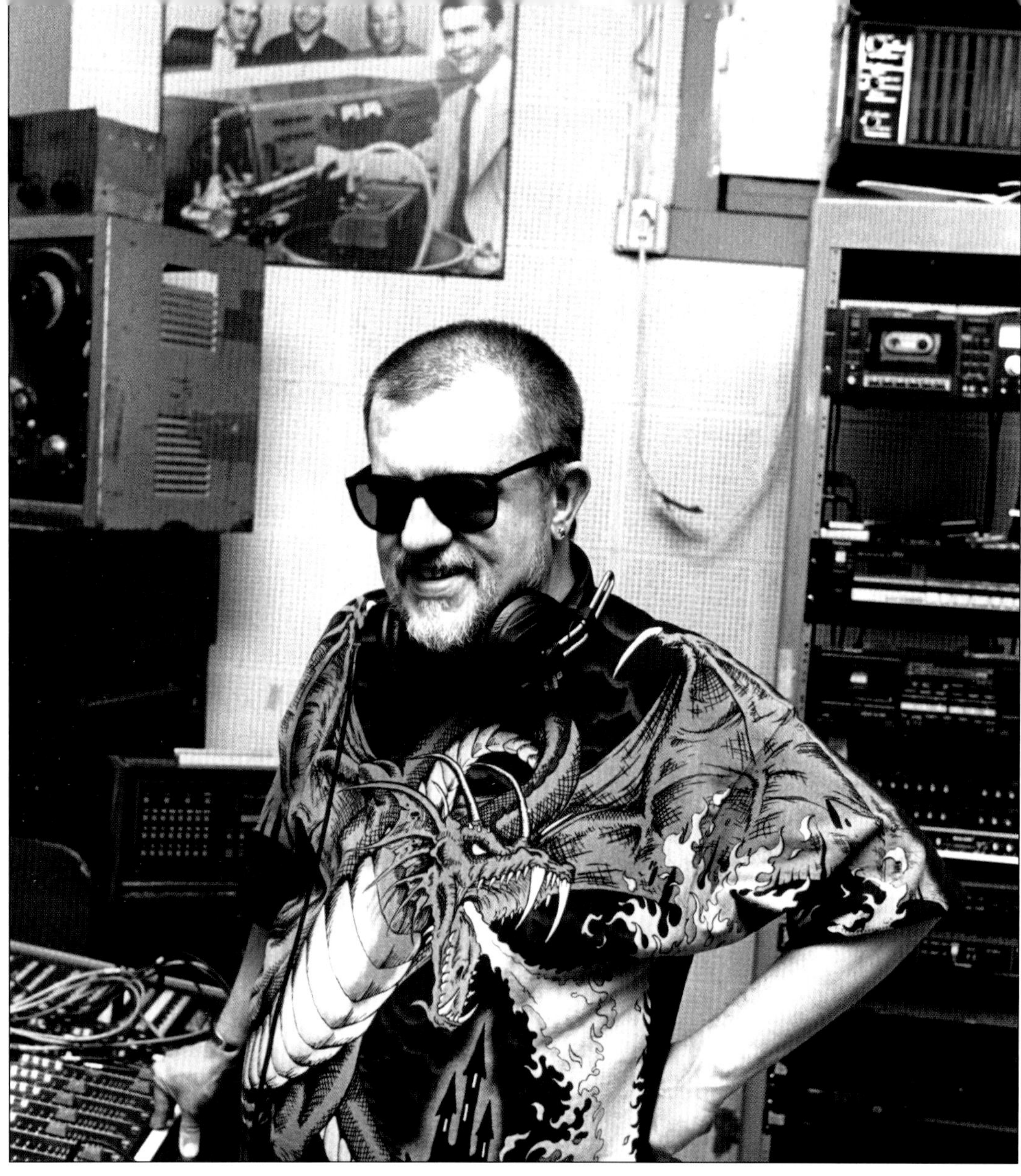

JIM DICKINSON

MUSIC VISIONARY

"Dickinson was a beautiful piano player ... working with Dickinson, and just getting the feel, really, of the South, and the way we were automatically accepted down south, was wonderful."

Keith Richards in his 2010 autobiography Life

Dickinson played piano on the *Sticky Fingers* track "Wild Horses," a mainstay ballad for Rolling Stones and rock n' roll fans everywhere. Dickinson moved to Memphis in his youth and created his first band, The Regents, while still a student at White Station High School.

Even at an early age, he backed up acts recording for Atlantic Records including Sam & Dave, Jerry Jeff Walker, Carmen McRae and Aretha Franklin. He toured with Arlo Guthrie in the 70s after recording "City of New Orleans." Bob Dylan, while accepting the Grammy Award for 1997's album of the year *Time Out of Mind*, would refer to Dickinson as "my brother."

Dickinson had his start with the Jesters' "Cadillac Man" at Sun Studio and would eventually help to create the sound and worldwide reputation of Ardent Studios. If he was a big man on stage, he was even larger than life behind the music and mixing board as producer for Big Star, Mojo Nixon, The Replacements and Screamin' Jay Hawkins.

As if he didn't give enough of himself to the music he loved, Dickinson unleashed his sons, Luther and Cody on the world as the North Mississippi Allstars and each has gone on to make more of the music they grew up on and the sound their daddy helped create.

Photograph Redferns/Ebet Roberts • **Story** by Richard Alley

KALLEN ESPERIAN

OPERA SOPRANO

Kallen Esperian is many things: a world famous operatic soprano, a strikingly beautiful woman, an adoring mother, and someone who loves Memphis. Esperian could live anywhere. She has performed at virtually every opera venue in the world, and has her choice of city and nation to call home. She chooses Memphis. Esperian made her debut as Mimi in *La Boheme* in Philiadelphia in 1986. Since then she has performed everywhere from the Royal Albert Hall in London, to the Met in New York City, to an appearance with Luciano Pavarotti in China. Still, she comes home to Memphis.

Anyone who expects diva-like behavior from Kallen Esperian is in for a pleasant surprise. She is delightfully down to earth, even recording versions of Led Zeppelin and Queen songs for a local radio show, simply because it made everyone smile. While she has many things about which she could boast, the one thing that Kallen Esperian loves to brag about is the fact that she is the only person she knows who has been sweated on by Luciano Pavarotti.

Photograph AFP/Getty/Hasan Mroue • **Story** by Dennis Phillippi

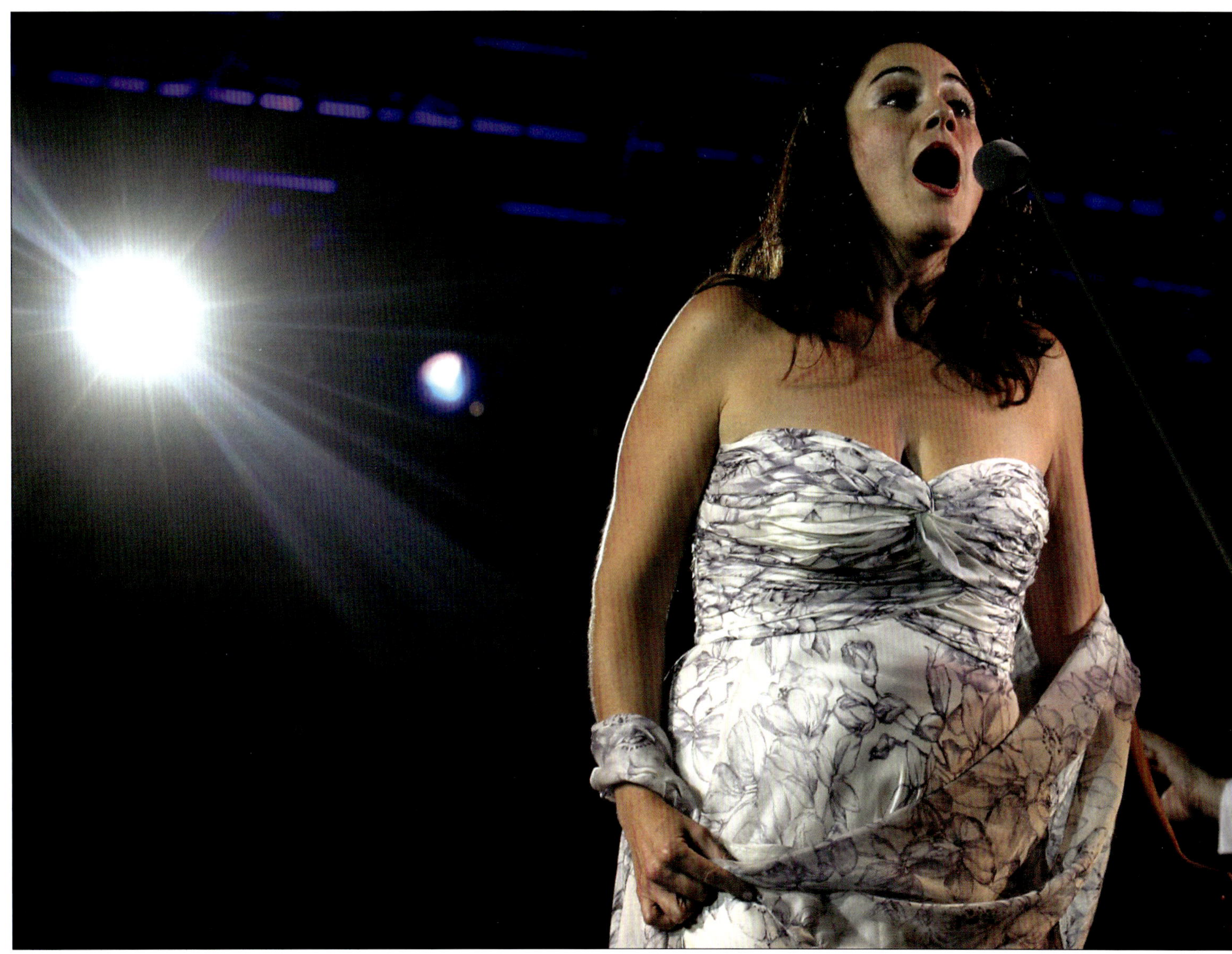

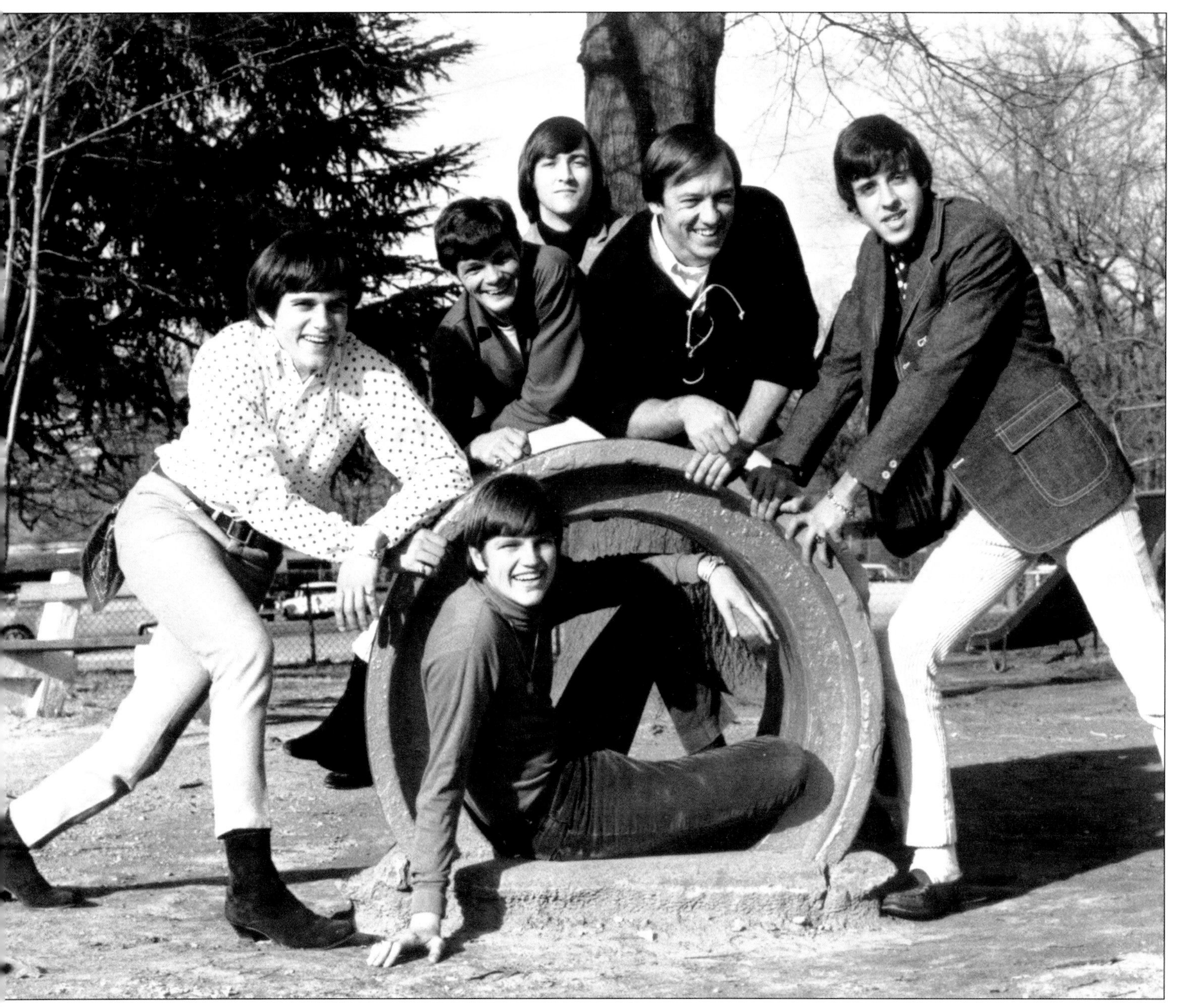

THE GENTRYS

BAND

In 1963, several students from Treadwell High School formed The Gentrys and began to make a name playing local dances. After winning a Battle of the Bands contest, they had a record contract. Soon they were blasting that Memphis garage band sound across the country with "Keep On Dancing," a song consisting of one short section repeated to fill the track. The Gentrys toured with the Beach Boys and Sonny & Cher and appeared in the 1966 film *It's a Bikini World*.

After the group split up, vocalist Jimmy Hart reformed the band in 1969, but they failed to recapture the former glory. Hart would go on to be a successful professional wrestling promoter, and guitarist Larry Raspberry would form Larry Raspberry and the Highsteppers.

Photograph MGM Records

W.C. HANDY

FATHER OF THE BLUES

W.C. (William Christopher) Handy wasn't the first musician to play the blues, but he is given credit for being the first to dress it up, take it out of the Mississippi Delta, push it through a horn, and show it off. He was both an educated musician and a music educator, and before bringing his band to Memphis and Beale Street in 1909, he had already toured the country at the head of various musical groups. Here he refined a uniquely American musical style, known only regionally, and took it from Memphis to New York to the world, and to fame and fortune. He died in New York in 1958. His first blues composition was for E.H. Crump's 1909 Memphis mayoral campaign. The song was then revised and released in 1912 as "Memphis Blues," widely considered the first official blues song. Although he had a long and prolific career as iconic musician and publisher, that first composition and two others composed here, "St. Louis Blues" in 1914 and "Beale Street Blues" in 1916, were his most famous. In fact, before the release of "Beale Street Blues" and its subsequent popularity, the street was named Beale Avenue.

Photograph W.C. Handy (left) with Cab Calloway, Time & Life Pictures/Getty Images • **Story** by Dan Conaway

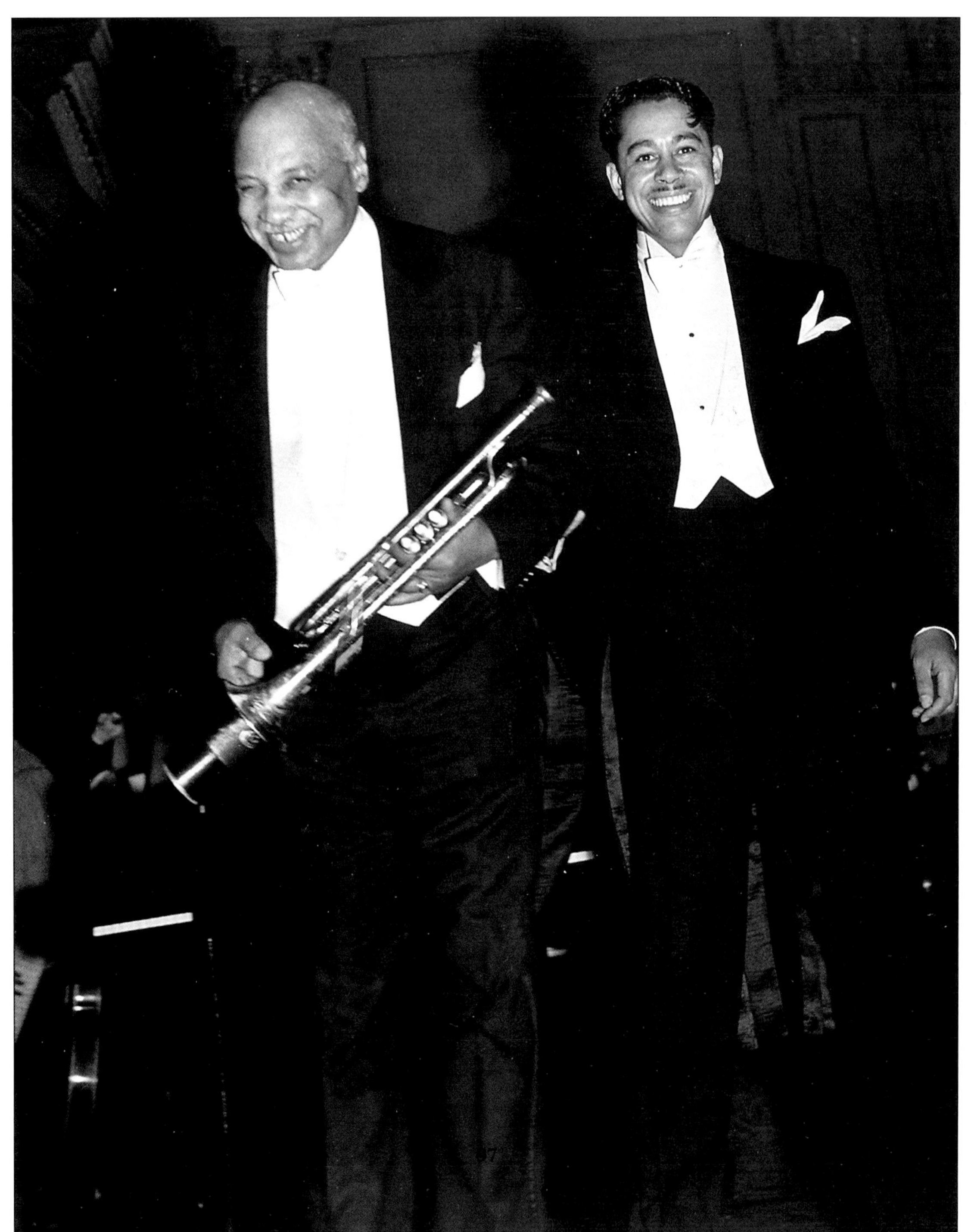

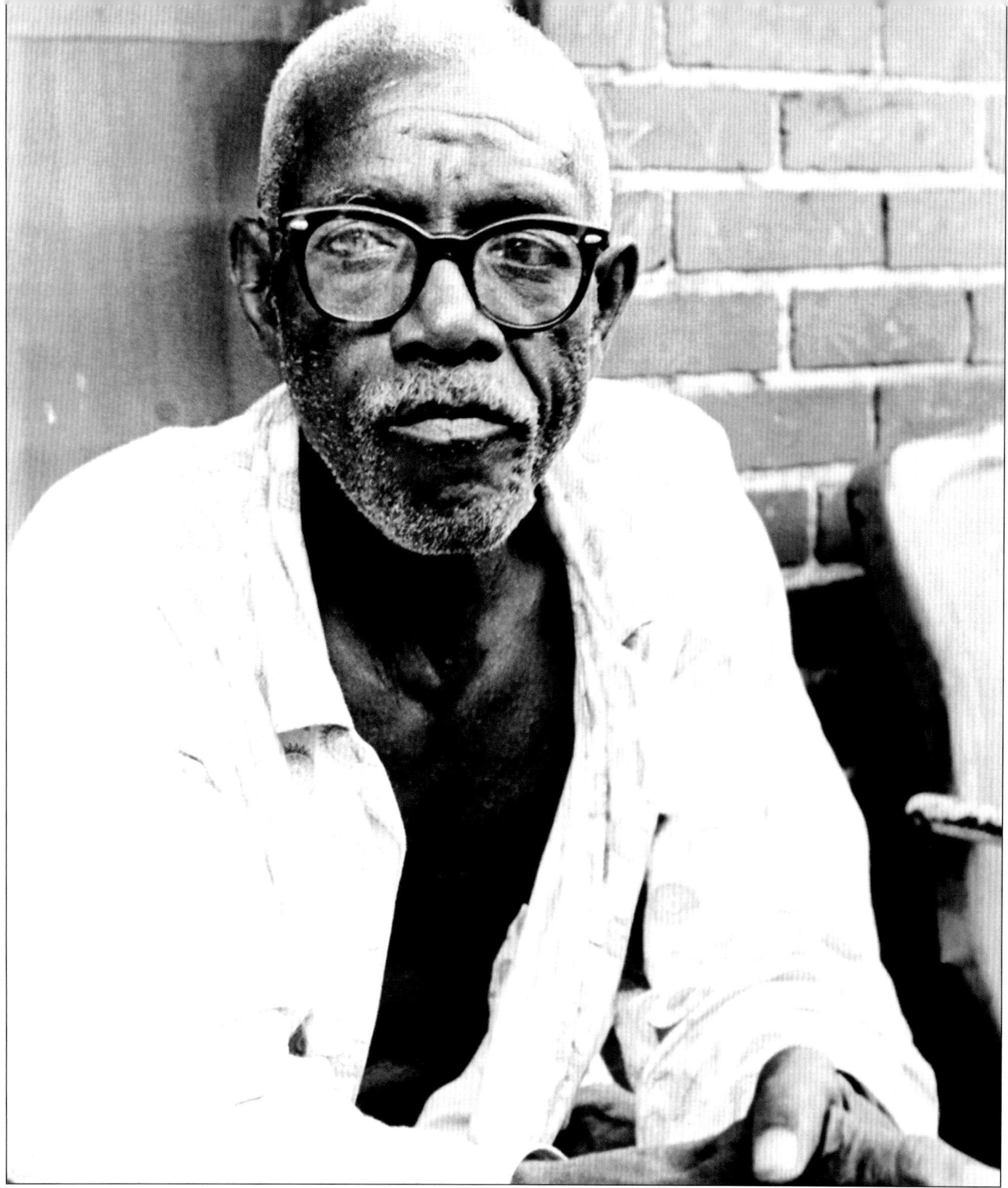

FURRY LEWIS

BLUESMAN

When Walter E. Lewis moved to Memphis with his family at age 7, he moved into one of the best communities for fostering a young musician. Nicknamed "Furry" by childhood friends, he was playing regularly at taverns and parties by age 15. He was asked several times to play with W. C. Handy's Orchestra, and Memphis allowed him to meet many of the era's best musicians, including Bessie Smith. In order to have steady money while pursuing music, Lewis took a job as a Memphis street sweeper (a job he kept until 1966). He recorded in Memphis in the late 20s, even once with Terry Manning at the record producer's home on Beale Street. Brought out of retirement by the 1960s folk blues revival, Lewis was the featured performer in the 1972 Memphis Blues Caravan. He died in 1981, and his grave in South Memphis bears two markers. The second one was purchased by his fans.

Photograph by Dick Waterman

ROBERT LOCKWOOD

BLUESMAN

Born in 1915, the same year and within a 100-mile radius of the births of Muddy Waters, Willie Dixon and Memphis Slim, Robert Lockwood's first musical instrument was the family pump organ. By age 11, he was learning guitar from Robert Johnson (yes, *that* Robert Johnson). Popular stories say that Lockwood learned Johnson's technique so well that when they played on either side of the bridge over Sunflower River in Clarksdale, Miss., citizens on the bridge couldn't tell which guitarist was Johnson. Lockwood did his first recordings in 1941, including "Take a Little Walk with Me" and "Little Boy Blue." Always traveling, Lockwood often stopped in Memphis to play with Howlin' Wolf and other musicians. Inducted into the Blues Hall of Fame in 1989, Lockwood died in 2006, at the age of 91.

Photograph by Dick Waterman

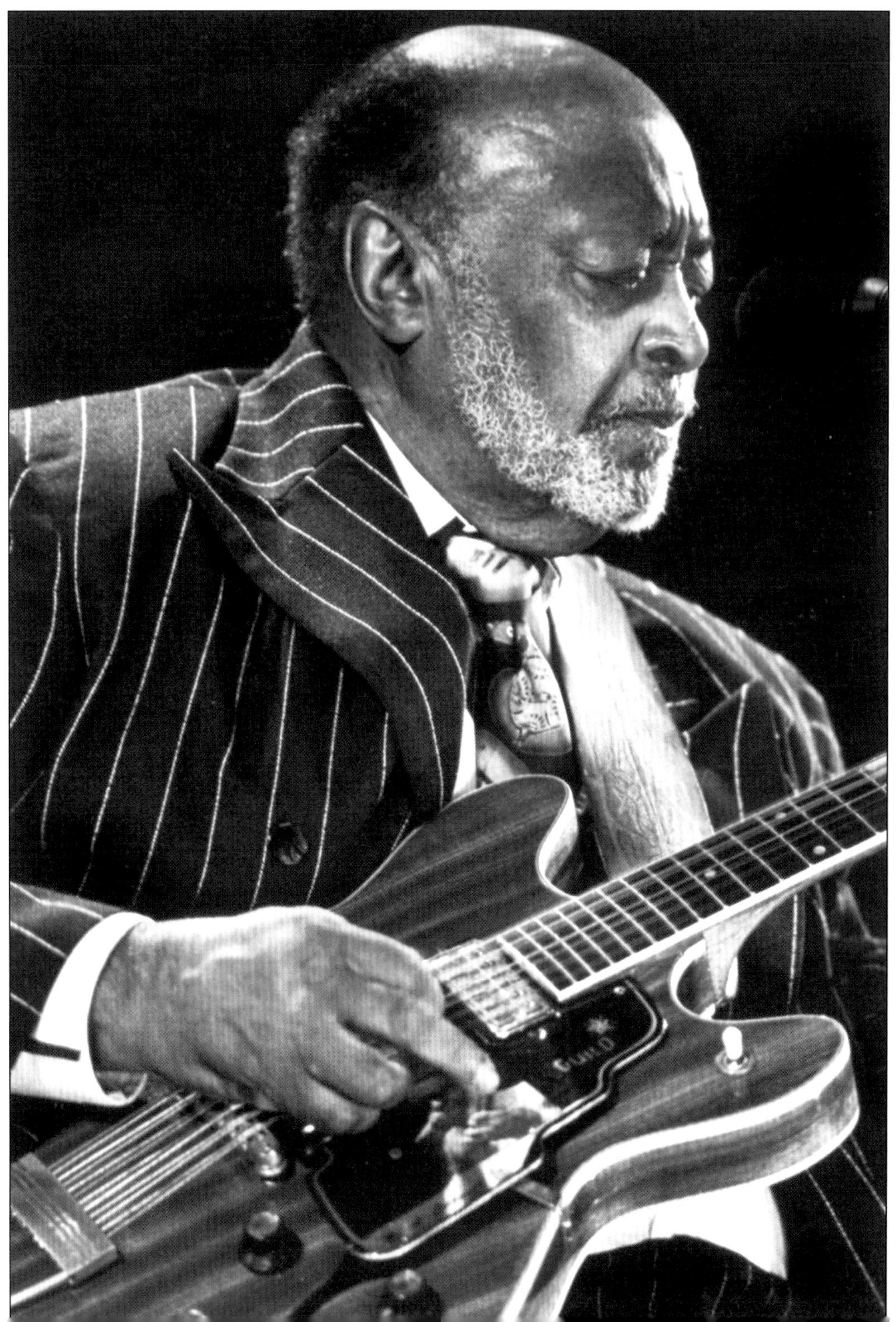

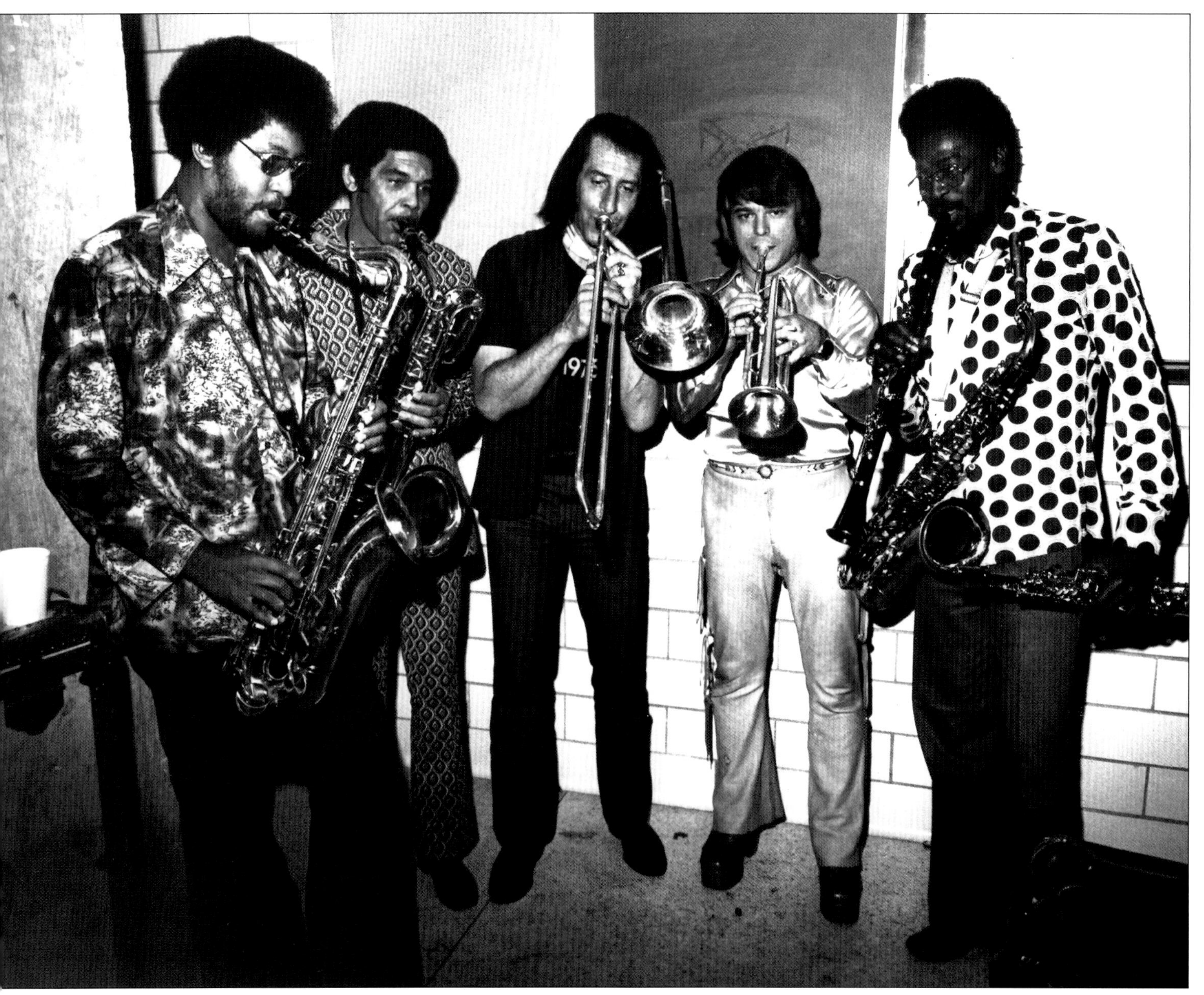

THE MEMPHIS HORNS

"Arguably the greatest horn section ever"

Ron Wynn

It would be easier to list the legendary performers the Memphis Horns have not backed than to list the ones they have. The tight horns that defined that Memphis sound in the 60s and 70s can be heard backing virtually every Stax recording artist including Isaac Hayes, Otis Redding, Rufus Thomas, Sam & Dave, and Aretha Franklin. With the legendary label's demise, the section anchored by Wayne Johnson and Andrew Love appeared on records by The Doobie Brothers, U2, Al Green, Neil Diamond, Elvis Presley, Sting, Peter Gabriel and Neil Young. Recently they backed Alicia Keys on "Another Way to Die" for the 22nd James Bond film *Quantum of Solace*.

Photograph Redferns/Gilles Petard

MEMPHIS SLIM

BLUESMAN

John Len Chatman was born in Memphis to a music-playing, juke-joint-owning father, and his love of music was born early. Playing in honky tonks around West Memphis and other Southern locations, he settled in Chicago in 1939 and began recording music in 1940, taking on the name Memphis Slim. In 1949, Slim released the song "Nobody Loves Me," a blues classic that has been covered (as "Every Day I Have the Blues") by notable artists such as B.B. King, Ella Fitzgerald, Jimi Hendrix, and many others. Later in life, Slim moved with his piano to Paris and was honored by the French government as Commander of Arts and Letters. The U.S. also honored him as Ambassador-at-Large of Good Will. He passed away in Paris in 1988, and was inducted into the Blues Hall of Fame in 1989.

Photograph Redferns/Jan Persson

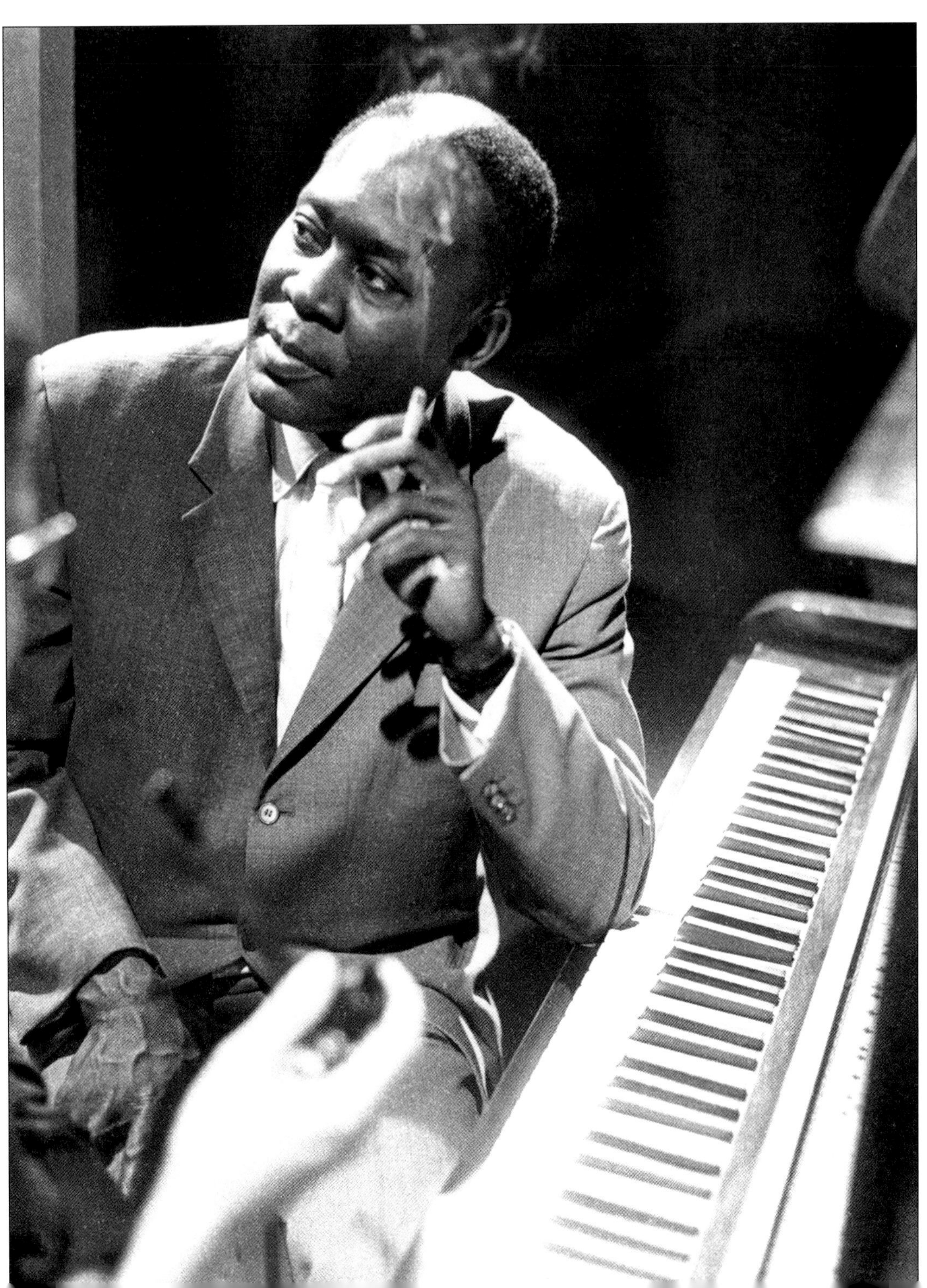

PHINEAS NEWBORN, JR.

PIANIST, SAXOPHONIST

"In his prime, he was one of the three greatest jazz pianists of all time."

Leonard Feather

Phineas Newborn, Jr., studied music with his father, and learned to play the piano, trumpet, and both tenor and baritone saxophone. Playing in a band with his father, he and the rest of the group recorded backup for B.B. King in his recording sessions at Sun Records in 1950. Newborn did some of his own early recordings with Sun before moving to New York and making a huge impression on the jazz scene. Health problems often interfered with his career, but he is still remembered as one of the best jazz musicians, and continues to be an influence for younger musicians. Scott Yanow said, "Phineas is one of the most technically skilled and brilliant pianists in jazz."

Photograph Redferns/Bill Wagg

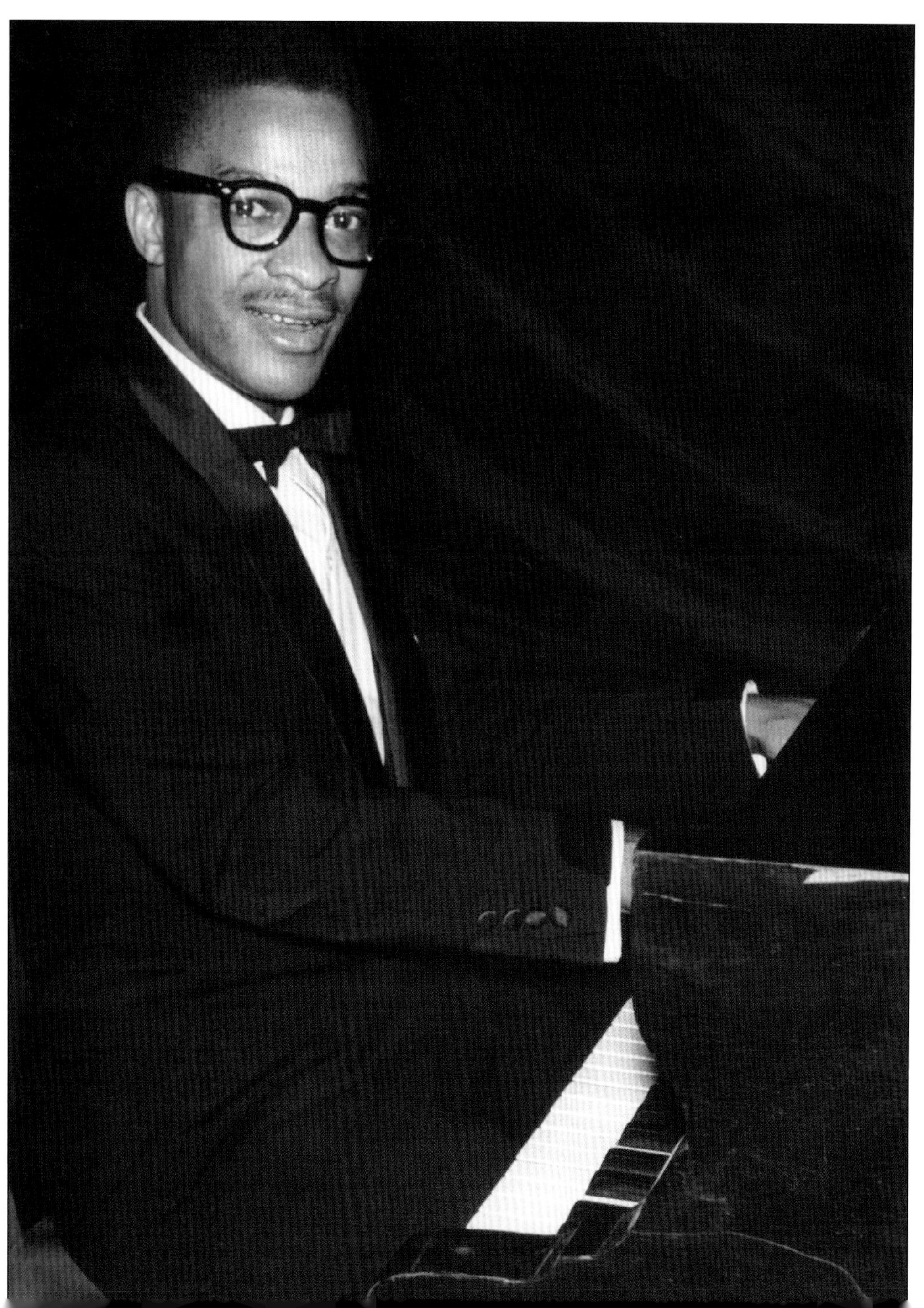

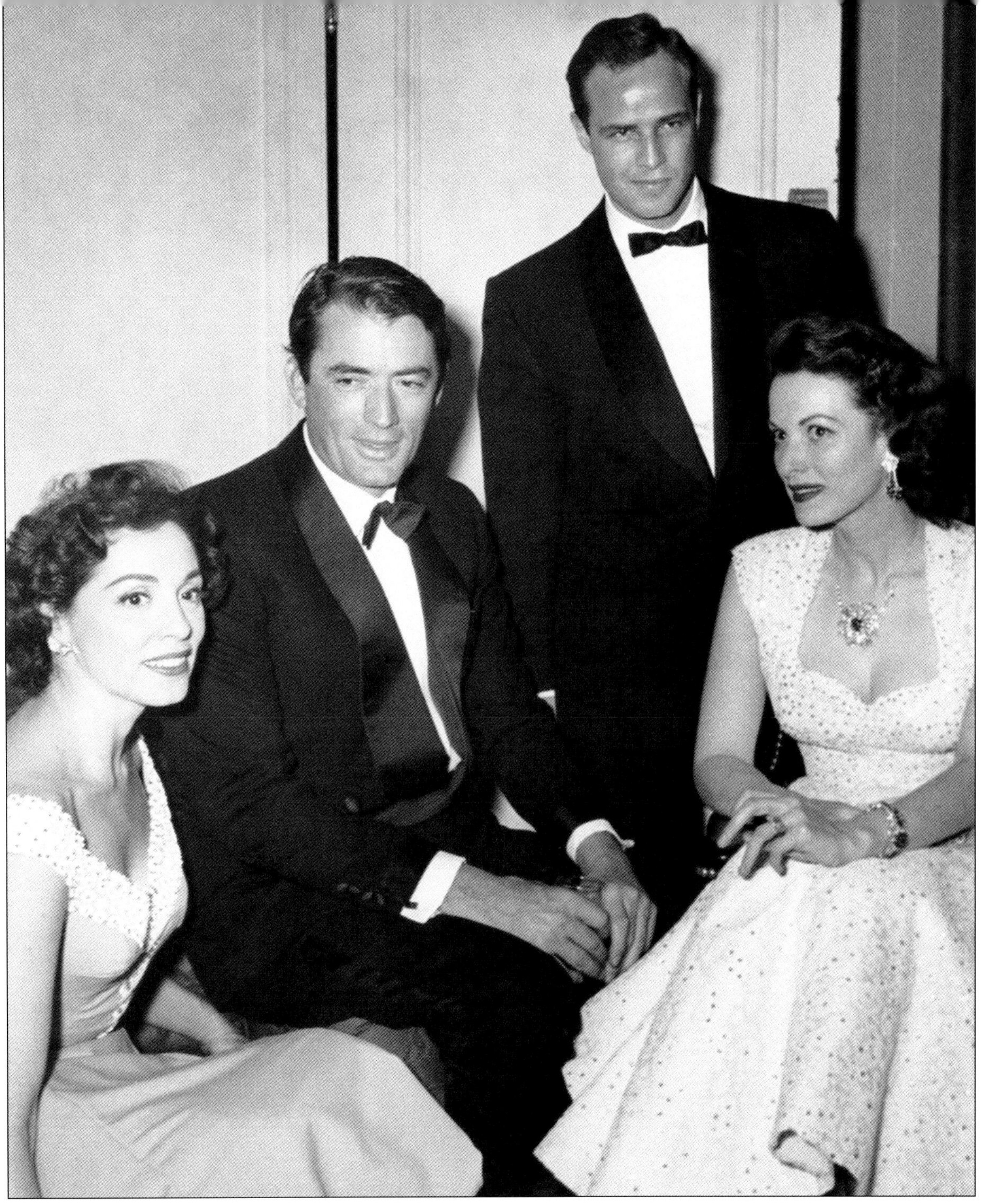

MARGUERITE PIAZZA

SOPRANO

In a prolific career and busy life, New Orleans-born soprano Marguerite Piazza has sung her way through success, personal challenges and cancer without missing a note. She debuted with the New York City Opera in 1944 at 18, the youngest member of the company. She first played Broadway in 1950, debuted with the Metropolitan Opera in 1951, and sang in everyone's living room as part of "The Show Of Shows" with Sid Caesar from 1950 to 1954. A Memphian since the height of her career, her voice has accompanied as many major charitable events around town as cufflinks have accompanied tuxedos. At the request of St. Jude founder, Danny Thomas, she hosted the first Marguerite Piazza St. Jude Gala, and has hosted 35 since.

Photograph Getty Archive (left to right: Marguerite Piazza, Cary Grant, Marlon Brando & Maureen O'Hara) • **Story** by Dan Conaway

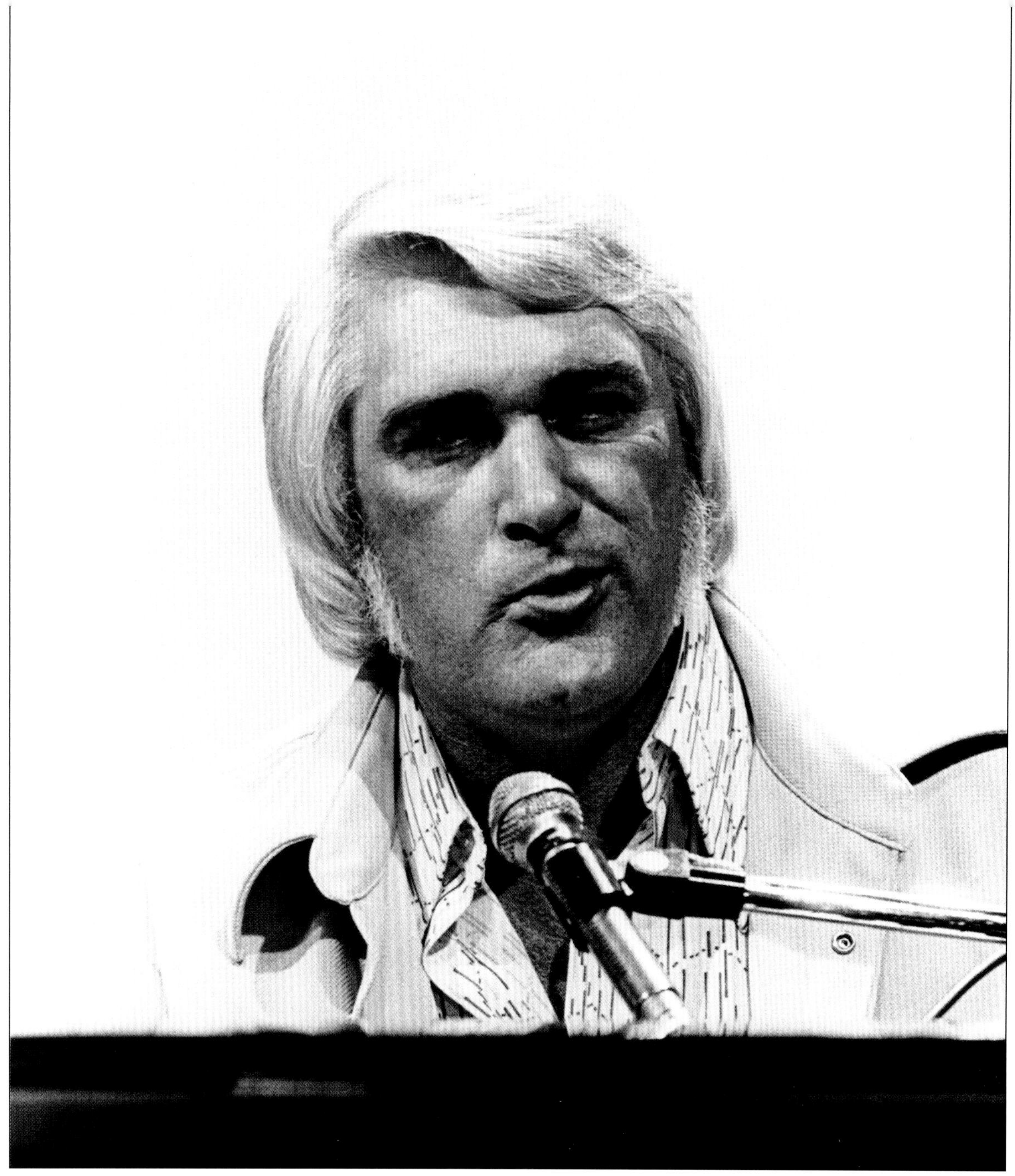

CHARLIE RICH

COUNTRY MUSIC STAR

"As a farmer, Charlie was a pretty good piano player."

Margaret Ann Rich

The son of cotton farmers, Charlie Rich put together his first group, The Velvetones, while in the Air Force. After his service, Rich returned to farming. The going was tough, so his wife, Margaret Ann took some recordings to Sun Studios, thinking, "I knew Elvis had gone to Sam Phillips so I thought maybe Charlie could try his luck." Phillips handed Charlie a stack of Jerry Lee Lewis singles and told him to come back "when he got that bad." Soon Rich was a session musician at Sun, backing the likes of Johnny Cash and Billy Lee Riley.

Breaking out on his own, Rich's fusion of jazz and country came to be known as "Countrypolitan" and his 1973 album *Behind Closed Doors* became a number one hit on both the country and pop charts. A string of hits followed and the Country Music Association named him 1974's Entertainer of the Year.

Photograph Redferns

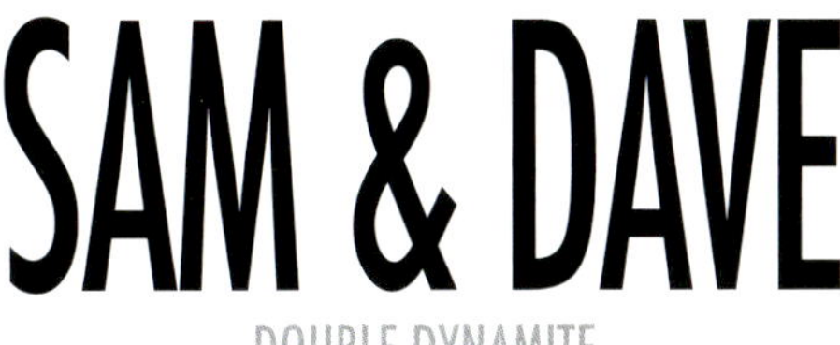

SAM & DAVE

DOUBLE DYNAMITE

"I think Sam and Dave will probably stand the test of time as being the best live act that there ever was. Those guys were absolutely unbelievable. Every night they were awesome."

Phil Walden, Otis Redding's manager

Sam Moore and Dave Prater first met while traveling around as gospel singers, and again while performing at amateur nights in Miami. They recorded many of their hits at Stax Records in Memphis, including "I Thank You," "Soul Man," and "Hold On, I'm Comin'," while working with the writing/producing team of Isaac Hayes and David Porter. Known for boundless energy onstage, Sam & Dave became known as "Double Dynamite" and "The Dynamic Duo." Between 1965 and 1968, the duo had ten consecutive Top 20 singles and three consecutive Top 10 albums, making them one of the most consistently successful soul acts on R&B charts, just behind fellow Memphian Aretha Franklin.

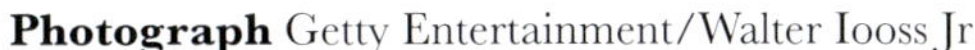

Photograph Getty Entertainment/Walter Iooss Jr

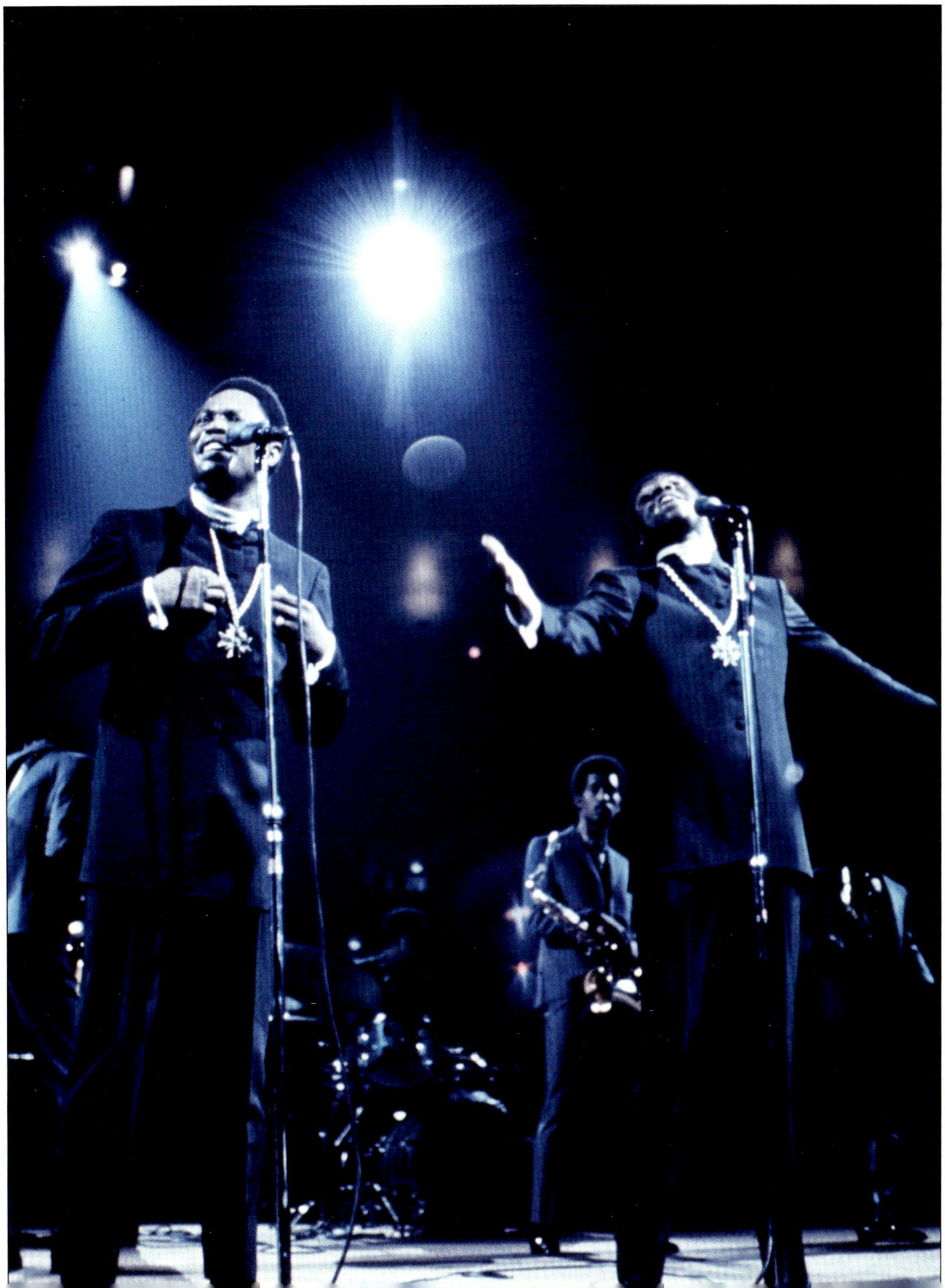

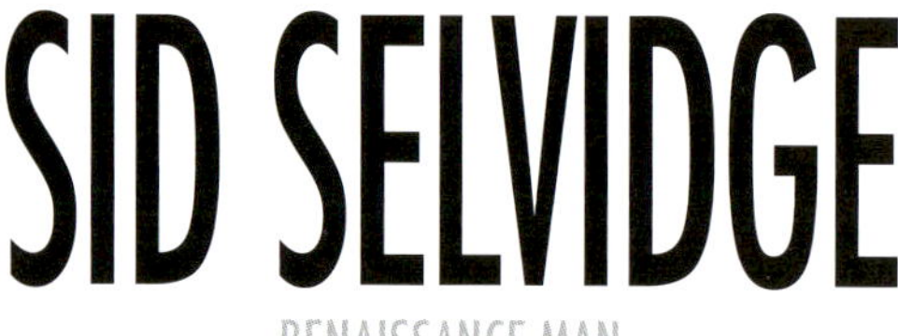

RENAISSANCE MAN

"You've got to do a little bit of everything, especially if you're going to be in this town."

Sid Selvidge

Sid Selvidge has done just about everything: radio DJ, musician, music producer and anthropology professor. And he has done it all in Memphis — teaching at Rhodes college, producing and performing on his own Peabody Records, and producing the radio show "Beale Street Caravan" to showcase local Memphis talent. Selvidge turned down big offers from record labels in order to stay in Memphis — and he's worked his entire career with uncompromising dedication, constantly learning and improving.

Photograph Redferns/Hayley Madden

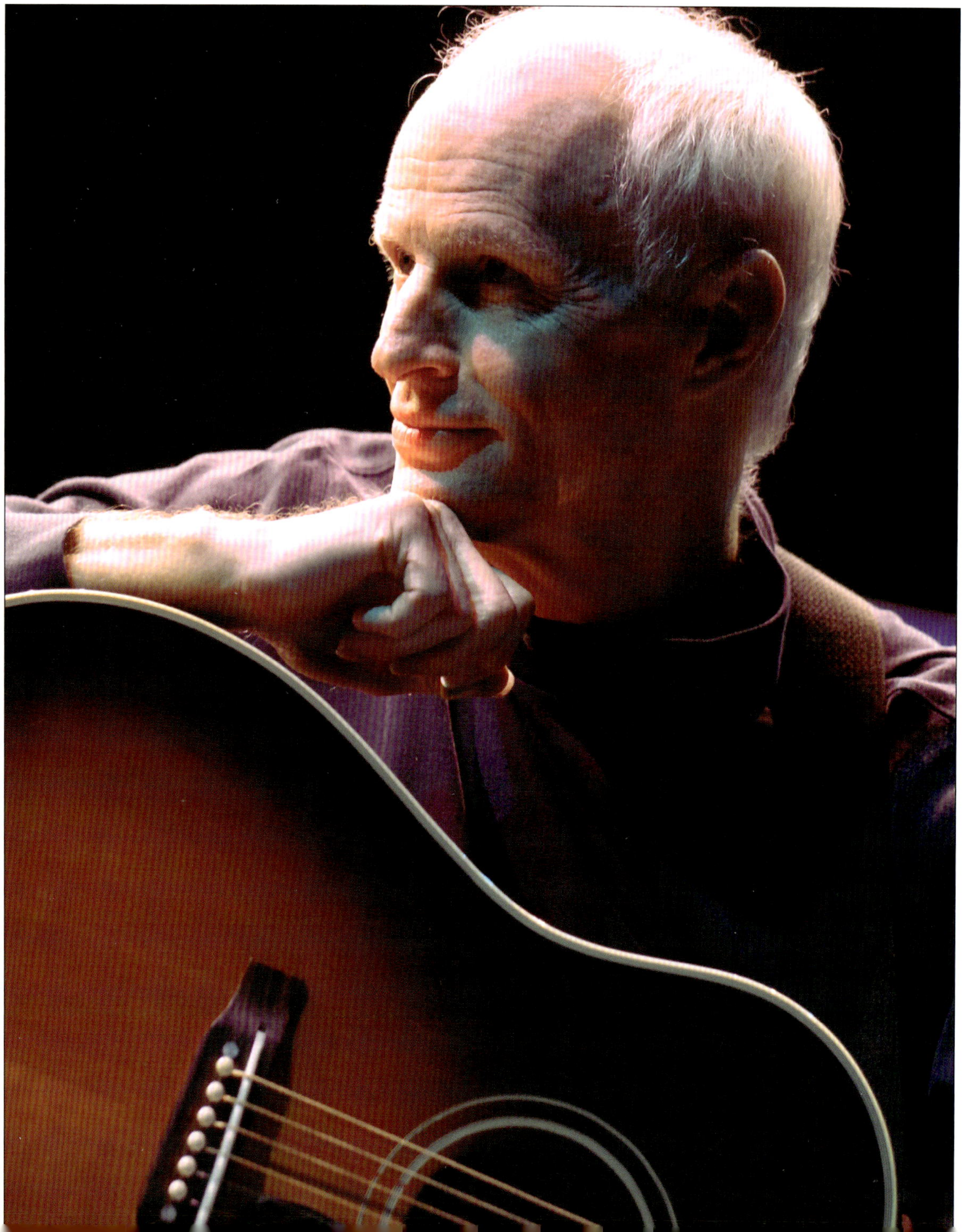

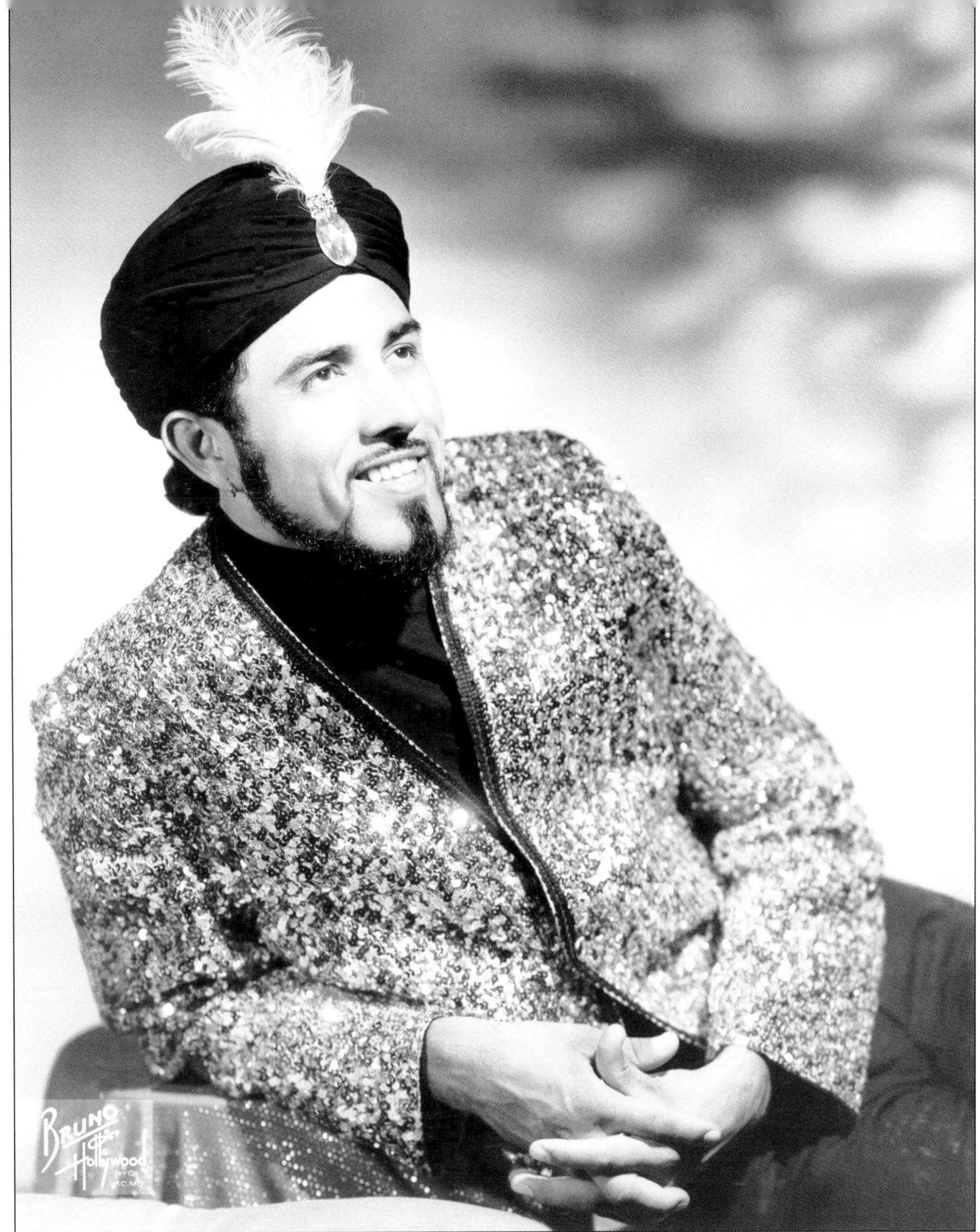

SAM THE SHAM

DOMINGO SAMUDIO

"There was no sustained advertising campaign to launch the record; the group is not particularly handsome; the name is old fashioned and cumbersome. So what is selling the record?"

Derek Taylor, KRLA Beat, 1965

Sam the Sham and the Pharaohs' self produced single "Wooly Bully" sold 3 million copies. It was June of 1963 when a Mexican-American former carny named Domingo "Big Sam" Samudio came to Memphis with his band "The Nightriders" (they were the house band for The Diplomat). Yet it wasn't until they changed their name to "Sam the Sham and the Pharaohs," and adopted campy robes that "Wooly Bully" began to outsell the giants of the British invasion. A string of novelty hits followed, but the band had more name and personal changes than it had records, adding three women to the group in 1967 as "The Shamettes." Sam won a Grammy in 1972 for Best Album Liner Notes. A long time resident of Memphis, he still performs but is primarily a motivational speaker and poet.

Photograph Michael Ochs Archives

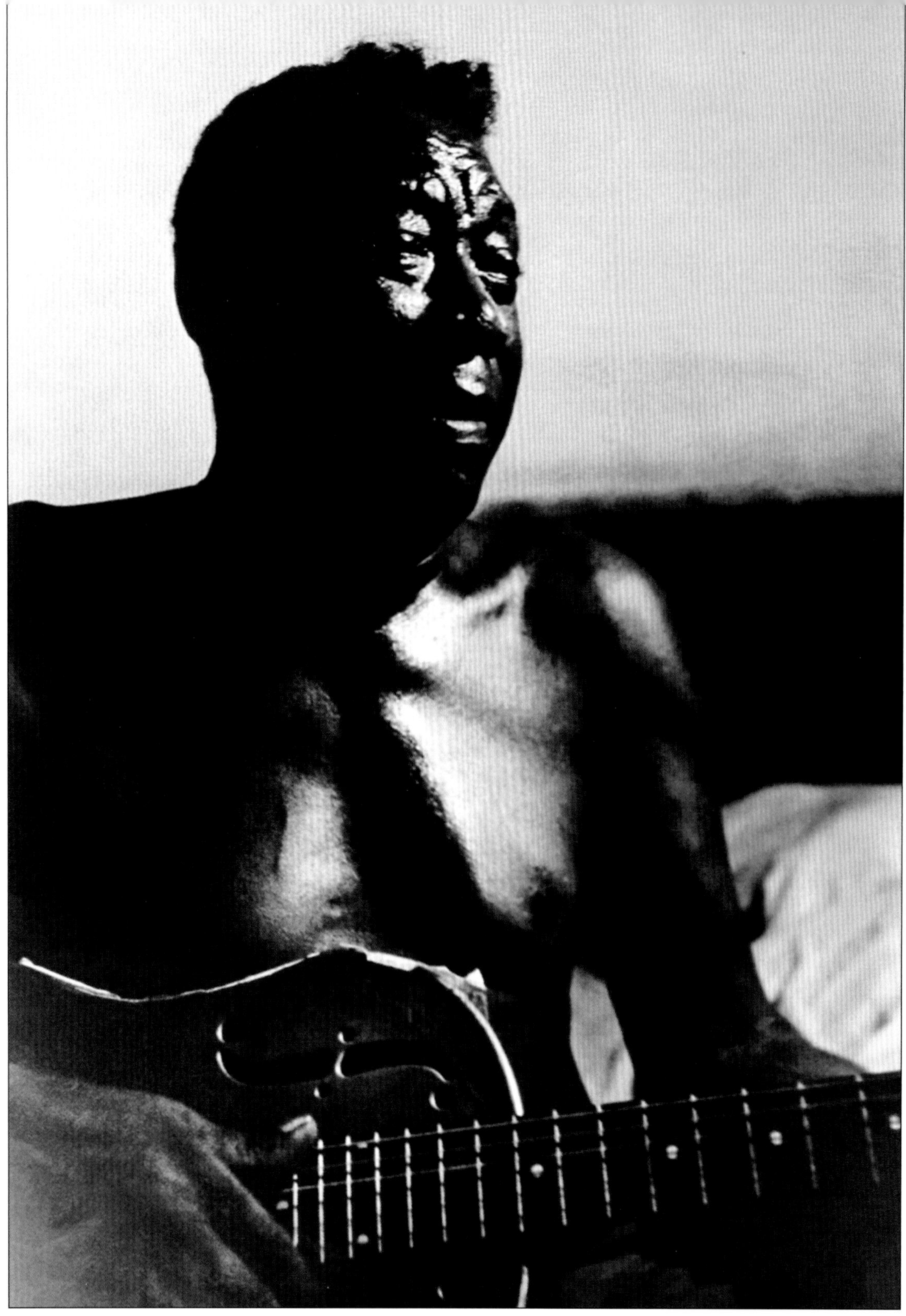

WILL SHADE

BLUES TRAILBLAZER

Will Shade first heard the Dixieland Jug Band in 1925. Wanting to combine Memphis-style blues with a jug band sound, Shade founded the Memphis Jug Band in 1927, which played for 40 years even though the jug band craze in Memphis lasted only about five. It wasn't the jug band, though, that established his fame. Shade's influence, that bluesy harmonica sound, can be heard in recordings by Big Walter Horton, Charlie Musslewhite, and Sonny Boy Williamson.

Photograph by Dick Waterman

THREE 6 MAFIA

RAPPERS, OSCAR WINNERS

Originally called the Backyard Posse when formed in 1991, Three 6, as they are generally known, consisted of DJ Paul, Juicy J, and Lord Infamous. All, by the way, stage names. The group has been through any number of line-up changes, at times including Koopsta Knicca, Gangsta Boo, and Crunchy Black. Also not their given names.

During the mid-nineties the group sold several EPs of their music on their own label before their breakout CD *Mystic Stylez*. They have subsequently released platinum selling CDs, including *Most Known Unknown*, which featured their well-known hit "Stay Fly." Three 6, of course, became part of the national mainstream with their smash hit "Hard Out Here For a Pimp" from the soundtrack of Craig Brewer's gritty rap drama *Hustle & Flow*, for which the group won the Best Song Oscar at the Academy Awards. Their reception speech at the Oscars is well remembered for its good natured, genuinely excited use of profanity. Followed by host Jon Stewart's quip, "To recap, Three Six Mafia: 1; Martin Scorsese: 0."

Three 6's current lineup appears to be DJ Paul and Juicy J. They continue to record top-selling CDs as well as produce music for other Memphis acts.

Photograph Getty Entertainment/Vince Bucci • **Story** by Dennis Phillippi

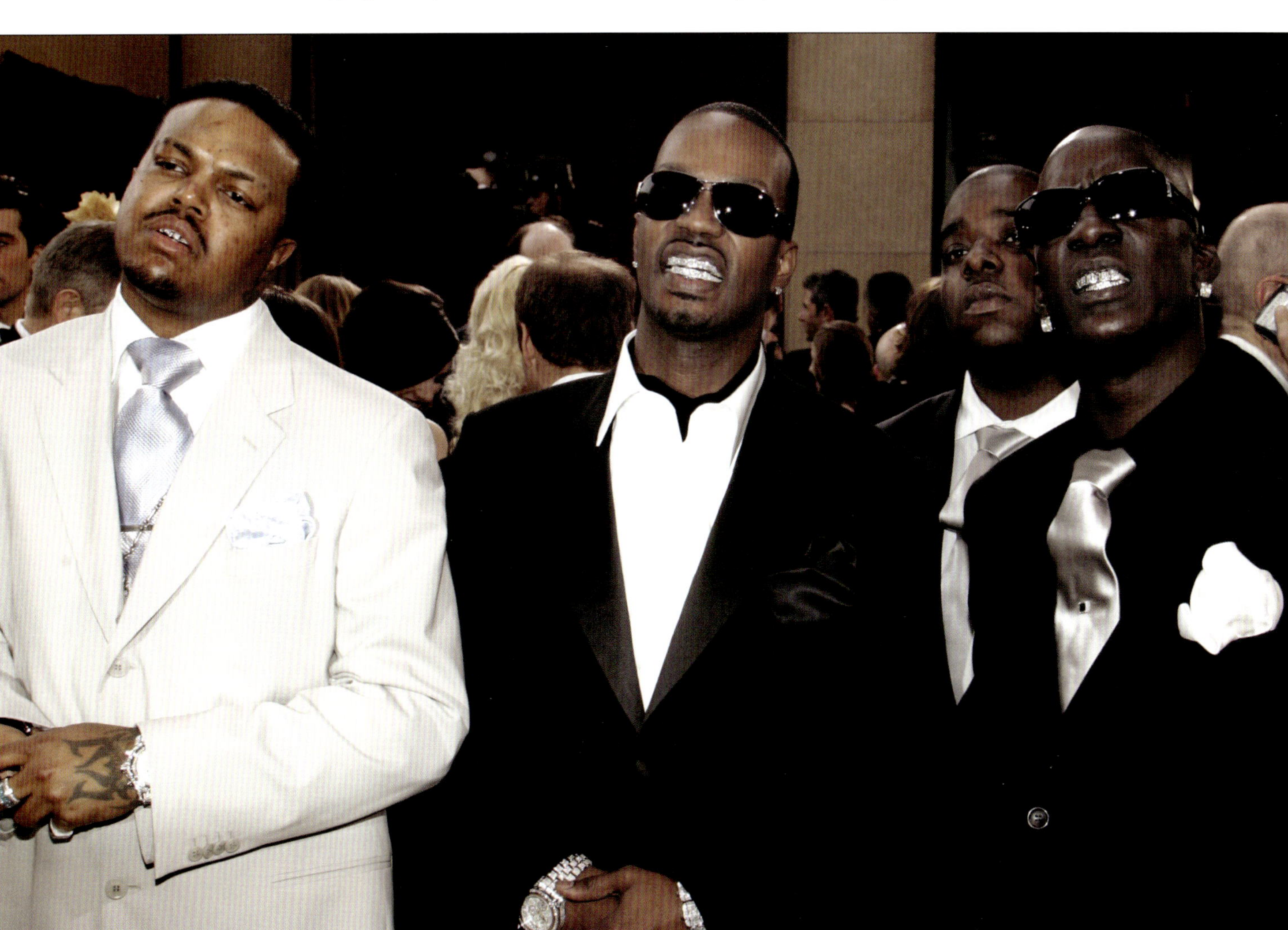

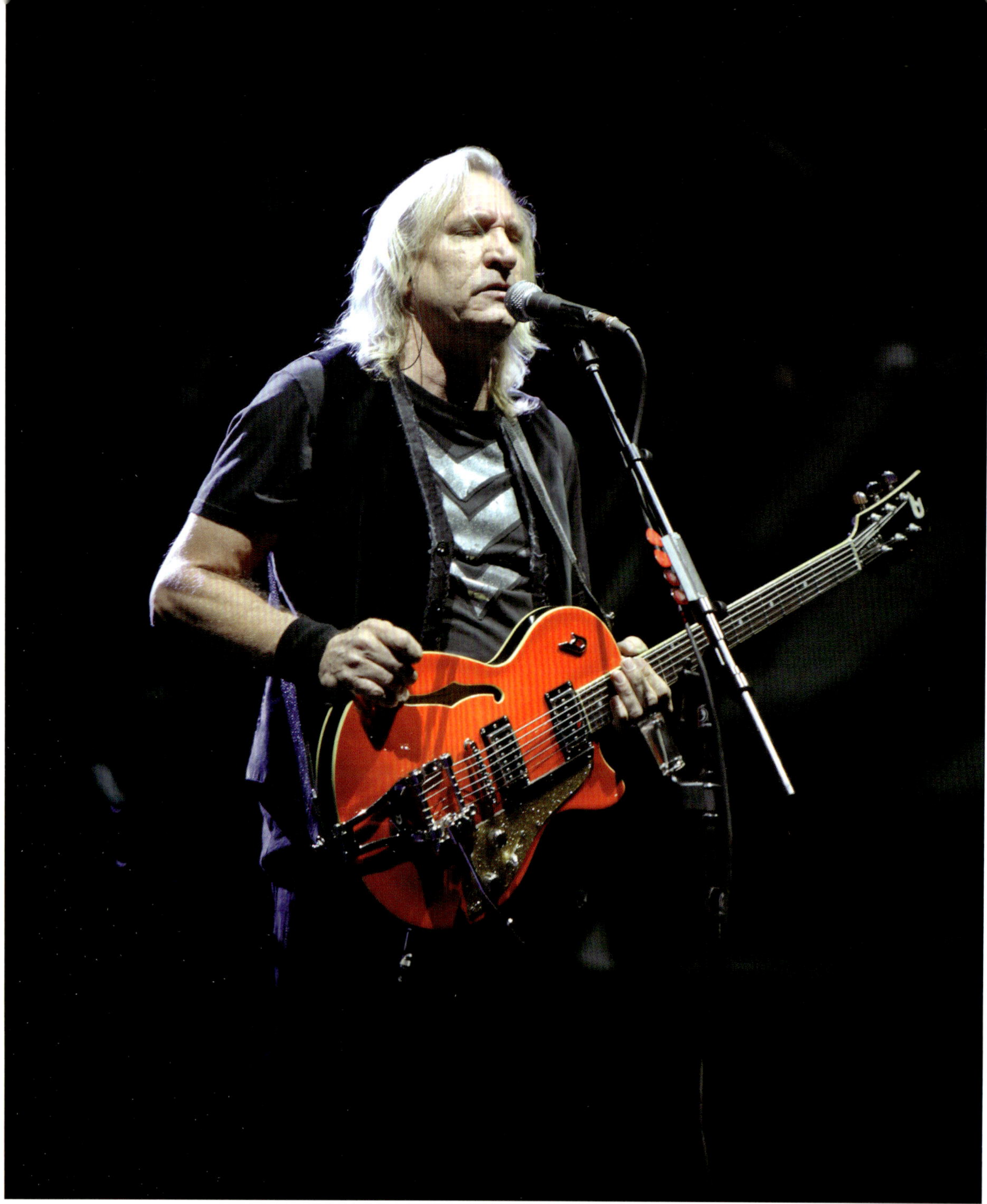

JOE WALSH

SONGWRITER, EAGLE

"I'm lucky I'm sane after all I've been through."

Joe Walsh, Life's Been Good

Joe Walsh didn't so much live in Memphis as he just stayed here — for several months, a few times over the years.

As he told *The Commercial Appeal* in 1995, "Memphis was and still is a real center of undiscovered talent and just tradition…I just decided to come to Memphis and spend some time there." He has recorded albums in Memphis with Memphis musicians and has been inspired. When asked about the title of an upcoming album, Walsh responded, "I'm thinking about it. I better come experience Memphis before I finalize one. I'm sure there is one floating around down there on Beale Street."

Joe Walsh loves Memphis, and Memphis – without a doubt – loves him.

Photograph WireImage/Anna Webber

ANITA WARD

DISCO ICON

Before her disco hit climbed the charts in 1979, Memphis native Anita Ward received a degree in psychology from Rust College and worked as a substitute teacher for Memphis elementary schools. While she was working on her first album, Ward was approached with a seemingly insignificant song. Originally written about teens on the telephone, the lyrics were re-written for an adult audience and a disco beat was added to create the now-famous track "Ring My Bell." The song reached #1 on the charts in Canada, the United Kingdom and the United States. As disco's popularity waned, Ward took time away from music to focus on raising her daughter. For New Year's Eve of 2005, she returned to Memphis to perform on Beale Street, and in 2011, Ward went back into the studio to work on her new album titled *It's My Night*.

Photograph ABC Photo Archives

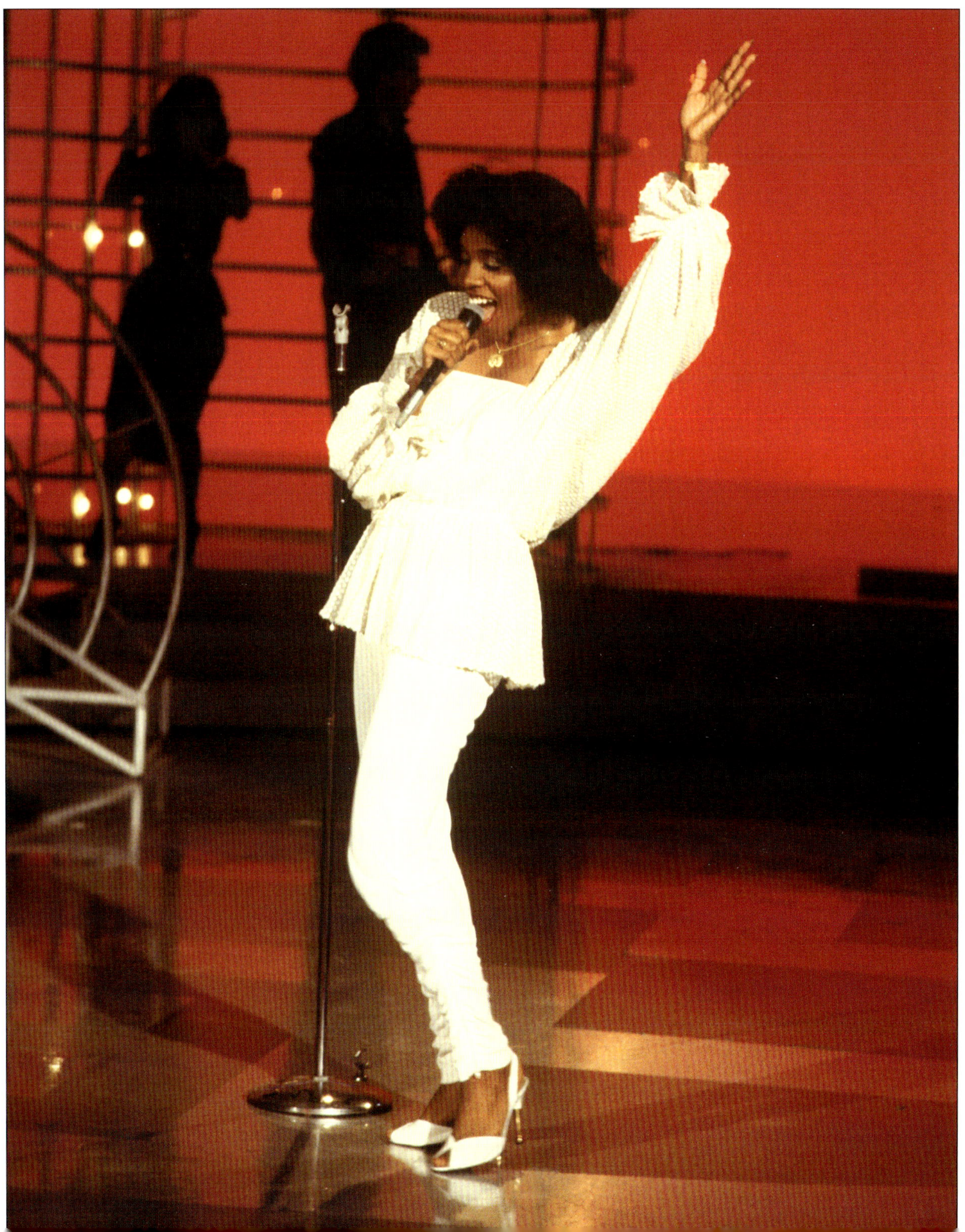

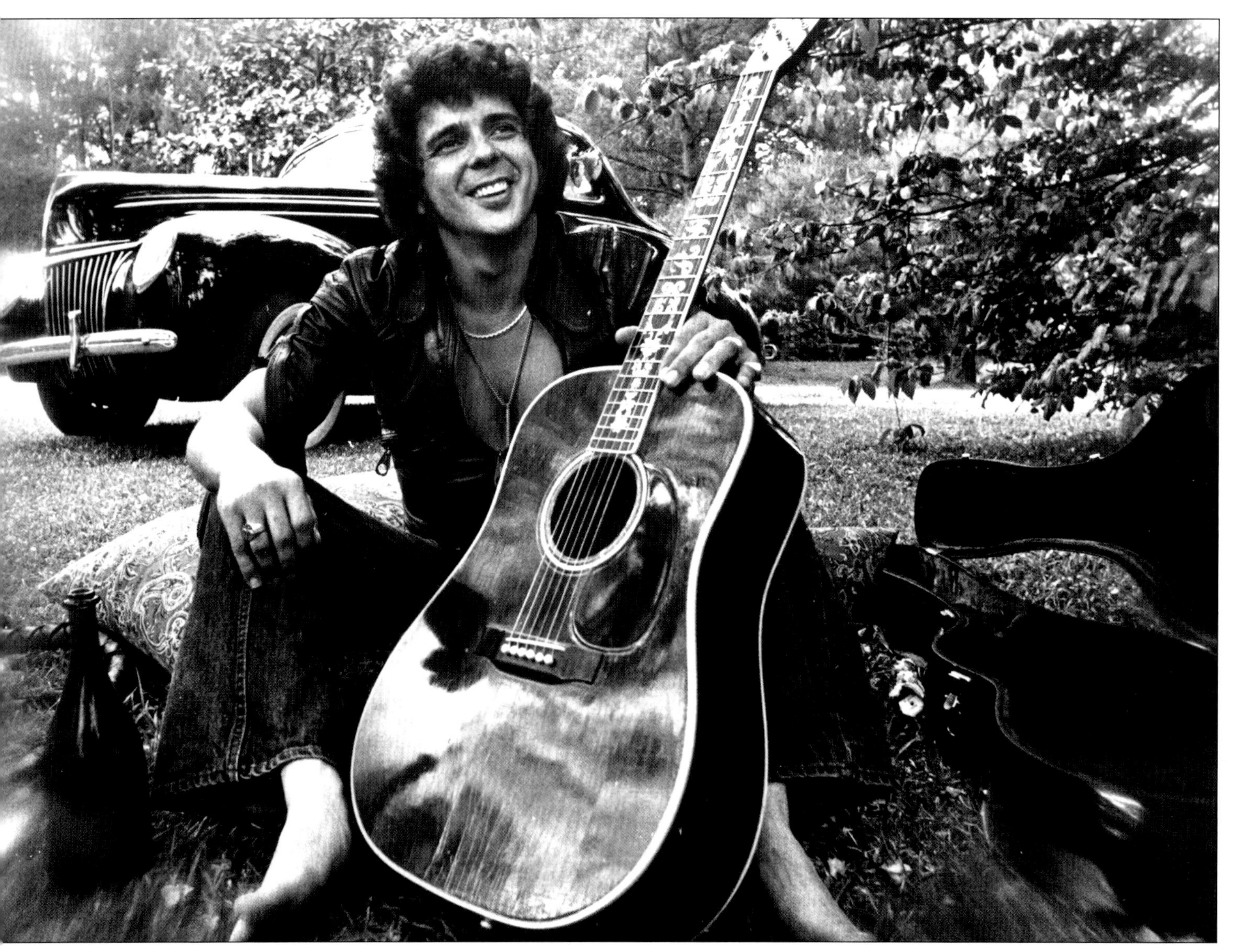

BOBBY WHITLOCK

SINGER, SONGWRITER

At the age of 16, Bobby Whitlock was the first white artist signed to the legendary Stax record label. His first professional recording was the clapping hands on Sam & Dave's "I Thank You." It was on a tour with Delaney & Bonnie that Whitlock met Eric Clapton. While the two worked on George Harrison's *All Things Must Pass*, Derek and the Dominoes was born. That partnership would produce one of the most influential rock albums ever recorded, *Layla and Other Assorted Love Songs*. Whitlock has gone on to a long solo career. He hosted a television show in Ireland, where he often brought in Stax mentor and fellow Memphian Steve Cropper.

Photograph Michael Ochs Archives

DEANIE PARKER

SINGER, STEWARD

"We were all youngsters...with a dream, with a vision, with an interest in expressing ourselves through music."
Deanie Parker

When Deanie Parker won a talent contest and an audition with Stax Records, she had no idea that it would lead to a life-long relationship with the Memphis company. After releasing a few singles as a singer, Parker switched to the other side of the microphone, working as the first director of publicity. Until Stax closed in 1976, Parker worked in just about every aspect of the business: songwriting, publicity, photography, artist relations and promotions.

Next, she worked for Memphis in May and the Regional Medical Center at Memphis. She returned to Stax in 1998, leading a successful fundraising campaign to create a Stax Museum and a Music Academy. The Academy opened in 2002 and the Museum the following year. She was the President and CEO of the Soulsville Foundation until she retired in 2007.

Photograph courtesy Stax Museum/jean-Pierre Leloir

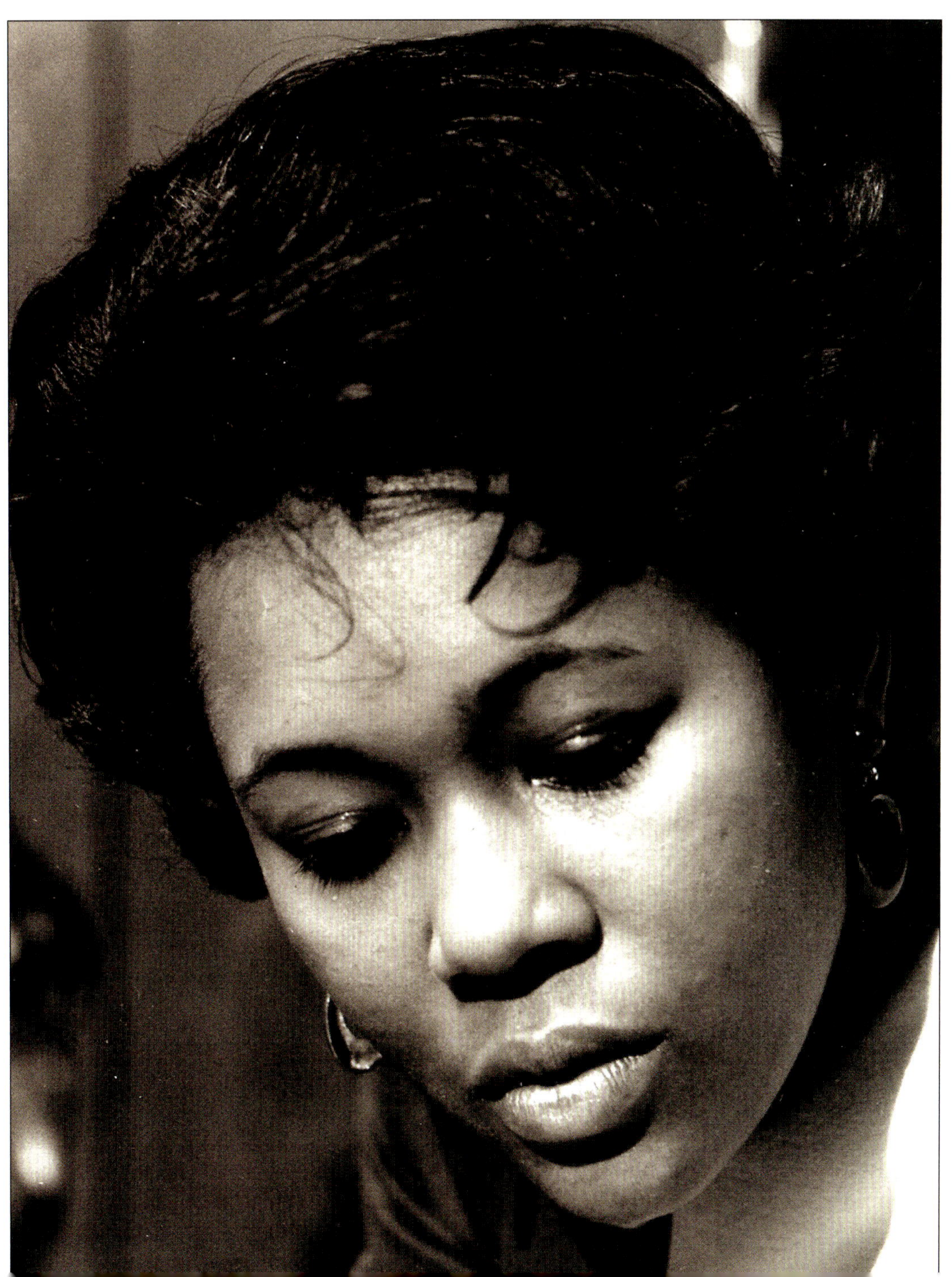

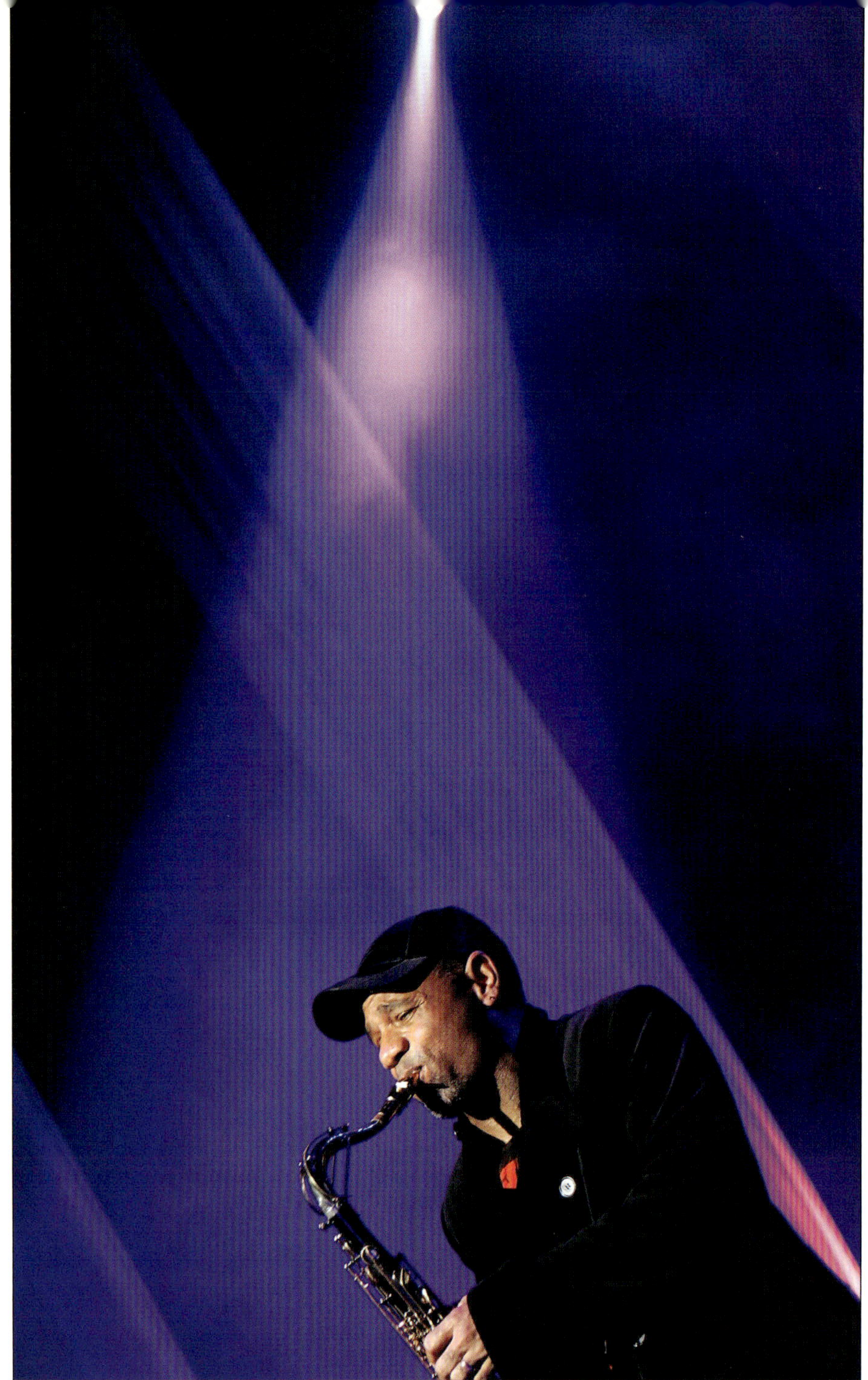

KIRK WHALUM

MUSICIAN, MINISTER

"The music I like to play and write encompasses the four elements I grew up with: Memphis R&B, gospel, rock, and jazz. The emphasis, though, is on melody, period."

Grammy-award-winning Kirk Whalum grew up around music: along with singing in his father's church choir, two of his uncles, Wendell and "Peanuts" were professional jazz musicians. After graduating from Melrose High School, he was part of the Ocean of Soul marching band at Texas Southern University. He has been a session player for some of the top names in the music business, such as Quincy Jones, Al Green, Barbra Streisand and Al Jarreau to name a few. On the road, Whalum opened for Whitney Houston for several years. His solo career has been no less impressive – with eleven Grammy nominations. It isn't all work, though; Whalum is an ordained minister and his 15-minute daily podcasts – *Bible in Your Ear* – take listeners through the entire Bible over the course of a year.

Photograph Getty Entertainment/Carlo Allegri

Sports

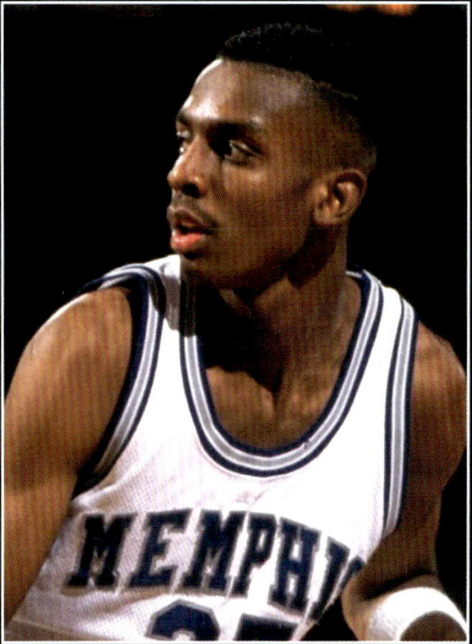

DEANGELO WILLIAMS

NFL RUNNING BACK

"Memphis is a big city.
You never see the same people twice."
DeAngelo Williams

Traditional wisdom in the NFL was that 5' 9" was too small to be a running back. Then they saw DeAngelo Williams play. The University of Memphis superstar holds the Division I NCAA record for the most career all-purpose yards at 7,573, as well as 34 games with 100+ yards rushing. He ranks fourth in all time rushing yards. The list goes on…and on….

In his final game for Memphis, Williams set a Motor City Bowl record with 238 yards and he scored 3 touchdowns. Williams has won awards for his sportsmanship on and off the field. He is currently playing, very well, for the Carolina Panthers.

Photograph Sports Illustrated/Darren Carroll

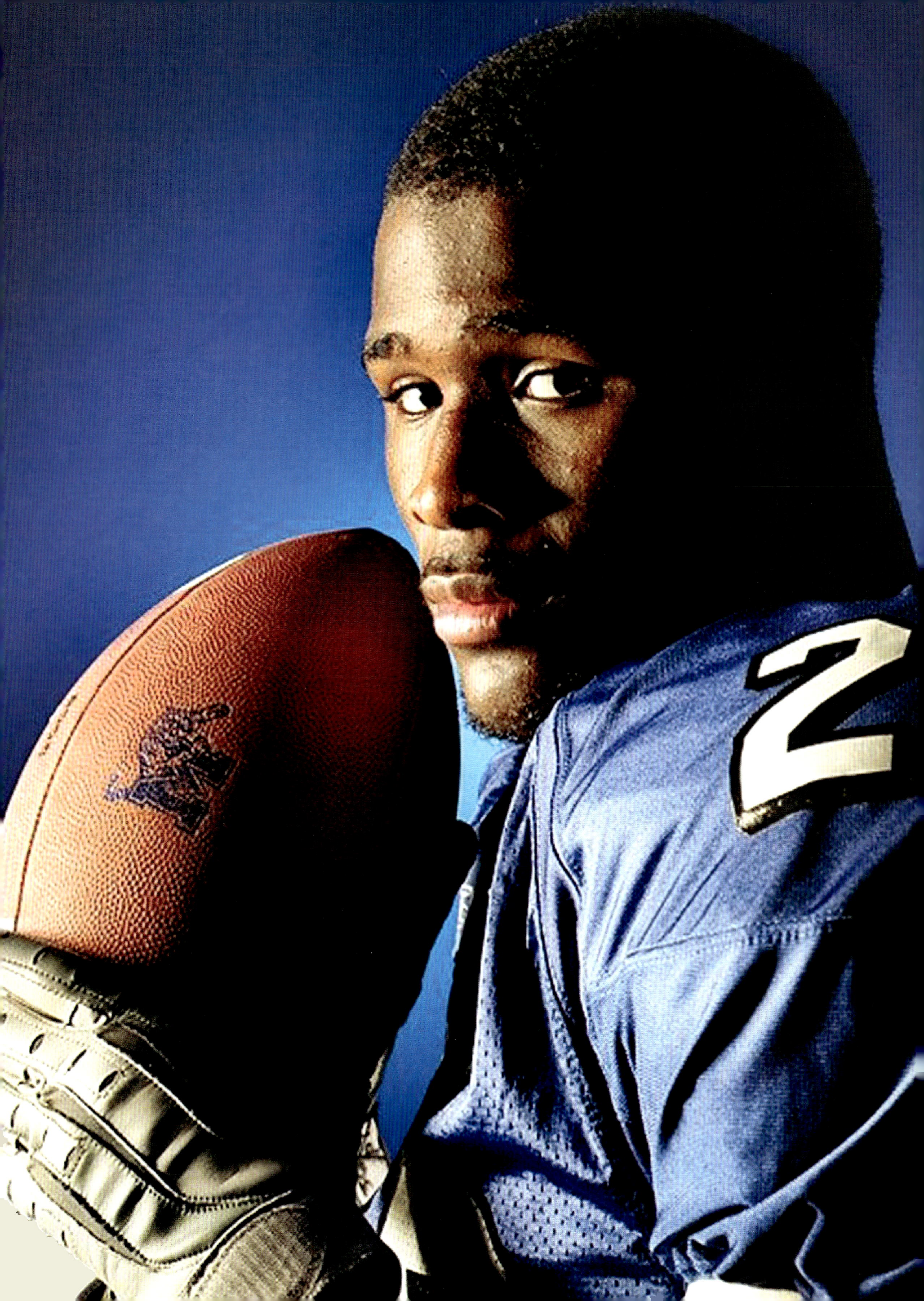

ANFERNEE "PENNY" HARDAWAY

BASKETBALL STAR

Anfernee Deon "Penny" Hardaway (born July 18, 1971) is a former professional basketball player who played in the NBA, specializing as a small forward, shooting guard, and point guard. His grandmother gave him the nickname "Penny." Growing up, he lived in the Binghampton section of Memphis and played for Treadwell High, before moving on to the Memphis State Tigers. His junior year (1992-1993) he was named an All-American and was a finalist for the Naismith College Player of the Year. He had a 3.4 GPA but skipped his senior year to play in the NBA. His most productive professional years came in his days as a member of the Orlando Magic, as well as the early portion of his stint with the Phoenix Suns. Hardaway was an all-NBA player early in his career. He last played for the Miami Heat, in 2007. In 1994, the University of Memphis retired his #25 jersey. Penny returned to the school in May 2003 and graduated with a bachelor's degree in professional studies. Penny is now retired and divides his time between golf and involvement in youth basketball in Memphis. He also donated a million dollars to the University of Memphis for a sports hall of fame. He continues to be a good ambassador for Memphis basketball, both college and pro.

Photography Sports Illustrated/Richard Mackson

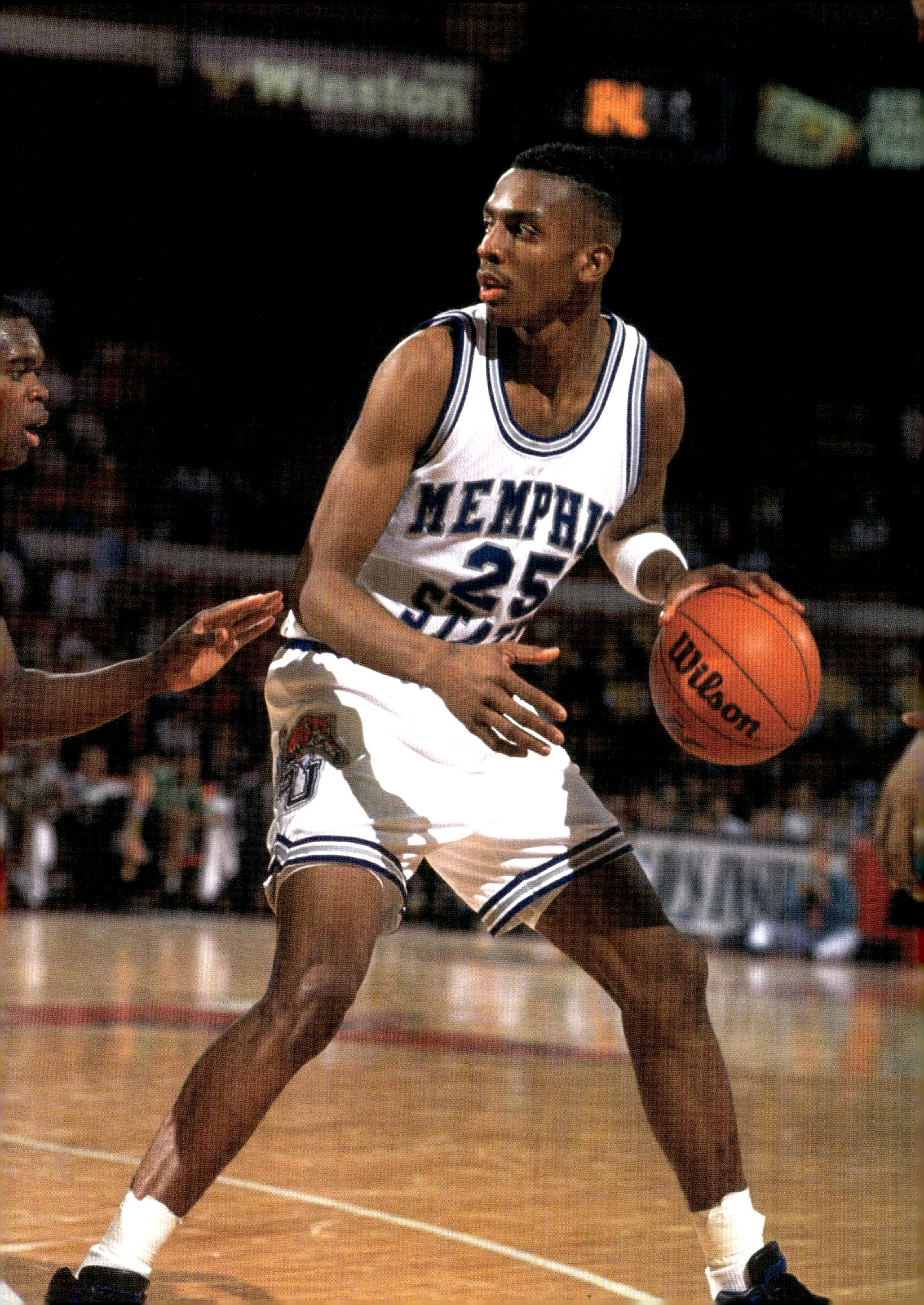
Winston
25
Wilson

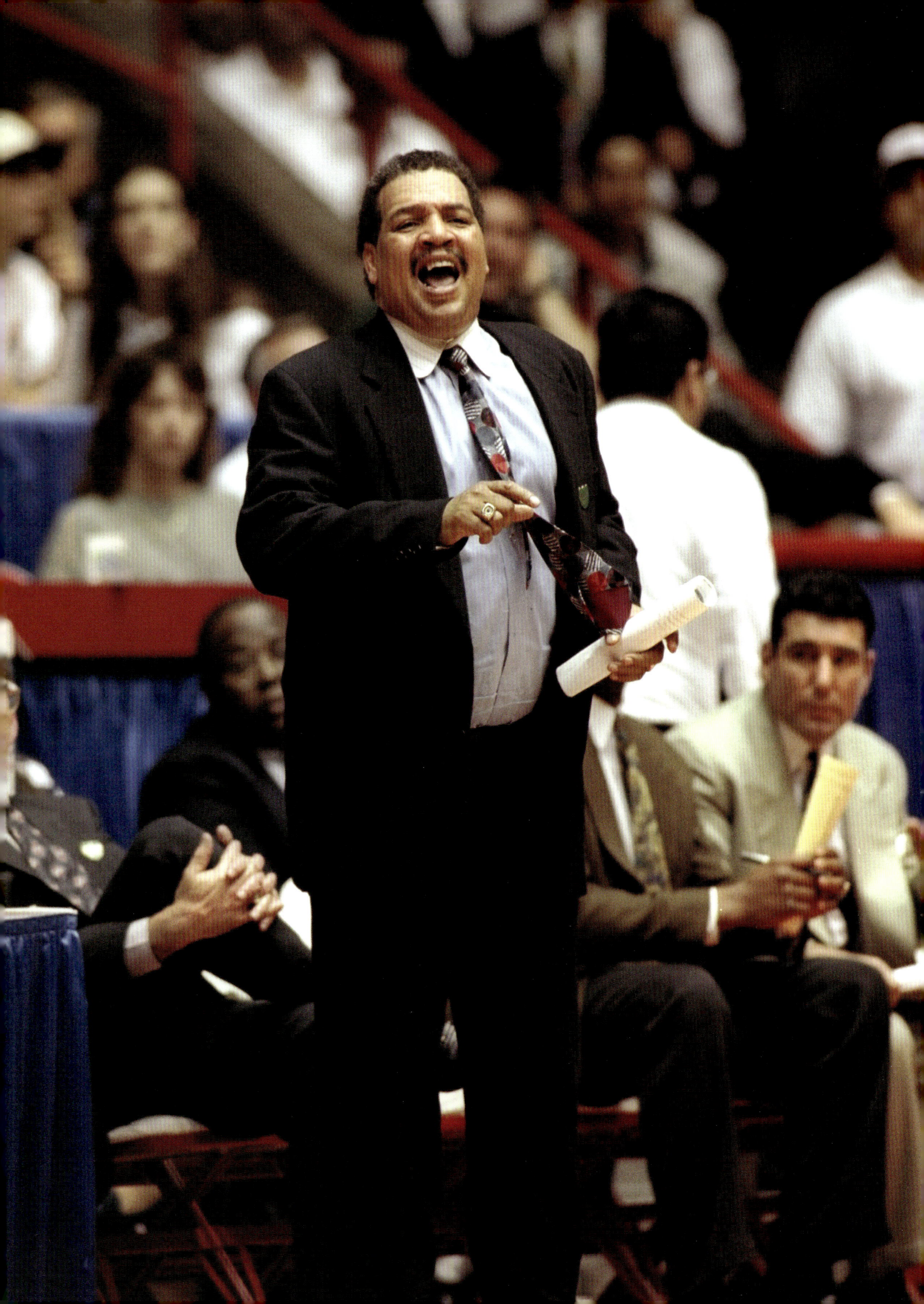

LARRY FINCH

MEMPHIS TIGER – PLAYER & COACH

His jumpshot was a thing of beauty. His hustle, drive and smile were inspiring. For a city rocked just years earlier with the assassination of Martin Luther King, Jr., this Orange Mound resident and Melrose High standout would lead his Memphis State team to hoop glory and provide the city with something even more important in the process.

Larry Finch's Memphis State Tiger basketball team provided a rallying point based on teamwork. And, of course, there was the game itself. Throughout his Tiger days, he hustled the court with a stellar cast of Tigers, including Melrose teammate and friend, Ronnie Robinson, and Larry Kenon. Finch would eventually lead his team to the Final Four and the championship game in 1973, as Finch hit for 29 points in the losing game against John Wooden's UCLA Bruins. He ended his college career that day as the highest scoring Tiger ever. Finch still ranks fourth with 1,869 total points.

After college and a brief stint in the NBA and ABA, Finch joined former Tiger head coach Gene Bartow at the University of Alabama Birmingham for several seasons before returning to his home town to become an assistant coach to Dana Kirk at Memphis State. It wasn't long before he found himself as head coach, posting 10 of 11 winning seasons and taking the Tigers to six NCAA tournaments, including the Final Eight in 1992. Finch amassed a head coaching record of 220 wins and 130 from 1986 to 1997, the winningest record for any Tiger coach.

After suffering a stroke in 1992, Finch's health declined. The city never forgot him, though, as fundraisers were held to offset medical bills. Finch died in April 2011.

Photography Getty • **Story** by David Tankersley

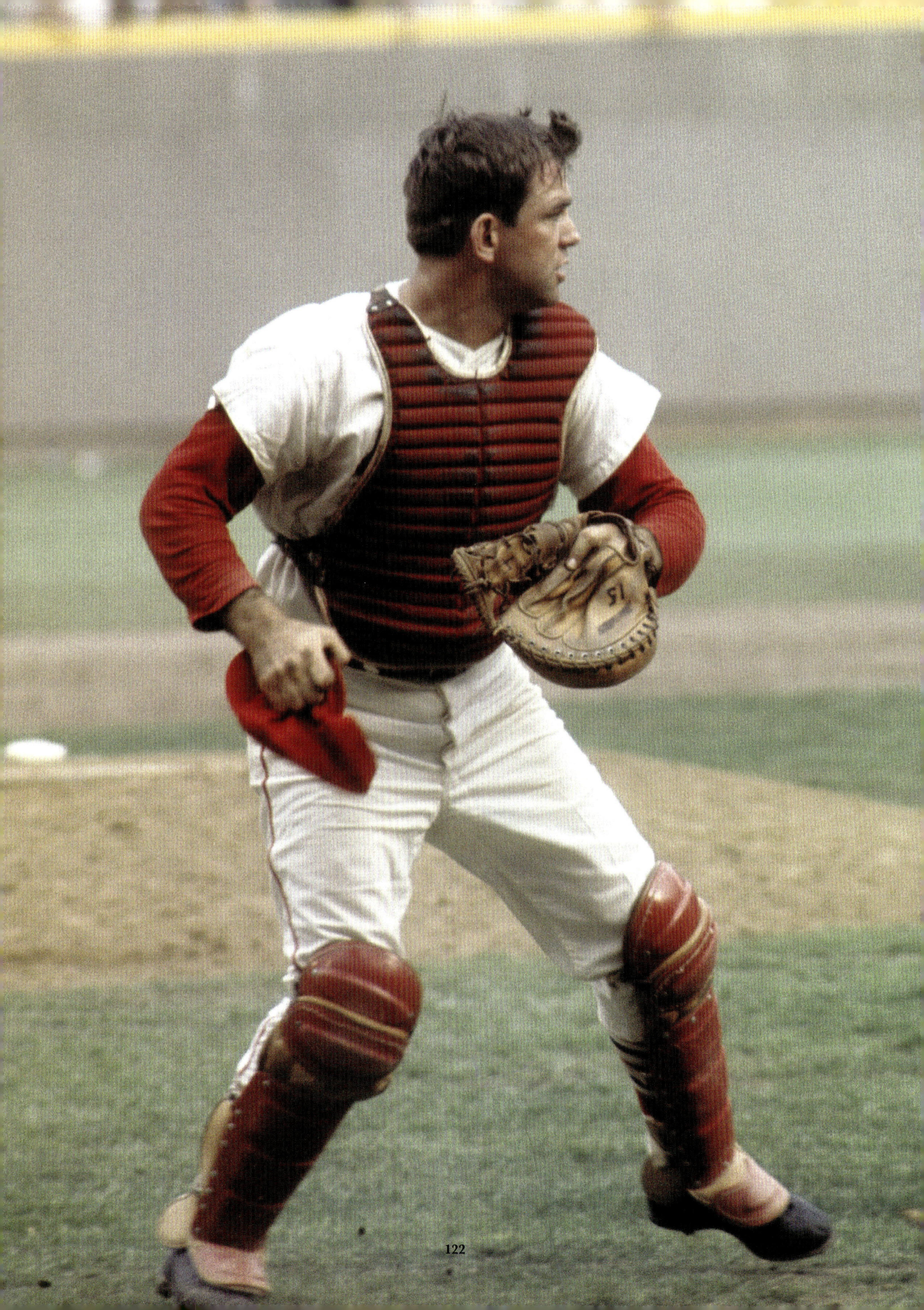

TIM MCCARVER

MAJOR LEAGUE BASEBALL CATCHER, ANNOUNCER

Born in Memphis in 1941, Tim McCarver attended Christian Brothers High School, and then it was on to a career in baseball. In his first year as a pro, at just 17, he bounced between several St. Louis Cardinals' farm teams, and was even briefly called up to the parent team. The pattern continued for the next several seasons, with McCarver even playing some minor league ball for the Cardinals in his hometown of Memphis. By his 4th season he was installed as one of the Cardinals' starting catchers. Over nearly two decades McCarver was, among other things, the favorite catcher of notoriously difficult pitcher Bob Gibson, and late in his career, of Steve Carlton. It was once said that McCarver and Carlton were so inseparable that when they died they would be buried sixty feet, six inches apart: the distance from the pitcher's mound to home plate. McCarver was also included in the trade that would have sent him and teammate Curt Flood to Philadelphia. Flood felt that the trade was against his best interest and fought it all the way to the Supreme Court, which ultimately resulted in free agency.

As a broadcaster, many fans adore McCarver's analysis and insight, though some consider him verbose. For a number of years the AA franchise of the Cardinals was the Memphis Chicks. They played at a ballpark named for McCarver.

Photograph Getty/Focus On Sport • **Story** by Dennis Phillippi

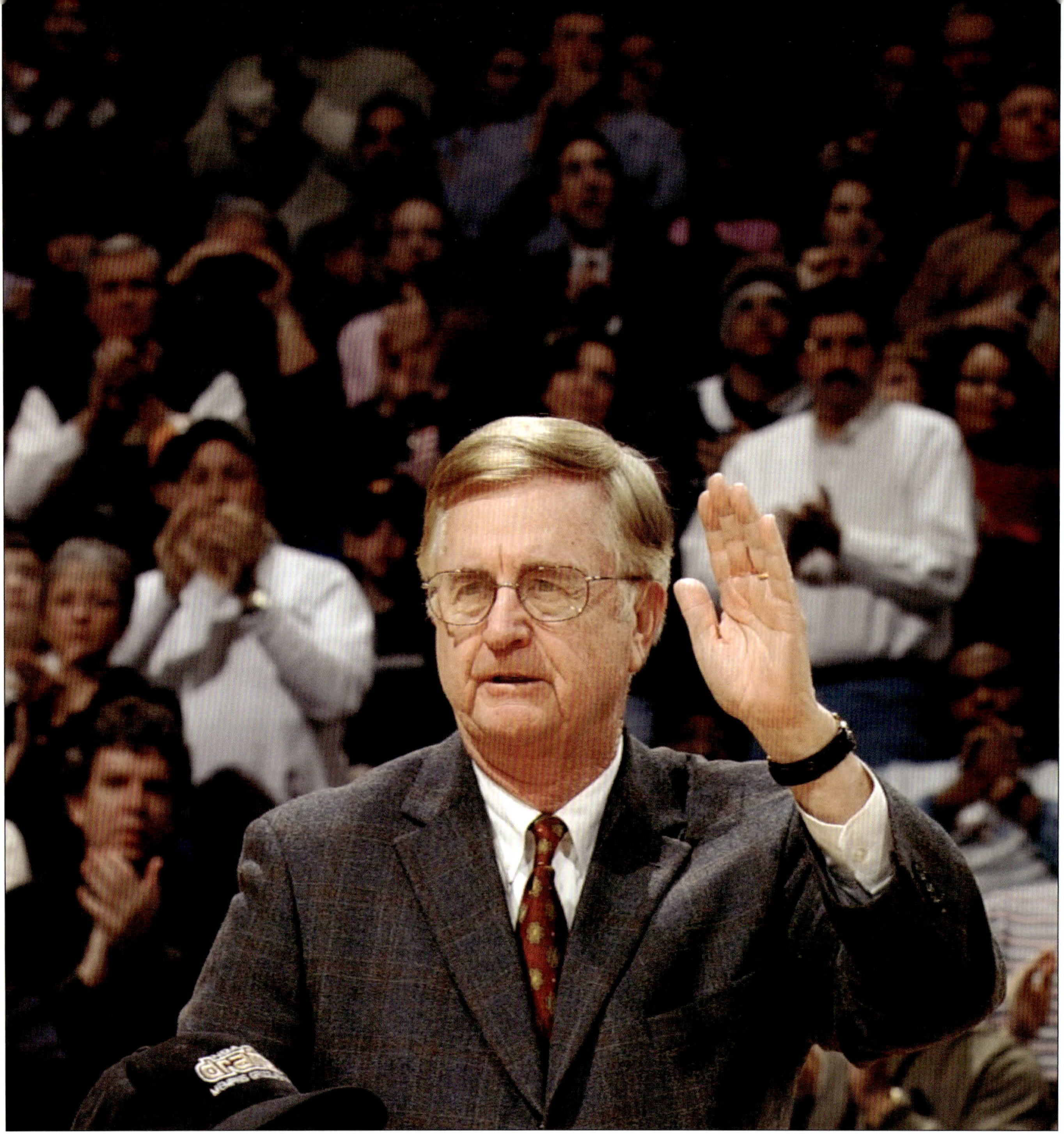

GENE BARTOW

BASKETBALL COACH

While Gene Bartow's time in Memphis may have been brief, just four seasons, he is considered by sports fans a Memphis treasure. In just his third season as the head coach of the then Memphis State Tigers men's basketball team, Bartow took them all the way to the NCAA final game. In that game Bartow's team, led by another Memphis treasure, Larry Finch, were unfortunate enough to run into UCLA's Bill Walton who went 21 of 22 and scored 44 points. It was arguably Walton's finest performance as a Bruin. Nonetheless, the Tigers would go decades without reaching the kinds of heights to which they were brought by Bartow. Ironically, Bartow would succeed legendary Coach John Wooden as the head coach of UCLA just a few seasons later.

Photograph NBAE/Getty Images • **Story** by Dennis Phillippi

ISAAC BRUCE

NFL WIDE RECEIVER

The stats on Memphis State wide receiver Isaac Bruce are mind boggling. He was named Rookie of the Year with the Los Angeles Rams and followed the team to St. Louis the next year. Since his first NFL reception, fans have yelled "Bruuuuuuce" every time he makes a catch. Certainly they did when he caught a 73-yard touchdown pass to win Super Bowl XXXIV. Amid the impressive stats, Bruce has also racked up little reported awards for sportsmanship and Man of the Year.

After thirteen seasons with the Rams, Bruce was picked up by San Francisco. In 2008, in a game against his former team, Rams fans wildly cheered "Bruuuuuuuce" as he caught his 1,000th career reception. In 2010 he was traded back to St. Louis so he could retire a Ram. Which says more about the man than a shelf of trophies.

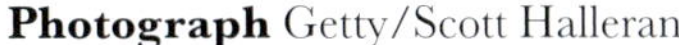

Photograph Getty/Scott Halleran

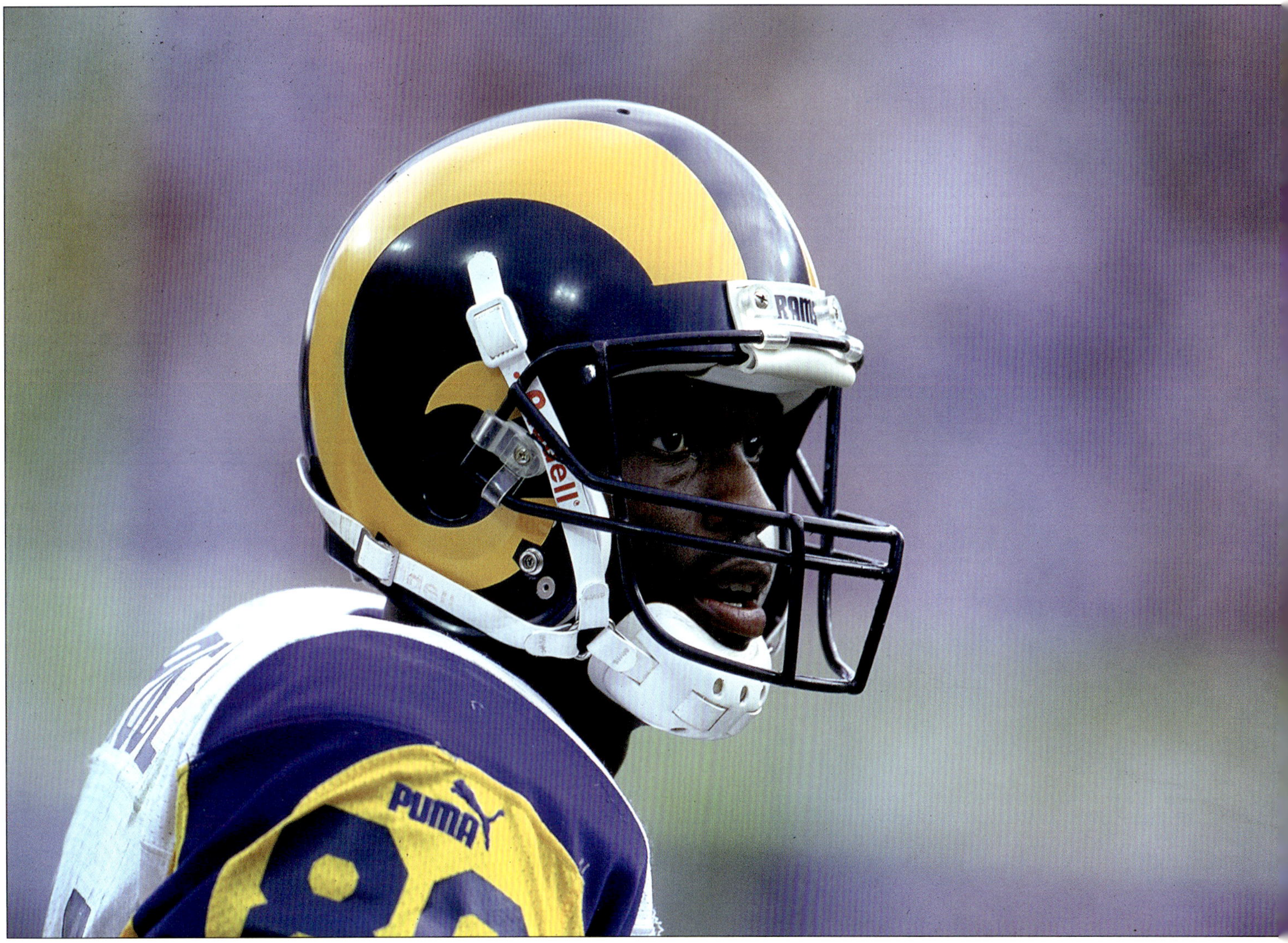

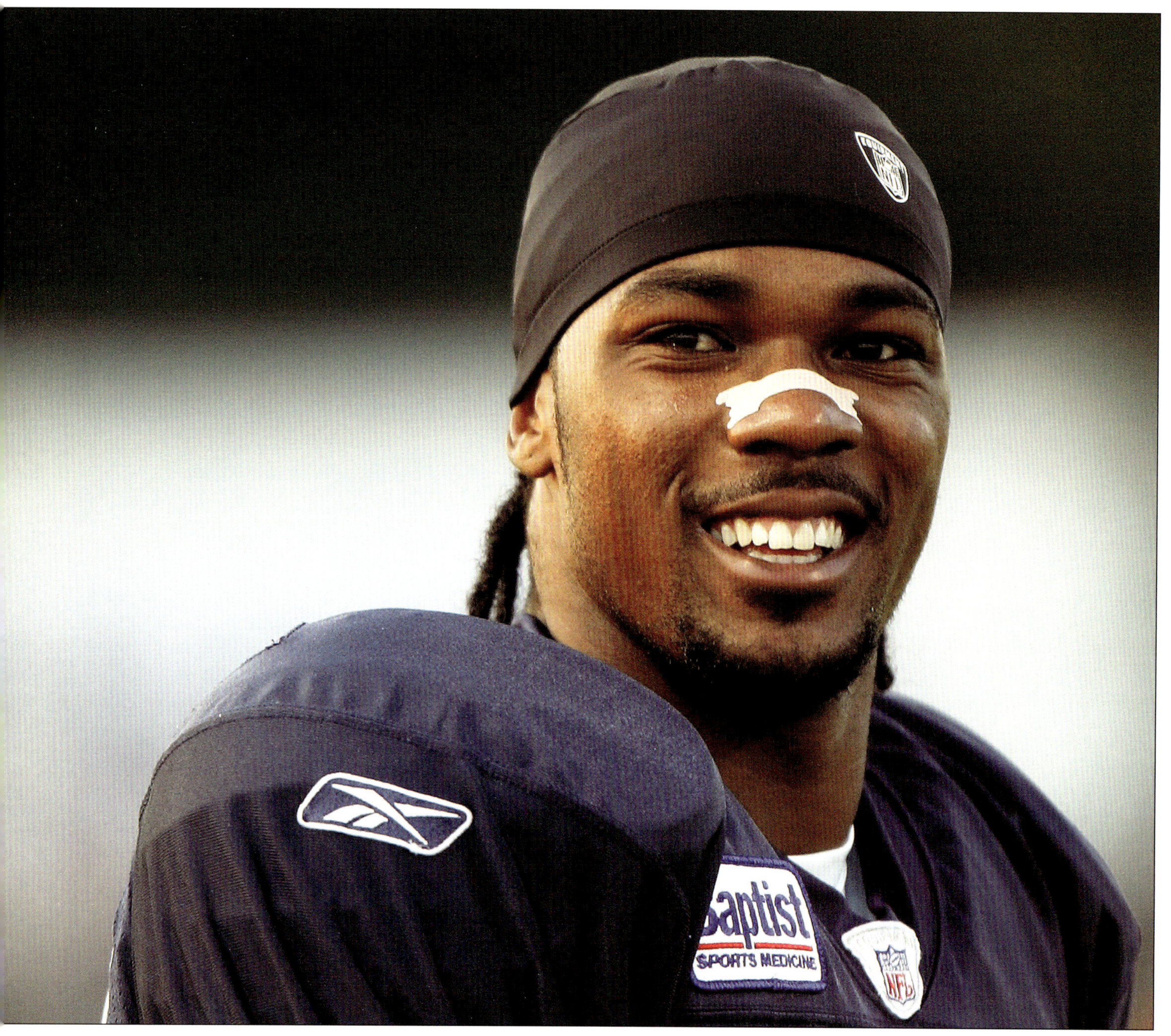

TYRONE CALICO

WIDE RECEIVER

After attending Millington Central High School in Tennessee, Tyrone Calico became the starting receiver for the MTSU Blue Raiders. At the 2002 NFL Scouting Combine, he ran the 40-yard dash in 4.34 seconds, the fastest of that year. He signed with the Tennessee Titans for the 2003 season and played until a knee injury forced him to stop in 2005. He now lives in Brentwood, Tenn., with his wife and daughter.

Photograph Getty Images Sport

BOB CARUTHERS

BASEBALL PIONEER

In 1884, Bob Caruthers, expert in billiards and poker, made his Major League Baseball debut as pitcher and right-fielder with the St. Louis Browns and led his team to its first pennant the following year. He lead the league with 40 wins. In 1886, he pioneered the art of absurd professional baseball contract disputes by conducting his from Paris, giving him the nickname "Parisian Bob." In 1887, he led the Browns to their third consecutive title despite having malaria. After being traded to the Brooklyn Bridegrooms, Caruthers again led the league in wins and led Brooklyn to the national league title in 1890. He ended his career with 218 wins and 99 losses.

Illustration courtesy of Sporting News

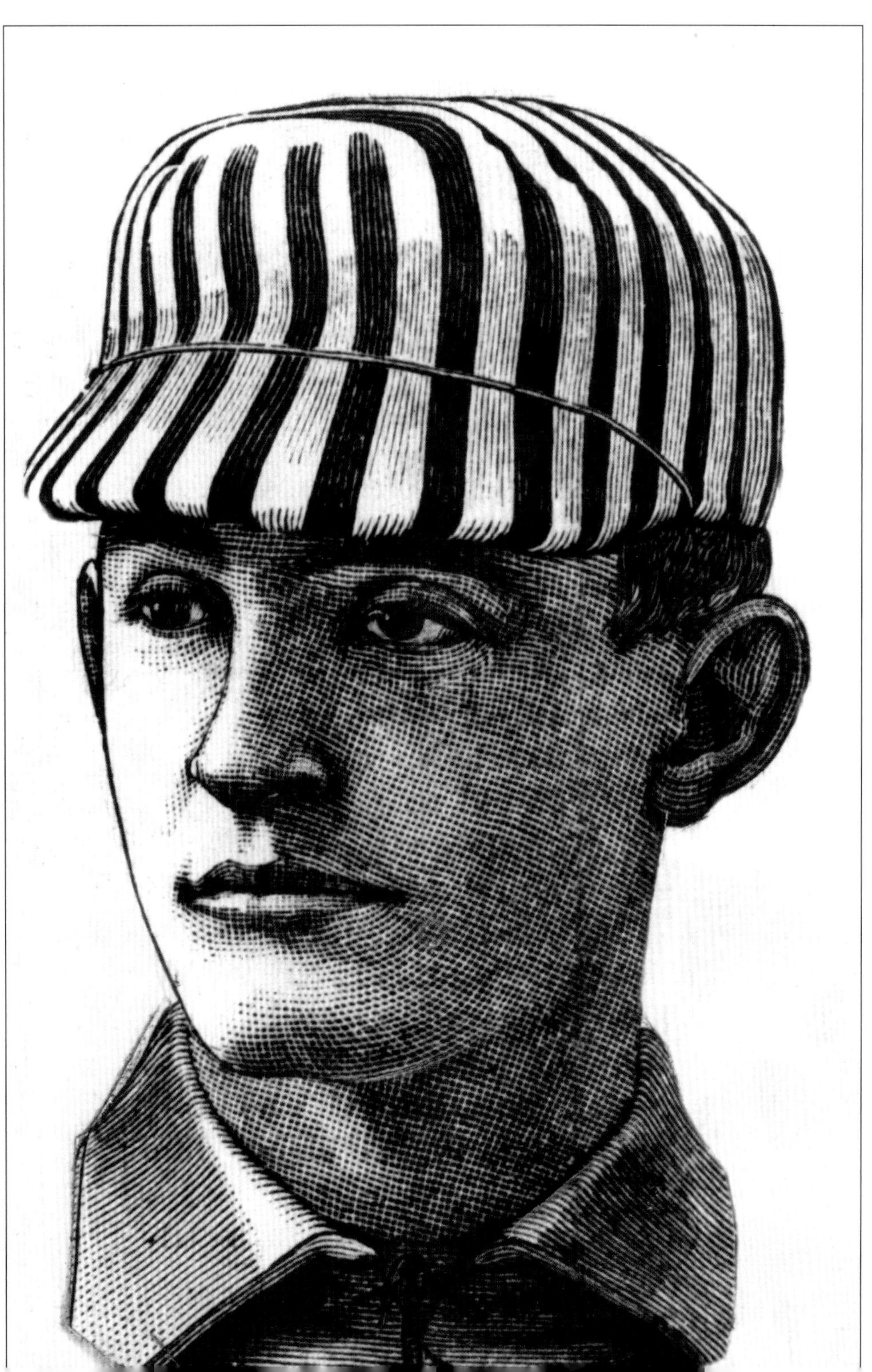

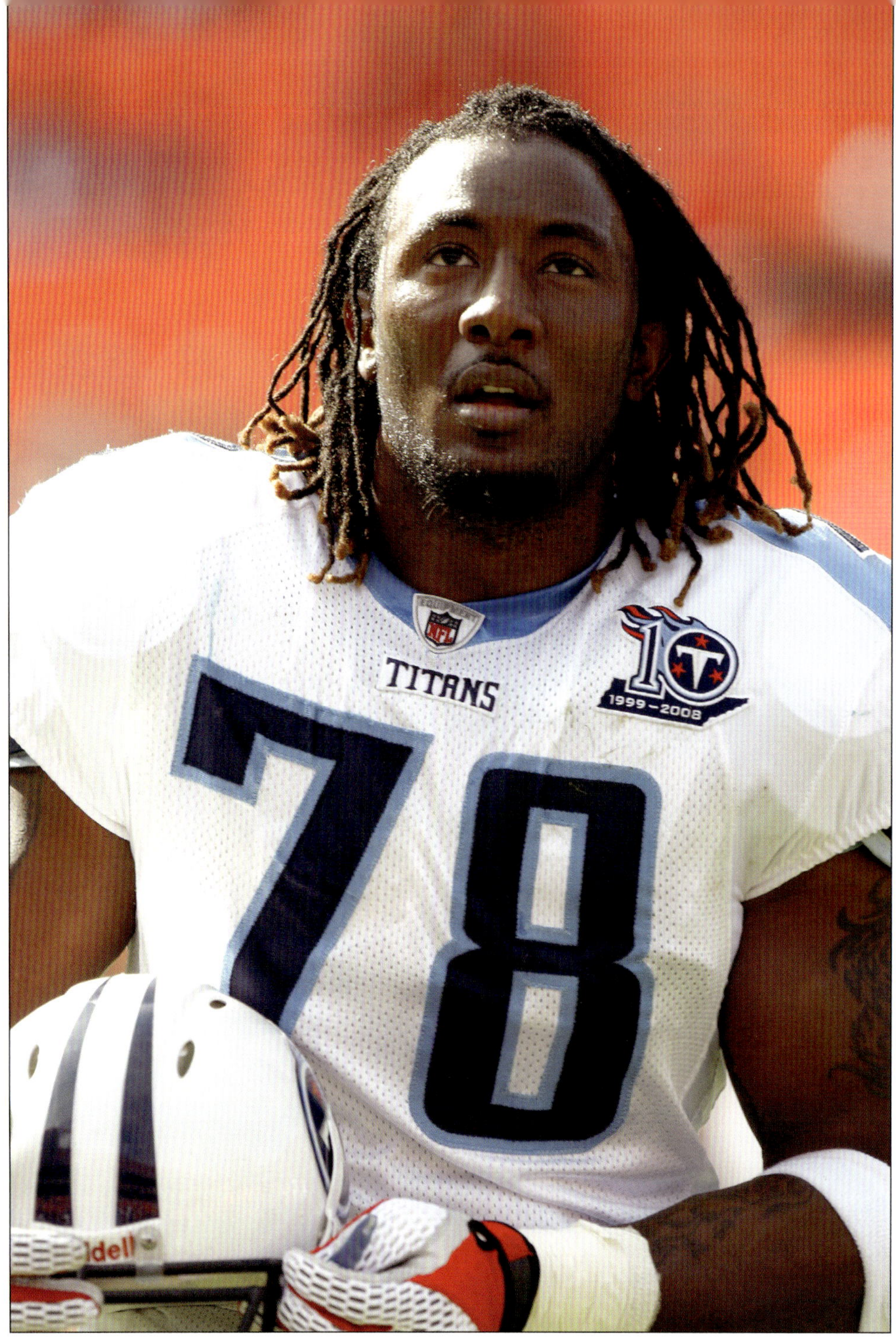

JACOB A.T. FORD

NFL LINEMAN, ARTIST

Genes are a funny thing. Tennessee Titans defensive end Jacob Ford is the son of internationally known jazz saxophonist "Sweet Daddy Goodlow" Ford, and Bessie Nelson West, a renowned artist. Ford, however, played football. At Melrose High School he earned All-Shelby Metro; at the University of Memphis he made the Freshman All-Conference USA honors. He dropped out of college, and football, for two years. Ford worked loading trucks. Soon he was back in school in Arkansas, and came back to Tennessee when drafted by the Titans, where he is one of the team's most established pass rushers. Dividing his time between Nashville and Memphis, Jacob enjoys drawing and painting landscapes – just like mom.

Photograph Getty/Jamie Squire

SHAUN MICHEEL

PROFESSIONAL GOLFER

Pro golfer Shaun Micheel feels that Memphis holds "his heart and home." Learning to play golf on a Memphis course near his childhood home, Micheel went pro in 1992. He won the Singapore Open in 1998 and the PGA Championship in 2003. In 2011, he hosted the 8th annual Shaun Micheel Make-A-Wish Golf Classic in Memphis to support the mid-South chapter of the famous foundation.

Photograph Getty/Stephen Munday

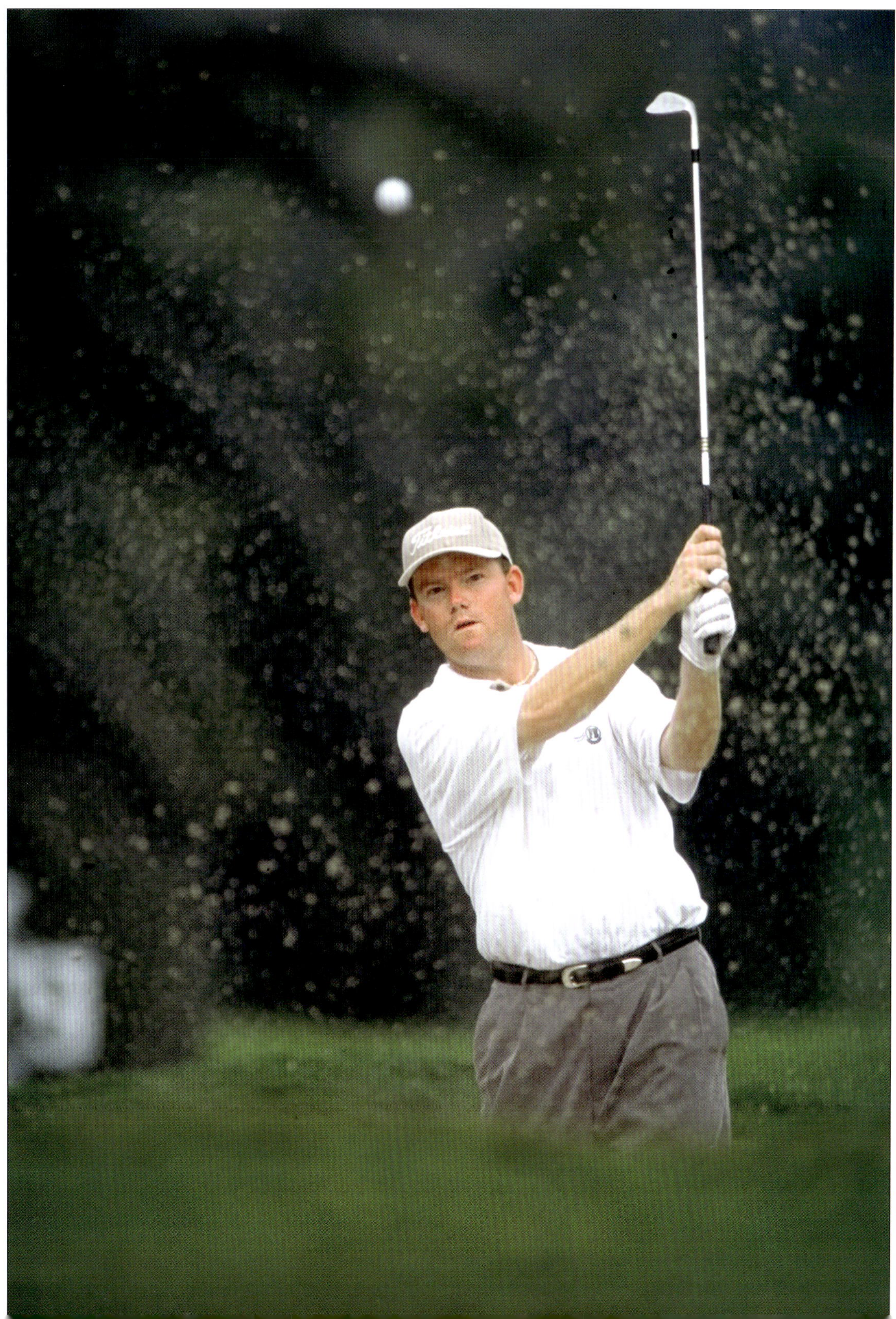

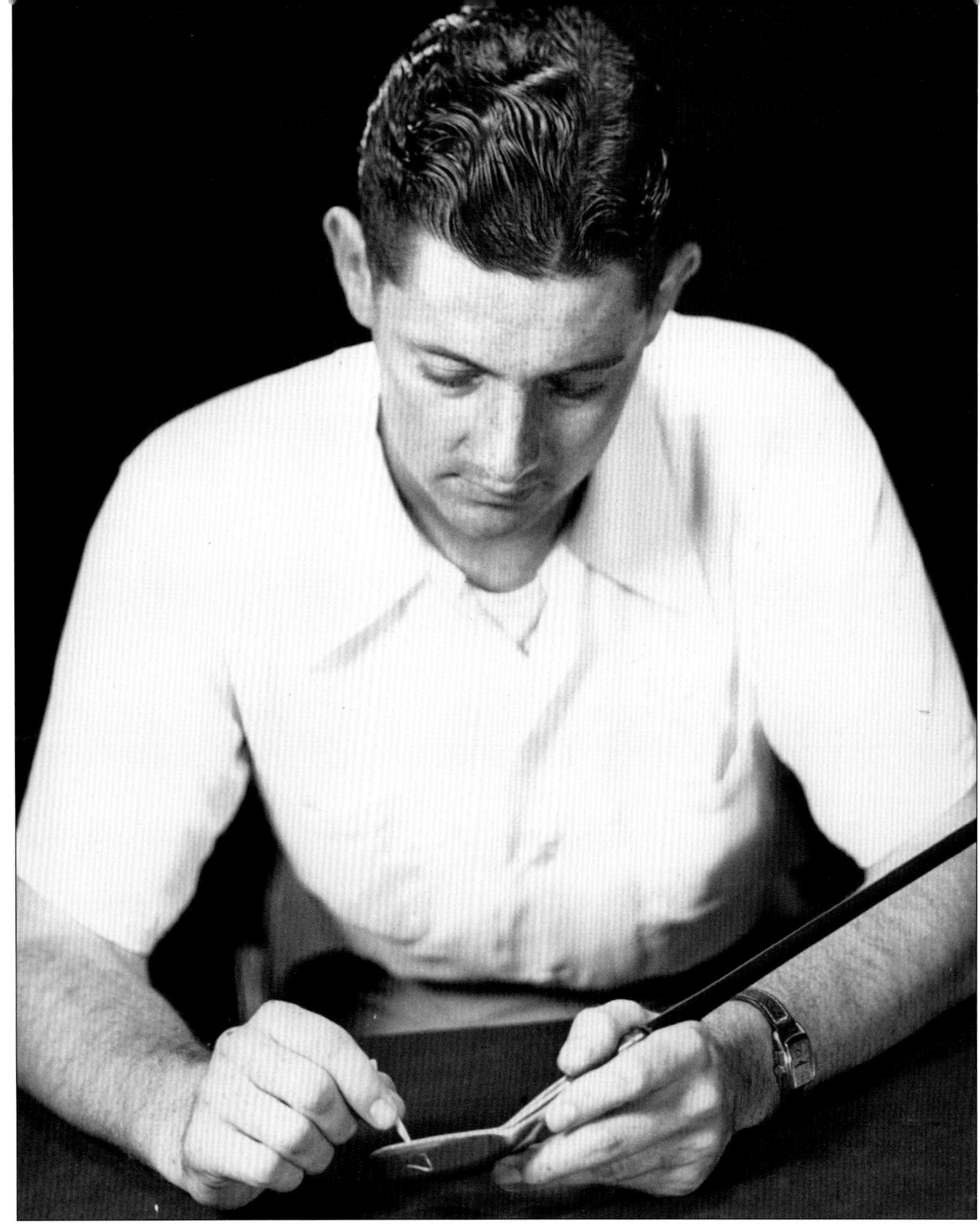

DR. CARY MIDDLECOFF

DRIVE-DRILLING DENTIST

Known for both the length of his drives and the length of time it took him to hit them, Cary "Doc" Middlecoff played his way into the World Golf Hall of Fame with 40 career victories on the PGA Tour when he retired in 1961, then eighth on the all-time list. As an amateur, he won the Memphis City Championship and the Tennessee State Amateur in his teens, won a collegiate tournament by 29 strokes while playing for Ole Miss, and played in the final group with Ben Hogan and Gene Sarazen in the 1945 North and South Open, beating them both to become the first amateur to win that tournament. And he almost never turned pro at all. His first profession was dentistry, and after serving as a dentist for 18 months of active duty in World War II, he decided he'd give his self-taught golf game a shot on tour. He gave himself two years to make it work. He never drilled another tooth, winning his first pro title in 1947 and winning at least one every year until he retired, including two U.S. Opens and a Masters. His playing style was – let's just say – deliberate. Iconic sportswriter Dan Jenkins joked that Middlecoff gave up dentistry because his patients couldn't hold their mouths open that long. Dr. Cary Middlecoff died in 1998.

Photograph Masters Historic Imagery/Augusta National • **Story** by Dan Conaway

CINDY PARLOW

OLYMPIC GOLD MEDALIST

The youngest gold-medal winning soccer player in the history of the Olympics was born in Memphis. Cindy Parlow played college soccer at the University of North Carolina. A four-time All-American, Parlow was a founding member of the Women's United Soccer Association. She played on the Women's Soccer Olympic Team in 1996, 2000 and 2004, resulting in one silver and two gold medals. She currently lives in Chapel Hill, North Carolina, and works as Director of Coaching for a Senior Girls' Program with a Triangle United Soccer Club.

Photograph Getty/Ben Radford

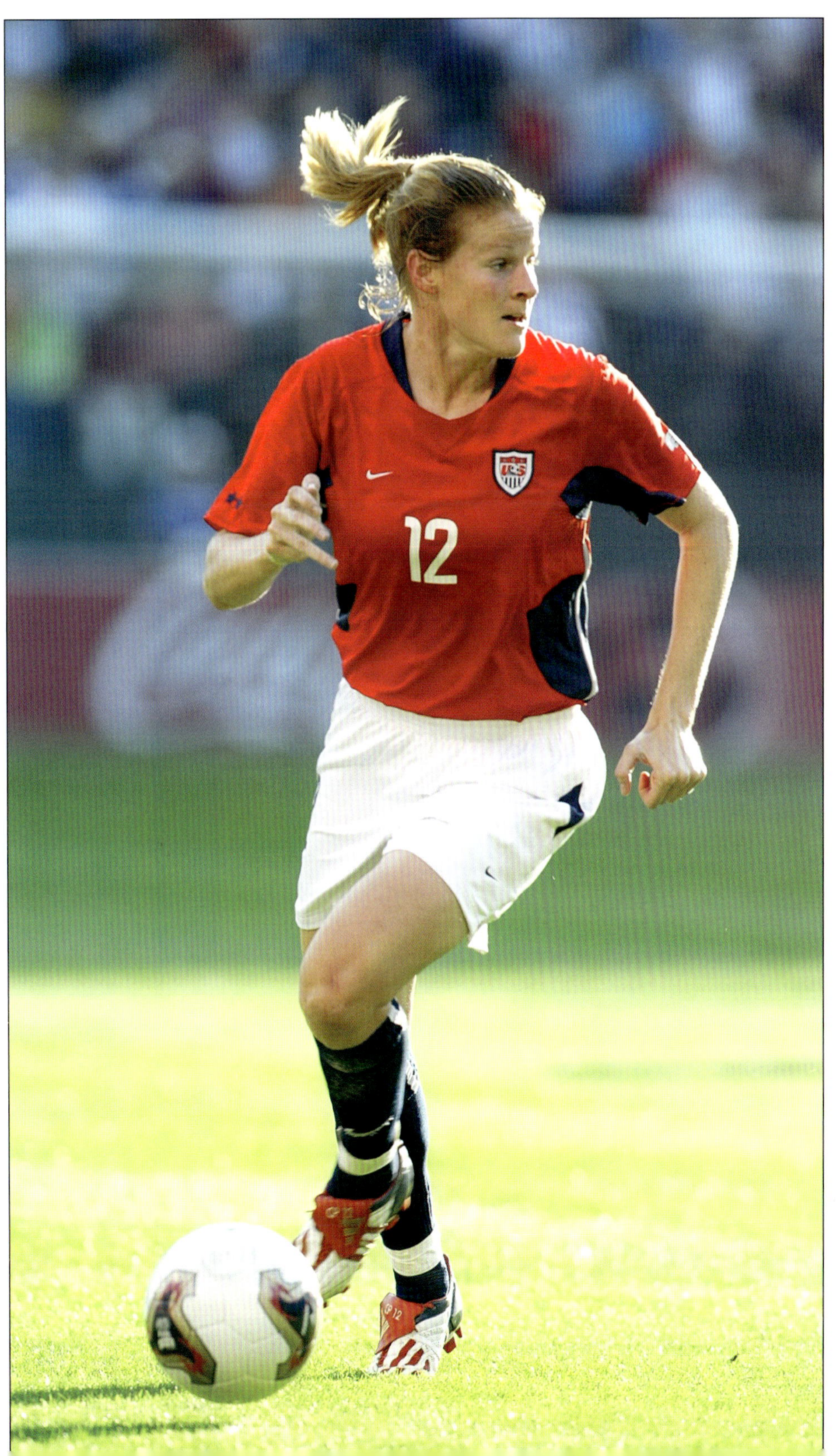

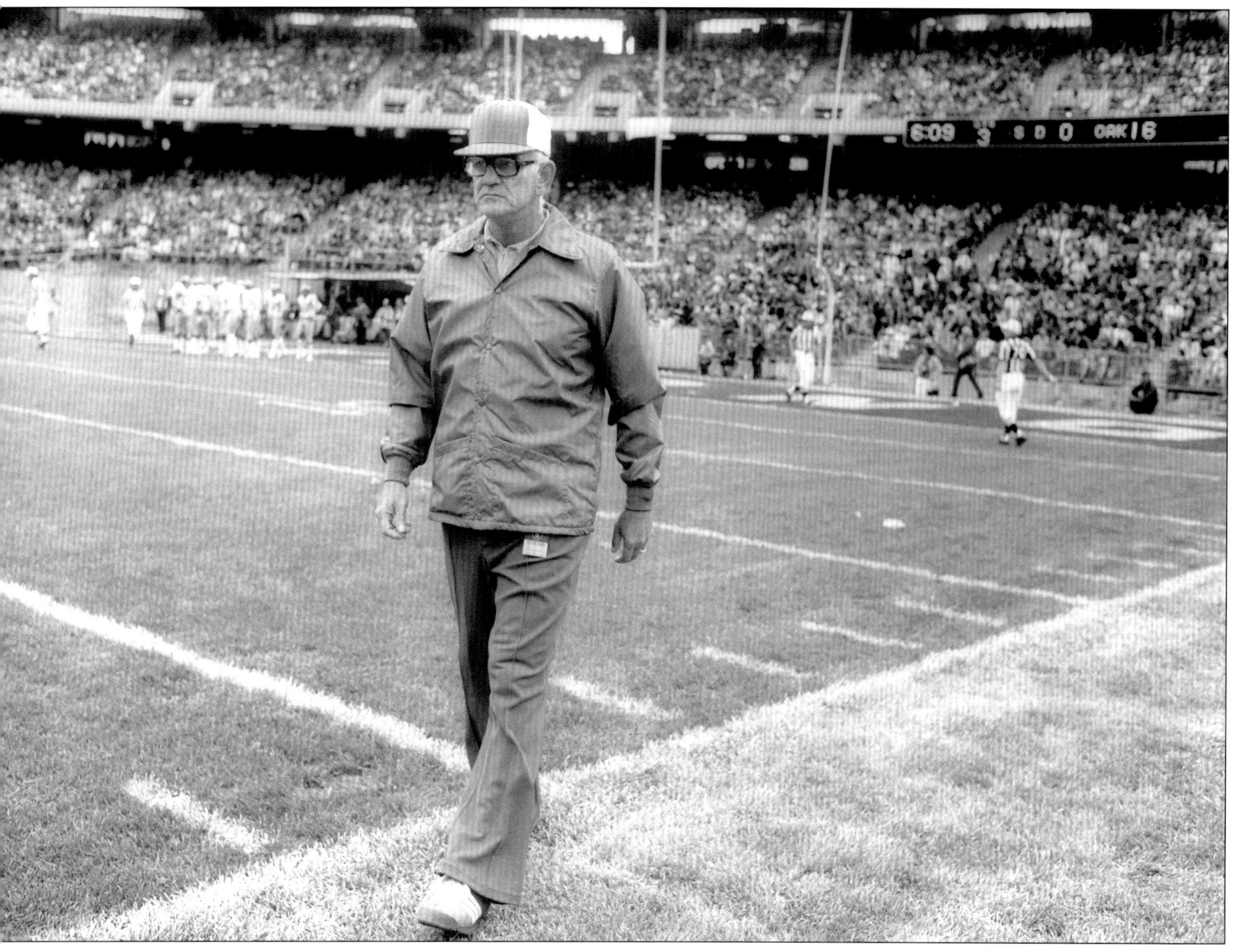

TOMMY PROTHRO

FOOTBALL COACH

Coaching legend Tommy Prothro was the son of Major-Leaguer Doc Prothro – who owned the Memphis Chicks after retiring from the majors. Tommy attempted a career in baseball, but his niche was the gridiron. He played for Central High School, then Duke, and was drafted by the New York Giants in 1942. He declined the offer in favor of a coaching career, which was put on hold by the Navy and World War II. Prothro resurrected a woeful Oregon State to success before moving on to UCLA. He went on to coach NFL teams Los Angeles Rams, San Diego Chargers, and Cleveland Browns. In addition to being inducted into the College and Pro Football Hall of Fame, Prothro did normal things, like competing in international bridge bournaments with the actor Omar Sharif as partner.

Photograph by Sports Illustrated

LOREN ROBERTS

BOSS OF THE MOSS

Renowned for his putting, Loren Roberts has 24 professional titles and counting. He didn't win his first title on the PGA Tour until he was 38, but starting with that one he won eight in nine years. He's holed 12 wins so far on the Champions Tour since joining in 2005, becoming the first to start a season with three straight wins in 2006. Barely missing a major title on the PGA Tour, losing the 1994 U.S. Open to Ernie Els in a playoff, he's won four majors on the Champions Tour, including two Senior British Opens.

Photograph Getty/Gary Newkirk • **Story** by Dan Conaway

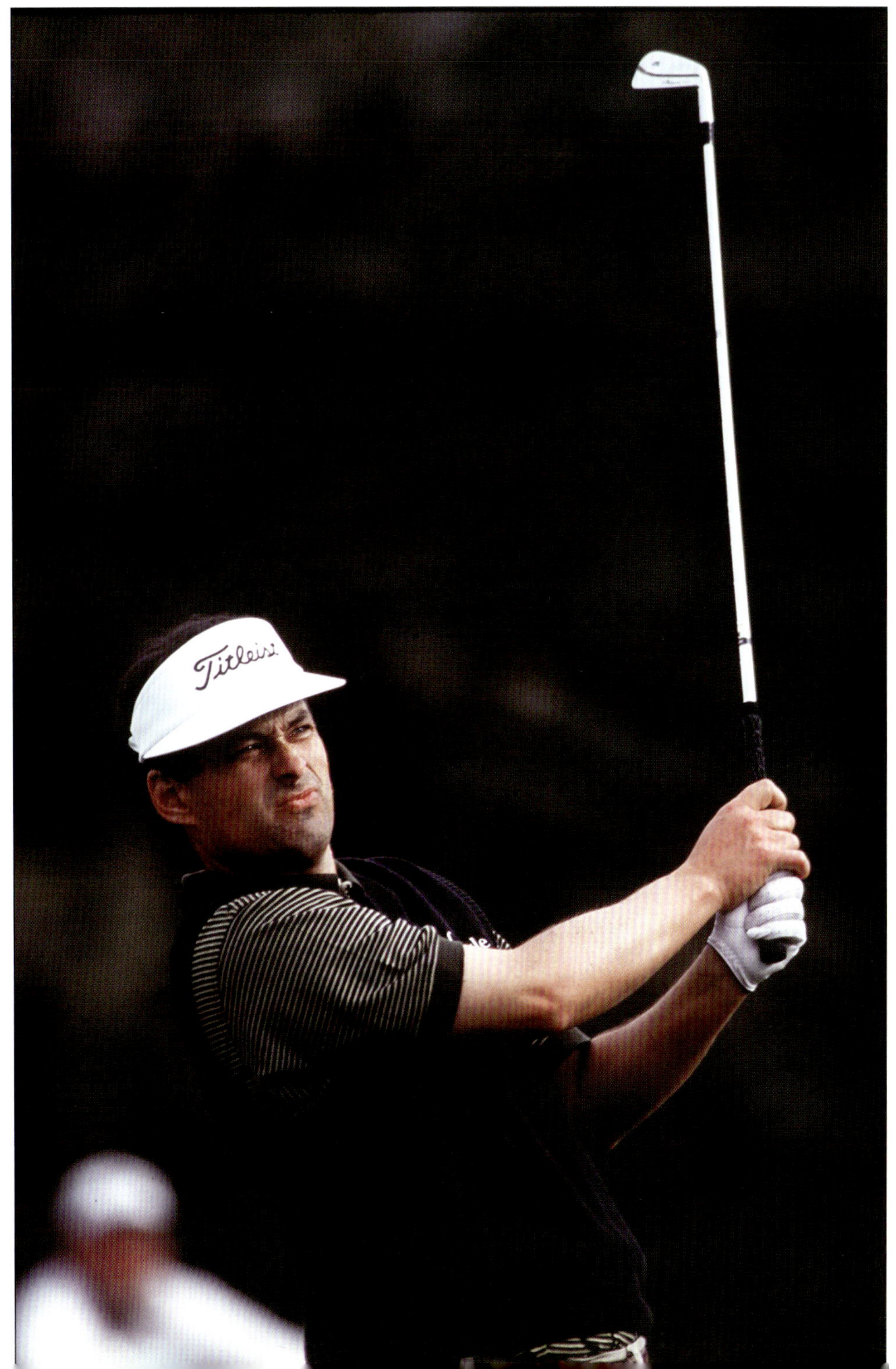

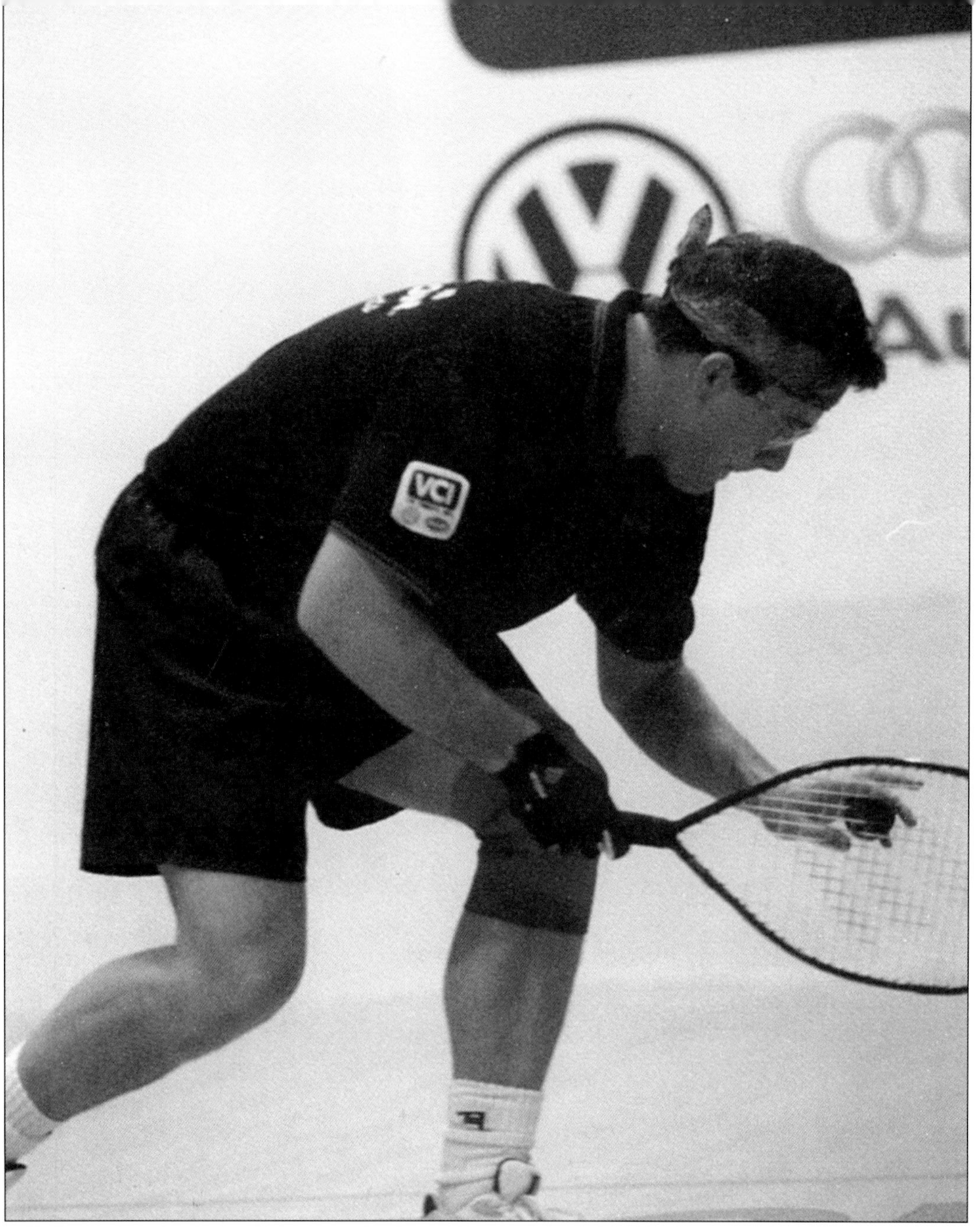

ANDY ROBERTS

RACQUETBALL

Memphis native Andy Roberts had the best kill shot in the game. And shortly after older brother Quinn introduced him to the sport of racquetball, Roberts discovered he could make a killing. During his teen years, he won tournament after tournament. "They'd give away motorcycles, televisions, cars," Roberts recalled. He would then turn around and sell the prizes. "I was making a pretty good living in high school," Roberts quipped.

When the scholarship offer came from Memphis State, Roberts (who would have to endure a serious pay cut) accepted and went on to win five national racquetball titles (three singles, two doubles). He was also named to the U.S. National Racquetball Team for eight consecutive years (during that span he lost only one match). The U.S. Olympic Committee named Roberts "Athlete of the Year" four times.

After graduation, Roberts returned to the money-making ranks. In his 11 years on the professional tour, Roberts dominated the sport. As a pro, he was never ranked below #4 in the world.

Roberts has been inducted into three Halls of Fame: the U.S. Racquetball Hall of Fame, the Tennessee Sports Hall of Fame, and the University of Memphis Hall of Fame.

Now an executive with FedEx, Roberts still calls Memphis home.

ELLIOT PERRY

BASKETBALL PLAYER

At a university known for great basketball point guards Elliot Perry still stands out. He played for four years at Memphis State where he was the only player in Metro Conference history to score over 2,000 points and dish out over 500 assists. As a collegian, he was the No. 2 scorer in Memphis State history with 2,209 career points. He was drafted by the Los Angeles Clippers in 1991 and played 11 years professionally. In the 1994-1995 NBA season, while playing for the Phoenix Suns, he came in 2nd for Most Improved Player. After his professional basketball career he returned to live in Memphis and became a minority share owner of the Memphis Grizzlies. Elliot Lamonte Perry was born in Memphis in 1969, grew up in Memphis, went to Treadwell High School here, and remains committed to the sports community in his hometown. He is also active as a mentor with the Boys and Girls Club of Greater Memphis. Elliot Perry, who credits Frederick Douglass as an influence, said, "I have always wanted to be a positive and central figure in my community, to use my platform to influence and help those who are in need."

Photograph Getty Sports/Otto Greule Jr

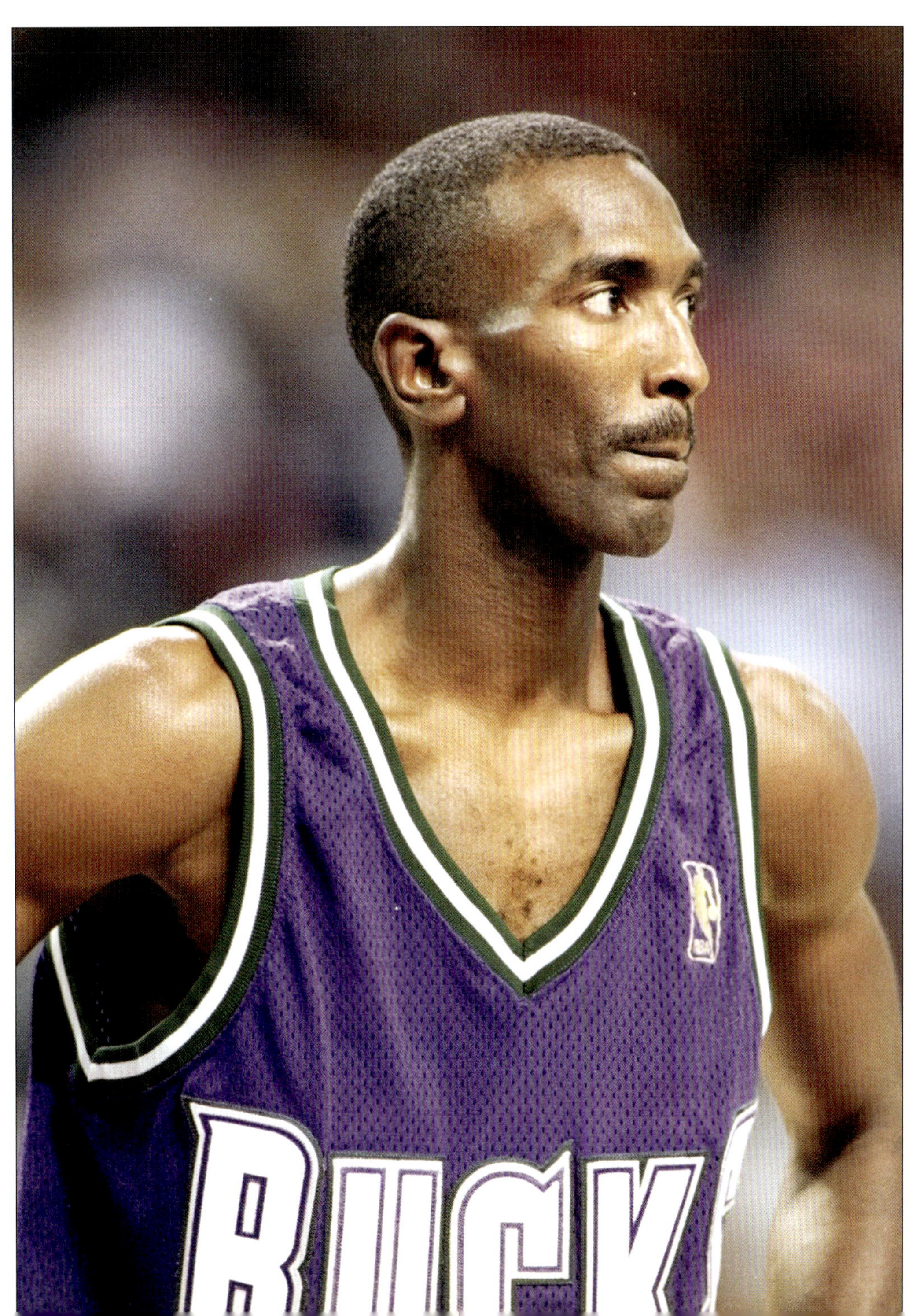

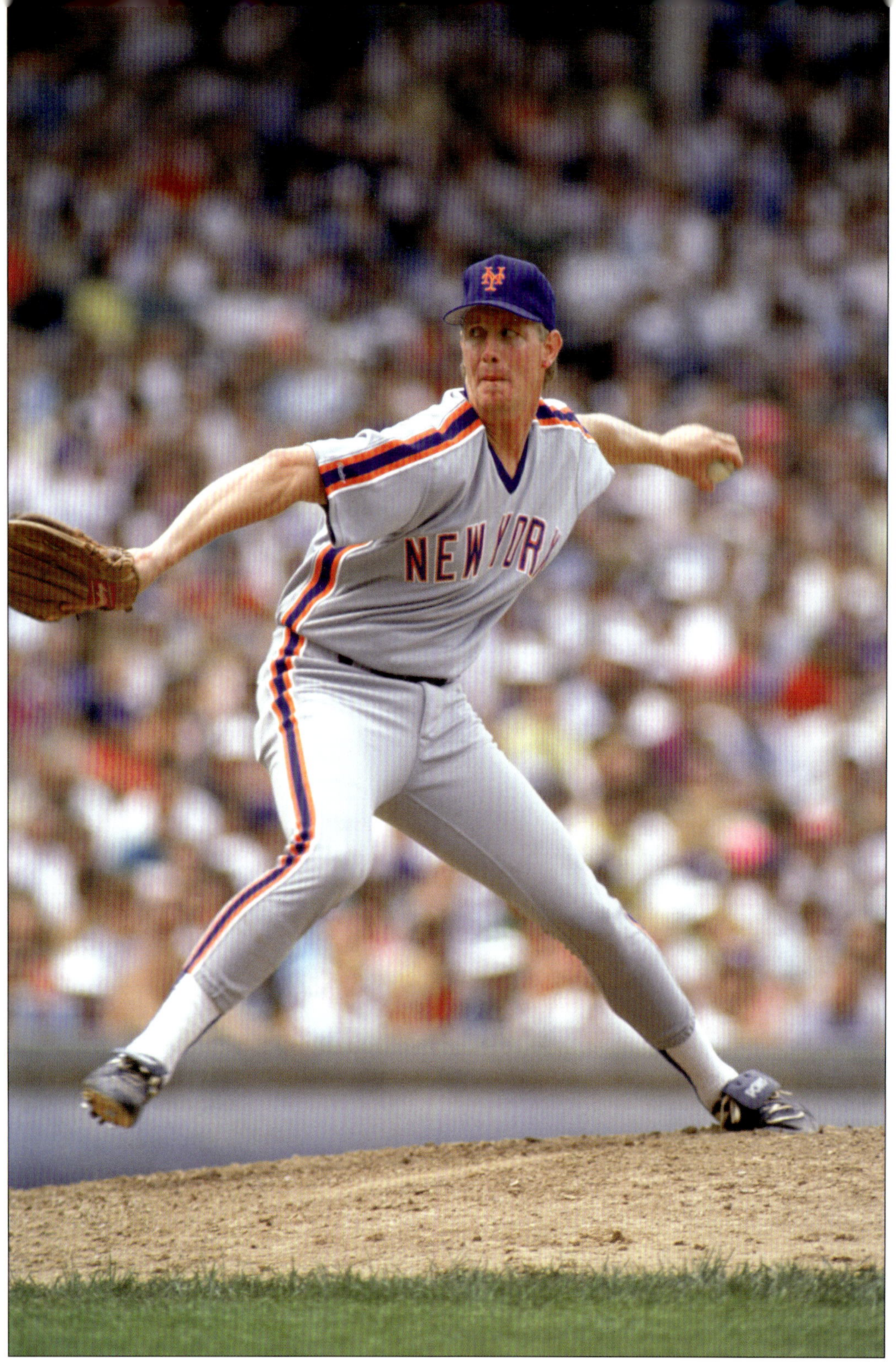

DAVID WEST

MAJOR LEAGUE PITCHER

A Memphian born and raised, David West was drafted into the Major Leagues not long after graduating from Craigmont High School. Drafted by the New York Mets, he pitched for them in 1988 before switching to the Minnesota Twins in 1989. He later pitched for the Phillies in the 1993 World Series.

Photograph Getty/Jonathan Daniel

REGGIE WHITE

MINISTER OF DEFENSE

Reggie White, a two-time NFL Defensive Player of the Year and Hall of Famer, was known for his prowess on the field, as well as a passion for his faith. Before he made a name for himself playing for the University of Tennessee Volunteers, White was an ordained minister at the age of 17. For this he was known as the "Minister of Defense." White was one of the highlights of the Memphis Showboats in the upstart USFL, but his career would take him beyond the new league to play for the Philadelphia Eagles, Green Bay Packers, and the Carolina Panthers. He was voted All Pro ten years in his 15-year career, along with the All-Decade team for both the 80s and the 90s. Although his NFL record for 198 sacks was surpassed by Bruce Smith's 200, his professional record stands at an unbeaten 221. The difference being made, of course, in Memphis. He died in 2004 at the age of 43.

Photograph Collegiate Images

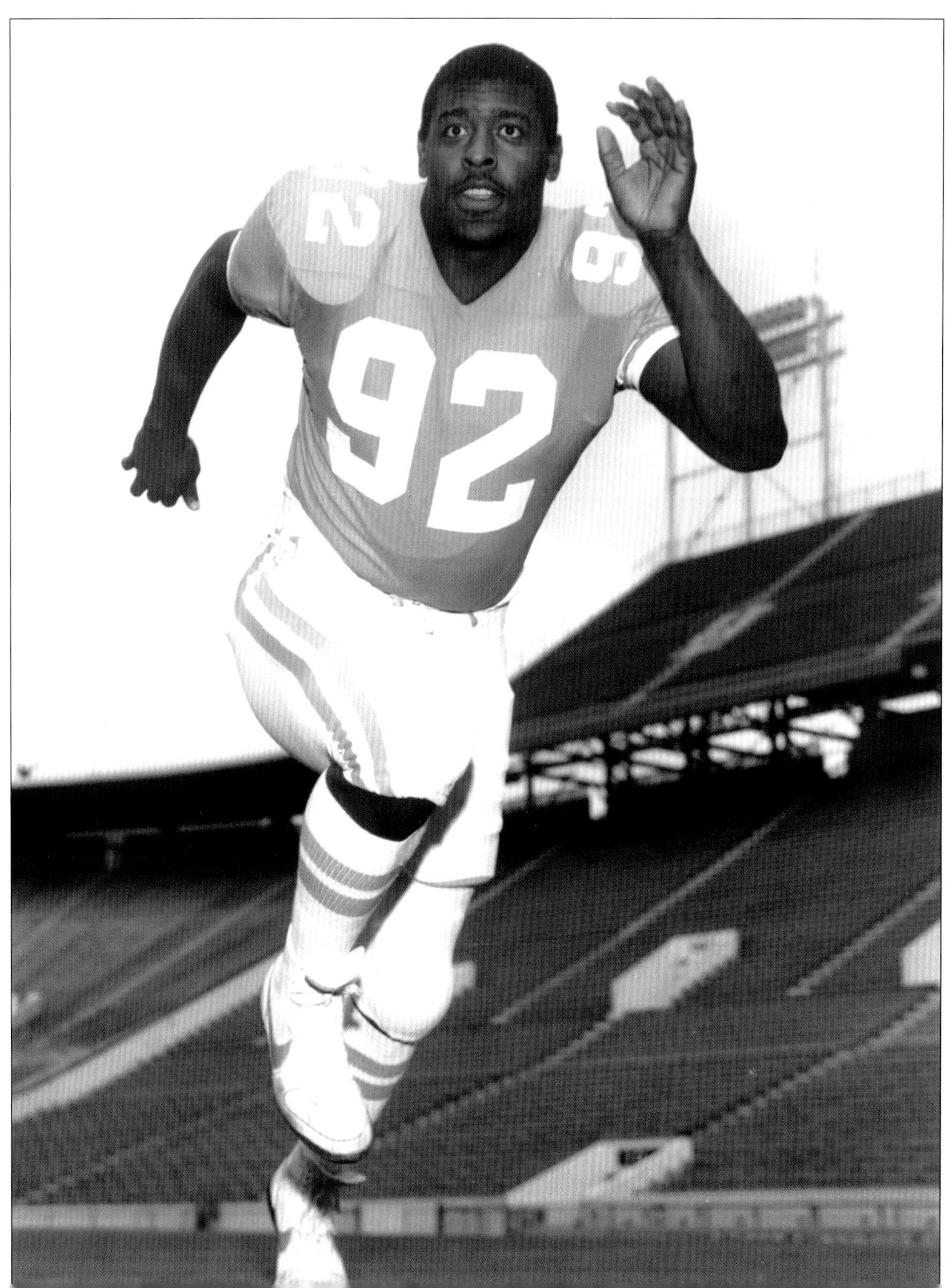

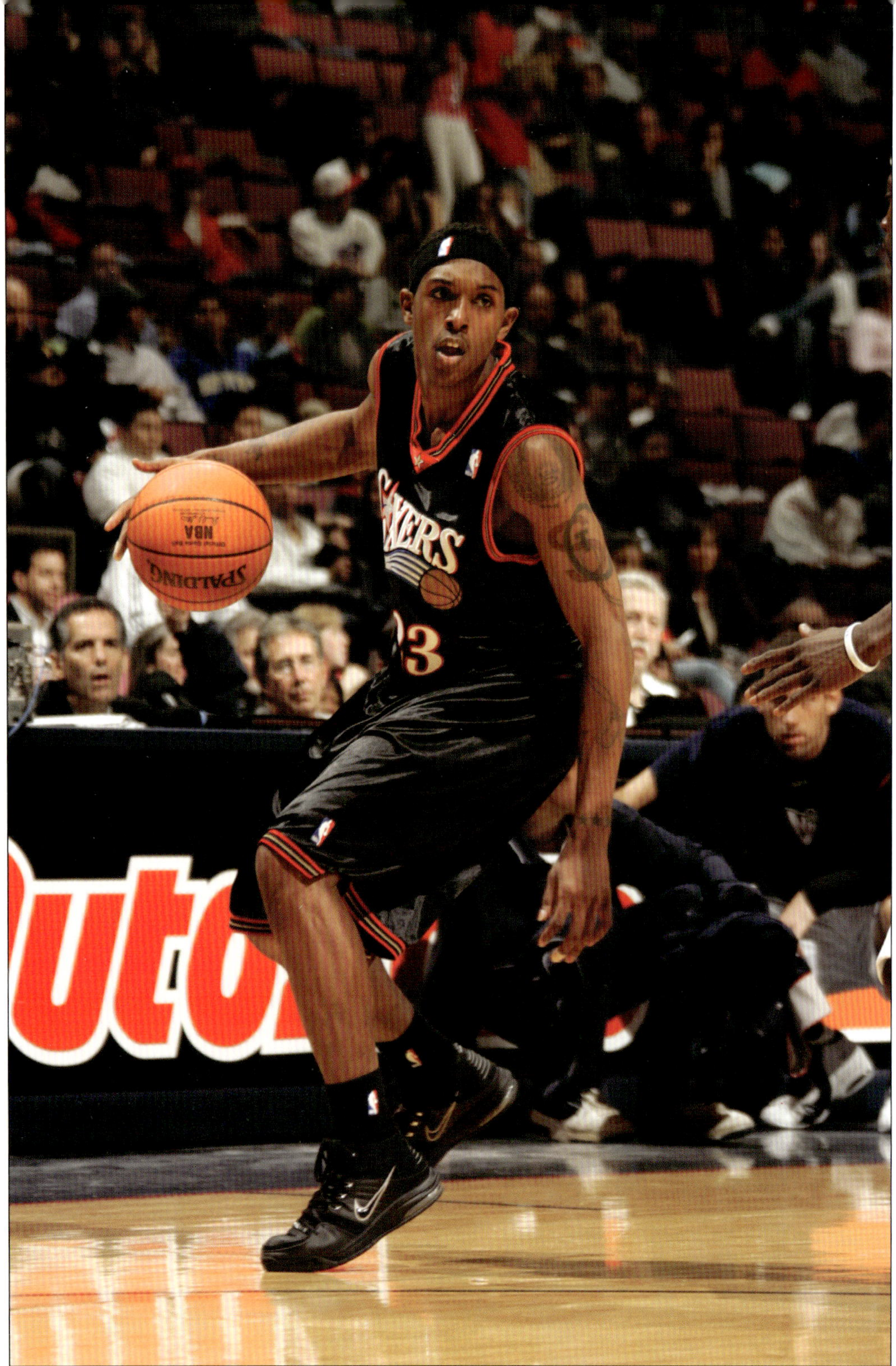

LOUIS WILLIAMS

MR. BASKETBALL

Louis Williams was born in Memphis, but he made his first dunk in Georgia as a 5'7" seventh grader. Named "Mr. Basketball" in Georgia where he was a four-time All-State selection, he was drafted to the NBA out of South Gwinnett High School in 2005 and plays for the Philadelphia 76ers. Williams still runs a basketball camp in South Gwinnett for 10-16 year olds.

Photograph NBAE/Getty/Ned Dishman

FRANCIS WINKLER

PROFESSIONAL FOOTBALL PLAYER

Born in Memphis, Francis Winkler attended Memphis State. After college, he was drafted by the Green Bay Packers and played defensive end for the 1968 and 1969 seasons.

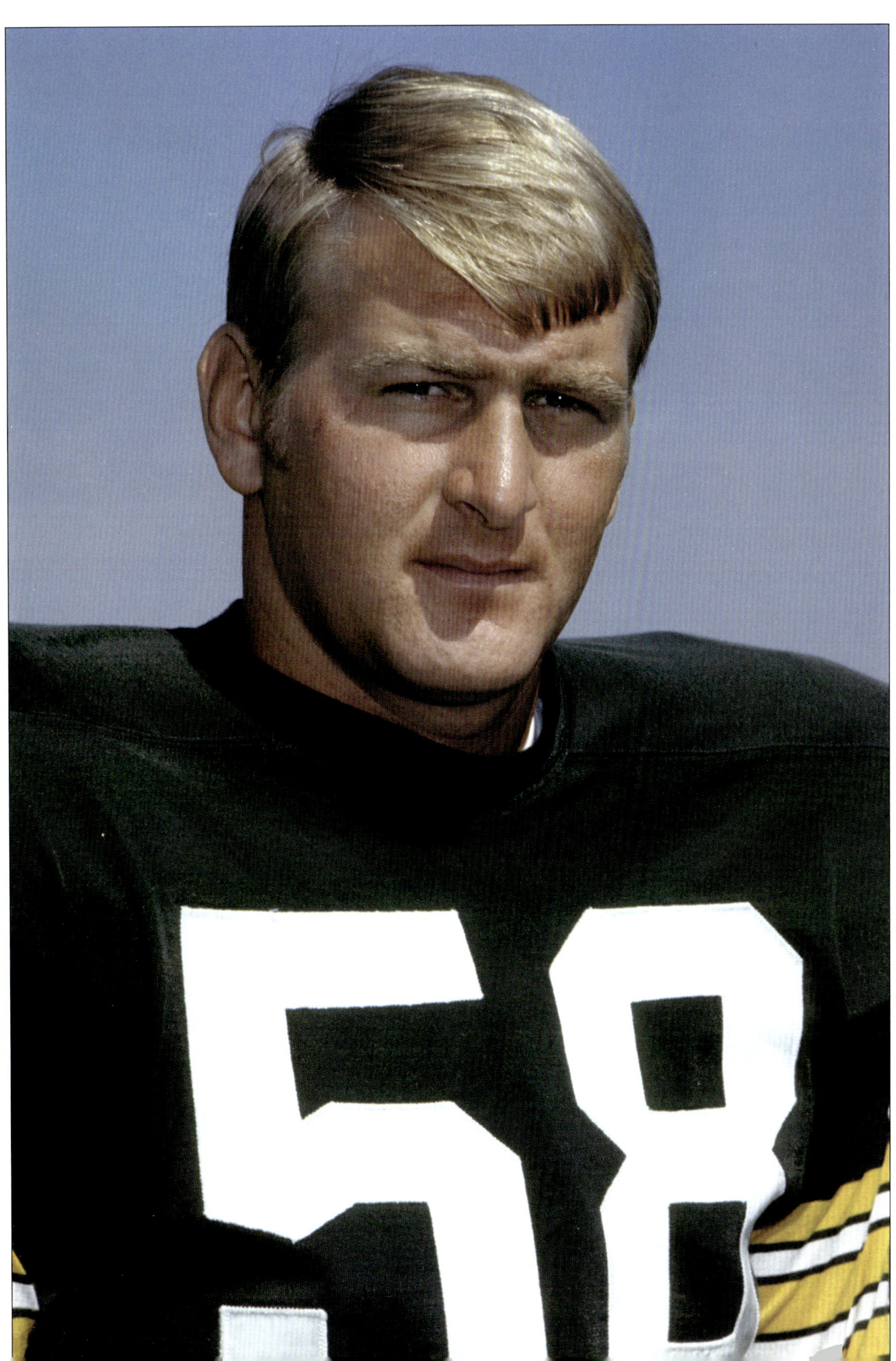

Innovators & Visionaries

Entrepreneurs

Writers & Journalists

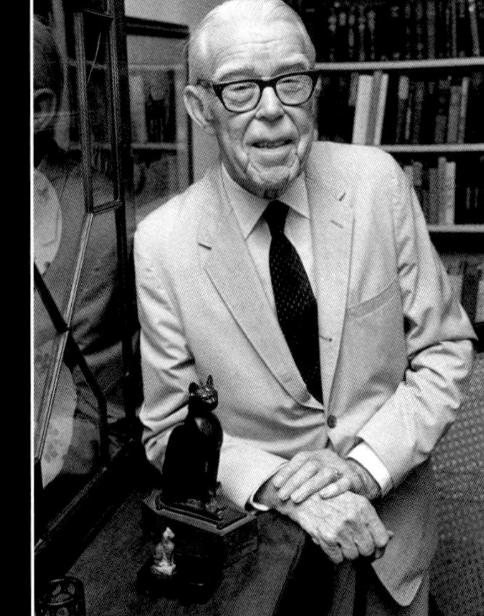

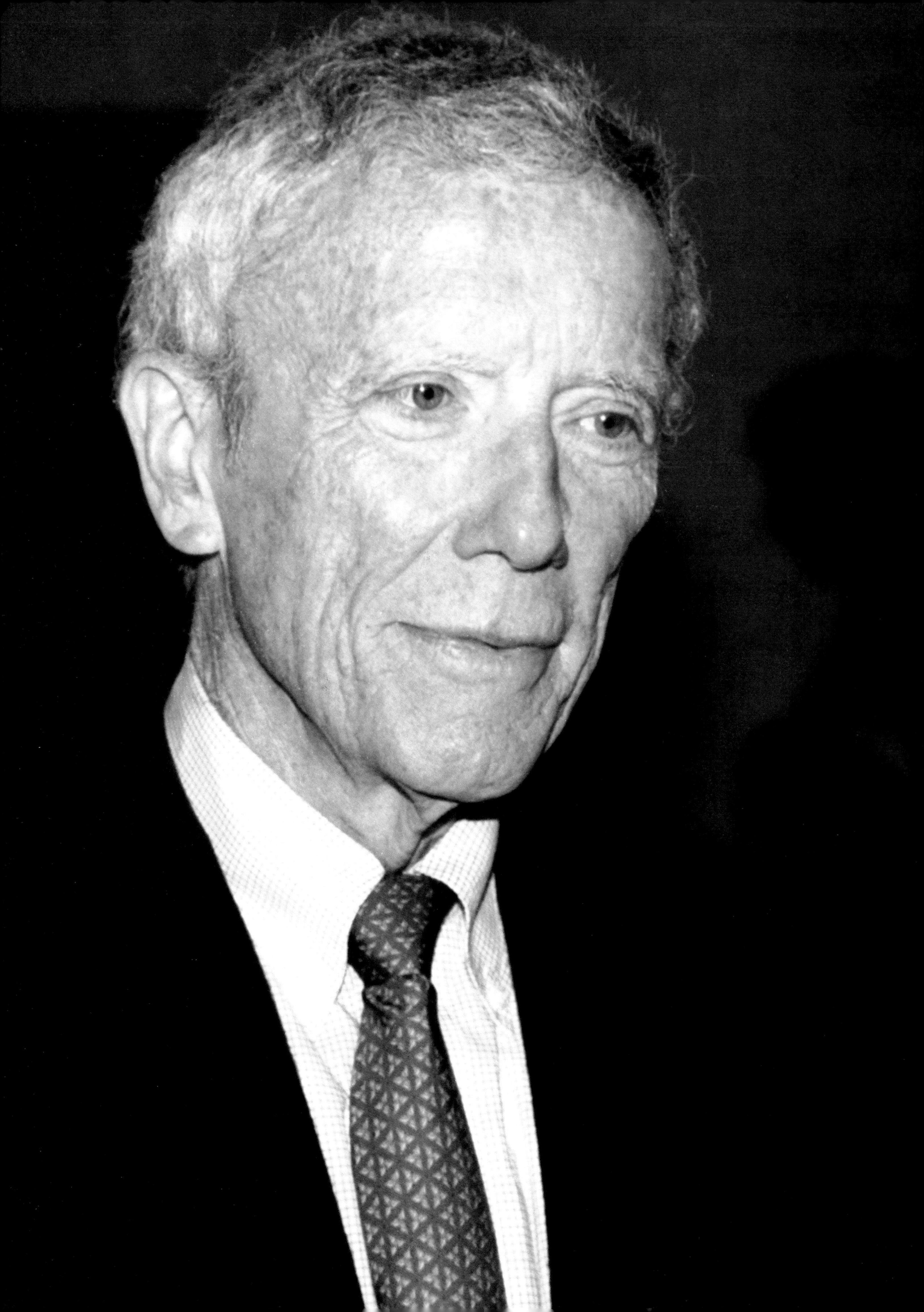

DR. JOHN SHEA, JR.

MEDICAL PIONEER

On May 1, 1956, Dr. John Shea, Jr., son of the founder of Memphis' Shea Clinic, performed the first stapedectomy operation to cure what was once the most common form of conductive hearing loss. Since that day, Dr. Shea has performed more than 25,000 stapedectomies and more importantly, they are now commonly performed all over the world. A year later he devised a new technique to make repairing perforated eardrums practical.

Not only has Dr. Shea pioneered medical techniques and specialized tools to perform them, he is a clinical professor at the Universities of Tennessee, Mississippi, North Carolina and Tulane. A member of more than 50 scientific societies and an honorary fellow of the Australian and English Royal Collage of Surgeons, he is married to Lynda Lee Mead Shea.

BENJAMIN HOOKS

LAWYER, ADVOCATE

Benjamin Hooks was always determined to fight segregation in the South. Born in Memphis, he attended DePaul University College of Law in Chicago because no law school in Tennessee would accept him. Always persistent, Hooks moved back to Memphis immediately following graduation, passed the Tennessee bar exam and set up his own law firm. He worked alongside Dr. Martin Luther King, Jr., joining the Southern Christian Leadership Conference and planning and attending sit-ins and boycotts. He became the executive director of the NAACP in 1977, a position he held until 1992. All his life he felt a religious calling, so in 1956 Hooks was ordained as a Baptist minister, and he preached regularly while keeping up his work as a lawyer and activist. Benjamin Hooks passed away in 2010.

Photograph Time & Life Images/Diana Walker

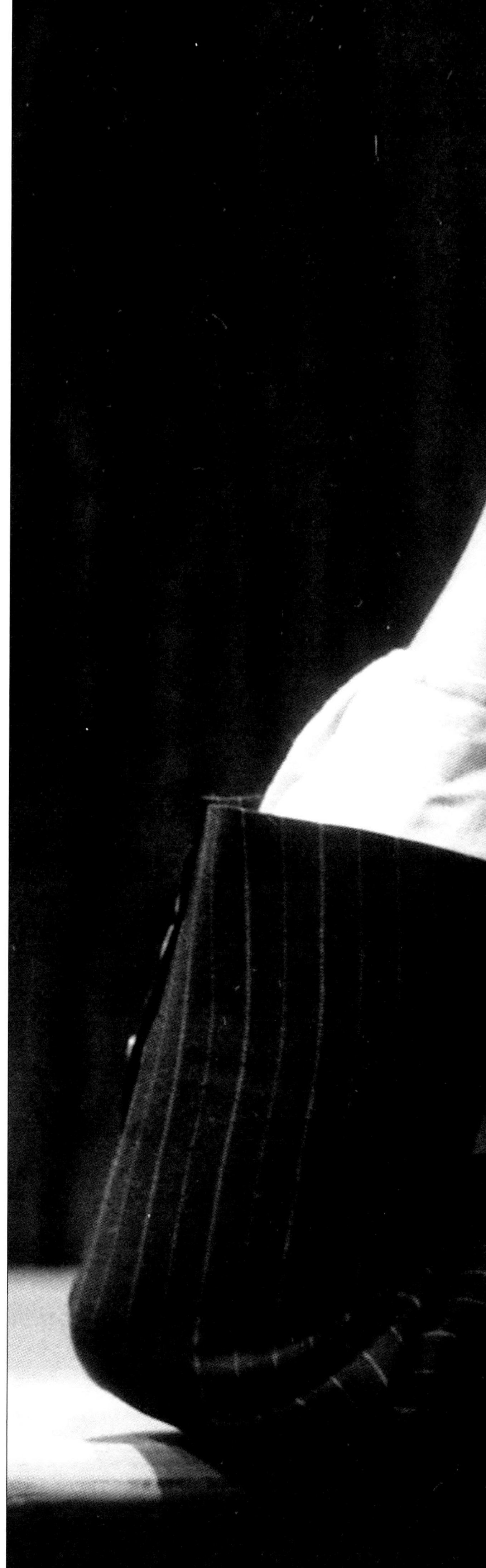

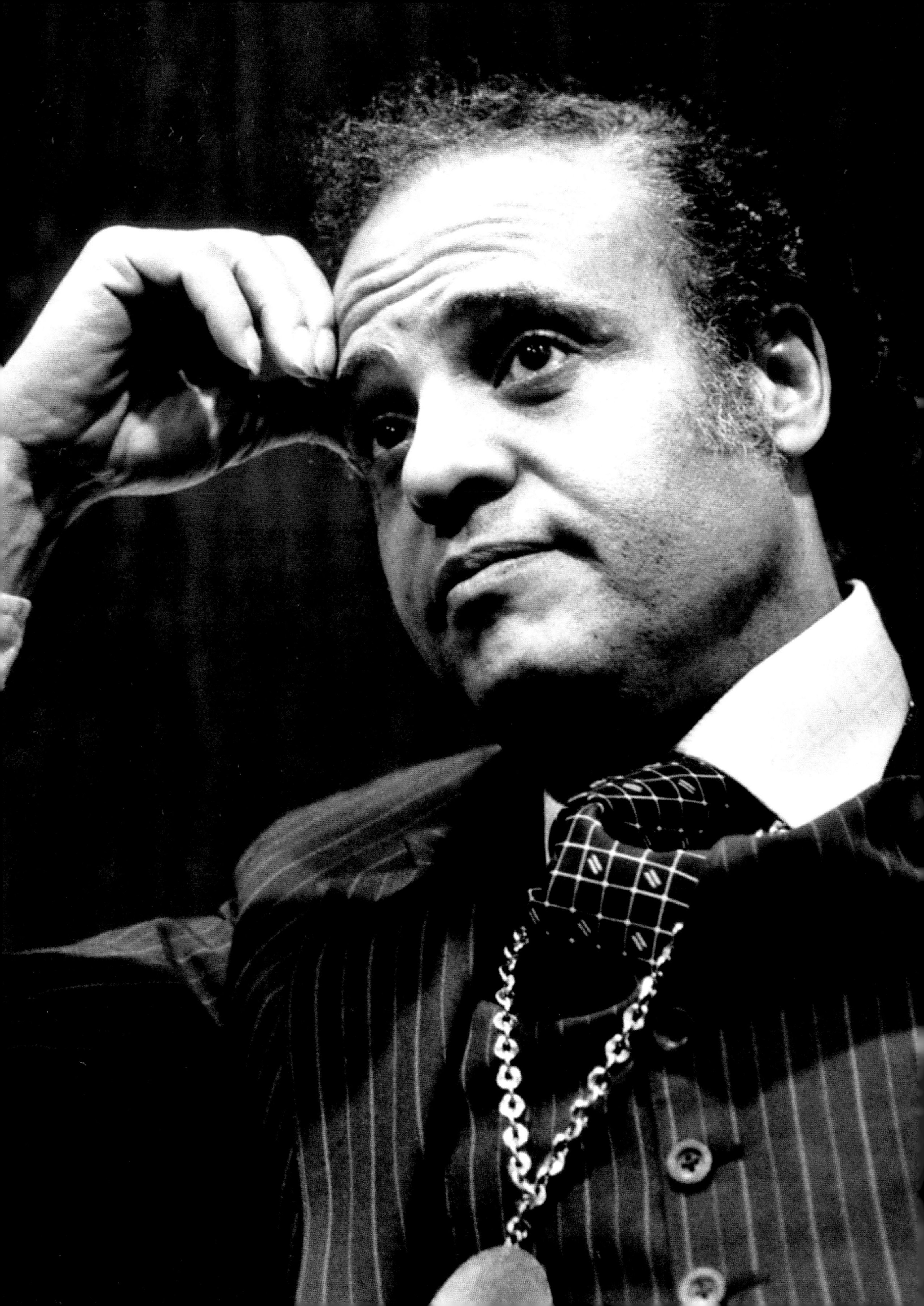

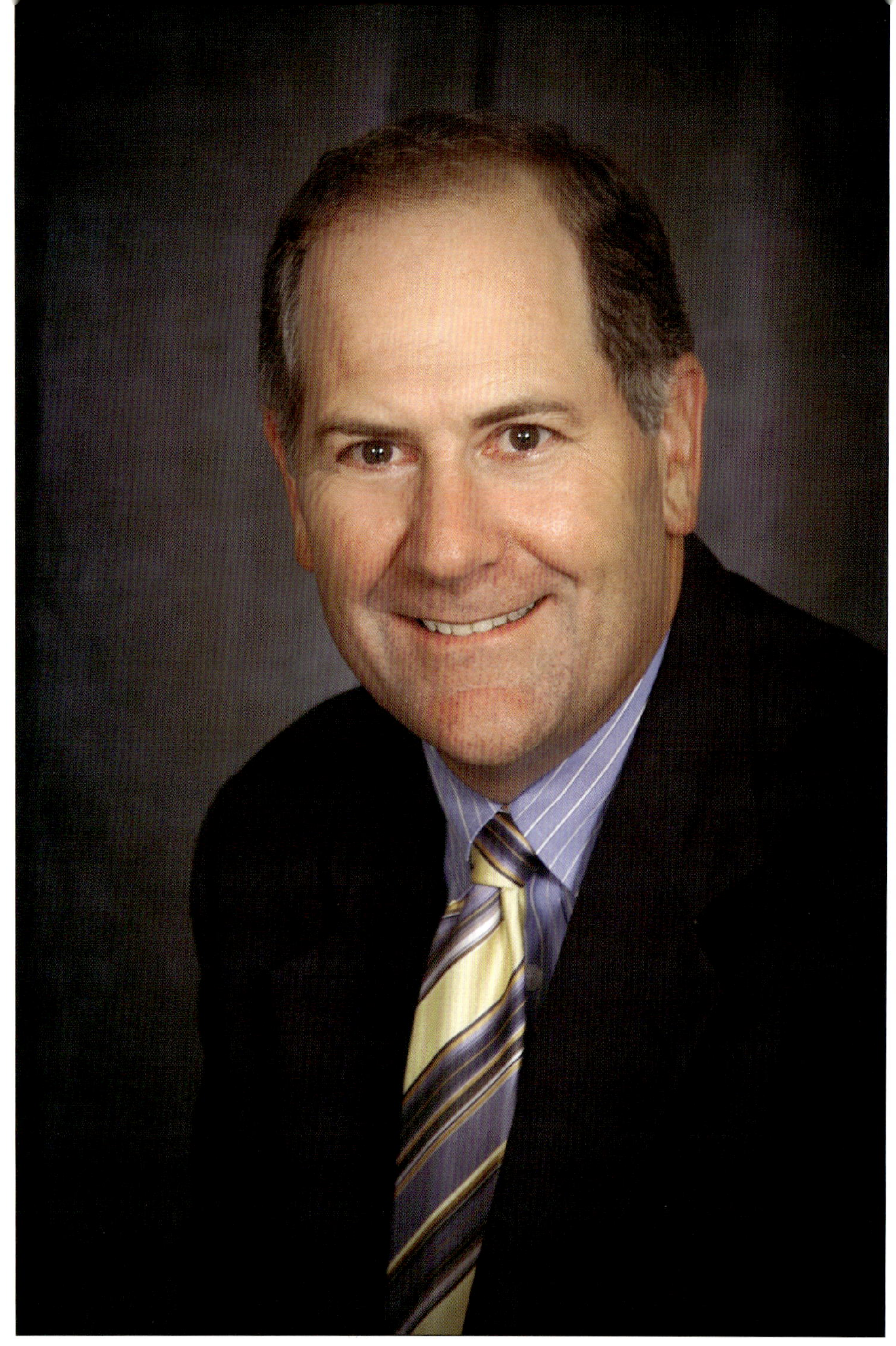

DR. STEVEN BARES

EXECUTIVE, VISIONARY

Dr. Steven J. Bares has worked diligently to position Memphis to capitalize on the growth of biomedical research — as well as the commercialization of life science technologies. He has served as president of the Memphis Bioworks Foundation since 2001. Dr. Bares has a Ph.D. in Physical Chemistry, a Master's of Business Administration and a B.S. in Chemistry. Dr. Bares is also the author of nine patents. In developing the foundation for math and science skills, Dr. Bares serves as the Chair of the Tennessee Charter School Association and is the co-founder of Tennessee's first Charter School. Dr. Bares is working hard to create more jobs and opportunities for professionals as well as students in his role in economic development for Memphis through the biosciences.

HUGO & MARGARET DIXON

ART COLLECTORS, PHILANTHROPISTS

The Dixons had no children so they left their priceless collection of art, as well as their beautiful house and grounds, to us. Born in Southport England in 1892, Hugo Dixon began working in the German offices of Geo. McFadden & Bro. in 1910. At the outbreak of World War I, Dixon and his fellow expatriates were interned as enemy aliens in Ruhrleben. The prisoners put on plays and art shows to pass the time and Dixon's love affair with the arts was cemented.

After the war, Dixon moved to Texas with McFadden and married Margaret Oates, of Vicksburg. When the company headquarters moved to Memphis, so came the Dixons. They bought 17 acres on Park Avenue and built a Georgian mansion and began to fill it with impressionist art. Dixon's sister designed the formal gardens. Hugo served on the boards of several museums and Margaret was a founder of the Memphis Garden Club. They were working towards converting their residence into a museum in 1974 when they died within months of each other. The Dixon Gallery and Gardens opened in 1976 and remains one of the few museums in the world that receives no government funding.

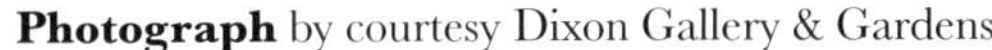

Photograph by courtesy Dixon Gallery & Gardens

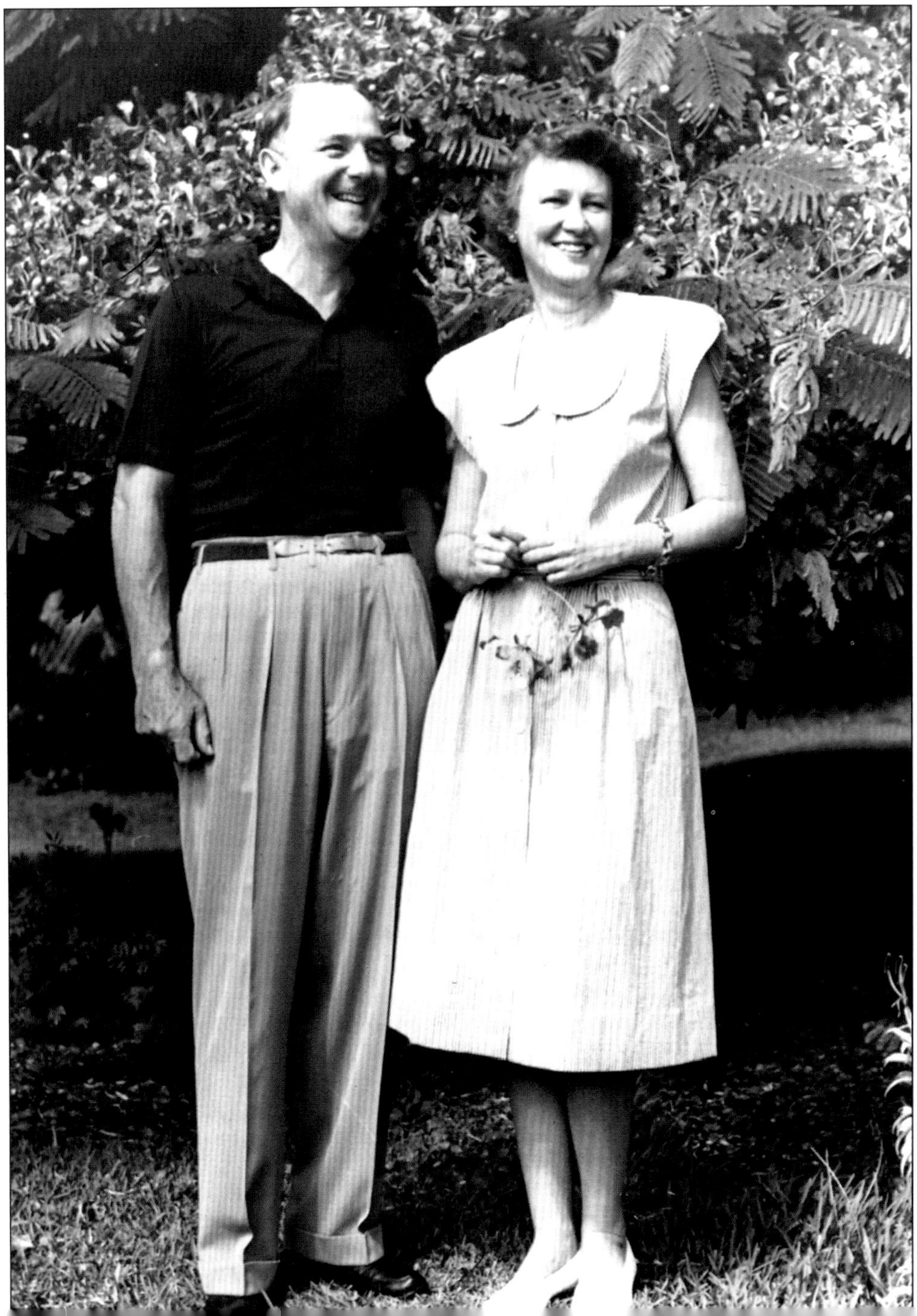

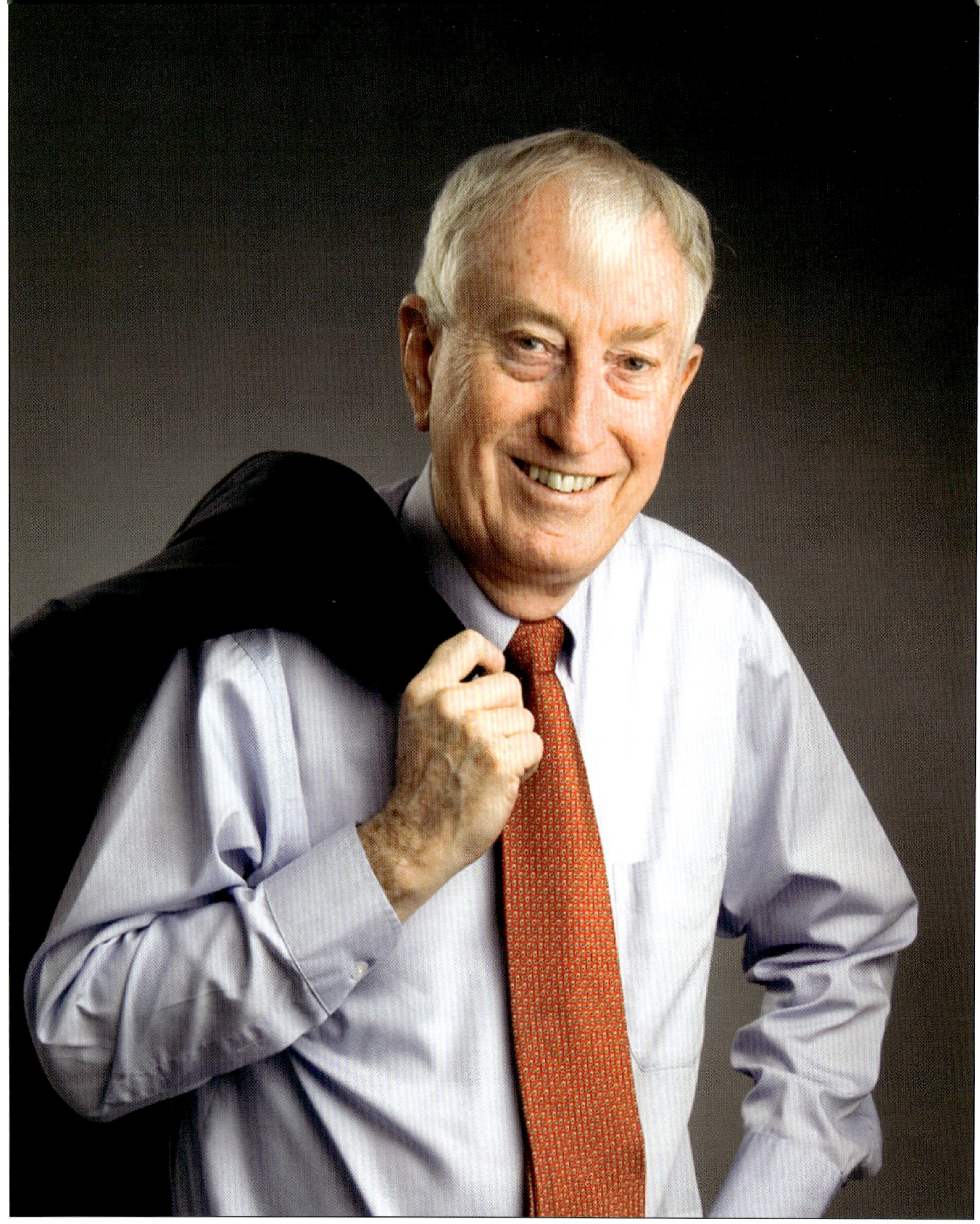

DR. PETER DOHERTY

NOBEL LAUREATE

Born in Brisbane, Australia, Peter Doherty, Ph.D., is a world-renowned immunologist who earned his Ph.D. in Pathology from the University of Edinburgh, Scotland. Doherty joined St. Jude Children's Research Hospital, located in Memphis, in 1988. He currently holds the Michael F. Tamer Chair of Biomedical Research at St. Jude and is a member of the Department of Immunology. In 1996, Doherty won the Nobel Prize in Physiology or Medicine with Rolf M. Zinkernagel, M.D., of Switzerland. Their discovery of MHC Restriction of T-Cell Recognition opened the door to an understanding of the immune system that has impacted autoimmune disease research, vaccine design, organ transplantation and the understanding of immune surveillance. Doherty is also a Fellow of the Royal Society, London; a member of the Institute of Medicine, a branch of the National Academy of Sciences; and a 1995 recipient of the Albert Lasker Basic Medical Research Award.

Photograph courtesy St. Jude

DR. KEVIN FOLEY

SURGEON, MEDICAL PIONEER

Dr. Kevin Foley, professor of neurosurgery at UT Health Science Center, went into the Army after completing his neurosurgery residency at UCLA. He served as an assistant chief of neurosurgery at Brooke Army Medical Center, and chief at both Tripler Army Medical Center and Walter Reed Army Medical Center. In 1992, he left the Army and began a private practice. He continues to conduct research on minimally invasive spine surgery, image-guided spinal navigation and spinal biomechanics. He has published 19 book chapters and over 70 articles.

Photograph by Commercial Appeal

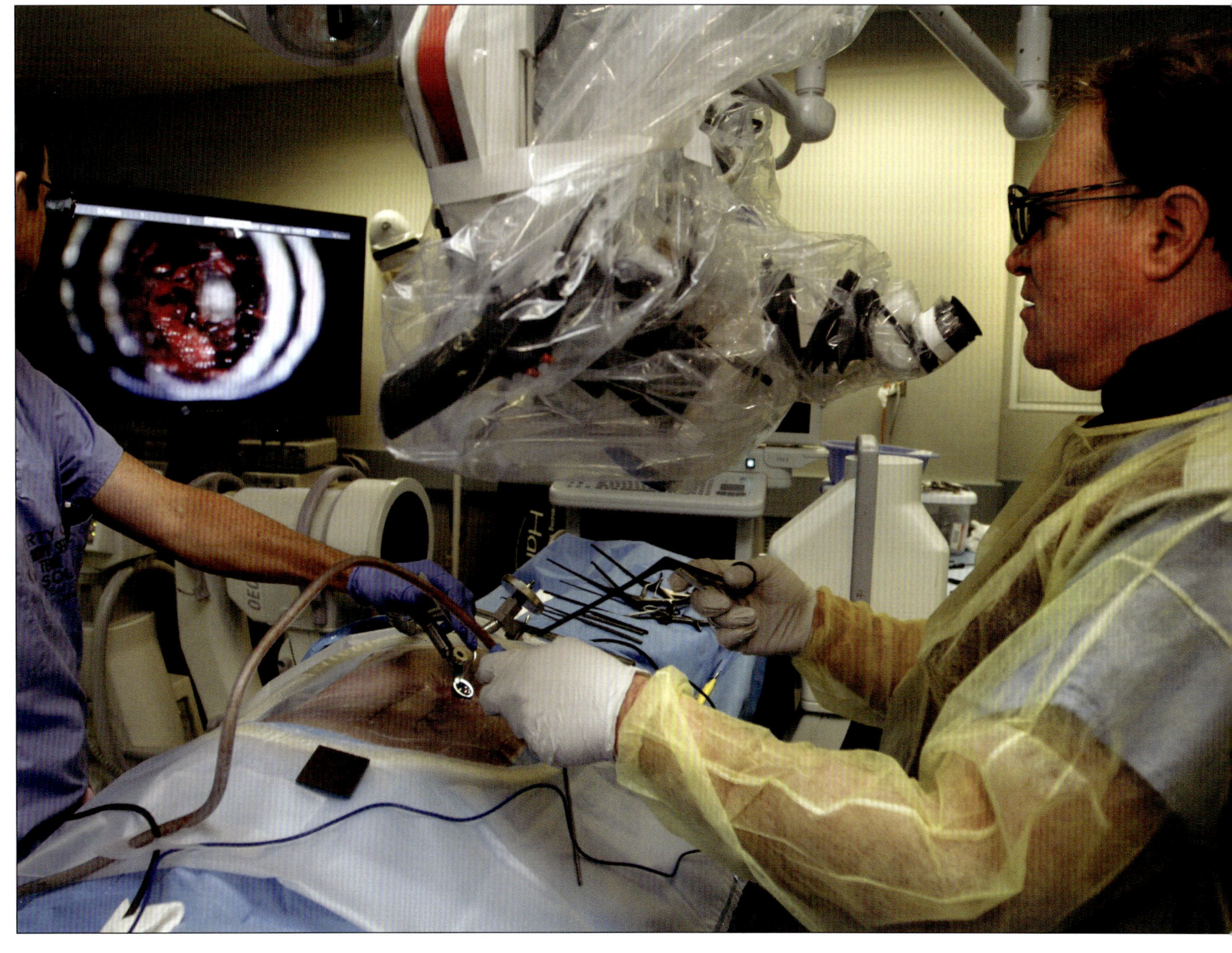

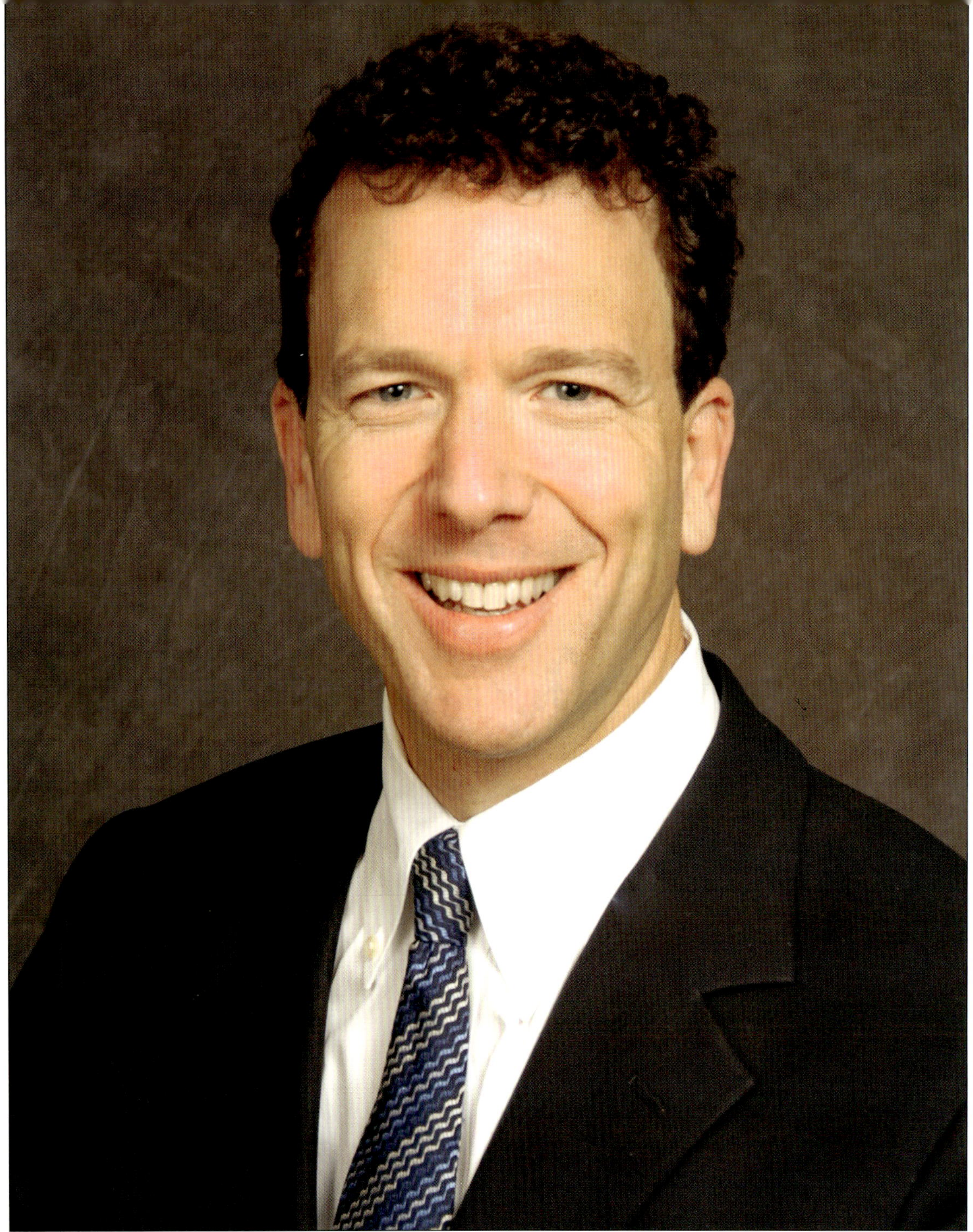

MICAH GREENSTEIN

RABBI RACONTEUR

The Senior Rabbi at Temple Israel in Memphis since 2000 is not only the leader of one of the country's largest Jewish Reform synagogues, he is also one of the most sought after speakers in every pulpit and on every dais in town. Micah Greenstein's message of love, understanding, respect, cooperation and shared responsibility – delivered with a wicked sense of humor and, if you're lucky, a touch of his singing voice – seems to resonate across denominations and audiences. He was chosen as principal speaker for the state of Tennessee at the National Cathedral in Washington in 2005, and has twice served as president of the Memphis Ministers Association.

Photograph courtesy Temple Israel • **Story** by Dan Conaway

PAT HALLORAN

PRODUCER, CIVIC LEADER

In 2010, Pat Halloran was honored with a star on Orpheum's Sidewalk of Stars. This is just one of many honors Halloran has received for his work with the Orpheum Theatre. Halloran has been President and CEO of the Memphis Development Foundation for over thirty years. During this time, he has been instrumental in completely restoring the Orpheum Theatre and turning it into a world-class performance facility. Constantly supporting theater both locally and nationally, Halloran has won three Tony awards as a producer for the Broadway musicals *Thoroughly Modern Millie*, *Spamalot*, and *Memphis*. He is also the author of *The Orpheum! Where Broadway Meets Beale*.

Photograph courtesy the Orpheum

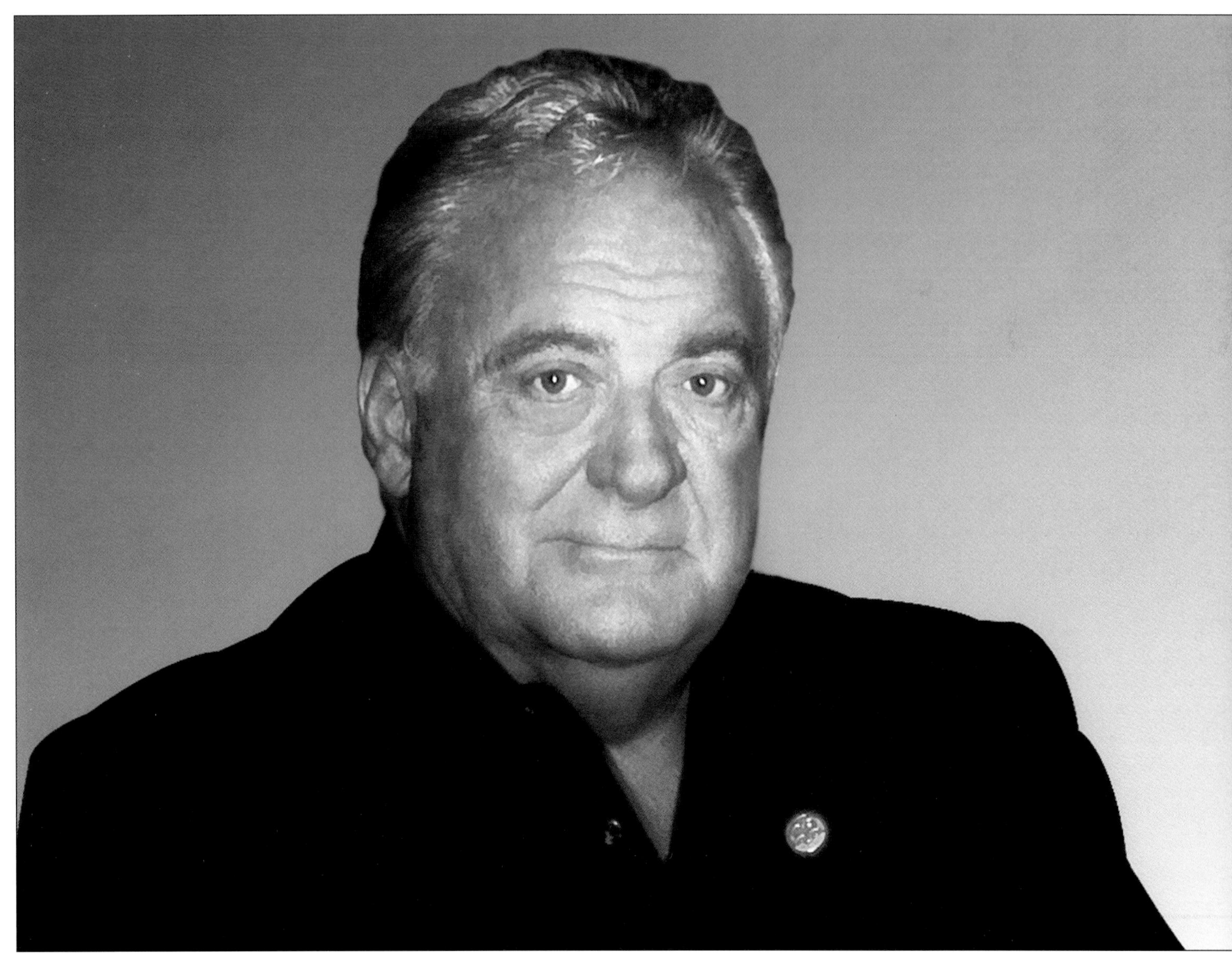

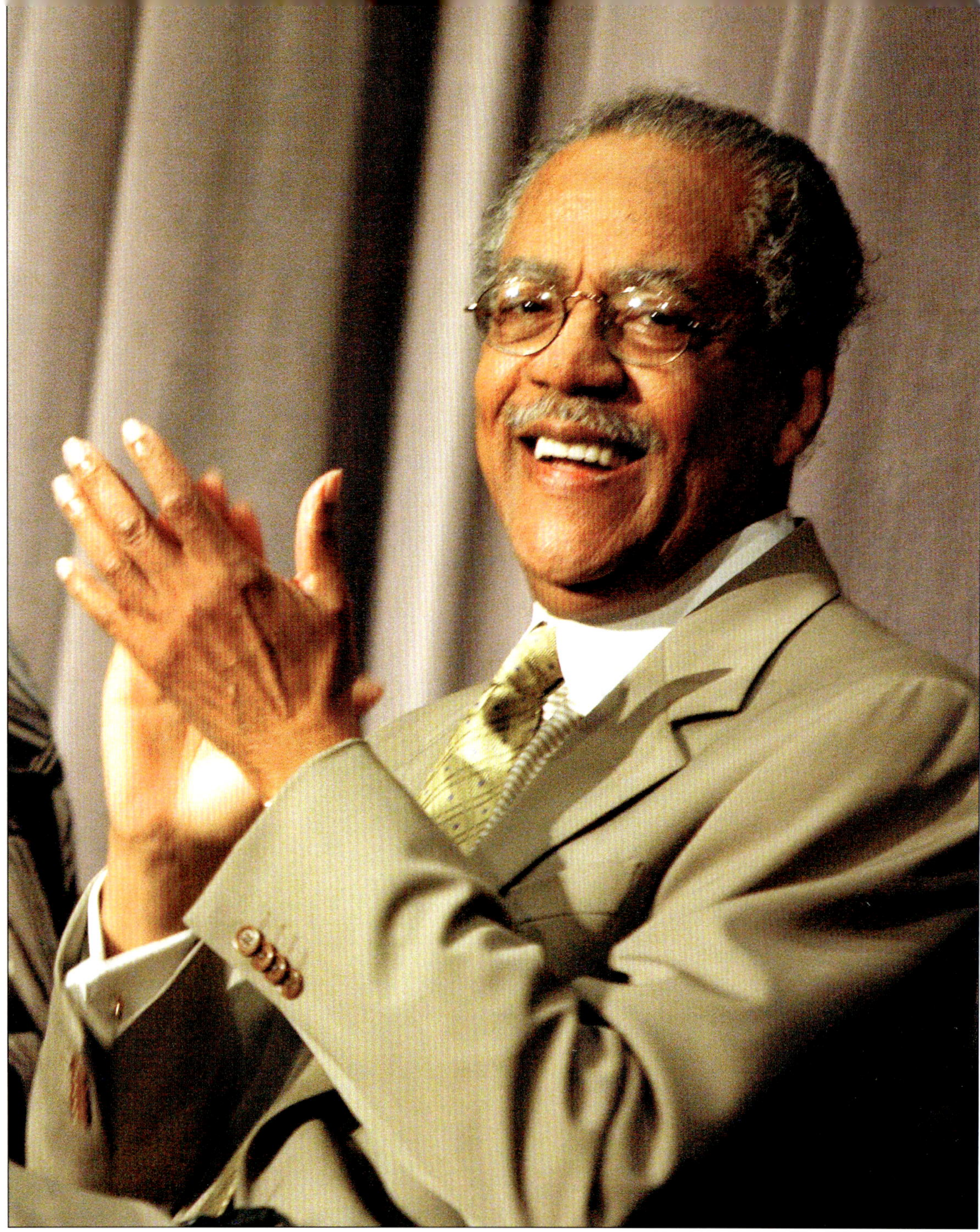

REV. SAMUEL "BILLY" KYLES

RELIGIOUS VISIONARY

Samuel "Billy" Kyles has a quiet demeanor. Soft spoken and exuding kindness, Reverend Kyles lives with history. It was Kyles who was instrumental in bringing Reverend Martin Luther King, Jr. to Memphis in the spring of 1968 in support of the striking sanitation workers. As a friend to King and a leading organizer in Memphis, Kyles stood side by side with the national leader as he marched along the streets of Memphis. Kyles sat with King and Ralph Abernathy, talking and joking in the Lorraine Motel room the fateful night of King's assassination. In fact, Kyles encouraged the entourage to move along, as his wife would be expecting them soon for dinner. With the unfolding history that began that tragic night, Reverend Samuel "Billy" Kyles grieved with the nation, but quietly and firmly kept marching. Since 1959, Reverend Kyles has led his congregation at Monumental Baptist Church, and through his leadership has continued the message of Dr. King. Kyles is a founding member of Operation PUSH (People United to Save Humanity) and was appointed by President Bill Clinton to serve on the Advisory Committee on Religious Freedom Abroad.

Photograph Getty/Kevin Winter • **Story** by David Tankersley

JACKIE NICHOLS

THEATRE DIRECTOR, VISIONARY

Jackie Nichols' name is synonymous with Memphis Theater. He graduated from Overton High School in 1965 and while there performed at Front Street Theater and with a group of fellow high schoolers in a troupe they called The Circuit Players. Over the past 25 years Jackie has created and run both the Circuit Playhouse (1969) and Playhouse on the Square (1975). Jackie also founded "Show of Hands," a performing arts troupe that puts on productions for the hearing impaired. More recently, in 2010, with generous donations from corporations, foundations and individual supporters, the new Playhouse on the Square, one of the finest theater spaces in the country, opened at 66 S. Cooper. The beautiful new building also offers staging opportunities for Ballet Memphis, The Memphis Symphony Orchestra, and Opera Memphis. "When I first saw people doing theater as a child, I thought, 'This is what I want my community to look like,'" Nichols said. "The people onstage are rich and poor, black and white, gay and straight. Other producers I've known are in it to see what they can get out of it. For me, I find joy in creating opportunities for people. Your soul needs to be fed. And the arts feed the soul of the city."

Photograph courtesy Playhouse on the Square

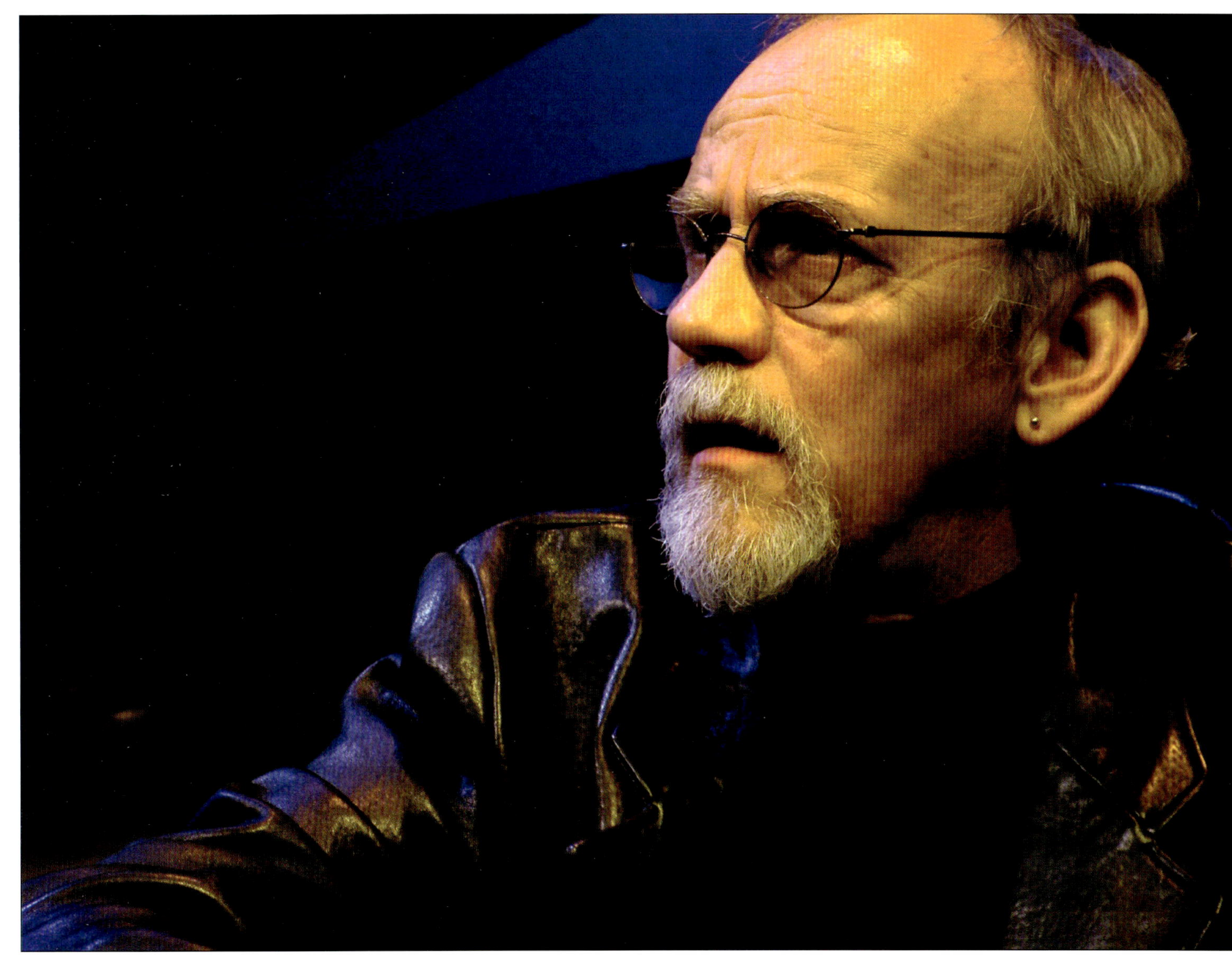

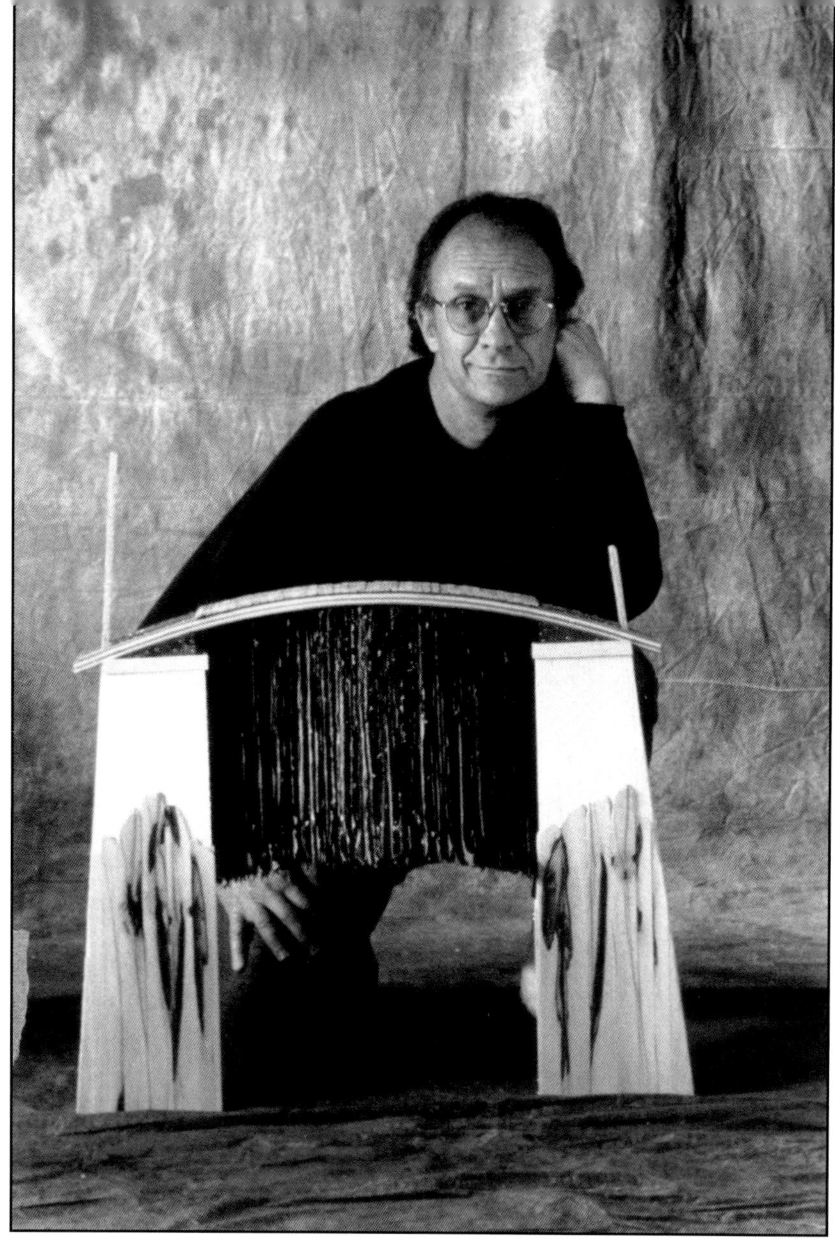

DOLPH SMITH

ARTIST, EDUCATOR

It's been a love affair between artist and community for more than 50 years. From flying barns to imaginary landscapes made of paper, Dolph Smith has created an artistic playground enjoyed by countless Memphians and art lovers across the world. And his influence and contributions have been more than strictly as practicing artist; Smith taught at the Memphis College of Art for thirty years, influenced countless young artists, and often traveled outside the city to teach at the Penland School and Arrowmont, to name but two.

His scope is represented by wistful watercolor landscapes of the South — barns and countryside rooted in rich colors and his own imaginary world of Tennarkippi made of wood, handmade paper, graphite and all manner of washes. His work — from purest drawing to one-of-a-kind handmade books — has roamed the world . There's no limit to the man's imagination, nor to his fans. Smith's work has been exhibited across the world.

It would take more than one gallery wall to begin to represent his honors through the years, but one stands out. Smith was selected as a recipient of a 2011 Governor's Art Award, Tennessee's highest honor in the arts.

Photograph courtesy of Memphis College of Art • **Story** by David Tankersley

MAXINE SMITH

CIVIL RIGHTS ACTIVIST

"I gave it my best shot."
Dr. Maxine Smith

Maxine Smith was born into a very different Memphis in 1929, and spent her life working toward the more egalitarian city, and nation, we have today. A graduate of Booker T. Washington High School, in 1957 she was denied enrollment in Memphis State because of her race. Never one to let things happen to her, Smith brought the injustice to the attention of the NAACP and by 1962 was its executive secretary.

Her work has been a virtual history of the civil rights movement: instrumental in organizing desegregation of the Memphis City Schools in 1960, the sanitation workers' strike in 1968, and Black Monday student boycotts which lasted from 1969 to 1972. In 1971 she was elected to the Memphis City School Board. She served as its president in 1991. She retired from the board in 1995 and has received some 160 awards for her lifetime of work on behalf of civil rights and educational issues. The Maxine A Smith Center at Southwest Tennessee Community College ensures that her legacy will continue.

Photograph by Commercial Appeal

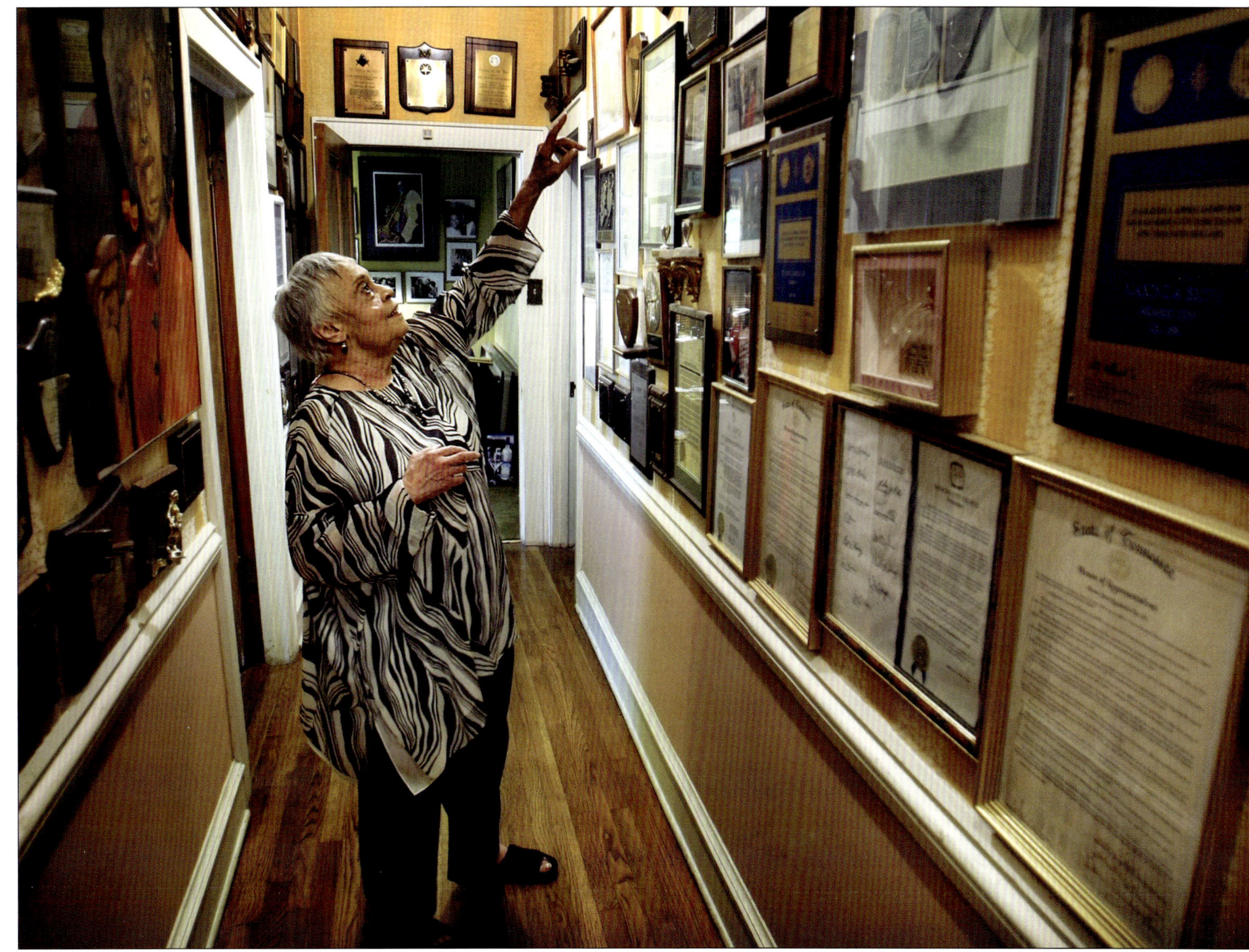

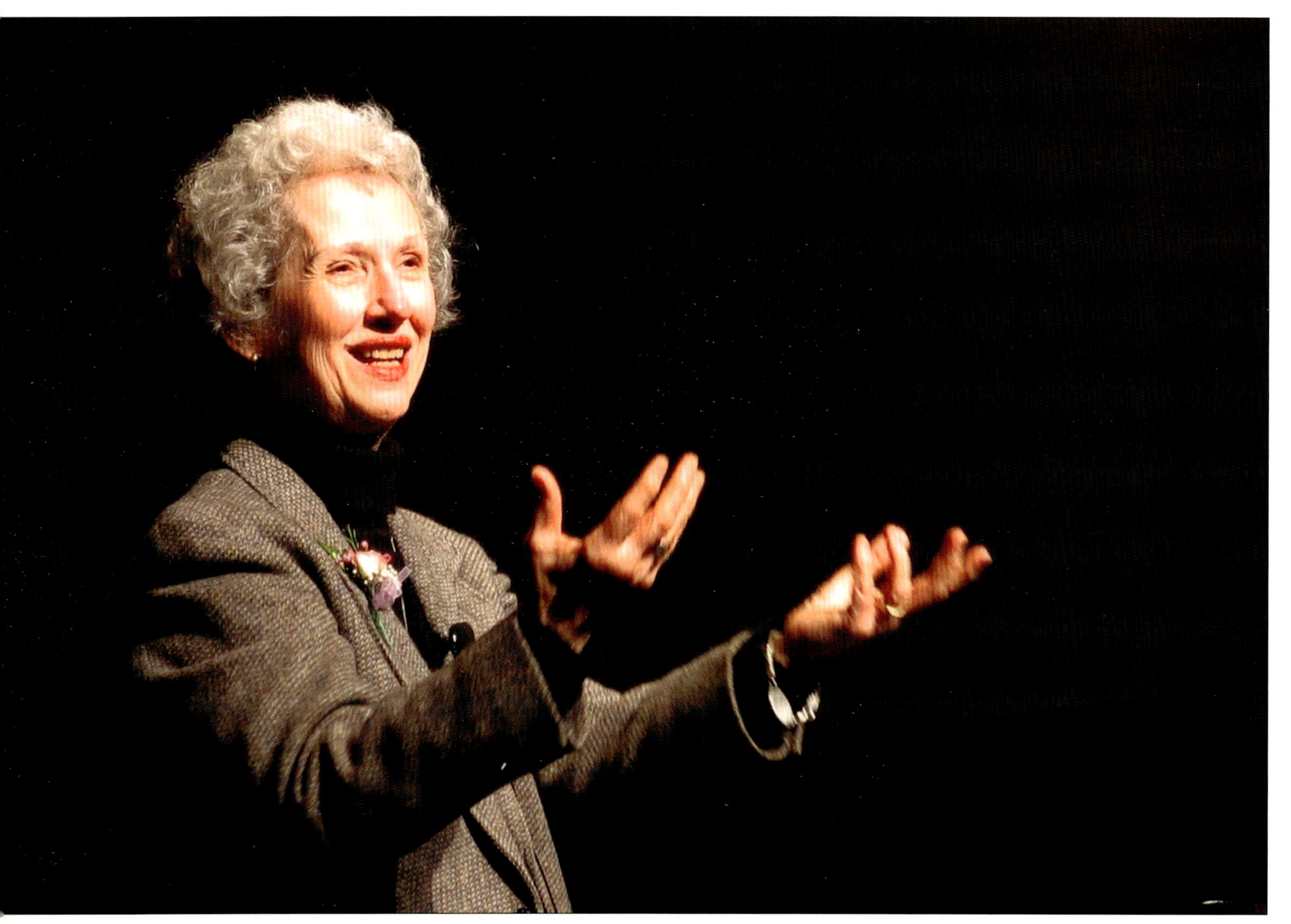

PHYLLIS TICKLE

ARTIST, EDITOR

Phyllis Tickle was born in Johnson City, Tennessee. She and her husband, Dr. Sam Tickle, moved to Memphis, and then eventually to Lucy, Tennessee, just outside of Memphis. The couple created one of the South's best small literary presses, St. Luke's Press, in 1972. They published Eleanor Glaze, David Spicer, Steve Stern, Jack Farris and Marilou Awiakta, among others. Phyllis was the founding editor of the Religion Department of *Publisher's Weekly*. She retired from there in 1994. She has published dozens of books, some family memoirs, some on spirituality. These include *The Tickle Papers*, *Prayer is a Place*, *The Shaping of a Life*, the 3-volume *The Divine Hours*, and *God-Talk in America*. In 2007 she received a Lifetime Achievement Award from The Christy Awards: "In gratitude for a lifetime as an advocate for fiction written to the glory of God."

In 2004, she received the honorary degree of Doctor of Humane Letters from the Berkeley School of Divinity at Yale University. In 2009 she received an honorary Doctor of Humane Letters degree from North Park University. Phyllis is a much sought-after speaker and spends a large amount of time traveling to speaking engagements. John Shelby Sponge said about one of her memoirs, "I have always loved Phyllis Tickle, and reading her personal story tells me why. She is real, honest, human, humorous, and deeply spiritual."

ERNEST C. WITHERS

PHOTOGRAPHER, JOURNALIST

We've all seen the photos. Men in work clothes and Sunday best lined up dozens strong and each holding a sign as iconic as the times themselves: I AM A MAN. The scene was Memphis, 1968, and the occasion was the sanitation workers' strike that would mobilize hundreds, earn respect for millions and bring Dr. Martin Luther King, Jr. to town for his final appearance.

The man behind the lens was Ernest C. Withers who worked as a photojournalist to document the civil rights movement, its triumphs and its tragedies. He had the most extensive archive of photographs from the era due to the unlimited access he was allowed to the inner sanctum of the leaders of the movement.

Born in 1922, Withers got his start as a photographer in the Army during World War II and later moved back to Memphis to open his own studio on Beale Street.

His vocation as a witness to the civil rights era began by being the only photographer to cover the entire Emmet Till trial, a black teenager murdered for allegedly whistling at a white woman in 1955. He photographed the integration of Little Rock's Central High School in 1957 and the funeral of Medgar Evers in 1963.

In addition to his startlingly frank photographs of the civil rights movement, Withers documented the raucous, musical times on Beale Street with images of B.B. King, Aretha Franklin, Ray Charles, Isaac Hayes, Al Green and Elvis Presley. Sports caught his eye and lens as well as he photographed the waning years of Negro League baseball.

Withers died on October 15, 2007, yet his memory lives on in photographs that illustrate man's inhumanity towards man and his overwhelming desire and ability to overcome such inhumanity. In 2011, the Ernest C. Withers Museum, honoring the man and showcasing his photographs, opened on Beale Street.

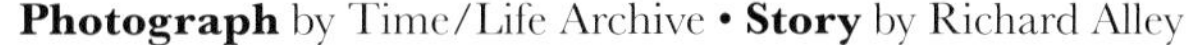

Photograph by Time/Life Archive • **Story** by Richard Alley

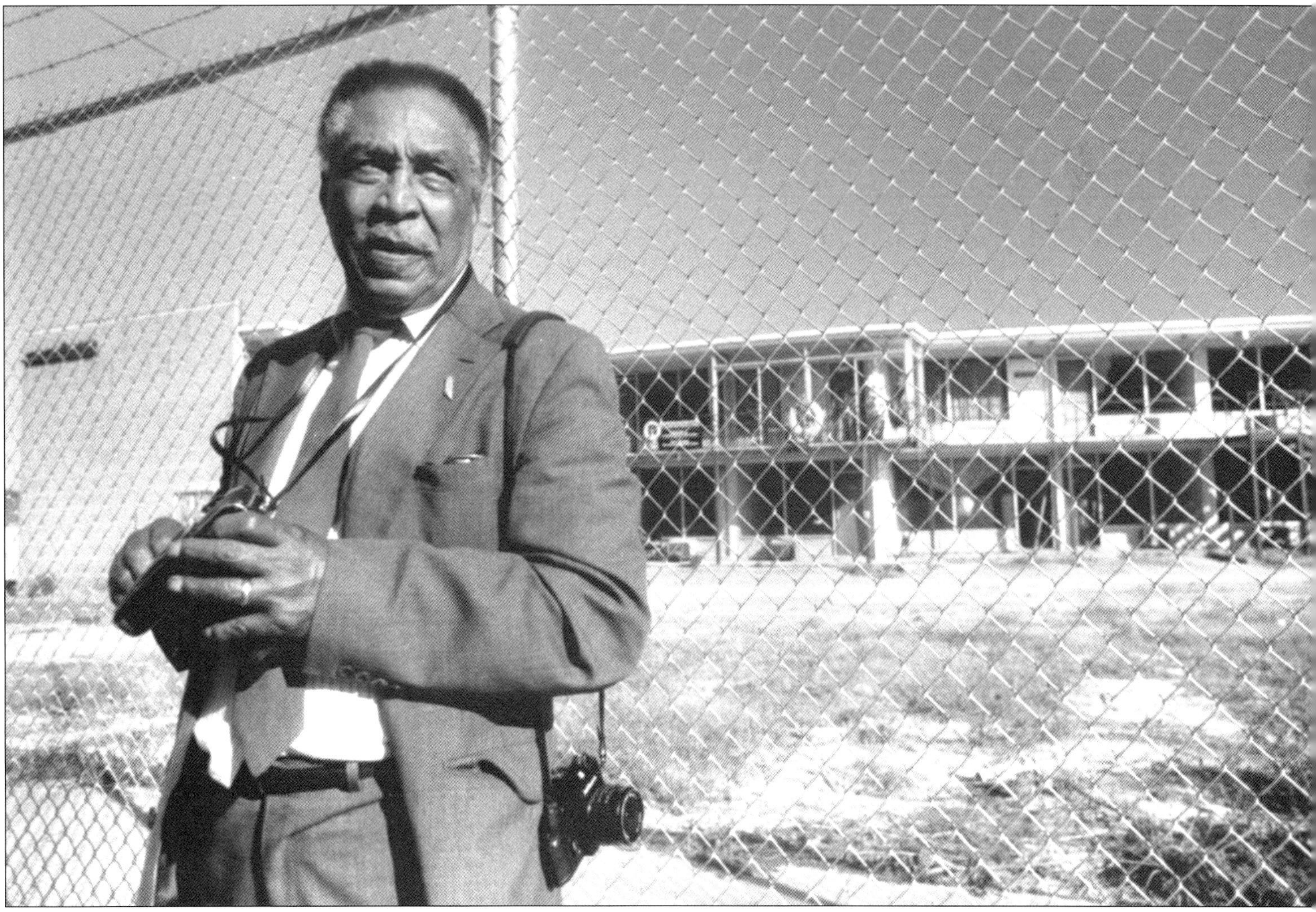

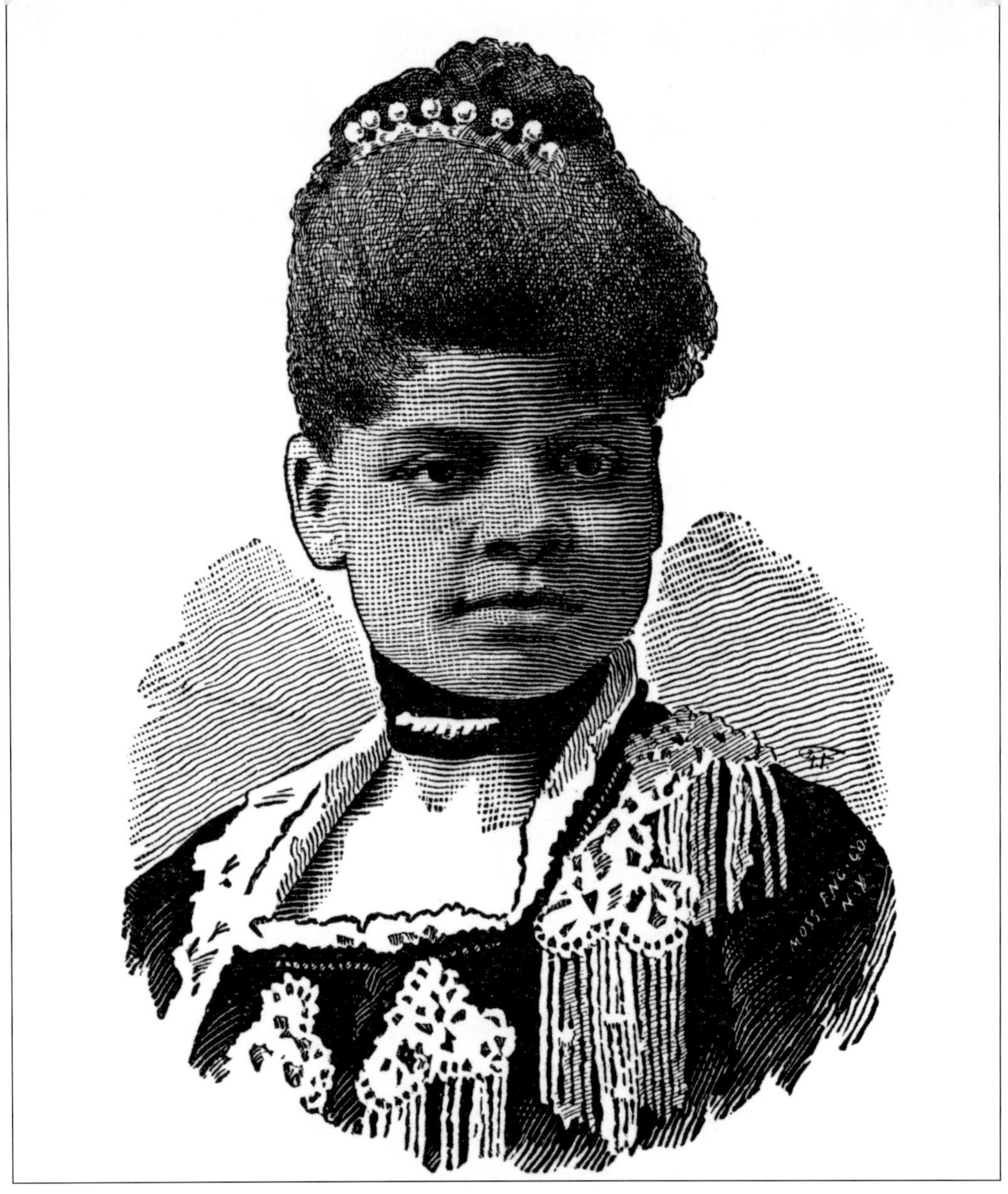

IDA B. WELLS

EDITOR, CRUSADER

In 1884, seventy-one years before Rosa Parks was forced to give up her seat on a bus, Ida B. Wells, a school teacher with five younger siblings to support, was told to get to the Jim Crow car of a train. She fought back. She bit the conductor's hand before being bodily removed to the applause of the white passengers. When her black lawyer was paid off by the railroad, she hired white lawyers that were harder to intimidate in court. She won the case locally, but lost her victory when it was overturned in the Tennessee Supreme Court.

She kept fighting. She became editor of the *Free Speech and Headlight* in 1889. When some friends were lynched for having a successful grocery store across the street from a white-owned store, she launched an anti-lynching campaign that made her world famous and included books, lecture tours, pamphlets, and boycotts. She married the editor of the first African-American newspaper in Chicago and was a founder of the NAACP. Until her death in 1931, Ida B. Wells never stopped fighting.

Illustration Getty

Memphis Icons

Movies, Television & Stage

Music

Sports

Entrepreneurs

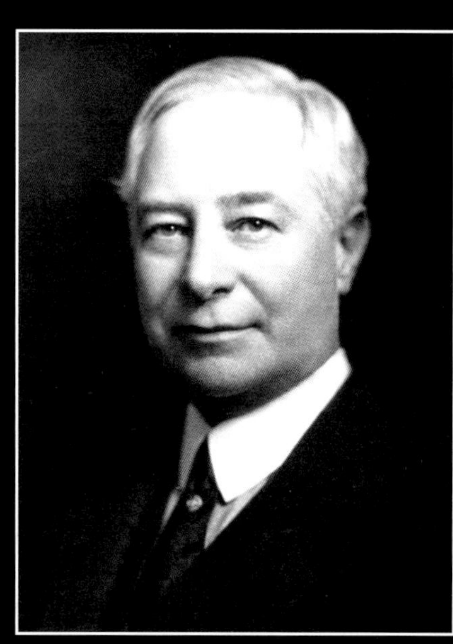

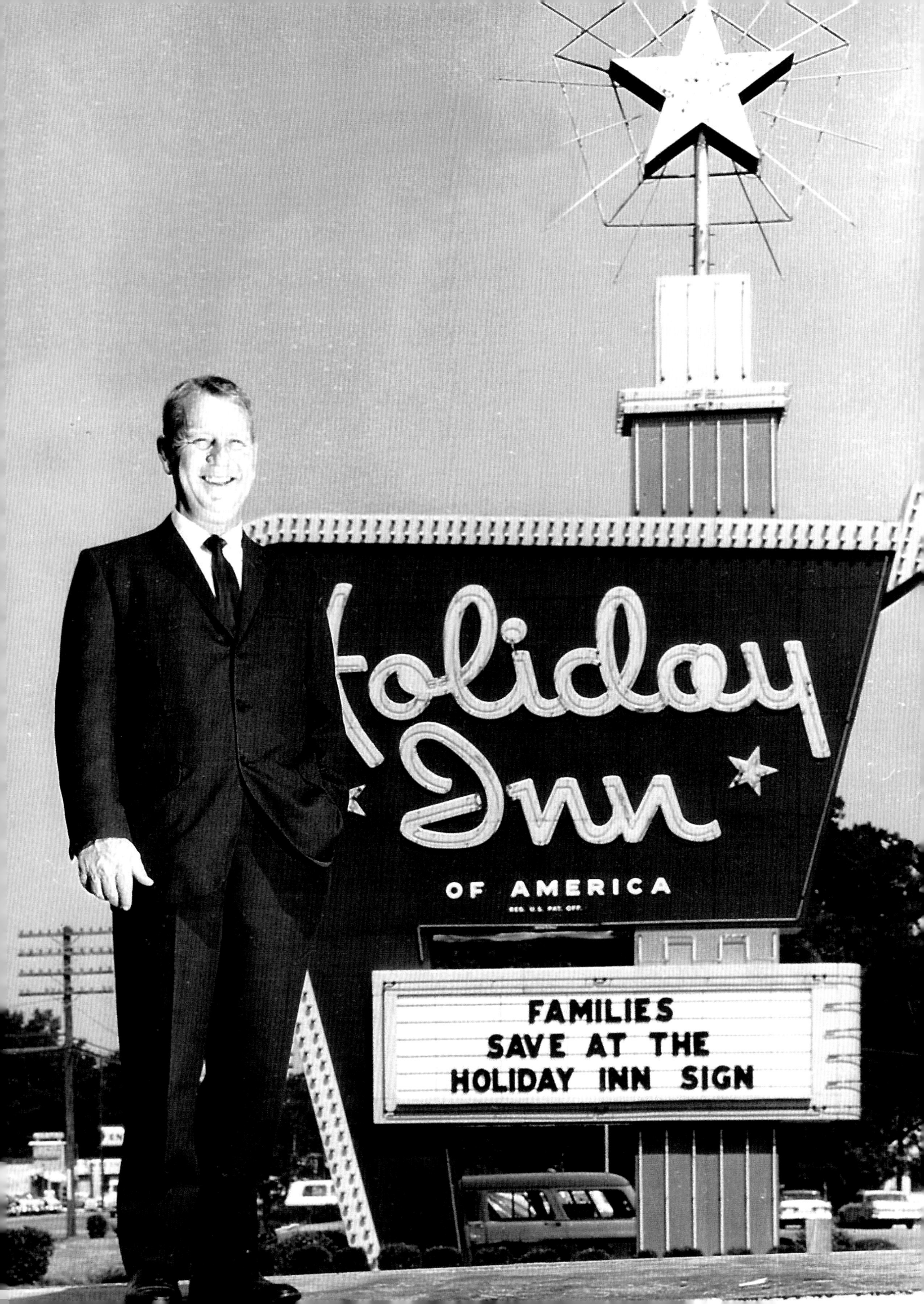

Holiday Inn
OF AMERICA
FAMILIES
SAVE AT THE
HOLIDAY INN SIGN

KEMMONS WILSON

THE WORLD'S INNKEEPER

Memphis seems to have a habit of changing the world's habits. Clarence Saunders changed the way we shop and Fred Smith changed the way we send packages. W.C. Handy changed our music and 50 years later, Elvis did it again. Kemmons Wilson changed the way we travel and our expectations for the experience. He taught generations to expect a clean, comfortable, family-friendly room at a good value with a TV and a phone in it and a restaurant and a swimming pool on the property. As basic as that now seems, before Kemmons Wilson every single one of those items was a crap shoot on a road trip. After a miserable road trip with his wife and five kids, Wilson came home with an idea. He started Holiday Inns, named after the Bing Crosby/Fred Astaire movie, in 1952. Before the first one went up on Summer Avenue, he told the sign company he didn't much care what the sign looked like but he wanted to make sure nobody could miss it. Mission accomplished. By 1958, that sign was in front of 50 locations, 500 by 1964, 1,000 by 1968 and more than 1,400 worldwide when Kemmons Wilson was on the cover of Time in 1972. Because of his standardization, consistency, centralized services and innovation, he was also a force in modern franchising and branding. Before his death at 90, Kemmons Wilson saw an entire industry built and transformed on his model worldwide. And kids stay free.

Photograph courtesy The Wilson Company • **Story** by Dan Conaway

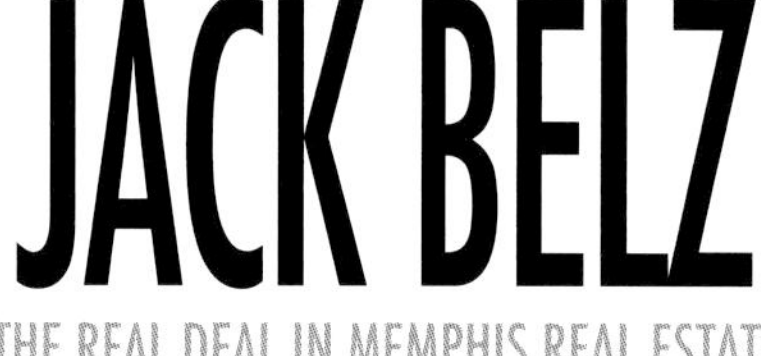

THE REAL DEAL IN MEMPHIS REAL ESTATE

Following his father Philip as patriarch to the Belz family, Jack Belz has led Belz Enterprises for decades, a company close to (or at the top) of Tennessee property owners. A quiet philanthropist and pioneer in the concepts of city gateway centers and factory outlet malls, Belz went very public with the world-class renovation and reopening of The Peabody in 1981, and the redevelopment of virtually everything around it. As surely as the ducks march to the lobby fountain in the South's grand hotel, Jack Belz's vision has led the march back downtown for people and businesses for 30 years. No one has meant as much to the city's central business district revitalization. The only one close is fellow visionary and downtown developer Henry Turley, and Turley has partnered with Belz in several successful ventures, including Harbor Town, Uptown and South Bluffs. In 1998, Belz and his wife established the Belz Museum of Asian and Judaic Art on South Main.

Photo courtesy Belz Enterprises • **Story** by Dan Conaway

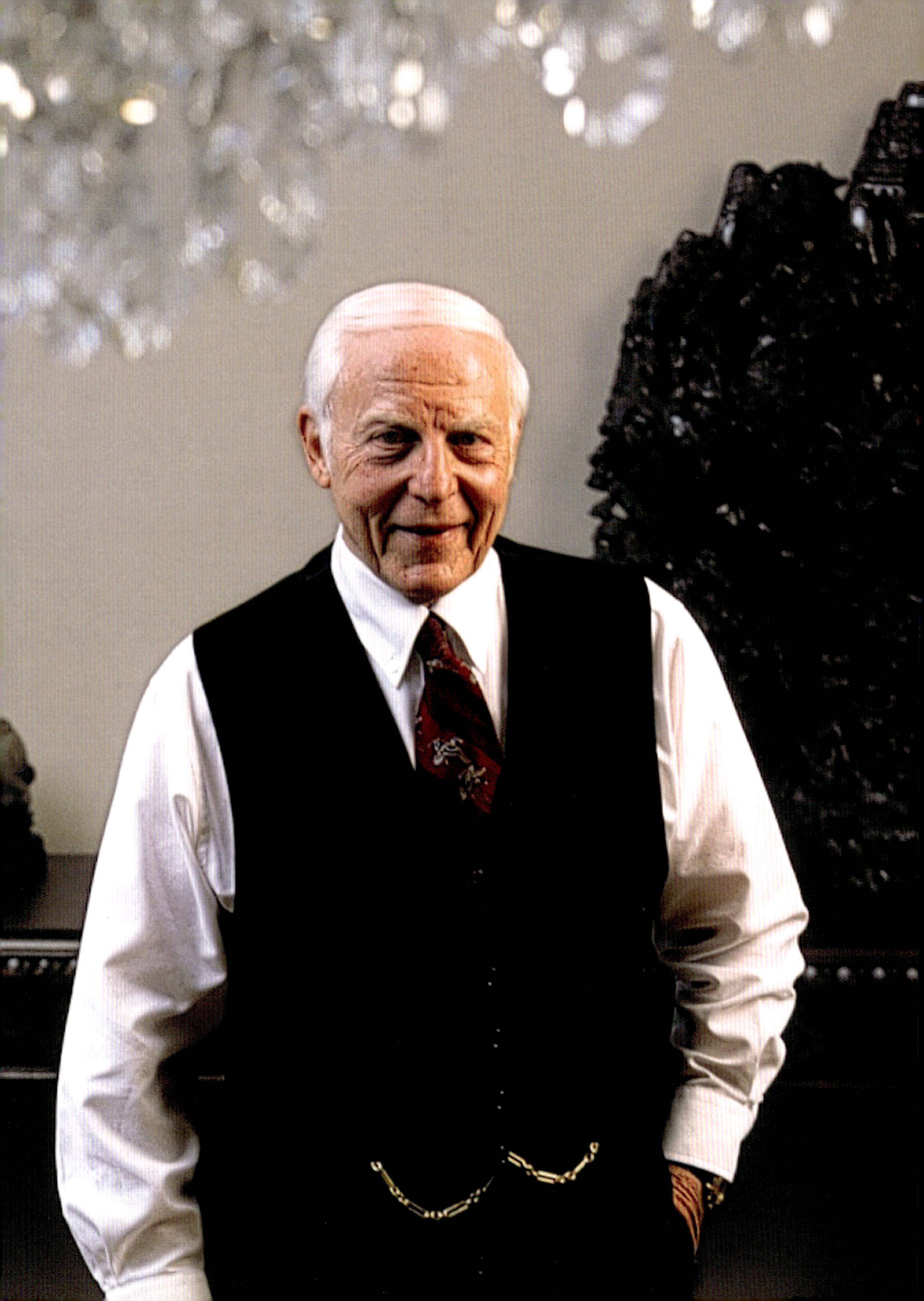

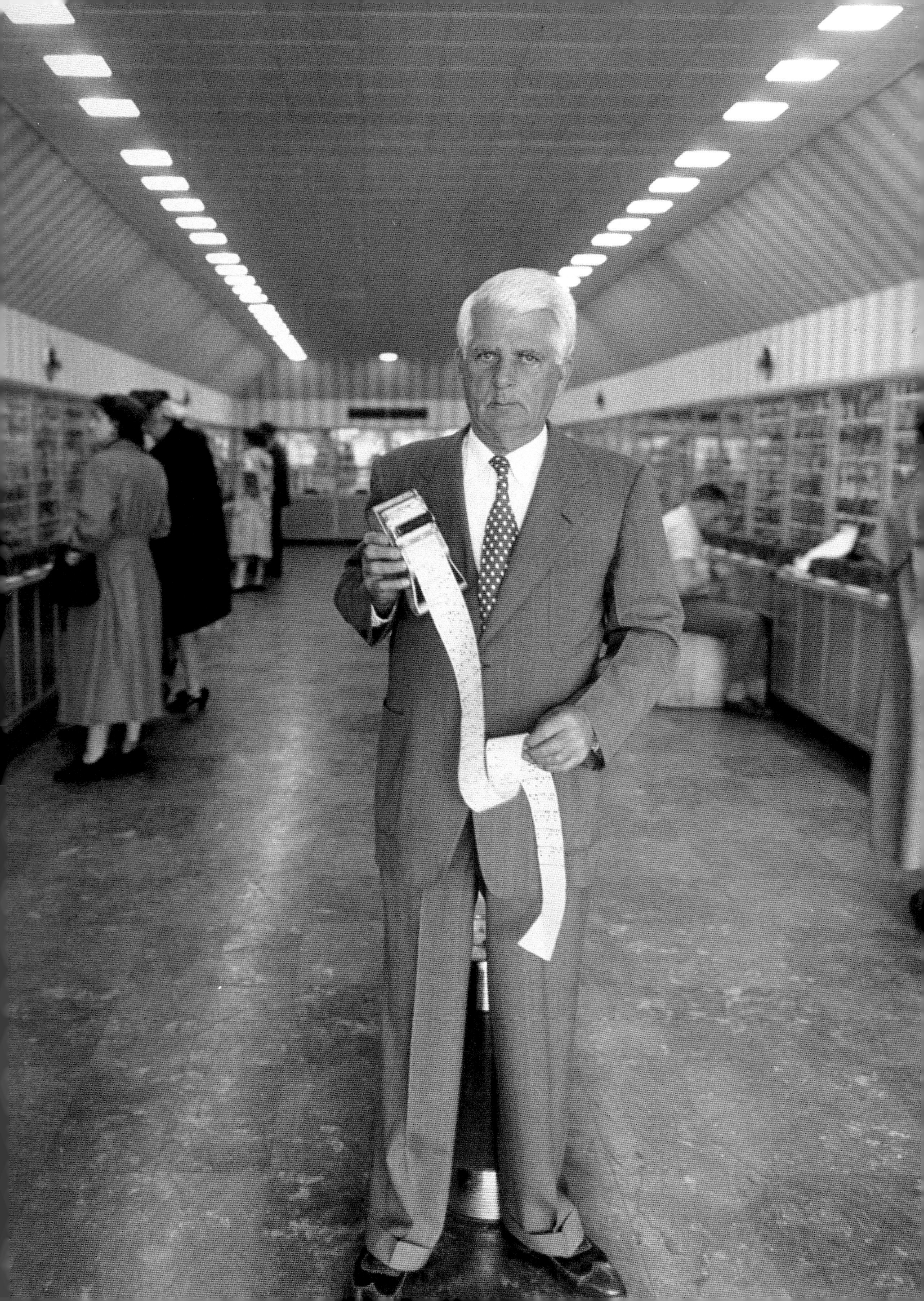

CLARENCE SAUNDERS

ALL THAT AND A BAG OF GROCERIES

The difference between Fitzgerald's Great Gatsby and Clarence Saunders is that Gatsby is fiction. Both were fabulously wealthy, self-made, flamboyant masters of the 1920s. One is a famous literary work. The other is a famous piece of work who changed the way everyone lives. Clarence Saunders invented – and patented – self-service grocery stores in 1916 with the first Piggly Wiggly at Jefferson and Main, parlaying it into a chain of thousands. He built a mansion, dubbed the Pink Palace from the color of its Italian marble, put in his own golf course, and never lived a single day or shanked a single wedge there. He lost everything in 1923 in a failed attempt to corner the New York Stock Exchange, and today his mansion is the Pink Palace Museum and his golf course is the exclusive Chickasaw Gardens neighborhood. He was far from through, however, and before his death in 1953, he made and lost at least two more fortunes, even starting a football team in Memphis and turning down an invitation to join the fledgling National Football League. Unable to use the Piggly Wiggly name after the 1923 debacle, he started another grocery chain with the snappy moniker of Clarence Saunders Sole Owner Of My Name Stores, lost it in the Great Depression, and then pioneered the automated store concept with two more chains, Keedoozle and Foodelectric.

Photograph by Time/Life Archive • **Story** by Dan Conaway

WILLIAM "BILLY" DUNAVANT

COTTON KING

Due to the early death of his father, William "Billy" Dunavant took over the family firm, TJ White & Co. in 1961 at the age of 29. That year the company sold 100,000 bales of domestically grown cotton, 90% of which was sold in the United States. Under Dunavant's visionary use of futures contracting – where the farmer agrees to a price before planting – the company, renamed Dunavant Enterprise, grew into the largest private company in Memphis and was in the top 100 largest private companies in the United States – selling four to six million bales of cotton in more than 80 countries. It handled the first sale of US Cotton to mainland China in 1972, and the largest single sale to China in 1990.

An avid hunter and tennis player, Dunavant built the Racquet Club of Memphis in 1972. Always innovating, in 2010, after 40 years dominating the business, Dunavant Enterprises sold its cotton operations to Allenburg Cotton, shifting their focus to worldwide logistics.

Photograph by Commercial Appeal • **Story** by Richard Murff

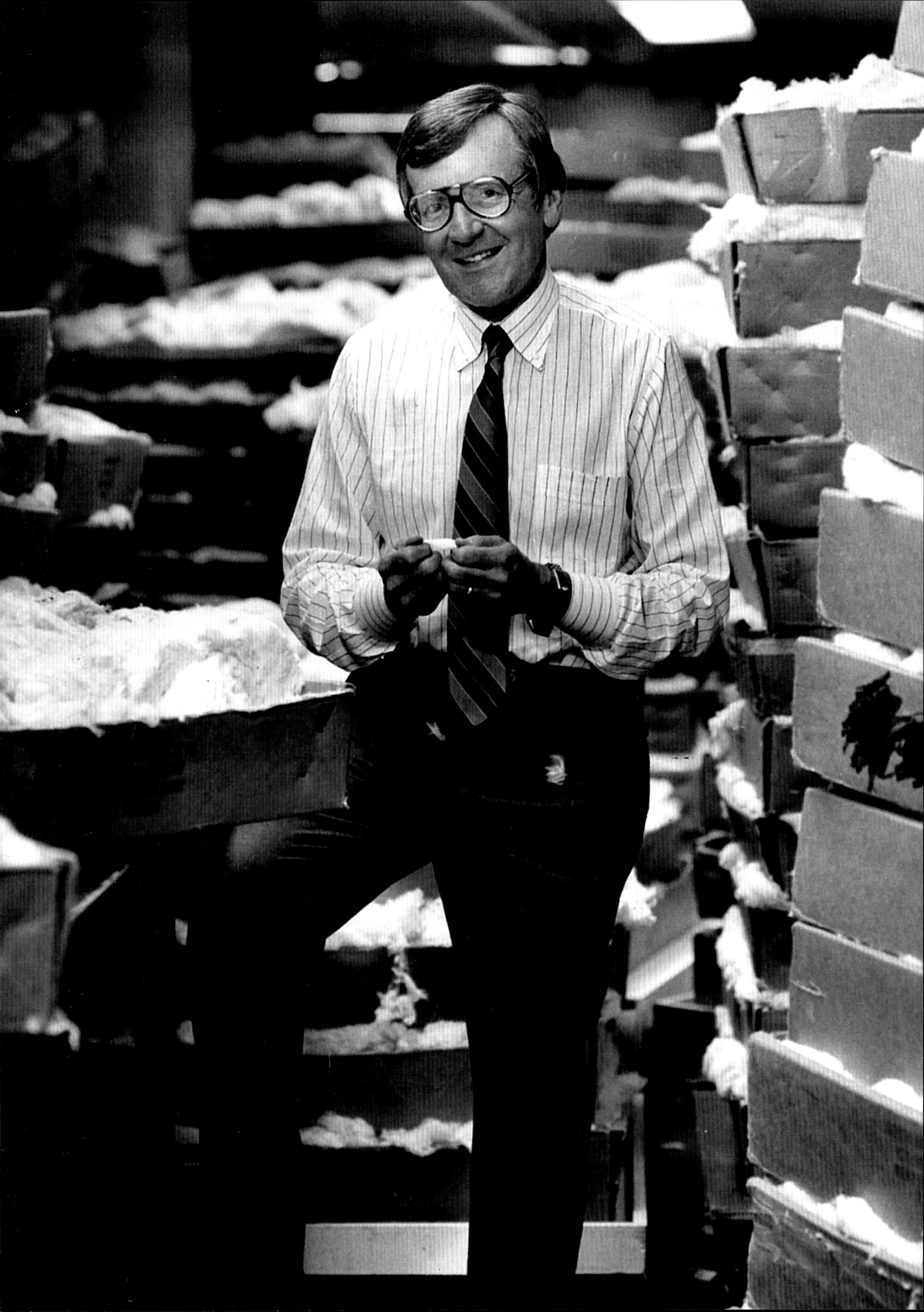

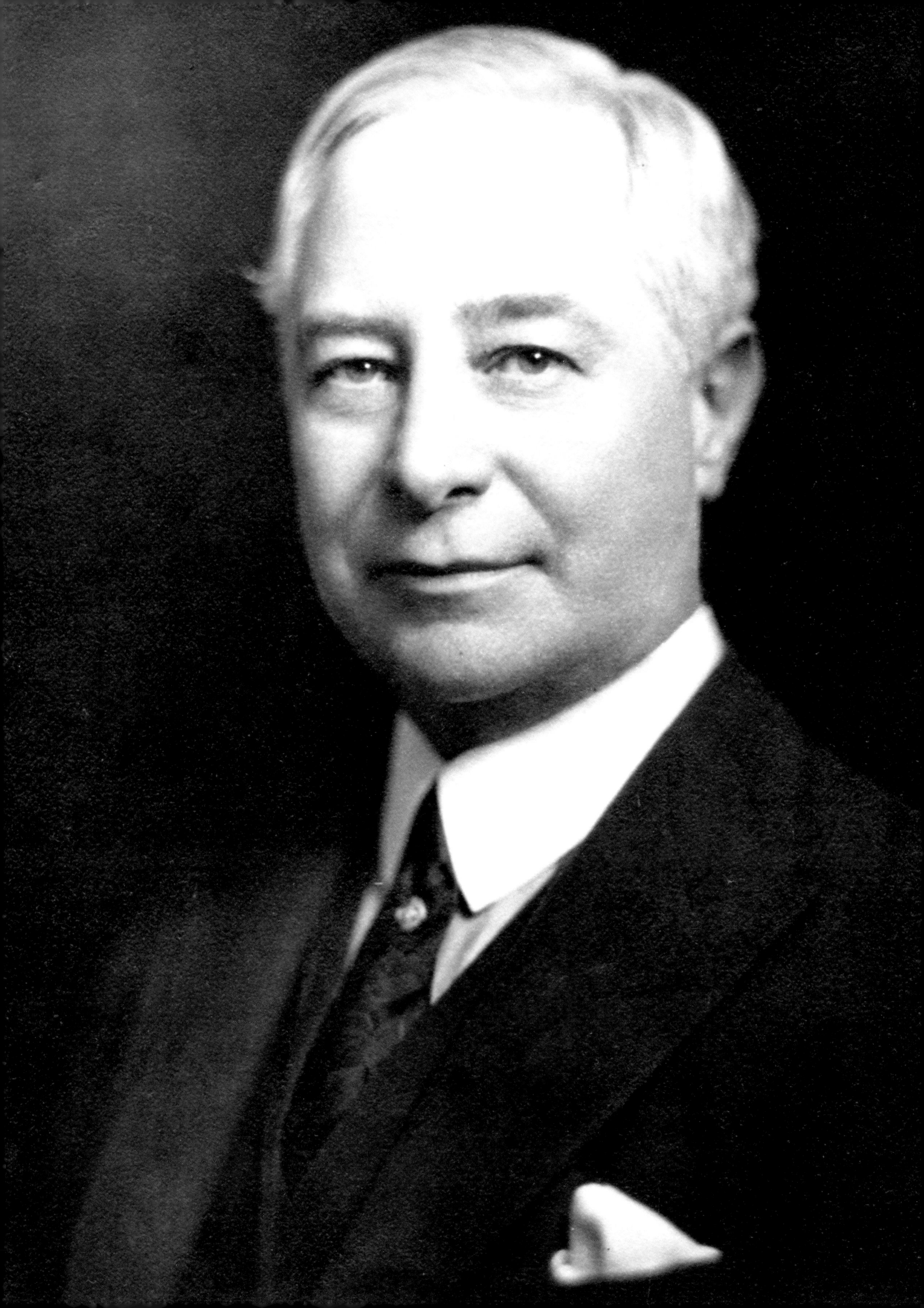

BARRON GIFT COLLIER

ADVERTISING & REAL ESTATE

Born in Memphis in 1873, Barron Collier quit school at age sixteen to work for the Illinois Central Railroad. Within four years, he started his own business, the Consolidated Street Railway Advertising Company of New York City. By age twenty-six, he was worth a million dollars. Collier was an unqualified success in streetcar advertising before he and the wife (Miss Juliet Gordon Carnes, also a native of Memphis) moved to Florida. They fell in love with the area, so they bought Useppa Island and created an exclusive resort. Then things really got going. By his death in 1939, Collier owned hotels, resorts, bus lines, banks, newspapers, a telephone company and a steamship line. He founded the eponymous Collier County, Florida and was the largest private landowner in Florida with some 1.3 million acres.

Photograph courtesy Collier County Library

ABE PLOUGH

MR. ANONYMOUS

Abe Plough attended Market Street School where a teacher taught him to calculate figures without pencil or paper. He said this "mental arithmetic" served him well in his business career. He never needed a pencil to calculate his acquisition of thirty companies for the Schering-Plough Corporation (at a cost of over $1 billion). On weekends Plough worked at a drugstore without pay because he wanted to learn the business — determined that it would be his future.

In 1908 a 16-year-old Abe Plough created Plough, Inc. with a horse and wagon bought for $125 borrowed from his father. With it he sold homemade remedies to the people in the rural areas outside of Memphis. Today Schering-Plough is a global pharmaceutical and consumer products company with brands like Maybelline, Dr. Scholl's and St. Joseph's Aspirin.

The company and many of its brands are instantly recognizable around the world. In charitable circles, Plough was known as "Mr. Anonymous" because so much of his considerable giving was done without fanfare and credit. Plough died in 1984, but his Plough Charitable Foundation continues to place gifts where they will do the most good.

Photograph Time & Life Images/Evelyn Hofer

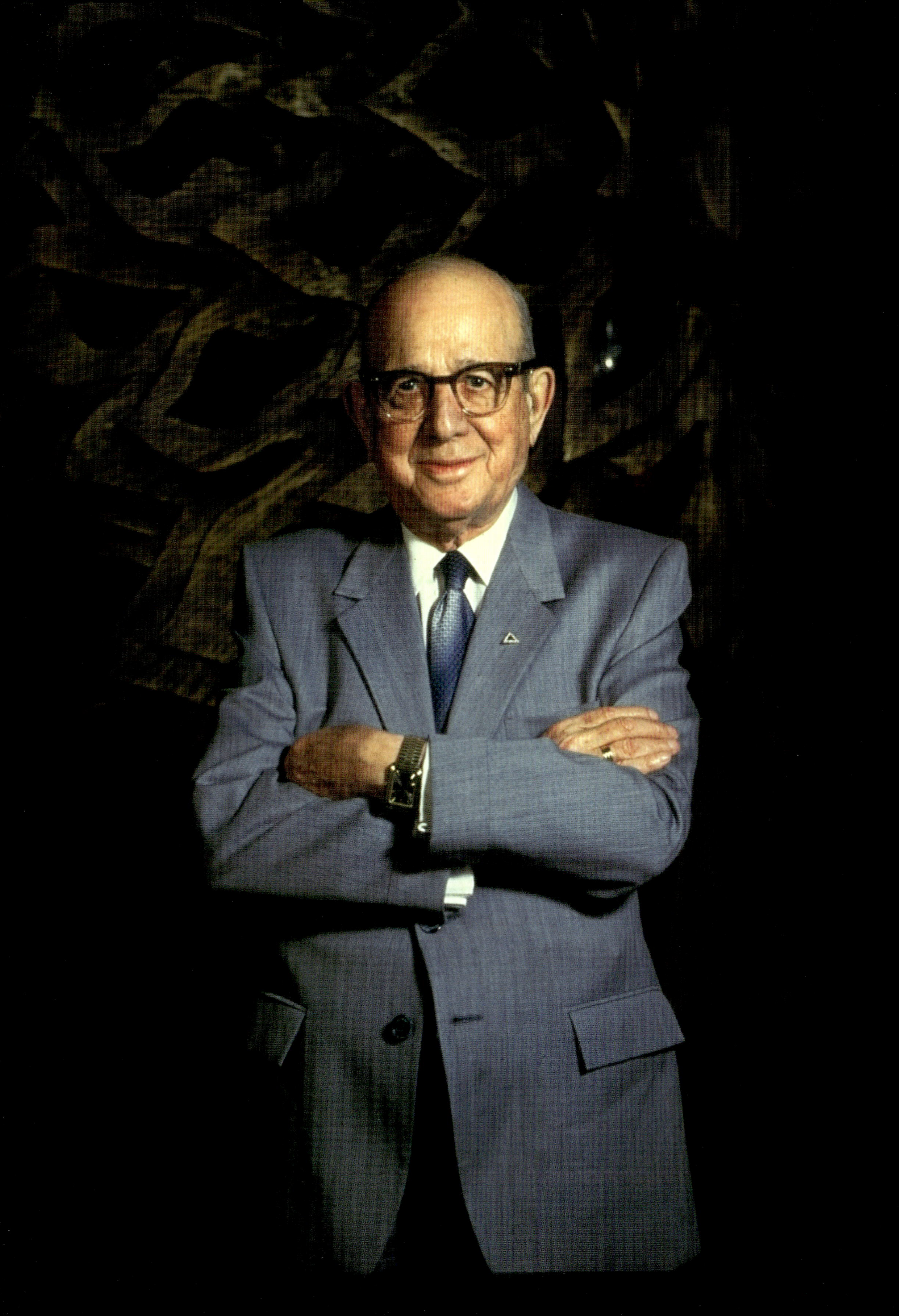

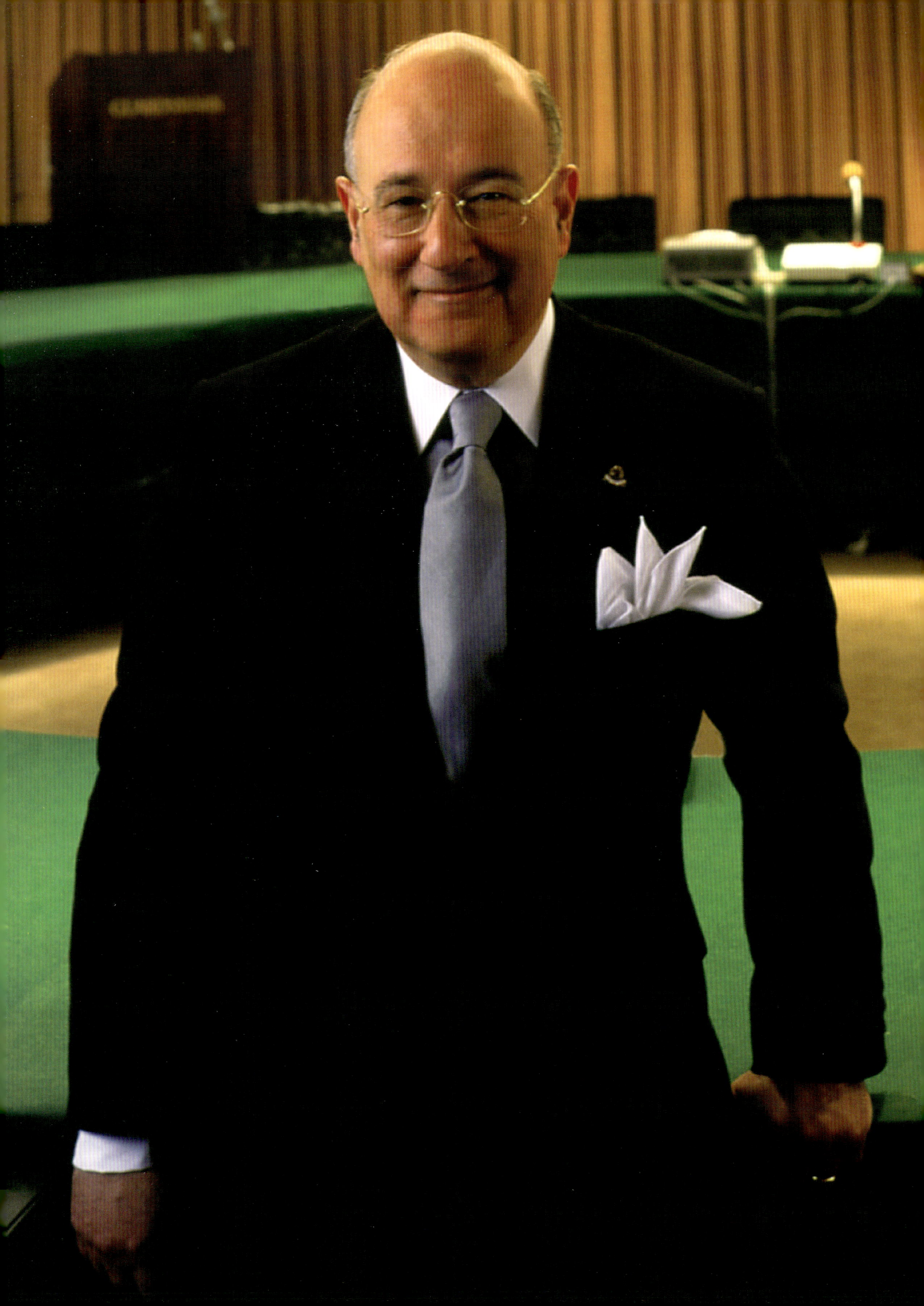

IRA A. LIPMAN

FOUNDER & CHAIRMAN, GUARDSMARK

Ira A. Lipman, Founder and Chairman of Guardsmark LLC, has literally changed the face of the security industry and continues to blaze trails in public awareness of threat, vulnerability and performance standards, industry regulation, and corporate ethics and diversity. In the course of his 50-year career, Lipman has been a clarion call of quality for the industry, pioneering and promoting policies, education and legislation to upgrade private security and protect the public from crime and terrorism.

Born in Little Rock in 1940, Lipman founded Guardsmark in Memphis in 1963 with a purpose – to bring standards and professionalism to a dangerously unregulated industry. With meteoric growth — and 10 percent compounded annual growth rate over 32 years without acquisition – Guardsmark stands today as one of the world's largest security service companies, operating approximately 150 branches and serving clients in more than 400 cities. For these inroads and accomplishments, Guardsmark is recognized as "the Tiffany's of the security industry," along with countless accolades from business ethics and public policy organizations and national publications.

Ira Lipman's and Guardsmark's ethical leadership and groundbreaking initiatives have been recognized with the American Business Ethics Award and the Committee for Economic Development Corporate Citizenship Award. Lipman personally received the Stanley C. Pace Award for Leadership in Ethics from the Washington, D.C.-based Ethics Resource Center.

An acclaimed author and speaker, Lipman has spoken at conferences and universities across America and written for the public on a wide range of security and ethics topics. He is author of the book *How to Protect Yourself from Crime*, published in four editions to date. He has also written numerous articles that have appeared in national publications and editorials published by *The New York Times* and *The Washington Post*.

His extraordinary leadership extends to the larger community as well, and he has served on the boards of more than 55 political, corporate and charitable organizations. These include various chairmanships and committees within the Council on Foreign Relations, United Way of America and the National Council on Crime and Delinquency.

Lipman holds three honorary LL.D. degrees – from John Marshall University, Northeastern University, and Ohio Wesleyan University. He has been honored with the University of Pennsylvania Wharton School Dean's Medal. With a name and a company synonymous with excellence, ethics and unremitting dedication, Ira Lipman's remarkable list of business, civic, and personal achievements are featured in more than 90 books.

Photograph courtesy Guardsmark

KAREN CARRIER

ARTIST, CHEF, RESTAURATEUR

"Karen Blockman Carrier's restaurants and cuisine reflect herself — vibrant, robust, funky, filled with energy and imagination."

The James Beard Foundation

Karen Blockman Carrier — a 1975 grad of The Memphis Academy of Art — has been a personal chef to such Hollywood big shots as Tom Cruise and Susan Sarandon. As many natives know, the way to Memphis' heart is through its stomach, and Carrier's innovative restaurants and one-of-a-kind cooking style make her a star in her own right. In 1983 Carrier launched Lunch Catering, in NYC, to the fashion photography industry. She later celebrated Independence Day in 1986, with the birth of her first restaurant, Automatic Slims "One Bar Under a Groove"— a Memphis meets Manhattan Juke Joint in Greenwich Village that melds soul food with Southern fried sensibilities.

Like all good Southerners, she eventually returned home to Memphis in 1987, to start a family and plant the seeds for a restaurant empire. *Food and Wine* Magazine described Carrier's restaurants as "in your face cooking; imaginative and full of surprises."

Another Roadside Attraction Catering was her first southern venture followed by Automatic Slims Tonga Club in Downtown Memphis (Carrier sold this restaurant after 17 years in 2008), The Beauty Shop Restaurant + Lounge, do Sushi + Noodles and her latest addition, The Mollie Fontaine Lounge. In all endeavors this chef-entrepreneur generates art and innovation.

Photograph by Jonathan Postal

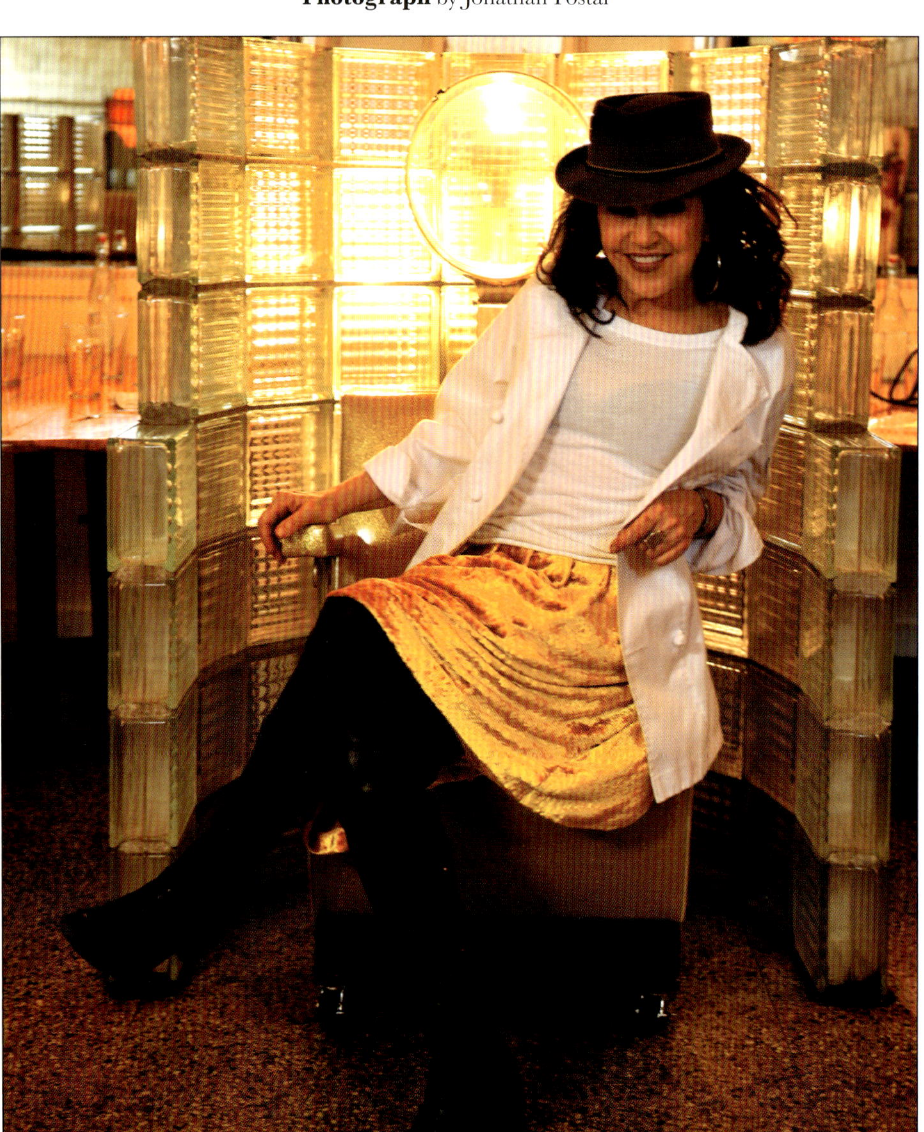

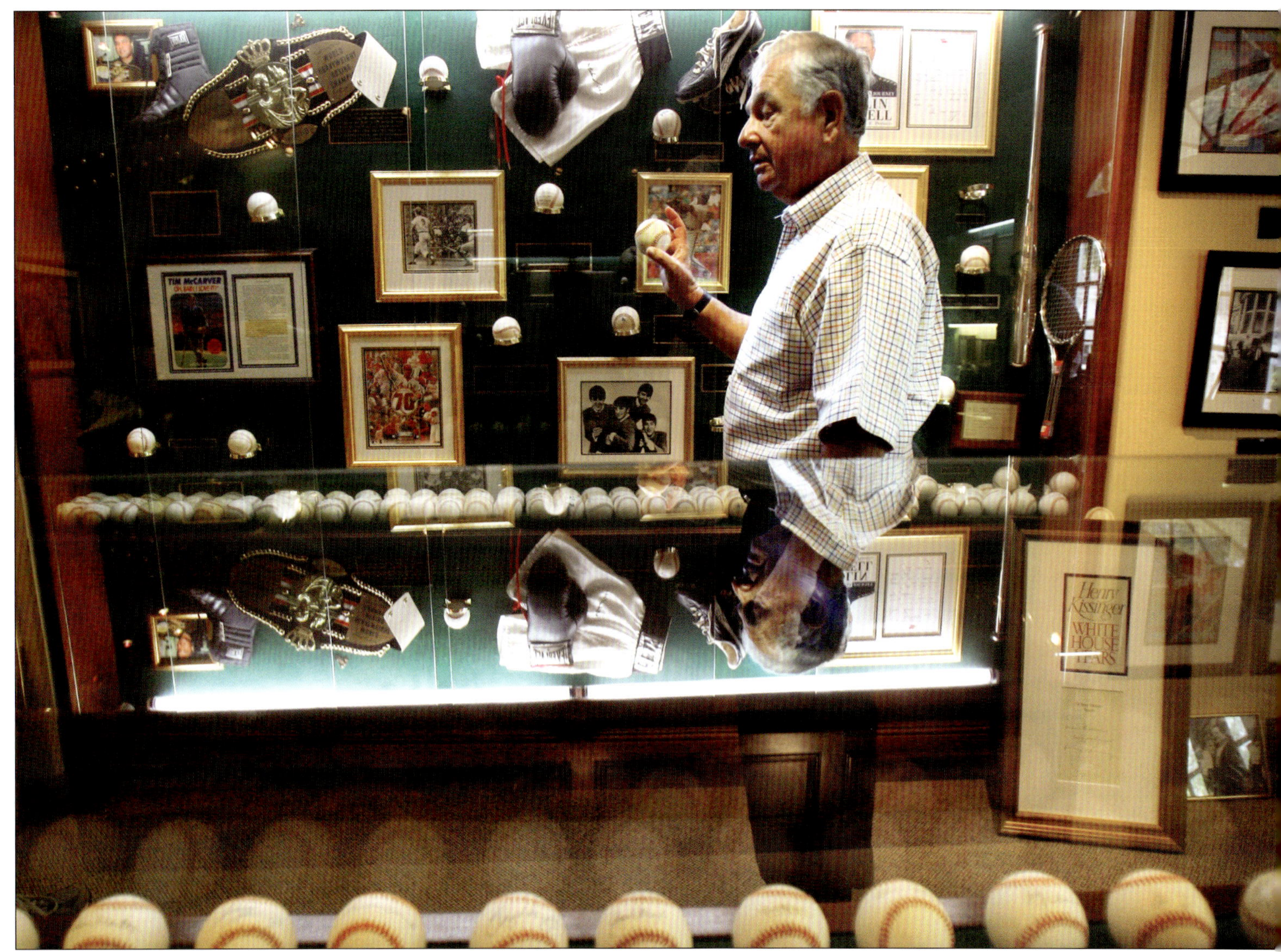

AVRON FOGELMAN

SPORTSMAN

It's the stuff of legend. A little league third baseman dreams of big league glory, and eventually gives up bat and glove for education and the worlds of finance and real estate, worlds in which Avron Fogelman became a most valuable player. Fogelman moves in the sphere of professional sports. He was the president of the basketball Memphis Pros at the age of 30. He bought the Memphis Grizzlies football team. And he brought minor league baseball back to Memphis, in 1978, with the Memphis Chicks. He even purchased the Memphis Rogues soccer team franchise in 1978, in spite of never having played the game.

And to top it off, he owned the Kansas City Royals from 1983 to 1991 — and has a World Series Championship trophy to prove it. If you can't play with them, own them.

Fogelman has been recognized by countless organizations for his charitable efforts — Special Olympics, Big Brothers and Big Sisters, the Memphis Sports Authority, the National Conference of Christians and Jews, and the NAACP.

A product of Memphis City Schools and graduate of Central High School, Fogelman is driven by a commitment to education and has long been a proponent of public education. Fogelman recently committed $1.25 million to the University of Memphis for the creation of the Avron B. Fogelman Center for Professional Career Development. The university's business school is named in his honor. His undergraduate alma mater, Tulane, plays basketball in the Green Wave-Avron B. Fogelman Arena.

For his contributions to sports, Avron Fogelman's name is ensconced in the shrines of the Tennessee Sports Hall of Fame. Not bad for a little league third baseman.

Photo by Commercial Appeal • **Story** by David Tankersley

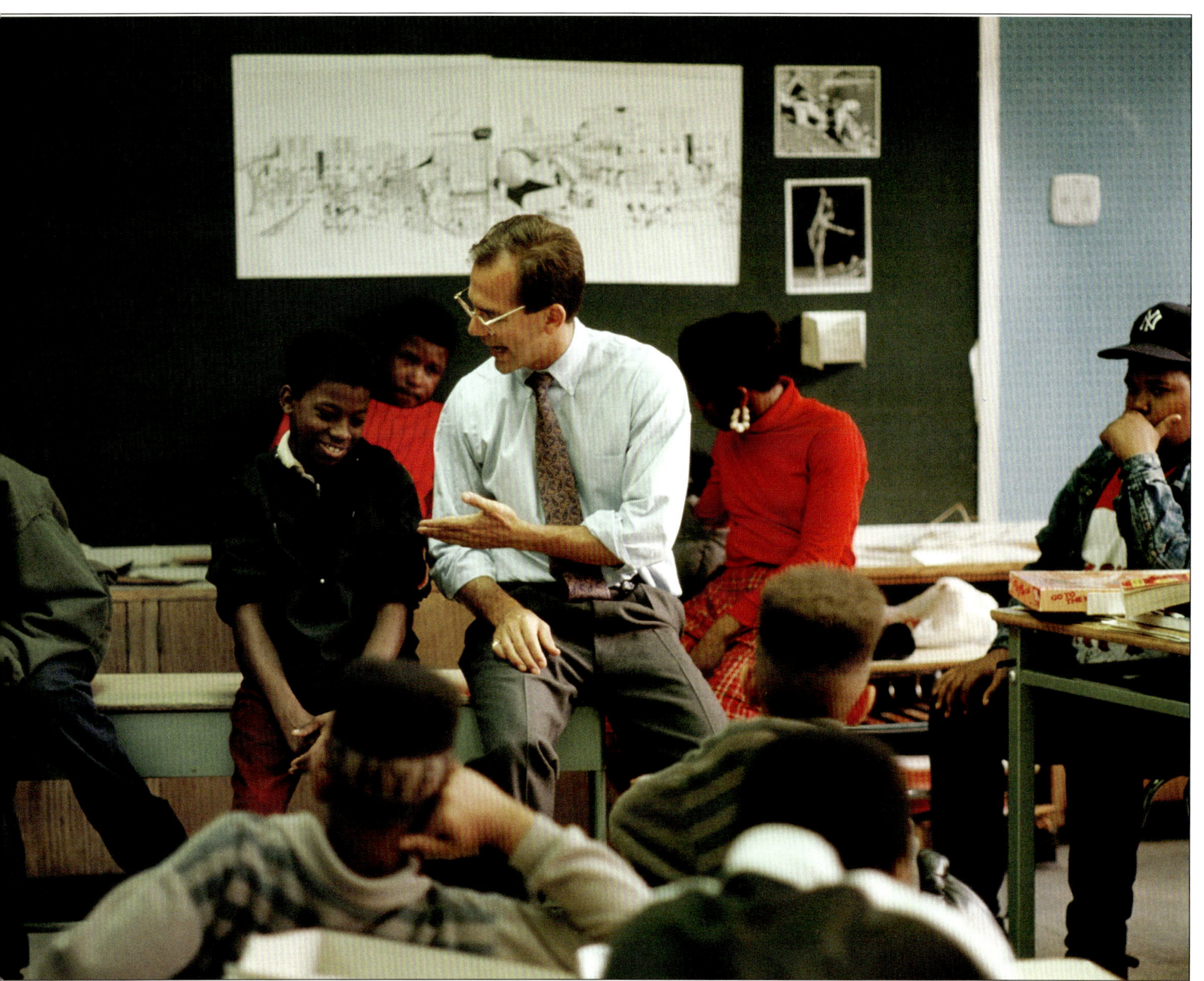

PAUL TUDOR JONES

ENTREPRENEUR, PHILANTHROPIST

On October 19, 1987 — Black Monday — when the rest of the world watched chunks of wealth evaporate, Paul Tudor Jones tripled his investment positions. An alumnus of Presbyterian Day School, Memphis University School and the University of Virginia, Jones was contemplating enrollment in the Harvard School of Business. But his cousin, Billy Dunavant, suggested he head to New Orleans to learn cotton futures trading. Tudor Investment Corporation was born.

Jones is the founder of Excellent Charter School — the country's all-boys charter school — in the Bedford Stuyvesant part of Brooklyn New York, as well as the Bedford Stuyvesant I Have a Dream Foundation for local college scholarships. He also founded the Robin Hood Foundation, a charitable organization backed by hedge fund managers, and owns the Grumeti Reserves in Tanzania. His ranch in Colorado is offered to disabled soldiers and citizens for trophy trout fishing.

Photo: Paul Tudor Jones spends a day in Brooklyn with some of the 109 students he has agreed to send to college.
Photo by Jodi Cobb/National Geographic/Getty Images

M.A. LIGHTMAN

ENTERTAINMENT MOGUL

Morris A. Lightman earned a degree in engineering from Vanderbilt but felt he was truly more of an entertainer. After coming upon a long line of moviegoers outside a theater one day, Lightman decided to open his own movie theater. Opening his first theater in 1915, he opened Memphis theaters The Memphian in 1935, the Malco in 1940 and the Crosstown in 1951 (among other Memphis drive-ins, and theaters in others cities and states). The name Malco, which now blazes brightly on each of the company's theaters, came from Lightman's initials. Malco theaters are still flourishing across the South, and the company is in its fourth generation as a Lightman-family-owned business.

Photograph courtesy Malco Inc.

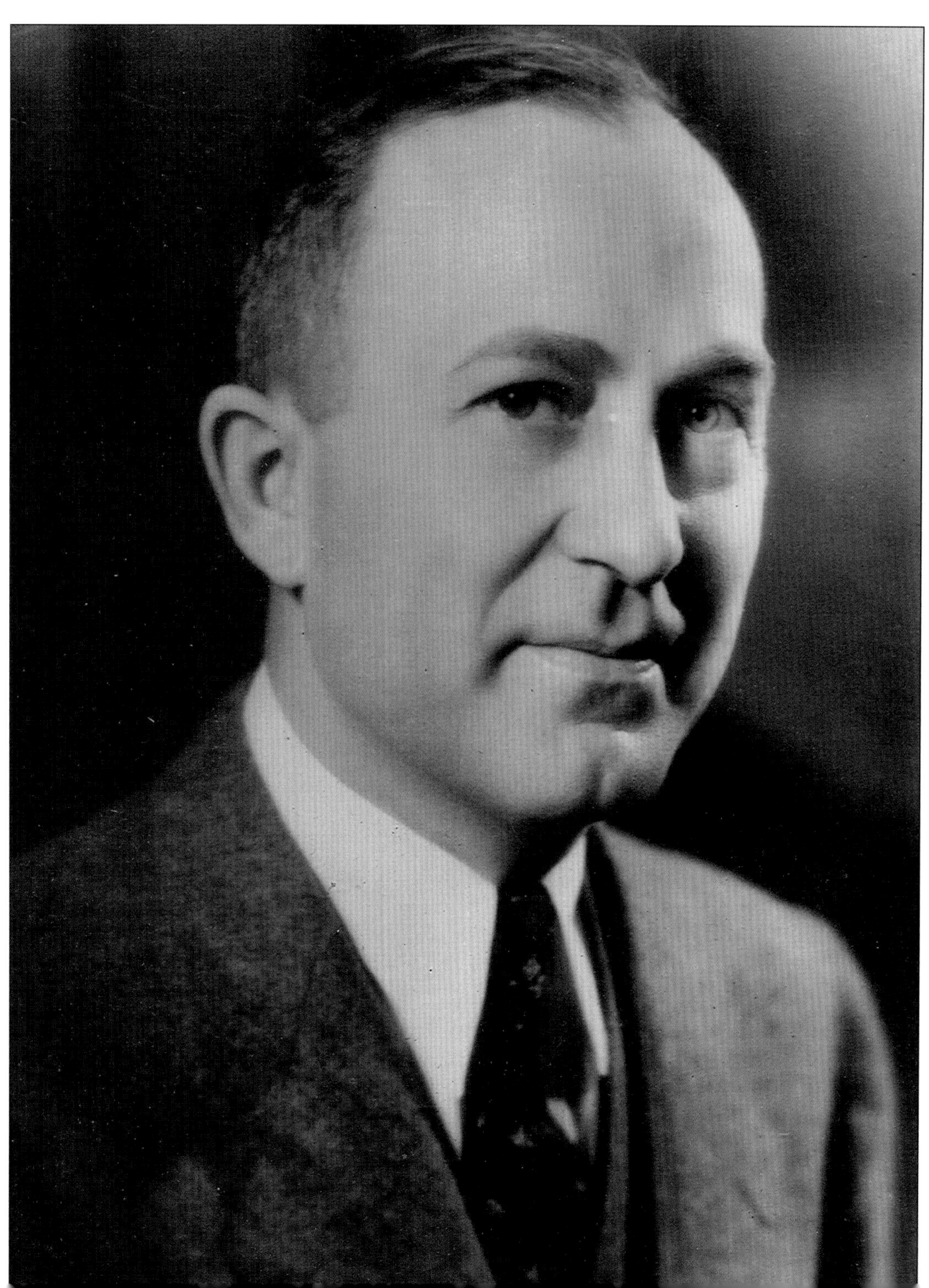

RON TERRY

BANKER

A native Memphian and graduate of public schools and the University of Memphis, Ron Terry started at First Tennessee's predecessor, First National Bank, in 1957 after serving as an officer in the Navy. Under his 20-year leadership, First Tennessee became the state's largest bank holding company. Shortly after Terry retired, the Comptroller of the Currency called First Tennessee one of the best-run banks in the country. Terry held national leadership positions in banking, including chairing an American Bankers Association committee that was a major force in developing legislation that reshaped the nation's financial services industry.

Terry was also one of Memphis' most influential civic leaders. He was founding president of the Beale Street Historic Foundation that protected and initiated redevelopment of that historic landmark. He chaired the 1981 Memphis Job Conference that set the agenda for a decade of the city's growth. He played the key role in providing capital to resurrect the Peabody Hotel, which sparked redevelopment of downtown Memphis. He created the First Tennessee Heritage Collection, First Tennessee's major collection of art by and about Tennesseans. And he initiated, personally financed and led the movement that founded the Shelby Farms Conservancy, which protects and develops the park.

Photograph courtesy of First Tennessee

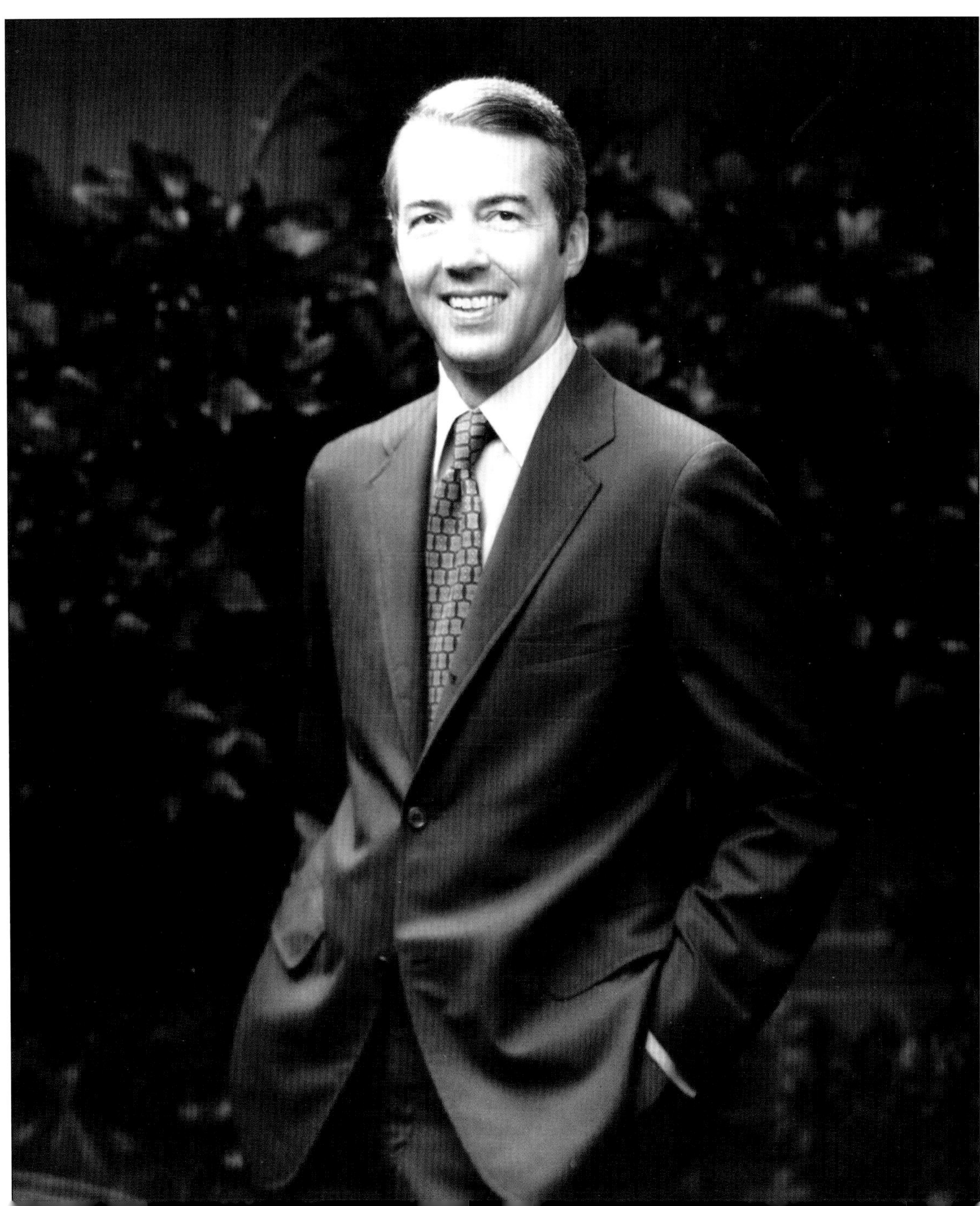

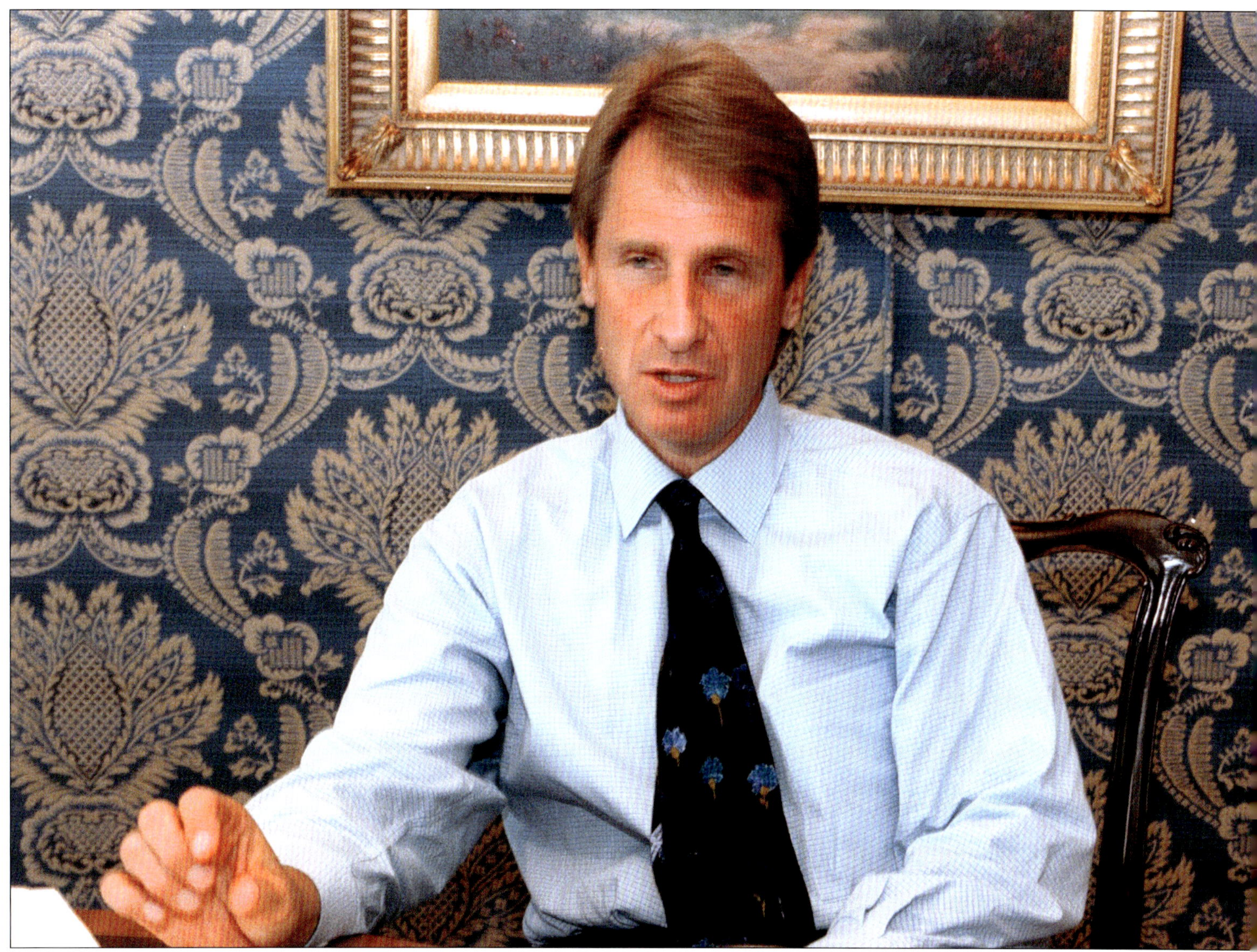

BRAD MARTIN

RETAILER, AUTHOR

The youngest person ever elected to the Tennessee General Assembly is now the Chairman of Saks, Inc. A graduate of the University of Memphis (where he was president of the student body), Brad Martin was elected to the General Assembly just two days after his 21st birthday. He served five terms as a member of the Tennessee House of Representatives, and in 1984 was the principal investor of a group acquiring Proffitt's, Inc. (the successor company of Saks). He served as the Chairman and CEO of Saks from 1989-2006, and continues to serve as the Chairman.

Now dividing his time between Memphis and the island of Grenada, Martin recently published a children's book, *Myles' Pesky Friends*, based on a story he used to tell his sons at night.

Photograph by Getty Images/Frances M. Roberts

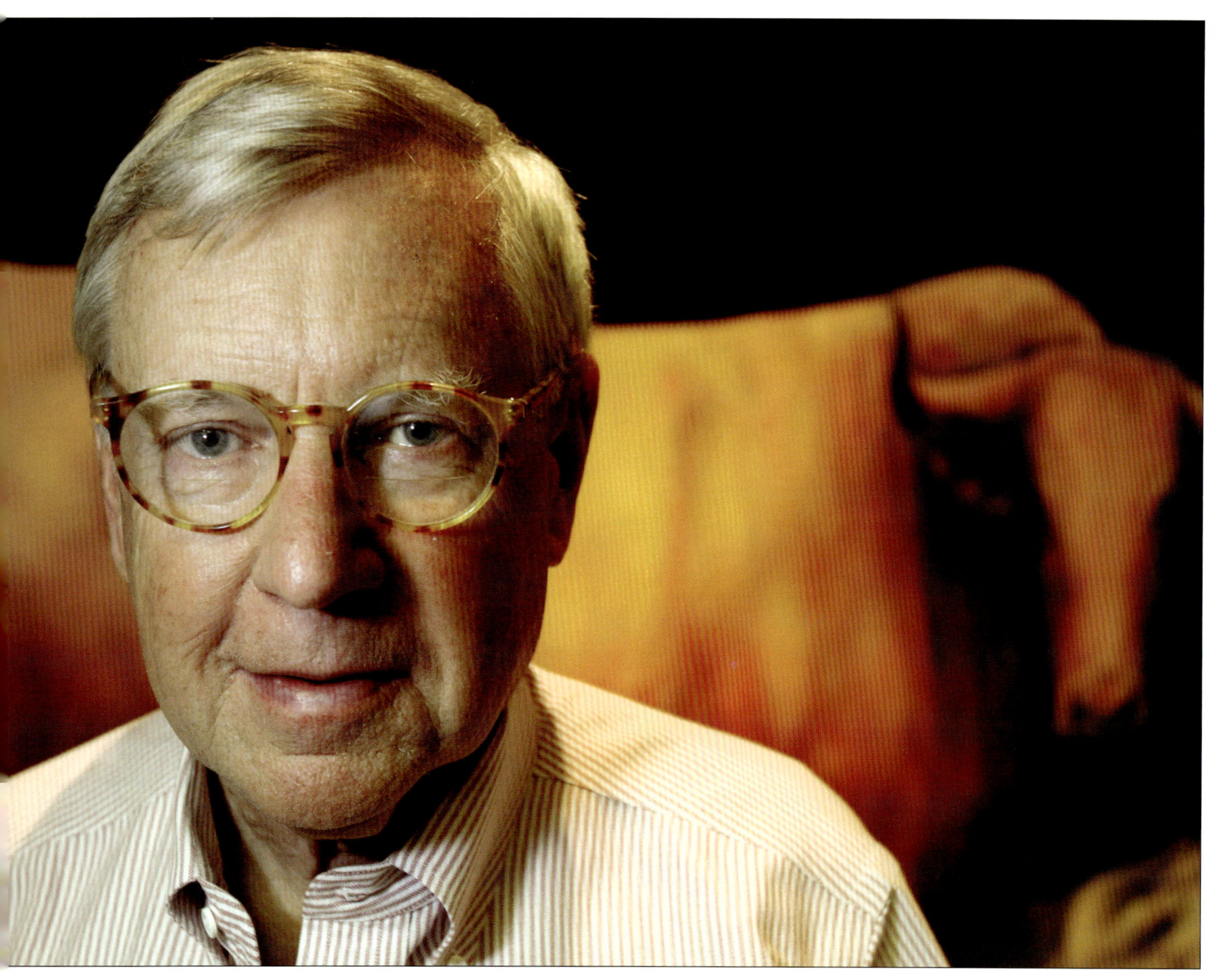

CHARLIE MCVEAN

TRADER,RESEARCHER,EDUCATOR

Model trains are prominently displayed everywhere in the East Memphis headquarters of McVean Trading and Investments. And much like a locomotive, the firm's leader, Charles McVean, chugs ahead with ideas and visions and lets very little stop him. Graduating from Vanderbilt University with honors in 1965, McVean went on to work for Cook Industries in Memphis, the Louis Dreyfus Corporation of New York, and Refco Inc. in Chicago before founding his own trading company in 1986. The firm trades in livestock and meats, grains and oilseeds, and conducts research in global macroeconomics.

But for all of his far-reaching interests in Beijing, Osaka and Geneva, McVean is decidedly and determinedly locally minded. He began the tutoring initiative aimed at 7th-12th graders, Peer Power Foundation, in 2004 "to prepare socioeconomically challenged youth to be professional, productive, and competitive contributors to our society." The son of a school teacher, his nonprofit organization is focused heavily on his alma mater, East High School.

In addition, McVean has funded the development of a human/electric hybrid bicycle, the Aerobic Cruiser, and headquartered the dealership along the Shelby Farms Greenline in an effort to promote personal health and a greener method of commuting. The cycle is billed as "The World's Most Sophisticated Electric Bicycle." As a direct result of this interest in pedestrian-friendly right of ways, he is intensely behind the reopening of the Harahan Bridge bike and walking path across the Mississippi River.

We hear every day "think globally, act locally." Charles McVean is an example of a Memphian who chooses to act tenaciously at both levels.

ALLEN MORGAN, JR.

CHAIRMAN EMERITUS, MORGAN KEEGAN & COMPANY, INC.

In 1969, at the age of 27, Memphis native Allen Morgan, Jr. founded Morgan Keegan & Company, Inc., a regional New York Stock Exchange member firm. The firm grew from one office and $500,000 in capital to its current size of over 300 offices in 19 states and a capital base of more than $900 million.

In April 2001, Morgan Keegan was acquired by Regions Financial Corporation, for approximately $800 million in stock and cash.

In 1994, Mr. Morgan was named Entrepreneur of the Year by the Society of Entrepreneurs in Memphis. In 1995, *Financial World* magazine honored him as one of three outstanding CEOs in the securities industry. He is also a past board member of two publicly traded companies, Catherine's Stores and Concord EFS.

Mr. Morgan has served on the boards of many civic and cultural organizations, including the Public Building Authority of Memphis and Shelby County, the State of Tennessee Building Finance Committee, the City of Memphis Mud Island Park Board, Methodist Hospitals, the Memphis Community Foundation, Trezevant Manor, Allen Morgan Health Center and St. Andrew's School.

He currently serves on the board of the University of North Carolina at Chapel Hill Foundation, Dixon Gallery & Gardens, and the Opera Memphis Foundation.

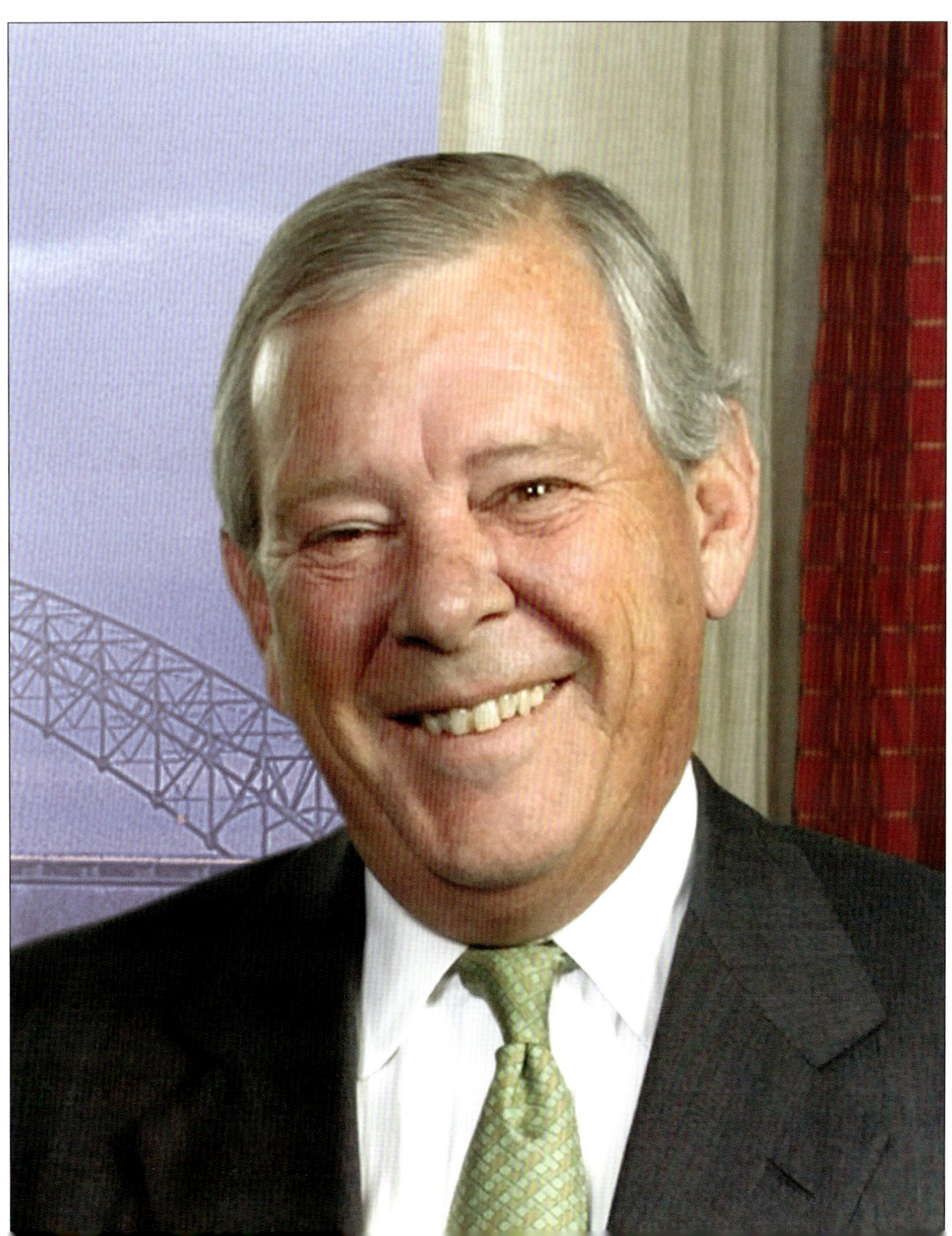

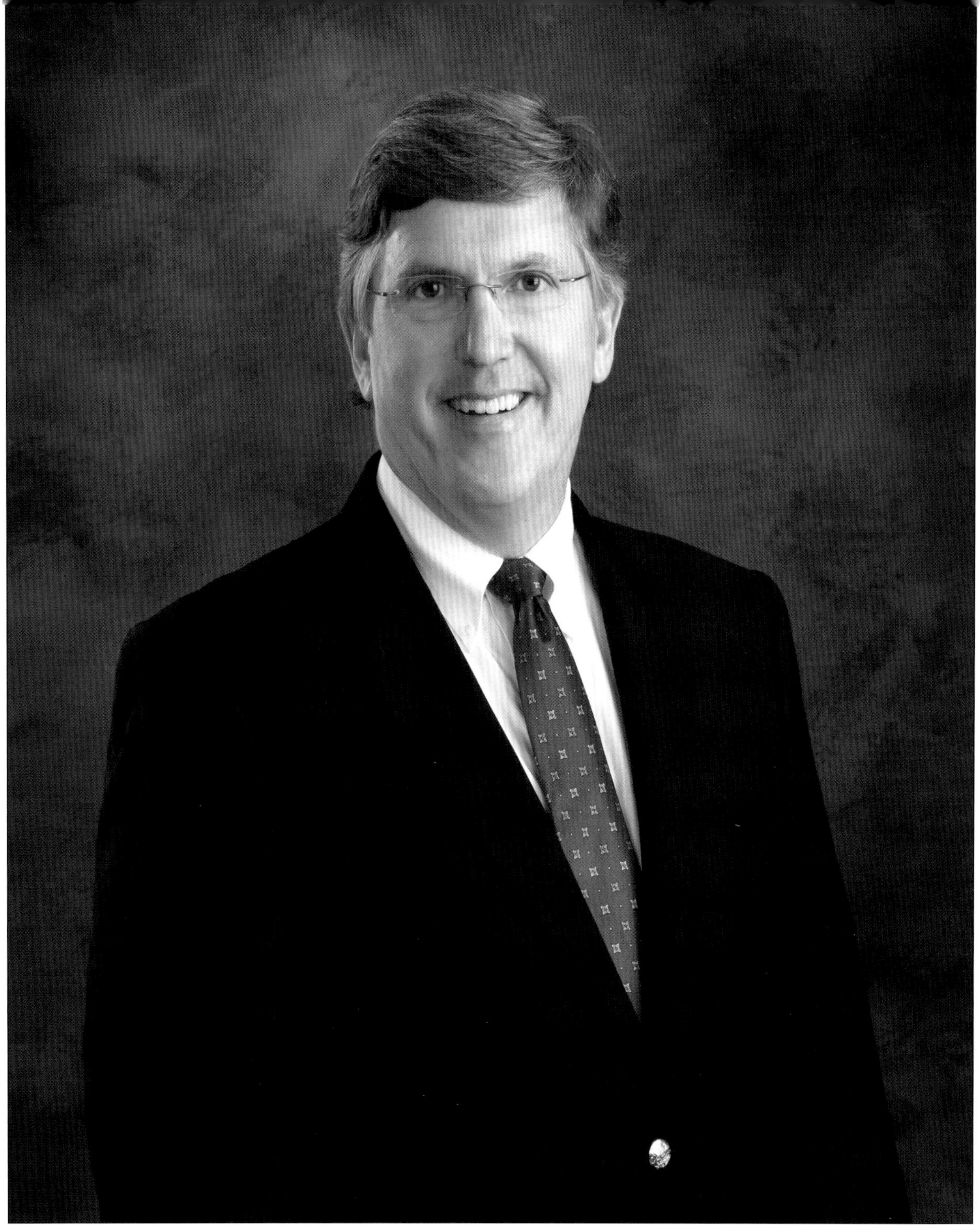

JAY B. MYERS

INTERACTIVE ENTREPRENEUR

Jay B. Myers is the Founder/CEO of Interactive Solutions, Inc.— a Memphis-based firm that specializes in video conferencing, distance learning, telemedicine and audio-visual sales and support.

Myers started ISI in 1996 and in the past 15 years has built it into an $18 million company with 61 employees and offices throughout the south. Interactive Solutions has been named to *INC* magazine's list of the fastest-growing private companies in the United States five times in the past decade. Myers and his company were also recently featured in *The Wall Street Journal*.

The company was named the *Memphis Business Journal's* Small Business of the Year in 2001. In 2003, it was the first recipient of the Kemmons Wilson Emerging Business Award.

Myers' book *Keep Swinging: An Entrepreneur's Story of Overcoming Adversity and Achieving Small Business Success* won the 2010 Ethan Award for entrepreneurial authors.

In 2011, Myers was inducted into the Christian Brothers High School Hall of Fame.

GAYLE ROSE

ENTREPRENEUR

The founder and CEO of Electronic Vaulting Services, Gayle Rose has made her mark in the business world. Rose's company is an industry leader in cloud back-up and recovery technology. She was the first female CEO to be featured on the cover of *Business Solutions* magazine. In 2005, she was named one of Tennessee's 100 Most Powerful People by *Business Tennessee* magazine. She is the co-founder of the Women's Foundation for a Greater Memphis, and in 2008, she was named Humanitarian of the Year by Diversity Memphis.

Photograph courtesy EVS

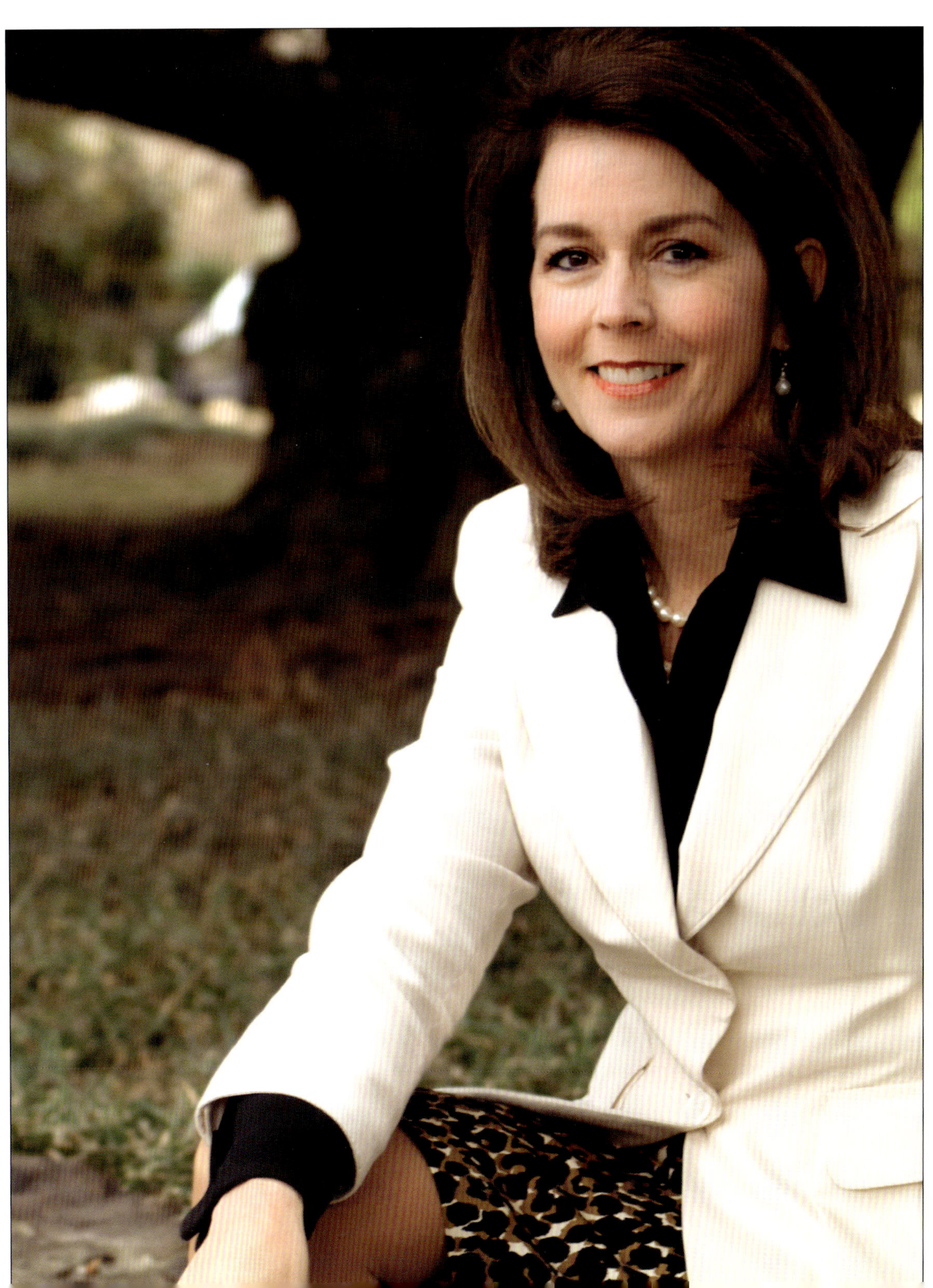

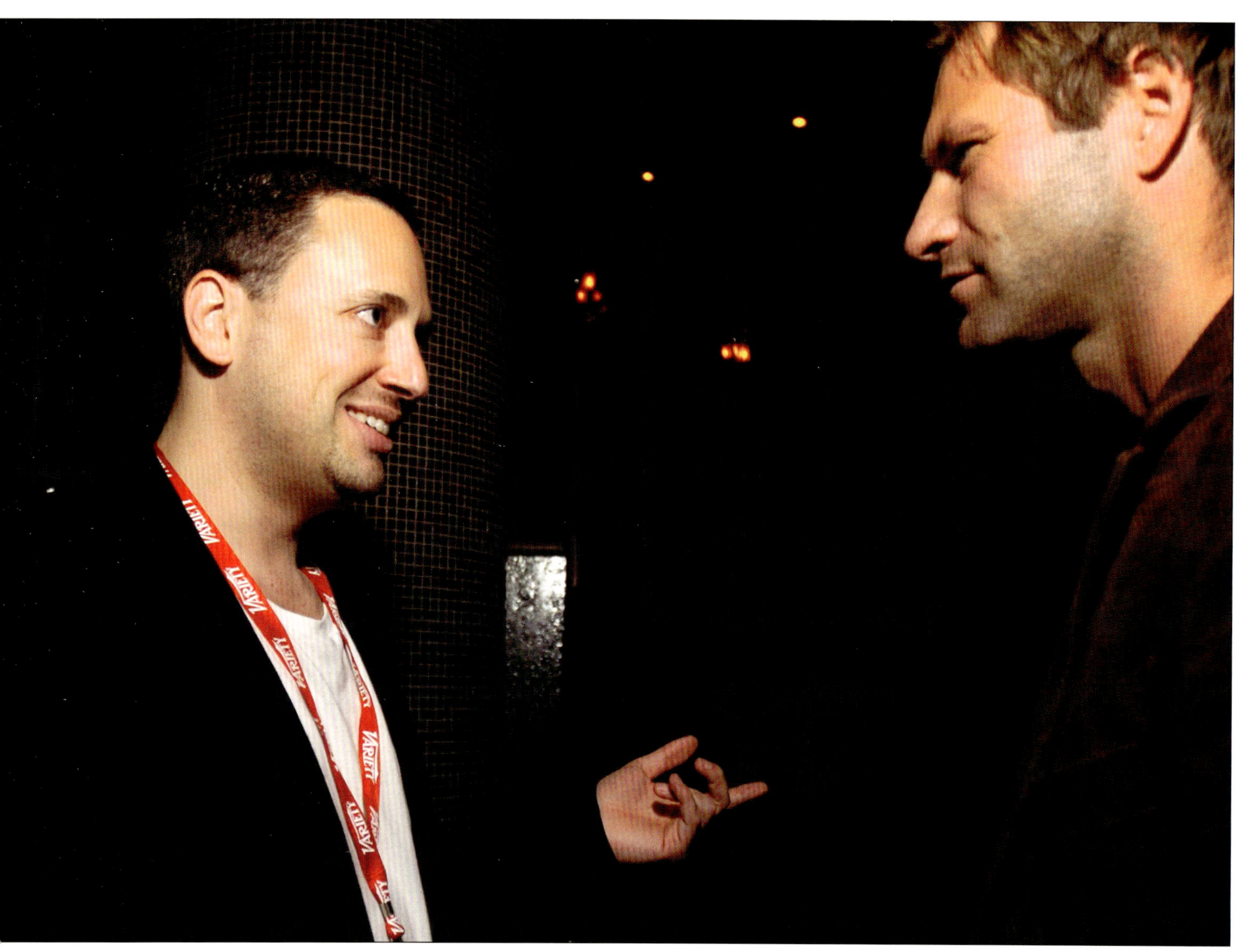

DAVID O. SACKS

PRODUCER

Having worked as the Chief Operating Officer of PayPal, Memphis-raised David O. Sacks left to fill his own dreams. In 2003, he formed Room 9 Entertainment, through which he co-produced and financed the critially acclaimed *Thank You For Smoking* with fellow Memphian Daniel Brunt. He is the founder of Geni.com — the world family tree — and Yammer.com, "the enterprise social network."

Photo: Producer David O. Sacks, left, talks to actor Aaron Eckhart at *Variety*'s Ten Producers to Watch Party/Getty

JOSEPH REEVES "PITT" HYDE

ENTREPRENEUR, PHILANTHROPIST, CIVIC LEADER

Joseph Reeves "Pitt" Hyde has innovation and entrepreneurship in his blood. His grandfather founded Malone & Hyde, which Pitt took over at the age of 26 due to his father's ill health. Under his guidance, the company became the third largest wholesale grocery retailer in the country. Looking for new opportunities, Hyde founded Auto Shack (which would later become AutoZone) in 1979. By always placing customer service first, AutoZone has become a Fortune 500 company and Hyde became the first after-market retailer to be inducted into the Automotive Hall of Fame in 2004.

Hyde has changed the face of Memphis sports. He was instrumental in bringing the Memphis Grizzlies from Vancouver. He supported the Memphis Redbirds at AutoZone Park. And AutoZone sponsors the Liberty Bowl.

He has been a wholehearted supporter of the National Civil Rights Museum, Ballet Memphis and the Memphis Brooks Museum of Art.

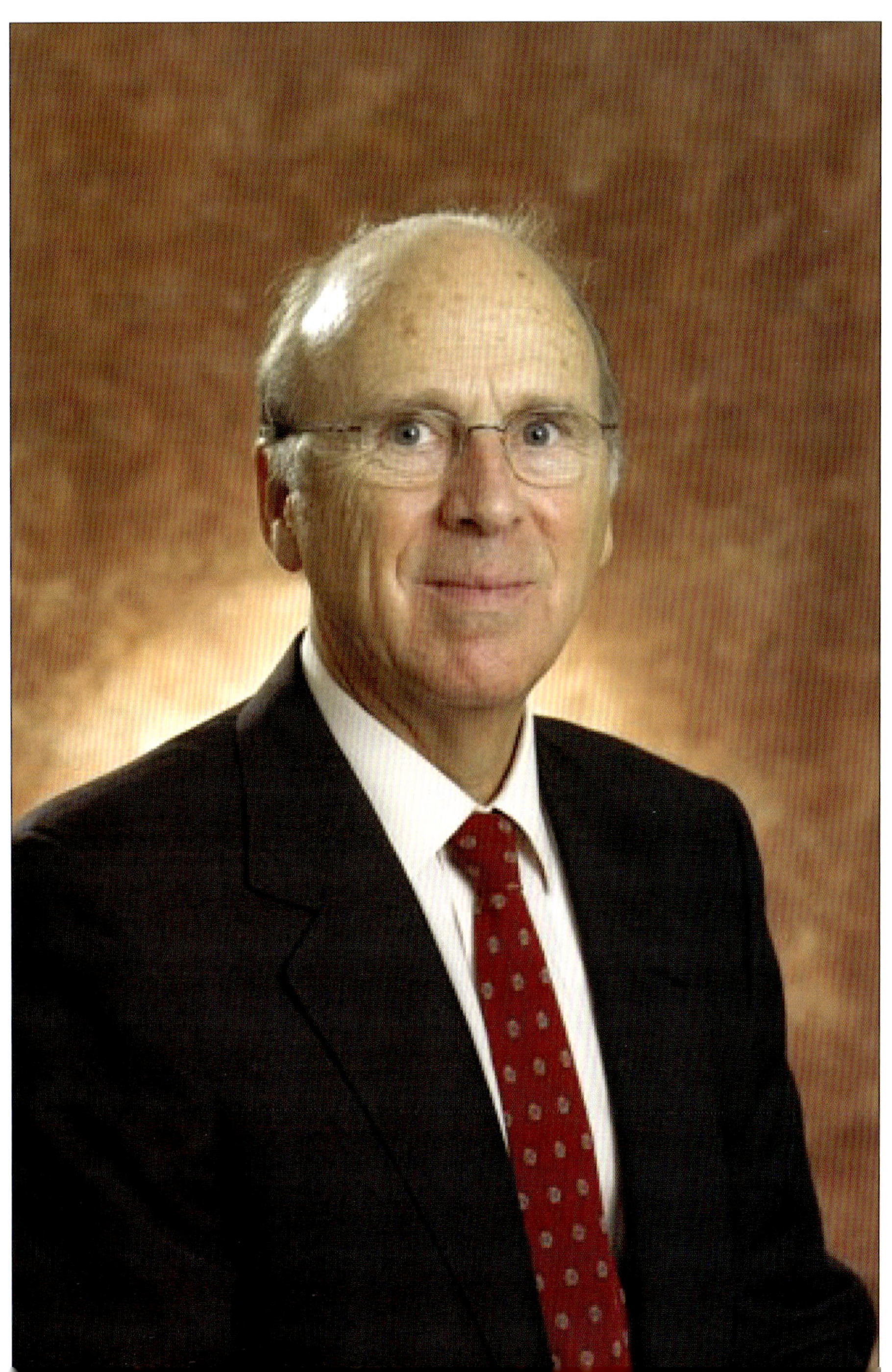

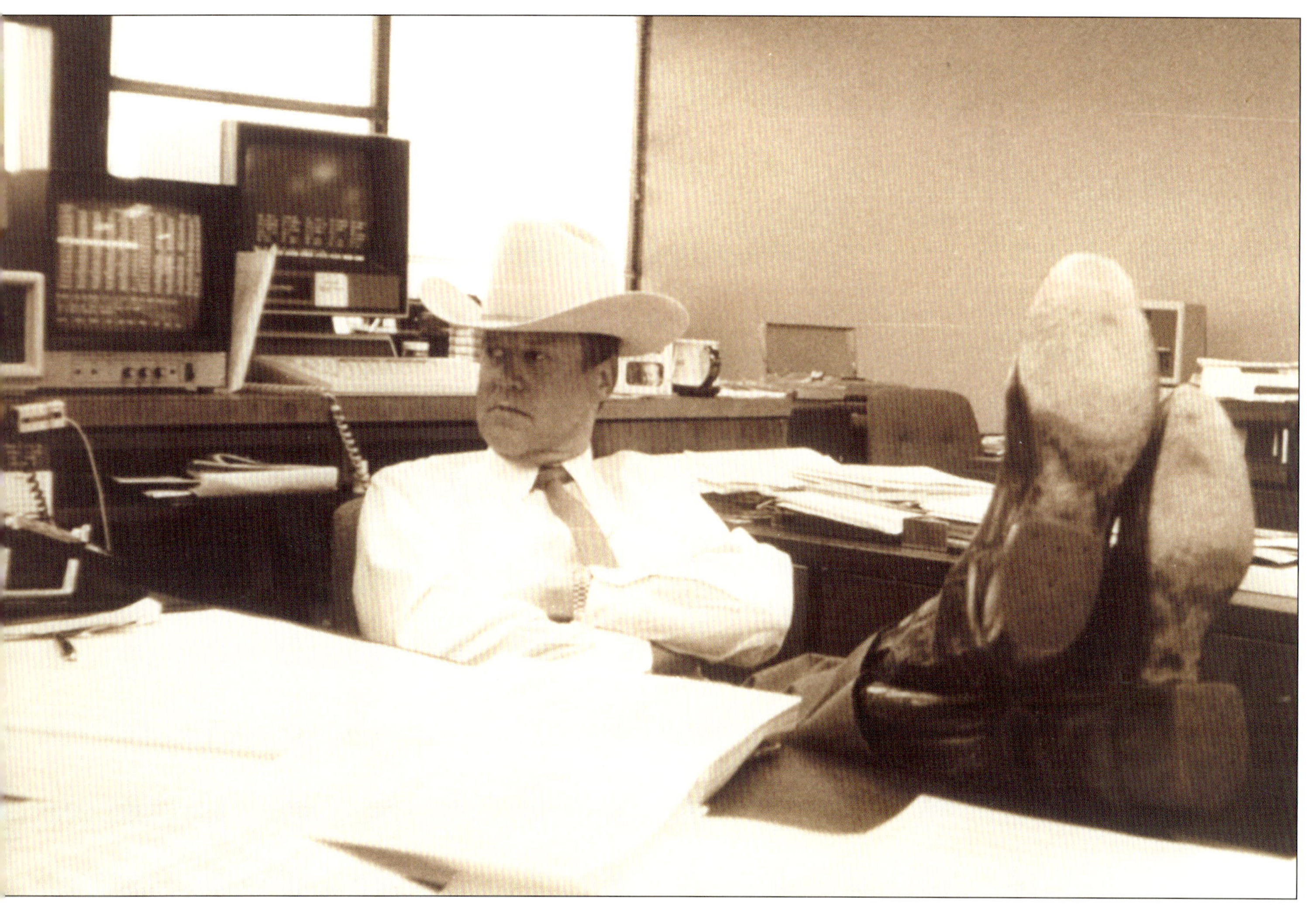

WILLARD SPARKS

FARMER

"Look beyond what everyone else knows."
Willard Sparks

Willard Sparks was a commodities man, an entrepreneur, an investor, a cattle rancher, a market mover and an economist. He called himself a farmer, and believed it. Sparks had horse sense by the bushel. He was right — a lot. A commodities empire consisting of 50 companies is not built on intuition alone. Sparks was a firm believer in higher, and enthusiastic, education.

Born in Dribble, Oklahoma, Sparks went to Oklahoma State and got a doctorate in agricultural economics from Michigan State in 1961. Two years later the man called "eight track" for his ability to multi-task was in Memphis as director of research and trading for Cook Industries. In the seventies, Sparks worked on a number of the first massive grain sales to the Soviet Union. In 1977, he founded Sparks Commodities. Sparks Companies followed. It consisted of dozens of companies, including a macadamia nut farm in Hawaii and Cattleco Inc., one of the largest cattle feed operations in the country.

Never forgetting that he was a farmer, or the power of education, Sparks created scholarships for agricultural students — as well as being primary donor and fundraiser for the Willard Sparks Beef Research Center. He died in 2005. Sparks was survived by his wife Rita and 40 years of Oklahoma State graduates.

Photograph courtesy Roger Sparks • **Story** by Richard Murff

CHARLIE VERGOS

FATHER OF THE DRY RIB & THE RENDEZVOUS

Both gruff and gregarious, larger than life with a heart larger than that, Charlie Vergos started cooking ribs in 1948 that were so good, you'd walk through an alley, down a set of steep basement stairs and wade through more mismatched memorabilia than a mile-square flea market just to tear into them. People from all over the world – from presidents to rock stars, the most famous to the most infamous – have been doing just that since then, and the experience was and is unique enough to define something called "the dry rib." Just as the wet and dry debate will continue, so will The Rendezvous, still in the basement off the alley, and still run by the Vergos family. After all, as their slogan states, "Not since Adam has a rib been this famous."

Photograph courtesy The Rendezvous • **Story** by Dan Conaway

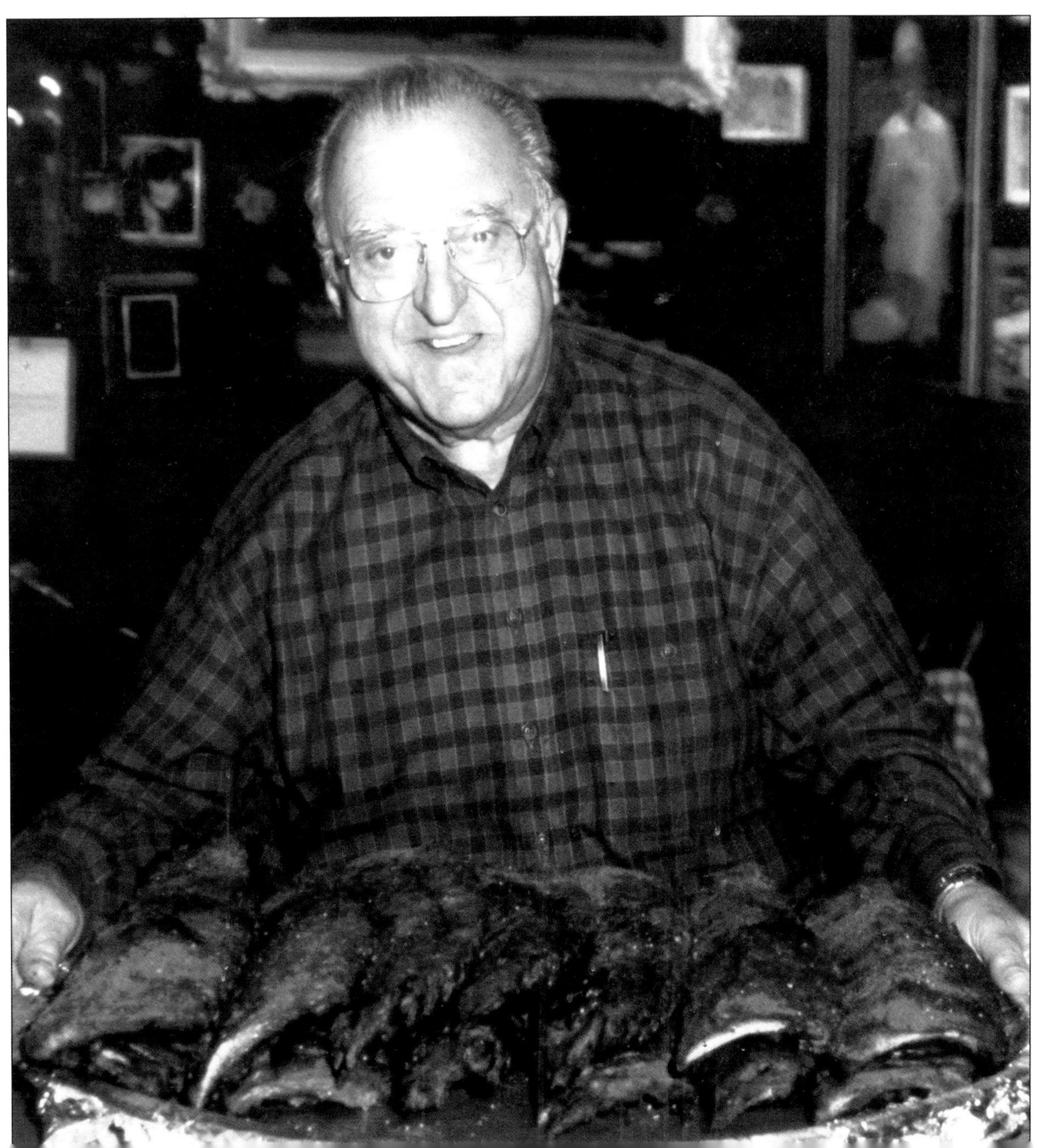

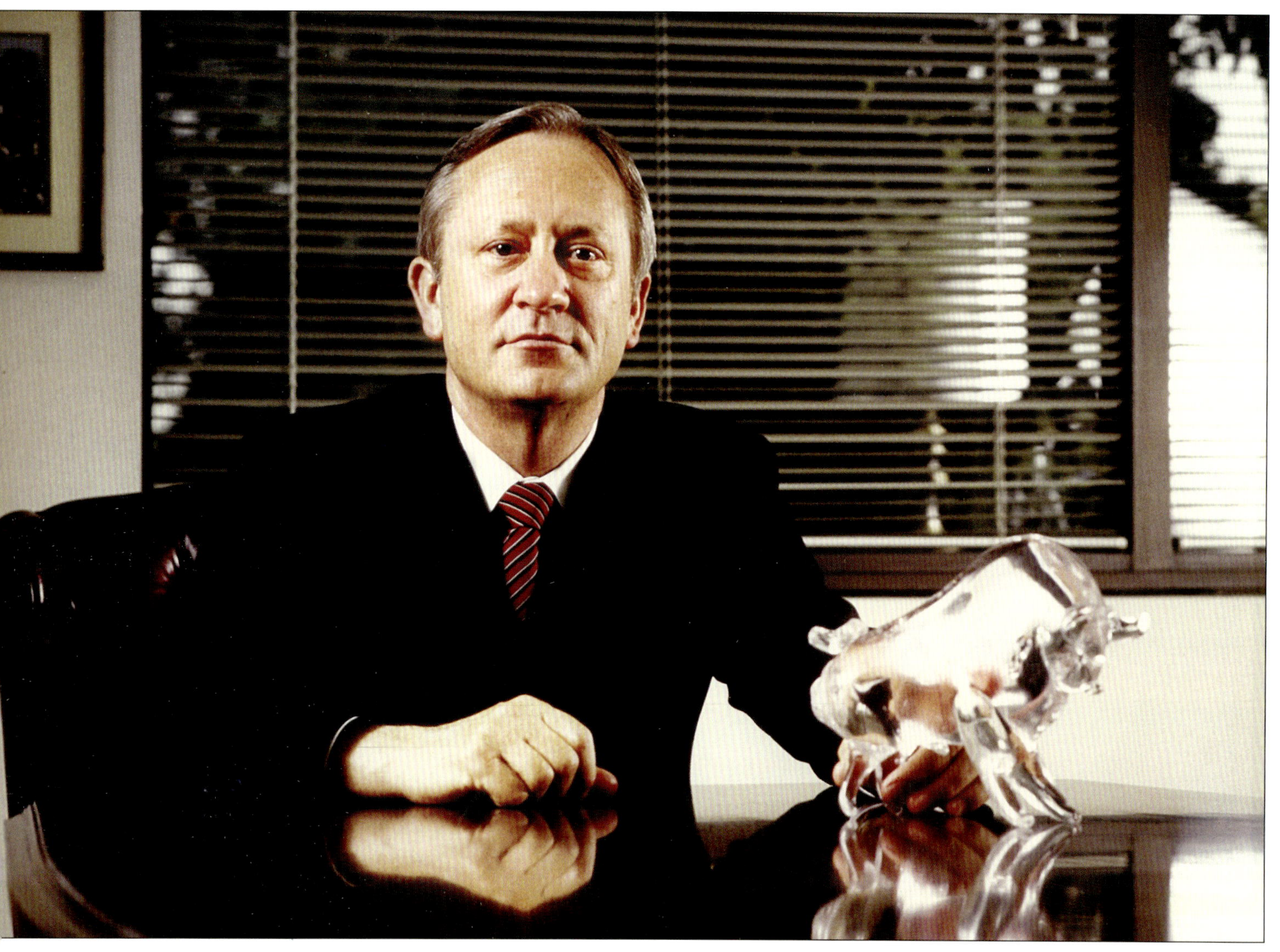

DUNCAN WILLIAMS

ENTREPRENUER, FINANCIER

"Many in the bond business got their start with Williams."

Memphis Press-Scimitar

Atlas Duncan Williams came from Bolivar, Tennessee to Memphis via Korea. After his military service, Williams joined the First National Bank of Memphis (now First Tennessee). Eventually, he succeeded Early Mitchell as chief of the bond division. After twelve years with the bank, Williams struck out on his own. In 1969, with six employees, he founded Duncan Williams, Inc. In that year, Memphis had grown to be the third-largest bond market in the United States. And Williams provided leadership for his company — and the industry — by sitting on the NASD's District Business Conduct Committee and its Nominating Committee (which he chaired in 1984).

The firm is now headed by his son, Duncan F. Williams. Under his leadership, the firm has taken the national stage, growing from 49 to 169 employees and opening offices in New York, Chicago, Jersey City, Houston, Charlotte, Atlanta, Cleveland, San Francisco, Los Angeles, Philadelphia, Nashville, Knoxville and Jackson (Mississippi).

Photo courtesy Duncan Williams

CHARLES WURTZBURGER

WRAPPER

"The Entrepreneur is the lifeblood, or fuel, in the marketplace."
Charles Wurtzburger

In its heyday, Cleo Wrap made enough wrapping paper, ribbons and bows to circle the earth 15 times. Founded in 1952 by Charles L. Wurtzburger and his father, Memphis Converting Company was renamed Cleo Wrap (after Cleopatra) in 1962. In the 25 years that Wurtzburger served as the company's president, it grew to be the largest manufacturer of wrapping paper in the country, and was once the largest employer in Memphis. Since his retirement Wurtzburger has been an active supporter of the Dixon Gallery & Gardens, The Hugo Dixon Foundation and a charter member of the Economics Club of Memphis. The title of his autobiography is aptly titled, *'S Wonderful*.

Photo by Commercial Appeal

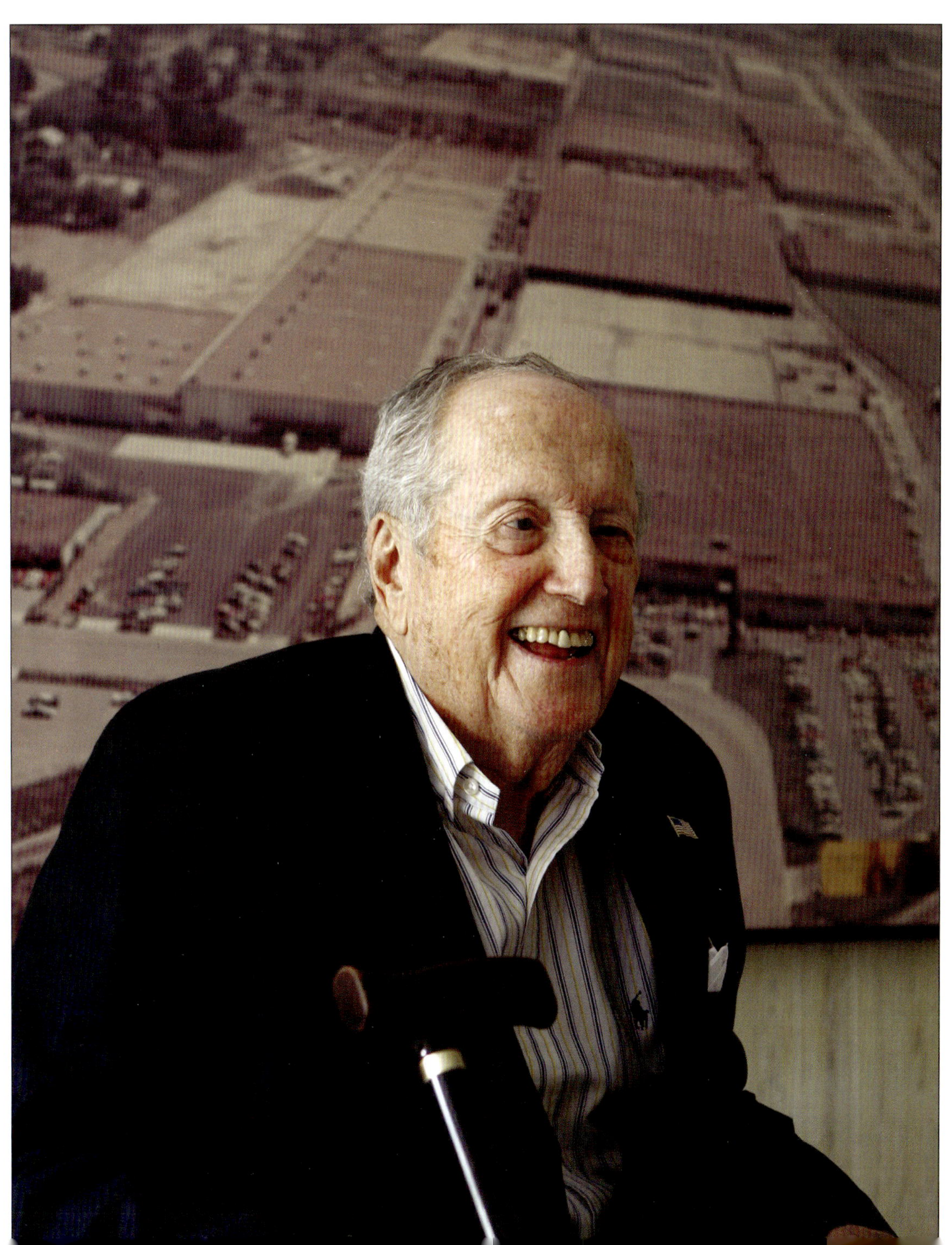

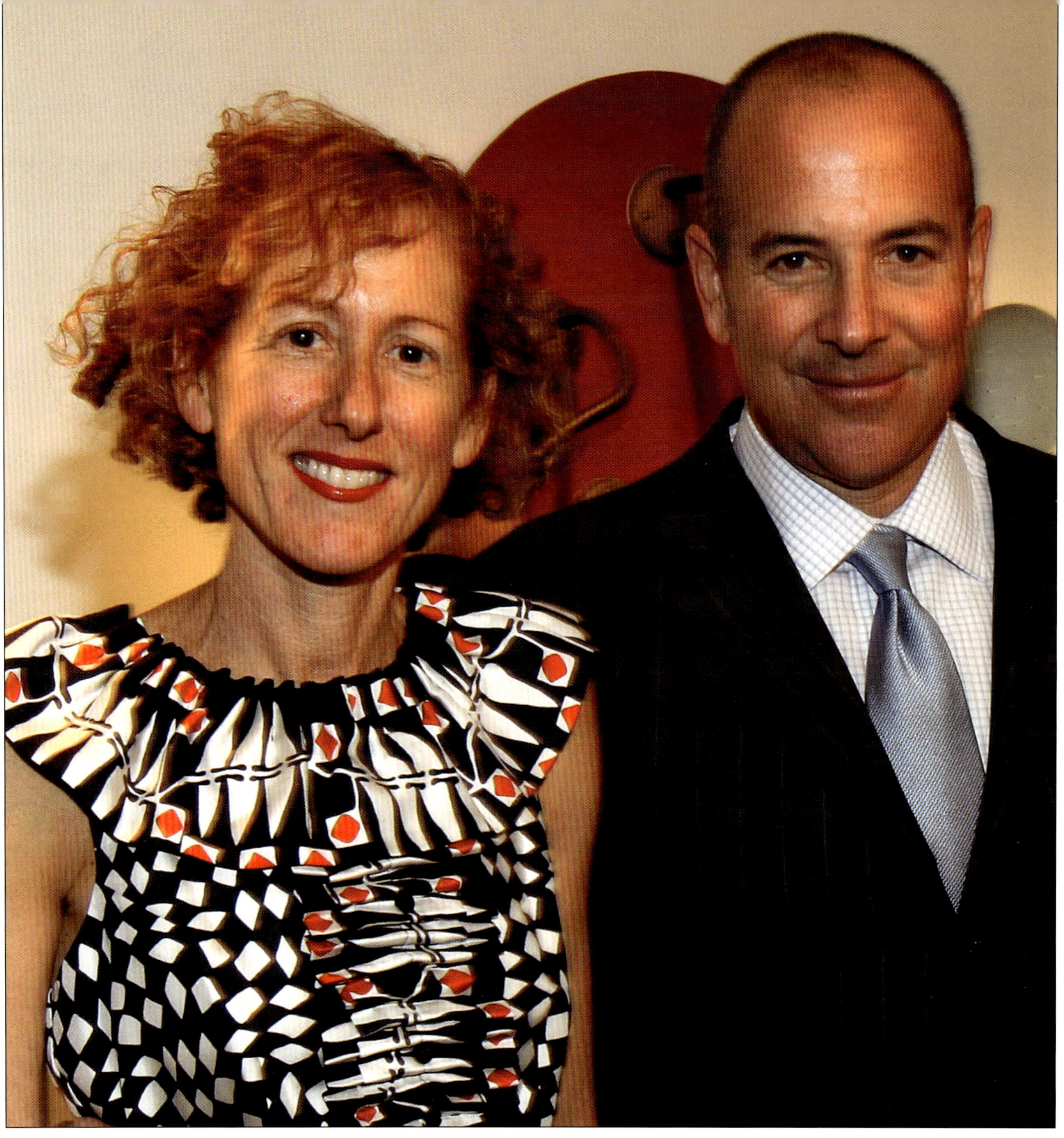

WENDY WURTZBURGER

ANTHROPOLOG(IE)IST

"I love the contrast of old and new, grand and rustic, formal and informal."

Wendy Wurtzburger

Like her father's company – Cleo Wrap – Wendy Wurtzburger started in Memphis and went global. She travels from Paris to Thailand to India for colors and items that delight not only her eye, but those of women around the world. Wurtzburger started as a retail buyer for department stores before joining Urban Outfitters in 1998. Now Co-President of the company's Anthropologie brand, Wurtzburger still seeks inspiration for the brand's "global flea market aesthetic."

Photo: Memphis native and Anthropologie Co-President, Wendy Wurtzburger, and CEO of Urban Outfitters Glen Senk/Getty

HUNTER HARRISON

RAILROADER

Hunter Harrison's railroad career began in 1963 when he joined the Frisco (St. Louis-San Francisco) Railroad as carman-oiler in Memphis while still attending school. He advanced through the ranks — and through many an acquistion. He was hired away by competing lines. By 1996, Harrison was President and CEO of Illinois Central. He worked until the railroad was the most efficient in North America.

He then served as VP, President and CEO of Canadian National Railway. In 2005, he authored the book, *How We Work and Why*, which chronicles how Canadian National railroaders think and operate. The book chronicles the real life stories of the people who have made it all possible.

Photo courtesy CN Railway

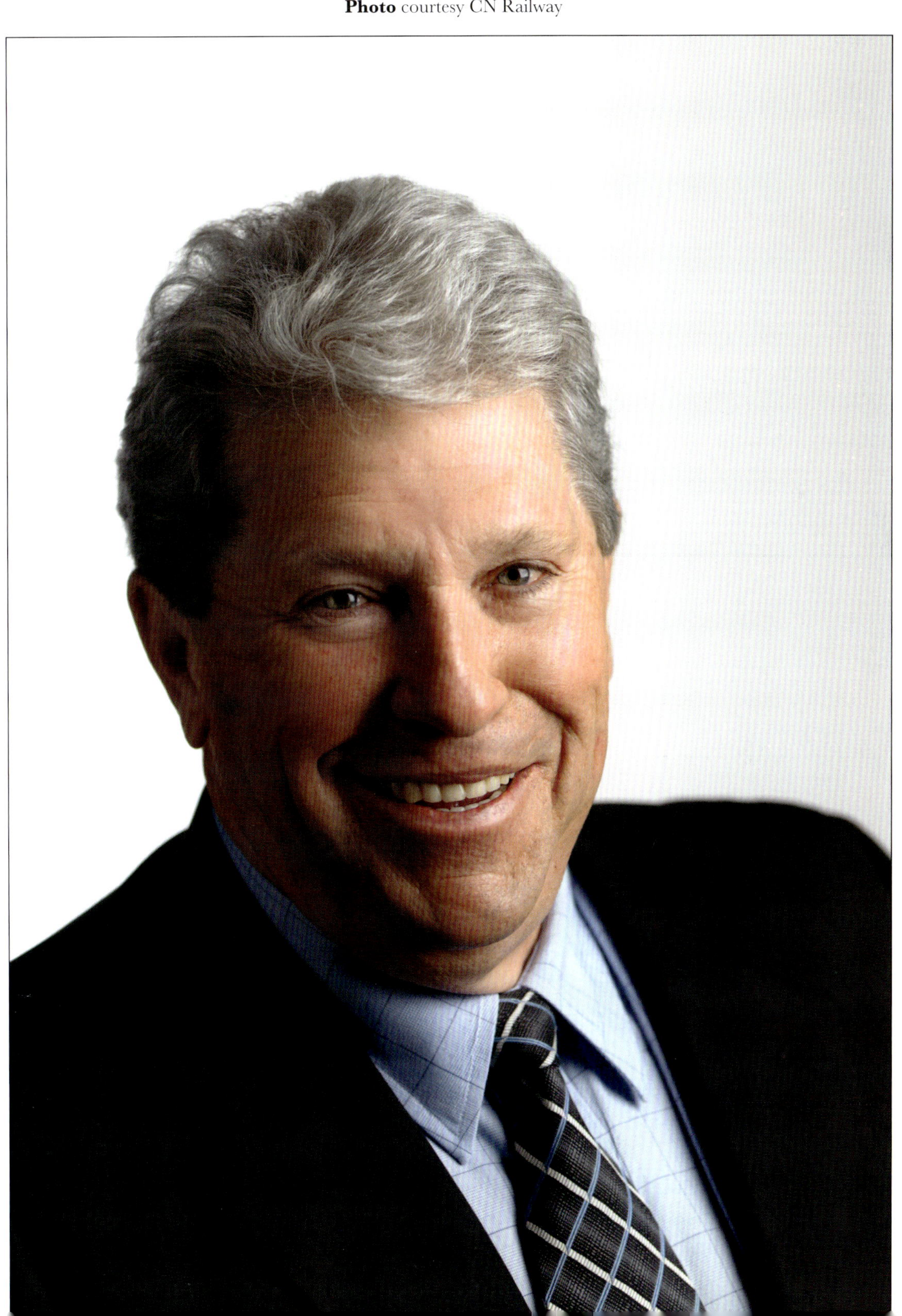

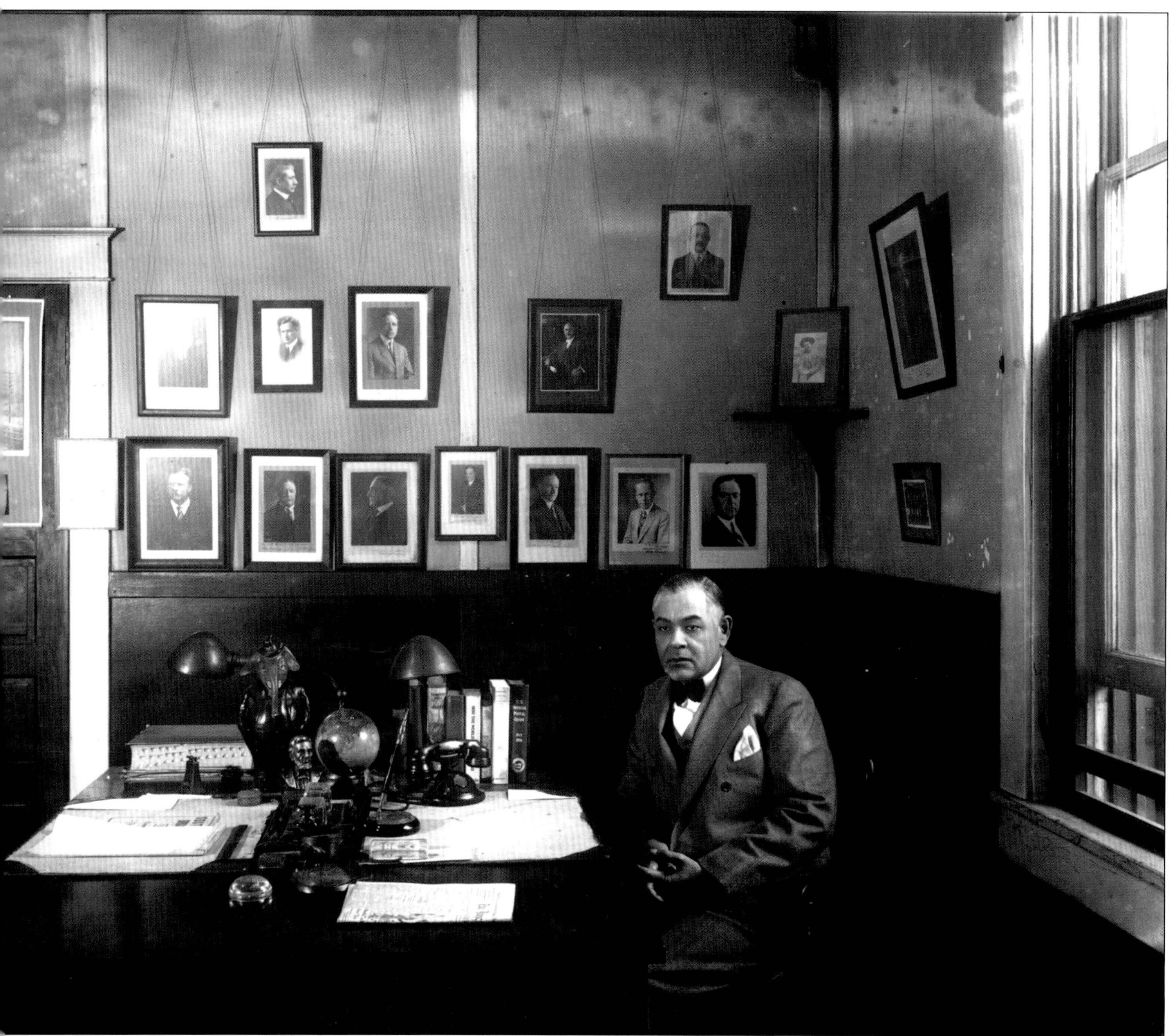

ROBERT REED CHURCH, SR.

THE SOUTH'S FIRST AFRICAN-AMERICAN MILLIONAIRE

Arriving in Memphis as a slave in 1851, Robert R. Church, Sr. would rise to regional and national prominence through the ownership of real estate, hotels and restaurants, and through his efforts to improve the lives and livelihoods of African-Americans. He would survive the yellow fever epidemics and being shot during the 1866 riots. He was the first citizen to buy a $1,000 bond to restore the city's charter after the 1878 epidemic. Starting as a saloon owner, he would become the South's first African-American millionaire, build the 2,000-seat Church Auditorium, and found a bank that would later become the largest African-American bank in the country. His son, Robert R. Church, Jr., was also an important Memphis business and civic leader.

Photograph courtesy Memphis Public Library • **Story** by Dan Conaway

Memphis Icons

Movies, Television & Stage

Music

Sports

Innovators & Visionaries

Entrepreneurs

Writers & Journalists

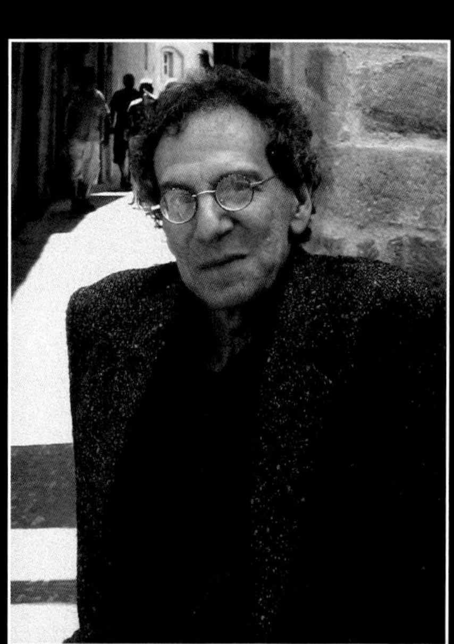

Law & Politics

Little-Known Memphians

Colorful Characters

Memphis Beauties

ALAN LIGHTMAN

PHYSICIST, ESSAYIST, NOVELIST

"If a person holds no ambitions in this world, he suffers unknowingly. If a person holds ambitions, he suffers knowingly, but very slowly."

Alan Lightman in Einstein's Dreams

Physicist, teacher, essayist and novelist, Alan Lightman was born in Memphis in 1948. His father was Richard Lightman, owner of the Malco movie theaters, and his mother, Jeanne Garretson, a dance teacher and volunteer Braille typist.

Along with classmate, Oscar-winner Kathy Bates, who remains a good friend, Alan graduated from White Station High School. He graduated magna cum laude from Princeton University in 1970, with an BA degree in physics. He earned his Ph.D. in theoretical physics from the California Institute of Technology in 1974, where he had received a National Science Foundation pre-doctoral fellowship. In his scientific work, Lightman has made fundamental contributions to the theory of astrophysical processes under extreme temperatures and densities.

In 1981 Alan began writing articles about science and publishing essays and short stories in magazines like *The New Yorker* and *Harper's*. His first novel, the universally acclaimed *Einstein's Dreams*, was published in 1994 and was an international bestseller (it was translated into more than 30 languages).

Lightman has continued to write both fiction and books about science. His 2000 novel, *The Diagnosis*, was runner-up for the National Book Award. More than two dozen independent theatrical and musical productions have been based on *Einstein's Dreams*, including a production at the University of Memphis in 2006.

In 1999, Lightman founded the Harpswell Foundation, a nonprofit organization whose mission is to empower a new generation of women leaders in Cambodia and the developing world, specifically through housing, education, and leadership training. He continues his charity work to this day, teaching part-time at MIT and publishing a new novel every few years. He has received dozens of awards for teaching and fiction writing. He has also received the Gold Medal for Humanitarian Service to Cambodia.

In 2009, Alan published his first volume of poetry, a book-length narrative in verse titled *Song of Two Worlds*. Alan Lightman said, "I have been very fortunate to have had a life in science and also a life as a writer, and I think my life as a writer will continue because I am still learning new things as a writer. But I would also like to change the world in direct ways, particularly with people who haven't had the opportunities I have."

Photograph Getty Images

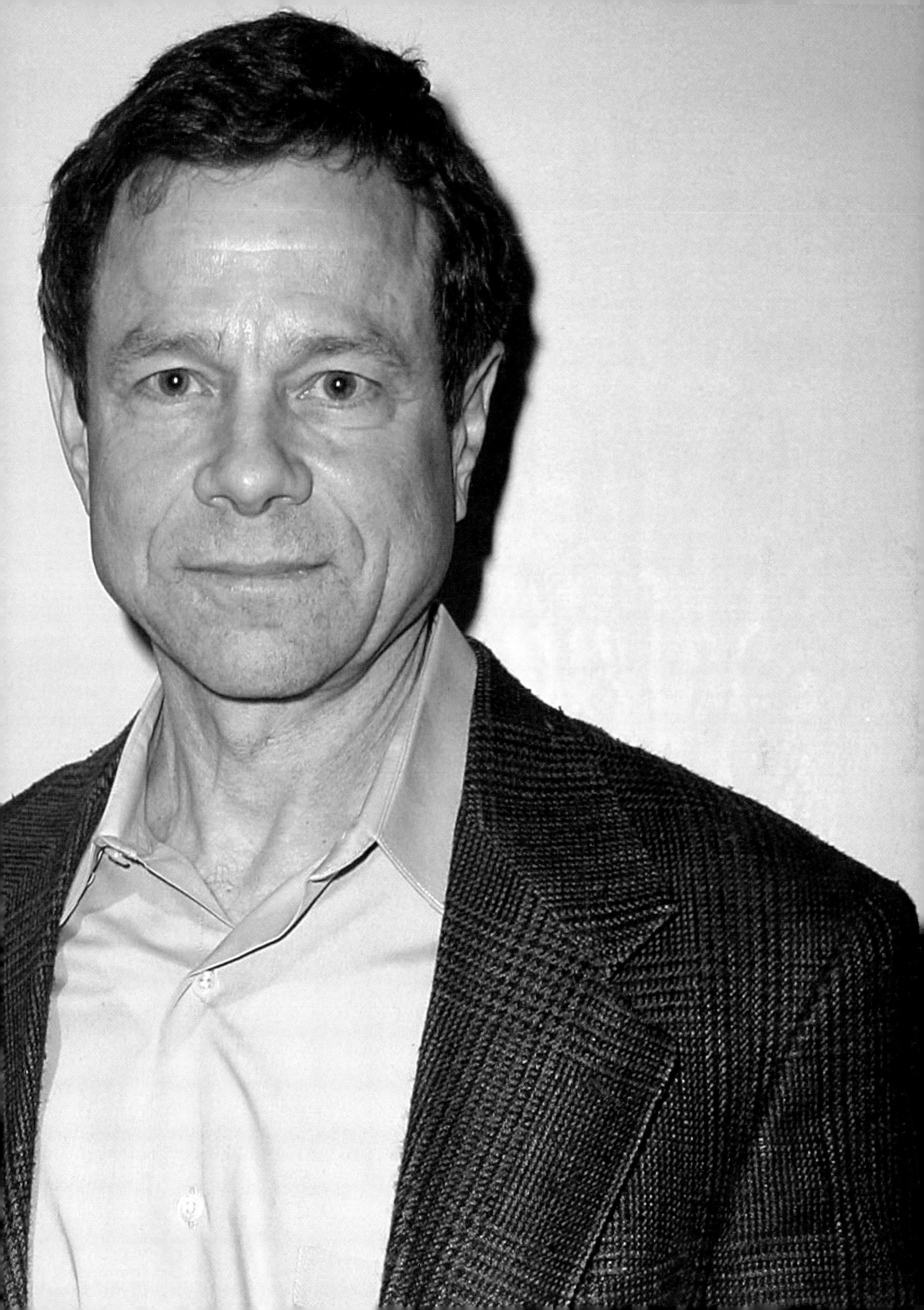

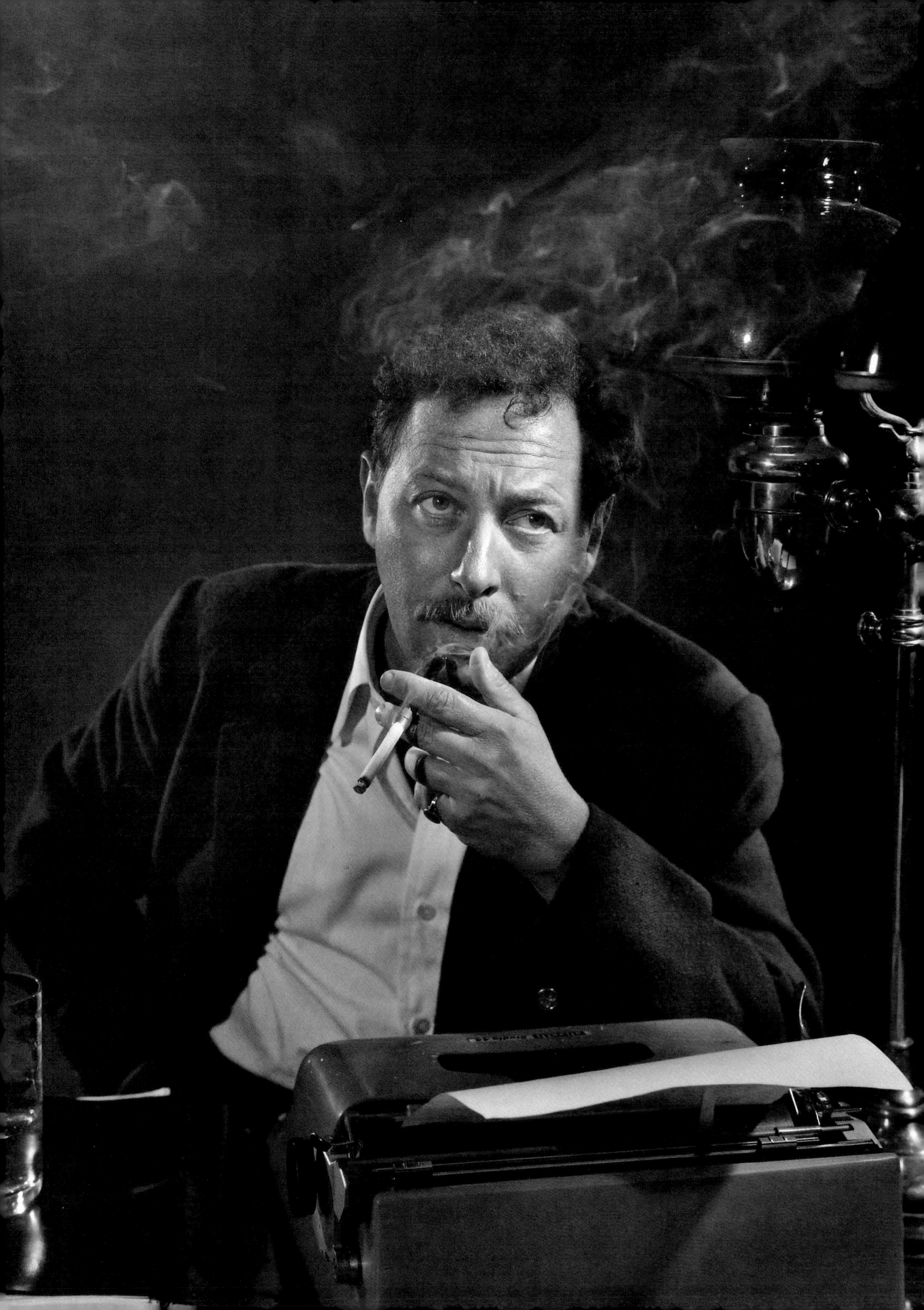

TENNESSEE WILLIAMS

PLAYWRIGHT

"You have been as brave as anyone I've known . . . ."
From Marlon Brando in a letter to Tennessee

Thomas Lanier "Tennessee" Williams III spent the summer of 1934 visiting his grandparents in Memphis, at their home on Snowden Avenue, a block from Southwestern at Memphis. In the college's library, he discovered the writings of Anton Chekhov, which enflamed him to want to write. Encouraged by a neighbor of his grandparents, Williams wrote his first script, the all but forgotten, *Cairo! Shanghai! Bombay!* It was produced by a local theater club in the backyard of a Memphis arts patron. Williams remembered it in his memoirs: "Then and there the theater and I found each other for better and for worse. I know it's the only thing that saved my life." Four years later he left Memphis for New Orleans where he could live openly as a gay man. In New Orleans, he wrote *A Streetcar Named Desire*. A 2008 movie starring Bryce Dallas Howard and Ann-Margret was made from a "lost" Tennessee Williams screenplay, *The Loss of a Teardrop Diamond*. It is set in Memphis in the 1920s.

Williams is generally regarded as the greatest playwright of the 20th Century. And it all started in Memphis.

Photograph © Yousuf Karsh

HAMPTON SIDES

AUTHOR, JOURNALIST

"Hampton Sides has long been one of the great narrative nonfiction writers of our time."
David Grann

A great deal of history is dealing with the dead, but Hampton Sides has a knack for bringing it to life. After graduating from MUS, Sides received his BA in history from Yale. A long-time journalist, Sides became an international bestseller with *Ghost Soldiers*, which told the story of the rescue of the Bataan Death March survivors and won the 2002 PEN USA award. He created the Ghost Soldiers Endowment Fund to preserve the memory of those soldiers. *Blood & Thunder* followed Kit Carson and his role in the American West. Sides' latest bestseller drew the writer back to his hometown for 2010's *Hellhound on His Trail.* Extensively using the new digital B. Venson Hughes collection, Sides brings a terrifying chapter in the city, and the country, vividly to life.

He is editor-at-large for *Outside* and his works have appeared in *National Geographic*, *The New Yorker*, *Esquire*, *Men's Journal*, and *The Washington Post.* Sides has been nominated for National Magazine Awards twice for his feature stories.

Photograph by Commercial Appeal

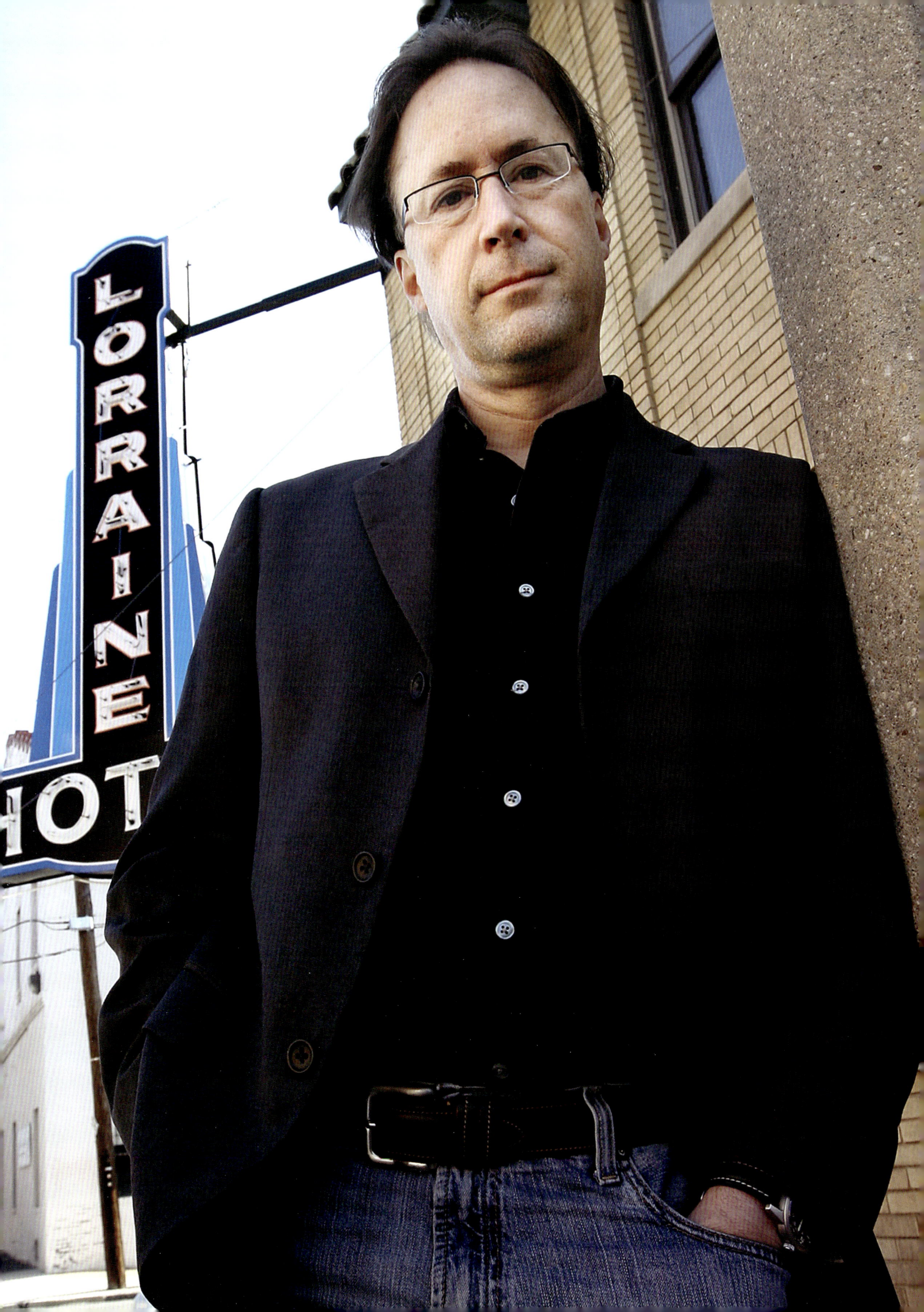
LORRAINE

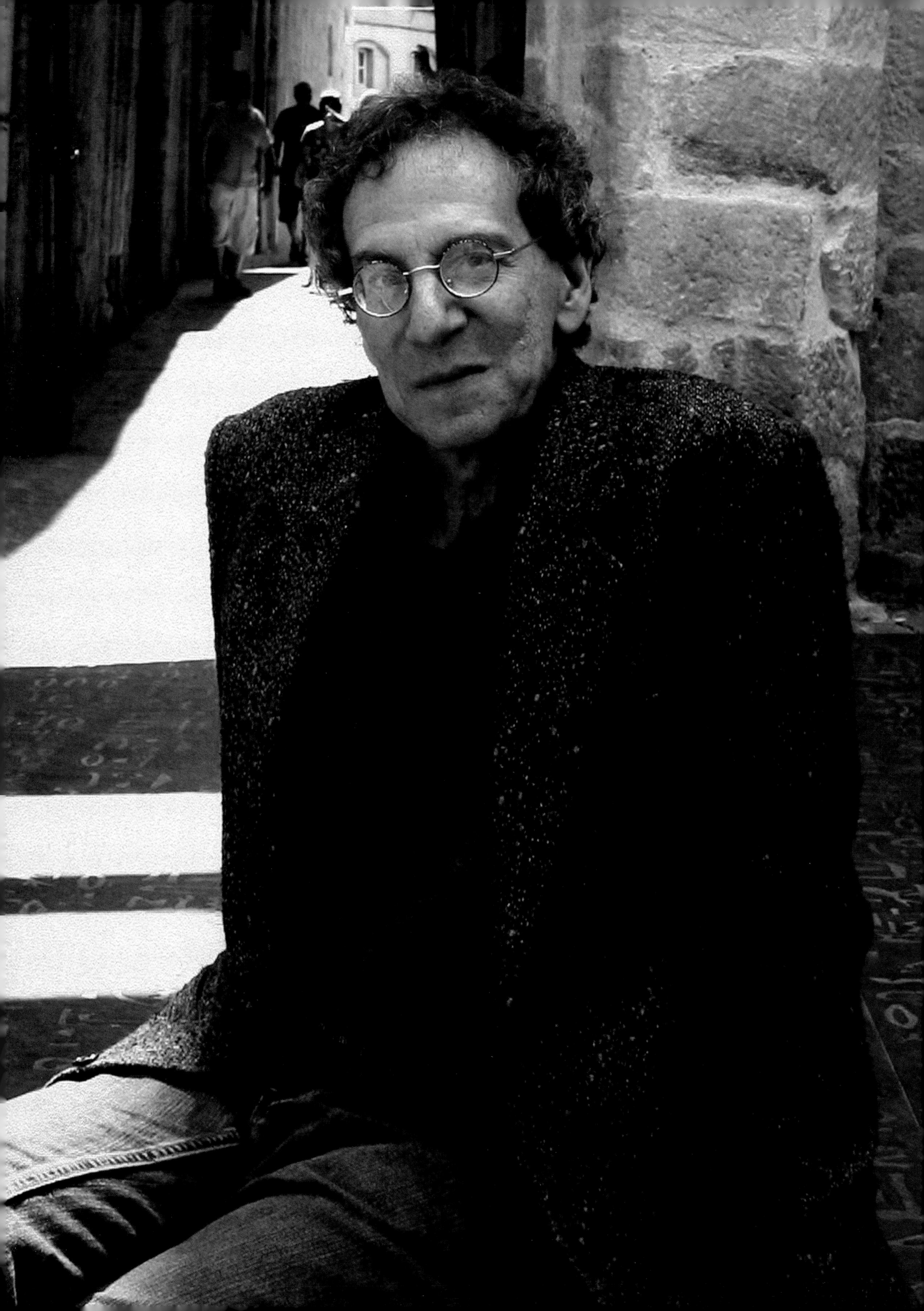

STEVE STERN

AUTHOR

"I'm much more a child of Kafka than of Isaac Singer," says Memphis author, Steve Stern. And about his schooling, "Nothing very distinguished. East High School in Memphis, 1965. Rhodes College, Memphis 1970, University of Arkansas, 1976. A lot of dropping in and out and washing up between degrees."

For the record, he was born in 1947, the son of a Memphis grocer. He left Memphis in the 1960s to travel and write. He lived for a time on a commune in Arkansas. He lived for a time in England. But he returned to Memphis and found the spark that inspired the rest of his literary output in the tales from the former Jewish ghetto area of downtown Memphis called The Pinch. His first book of Pinch tales, *Isaac and the Undertaker's Daughter*, came out in 1983. By decade's end Stern had won the O. Henry Award, two Pushcart Prize awards, published more collections, including *Lazar Malkin Enters Heaven* (which won the Edward Lewis Wallant Award for Jewish American Fiction) and the novel *Harry Kaplan's Adventures Underground*.

Stern was being hailed by critics such as Cynthia Ozick as the successor to Isaac Bashevis Singer. Stern's 2000 story collection *The Wedding Jester* won the National Jewish Book Award, and his novel *The Angel of Forgetfulness* was named one of the best books of 2005 by *The Washington Post*.

Stern has been called the finest writer to ever come from Memphis. "Most writers need to discipline themselves to go to their desks every day," said the writer Steven Millhauser, who is a friend. "Stern needs to discipline himself to stay away from his desk."

Photograph courtest Algonquin Books

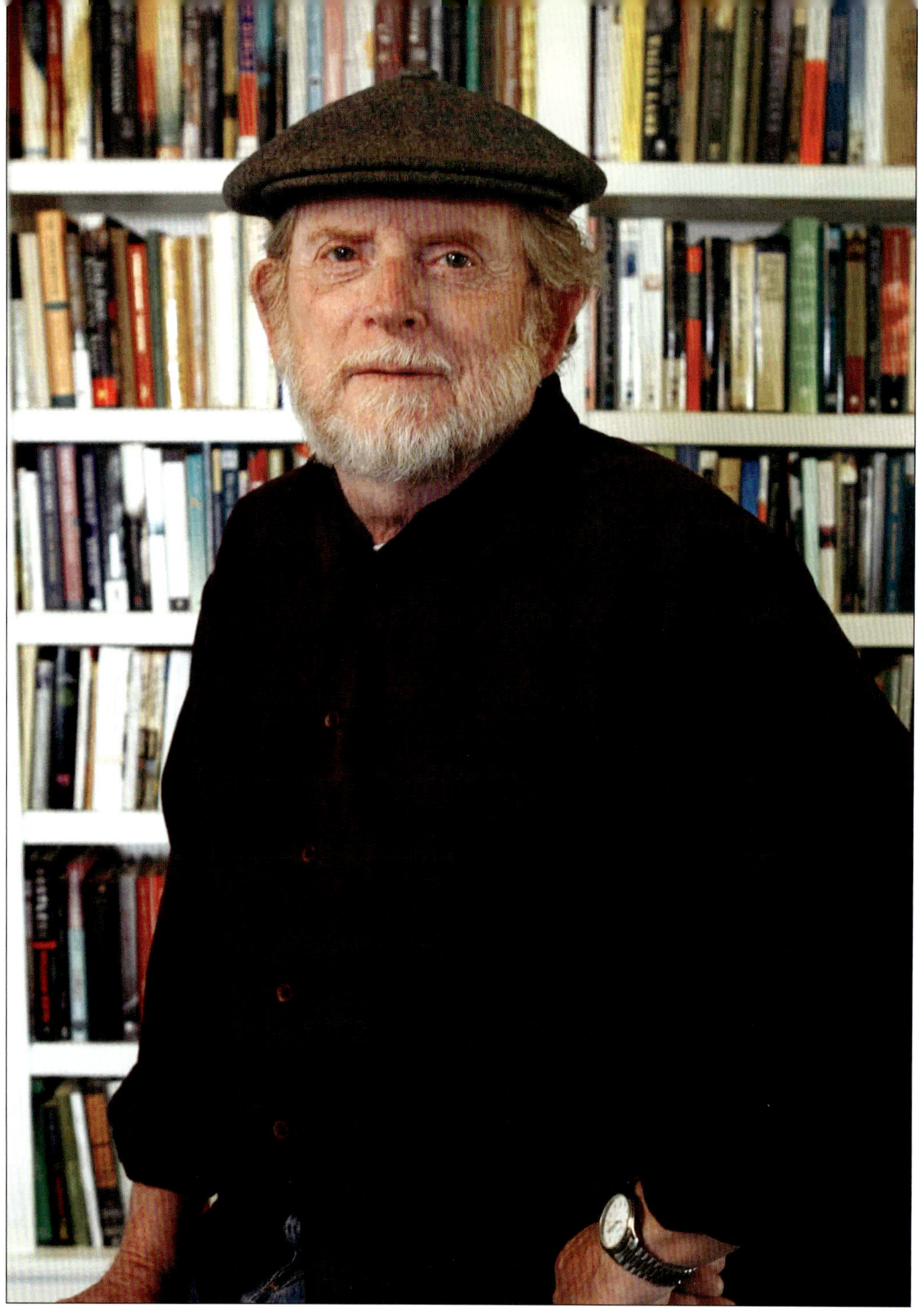

RICHARD BAUSCH

AUTHOR

"No writer has a finer insight into the delicate nuances of the human heart than Richard Bausch."

Pulitzer Prize-winner, Robert Olen Butler

After three years in the Air Force, Richard Bausch traveled around the country both writing and playing music. With a BA from George Mason and an MFA from Iowa, Bausch has taught at several universities, including his alma mater George Mason University. Among many other awards and honors, he received the National Endowment for the Arts grant in 1982, a Guggenheim Fellowship in 1984 and the American Academy of Arts and Letters' Award in Literature in 1993. His books *Take Me Back* and *Spirits and Others Stories* were both nominated for the PEN/Faulkner Award, and his novel *Peace* won the Dayton Literary Peace Prize. He currently lives in Memphis and holds the Moss Chair of Excellence in English at the University of Memphis.

JAMES CONAWAY

AUTHOR

His two novels are set in coastal Louisiana and spun from his stint as a police reporter in New Orleans. While he lived in Europe for several years, James Conaway is best known for his non-fiction portraits of America. *Napa: The Story of an American Eden* told the story of a "paradise in trouble, but not lost." The book's sequel *The Far Side of Eden* was a *Washington Post* Best Book of the Year for 2002. Conaway traveled America's vast public lands of the West in a van for *The Kingdom in the Country*. His hometown best remembers him as the author of *Memphis Afternoons*, a wide-eyed portrait of Memphis in the 1950s, and as the older brother of local advertising guru, Dan Conaway.

Conaway's work has appeared in *New York Times Magazine*, *Atlantic*, *Harper's*, *The New Republic*, *Gourmet*, *Smithsonian*, and *National Geographic Traveler*. He lives in Piedmont, VA. and Washington D.C.

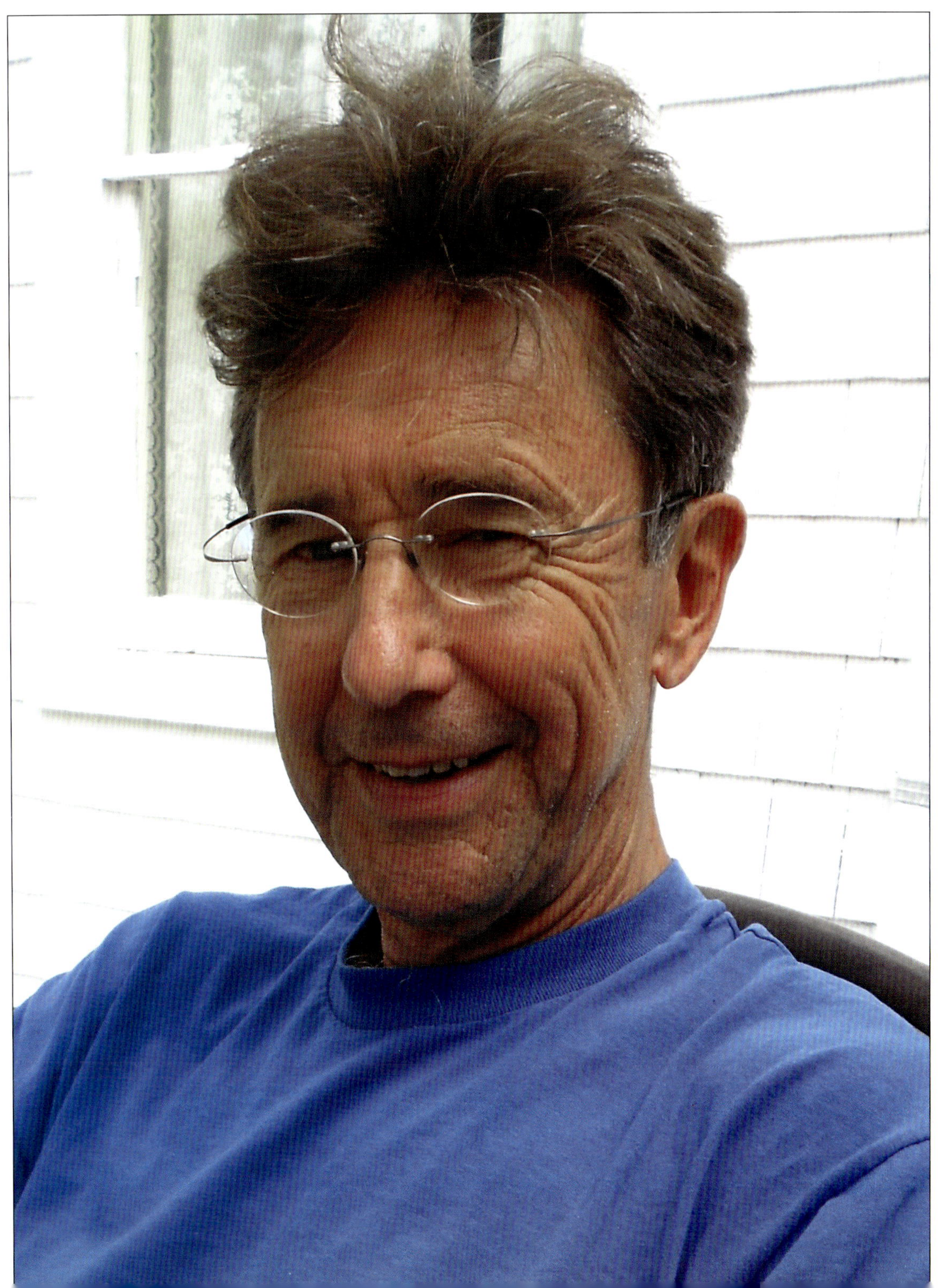

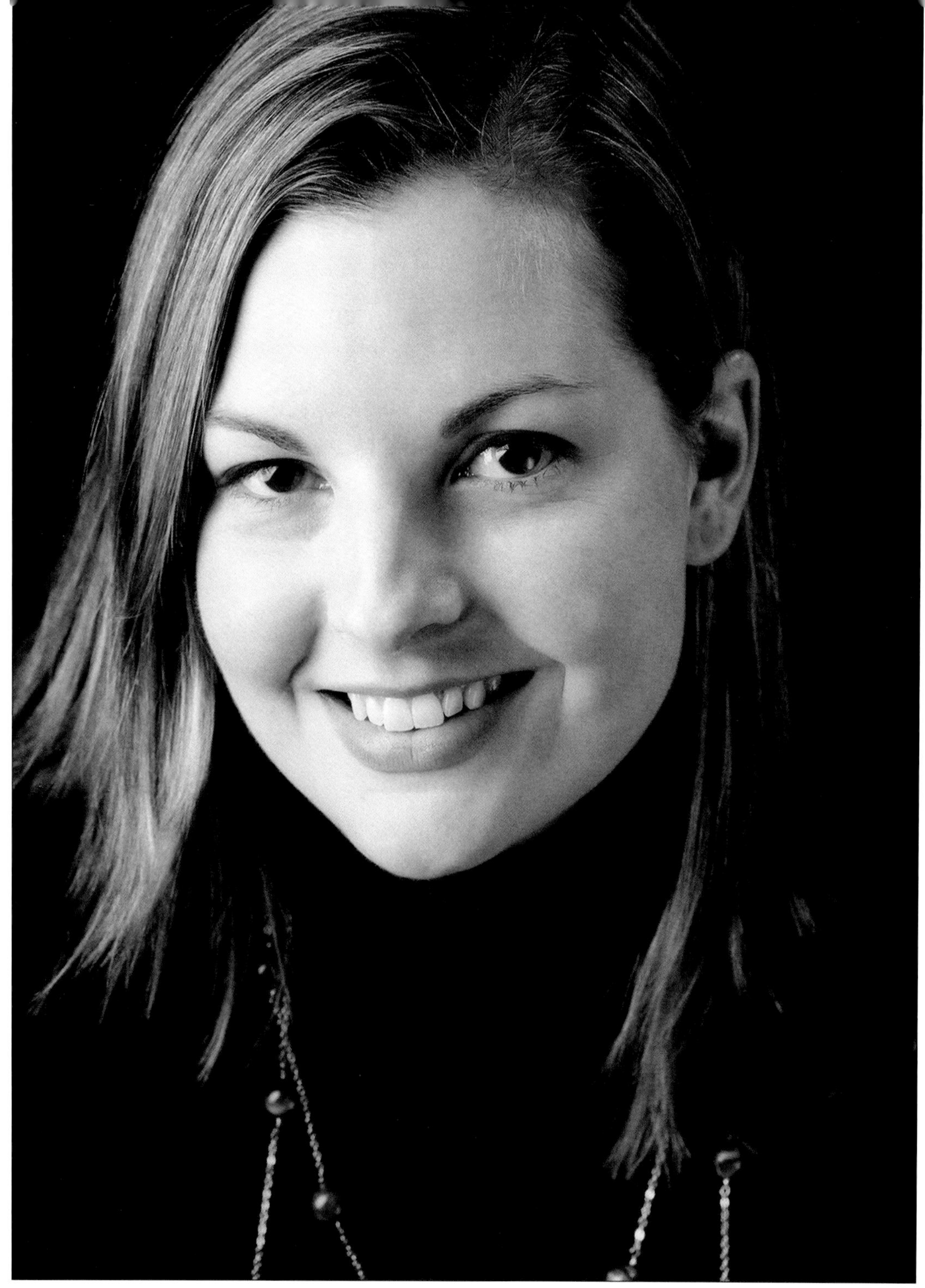

MOLLY CROSBY

AUTHOR, JOURNALIST

"Molly Crosby has the mind of a journalist and the heart of a poet."
Memphis poet Marilou Awiakta

Author and journalist Molly Crosby's first book, *The American Plague: The Untold Story of Yellow Fever, The Epidemic That Shaped Our Nation*, was hailed as "first-rate medical detective drama" and was chosen as a *New York Times* Editor's Pick. With a Master's Degree in nonfiction and science writing, Crosby's work has appeared in *Newsweek* and *USA Today*, and she has been heard on NPR many times. Her second book, *Asleep: The Forgotten Epidemic that Remains One of Medicine's Greatest Mysteries*, was published in 2010. Crosby lives in Memphis and is working on a third book.

ROBERT GORDON

AUTHOR

"Where Guralnick interprets a musical tradition that is already firmly embedded in the American psyche, Gordon gives voice to a clandestine tradition that otherwise might go forgotten."

music writer Matt Hanks

Robert Gordon was first published in 2nd or 3rd grade while a student at Shady Grove Elementary. The piece called "Acrostic Telephone" was printed in a student anthology. We know him better as the author of *Can't Be Satisfied: The Life and Times of Muddy Waters*, *It Came from Memphis* and *Elvis: The King on the Road*. He also produced and directed, with filmmaker Morgan Neville, a documentary based on his Muddy Waters book. Gordon was the Writer and Associate Producer of "The Road To Memphis" episode in Martin Scorsese's 7-part series *The Blues*.

It Came from Memphis, his book about Memphis music and culture, spawned two companion CDs, which Gordon produced. Among his accolades is a Grammy nomination for his liner notes to the Al Green box set, *Anthology*.

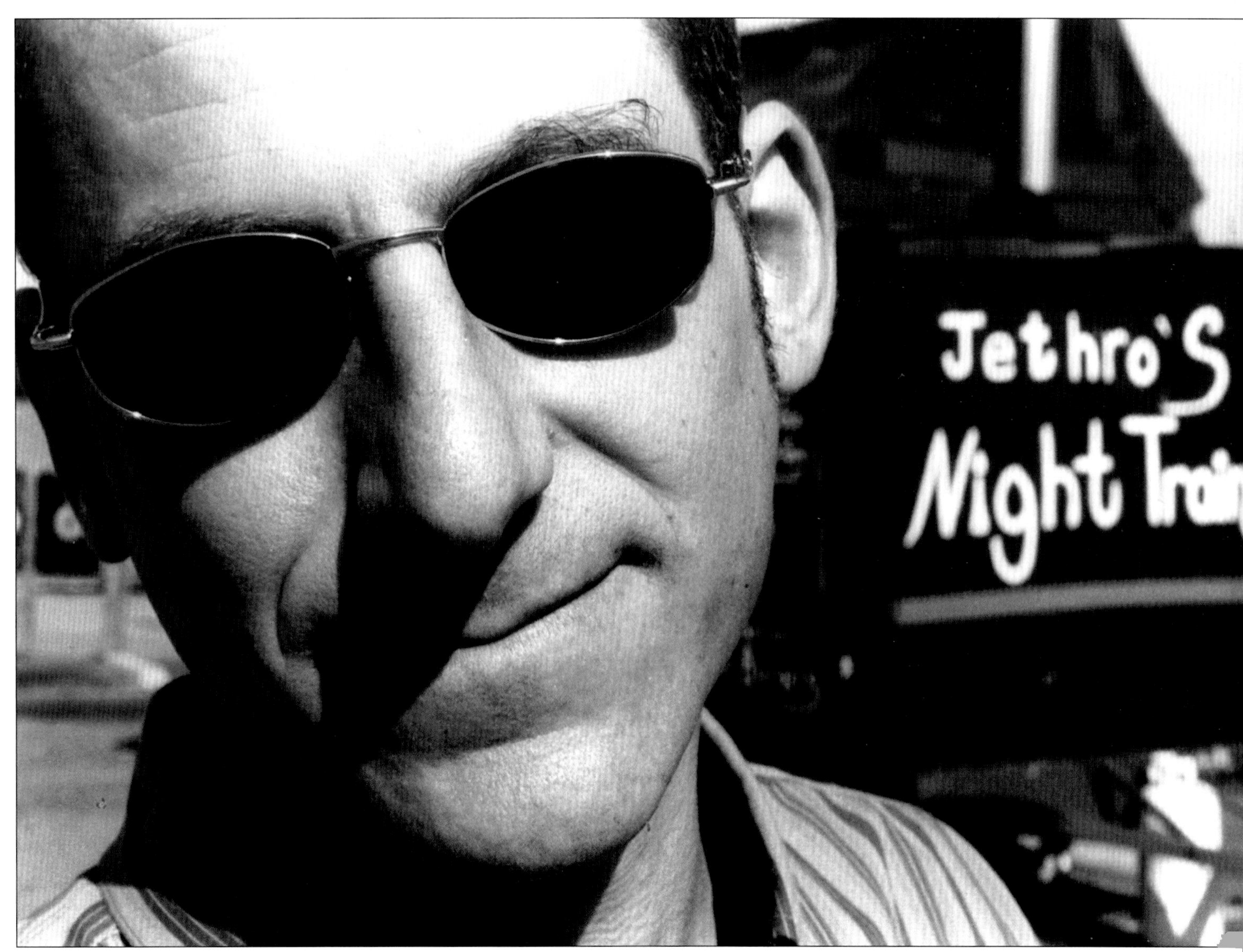

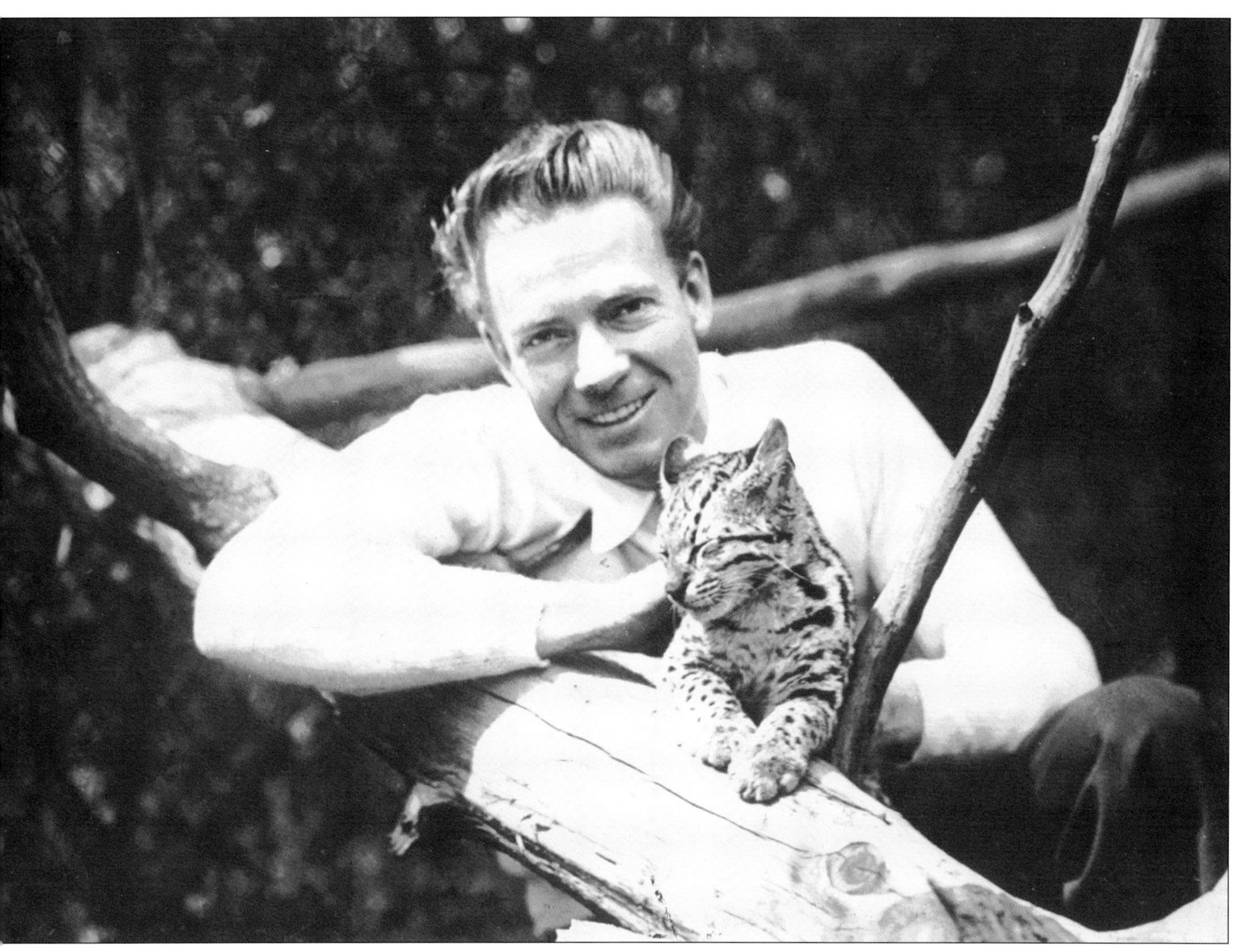

RICHARD HALLIBURTON

WRITER, ADVENTURER

Richard Halliburton wrote eight best sellers and countless syndicated articles, but to call him merely an author would be like calling Indiana Jones merely an anthropologist. However, while Indy's unbelievable fictional adventures are just that, Halliburton's unbelievable adventures were real and documented. Memphis raised and Princeton educated, he was never comfortable in traditional roles. For Halliburton, not just one descent into the Mayan Well of Death would do, but two. Like Lord Byron, he swam the Hellespont. Like Hannibal, he rode an elephant across the Alps. He re-enacted Robinson Crusoe's island ordeal, retraced Cortez's expedition to the heart of the Aztec Empire, and followed Homer's Odyssey and Odysseus across the Mediterranean. He climbed the Matterhorn, was the first to climb Mount Fuji in winter, and stood in the open cockpit of a biplane to photograph Everest while circumnavigating the globe. He lived with the French Foreign Legion, hid by day in the Taj Mahal to swim in its pool by moonlight, and swam the length of the Panama Canal after famously paying the lowest toll in its history for his passage: 36¢. He commissioned the *Sea Dragon*, a jaunty, 75-foot Chinese junk, to go from Hong Kong to the Golden Gate International Exposition in 1939, and, at the age of 39, he would go down with her in a typhoon. One of the world's most-famous, most-beloved characters in his day, his time, like the inspiration for his legion adventures, was past. The bell tower at Rhodes College was given by his parents in his memory, and his home, Hangover House, in Laguna Beach remains a symbol of his life, an adventure unto itself, hanging, seemingly suspended, above the Pacific Ocean.

Photograph courtesy The Commercial Appeal • **Story** by Dan Conaway

KRISTEN IVERSEN

AUTHOR, PROFESSOR

Kristen Iversen's first book, *Molly Brown: Unraveling the Myth*, won the Colorado Book Award and the Barbara Sudler Award for Nonfiction. It also led to extensive work with A & E Biography and The History Channel. *Shadow Boxing: Art and Craft in Creative Nonfiction* is the first textbook to cover the major subgenres of creative nonfiction — and Iversen is regarded as one of the best writers/instructors in the creative nonfiction world. Iversen's forthcoming book, *Full Body Burden: Growing Up in the Nuclear Shadow of Rocky Flats* (Crown 2012), a work of memoir and investigative journalism, chronicles her experiences with Rocky Flats, a highly controversial government facility that secretly produced the plutonium heart of every nuclear weapon made in America during the Cold War.

Iversen teaches at The University of Memphis, where she directs the MFA program. She is also Editor-in-Chief of *The Pinch*, an award-winning, nationally distributed literary journal.

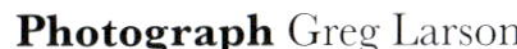

Photograph Greg Larson

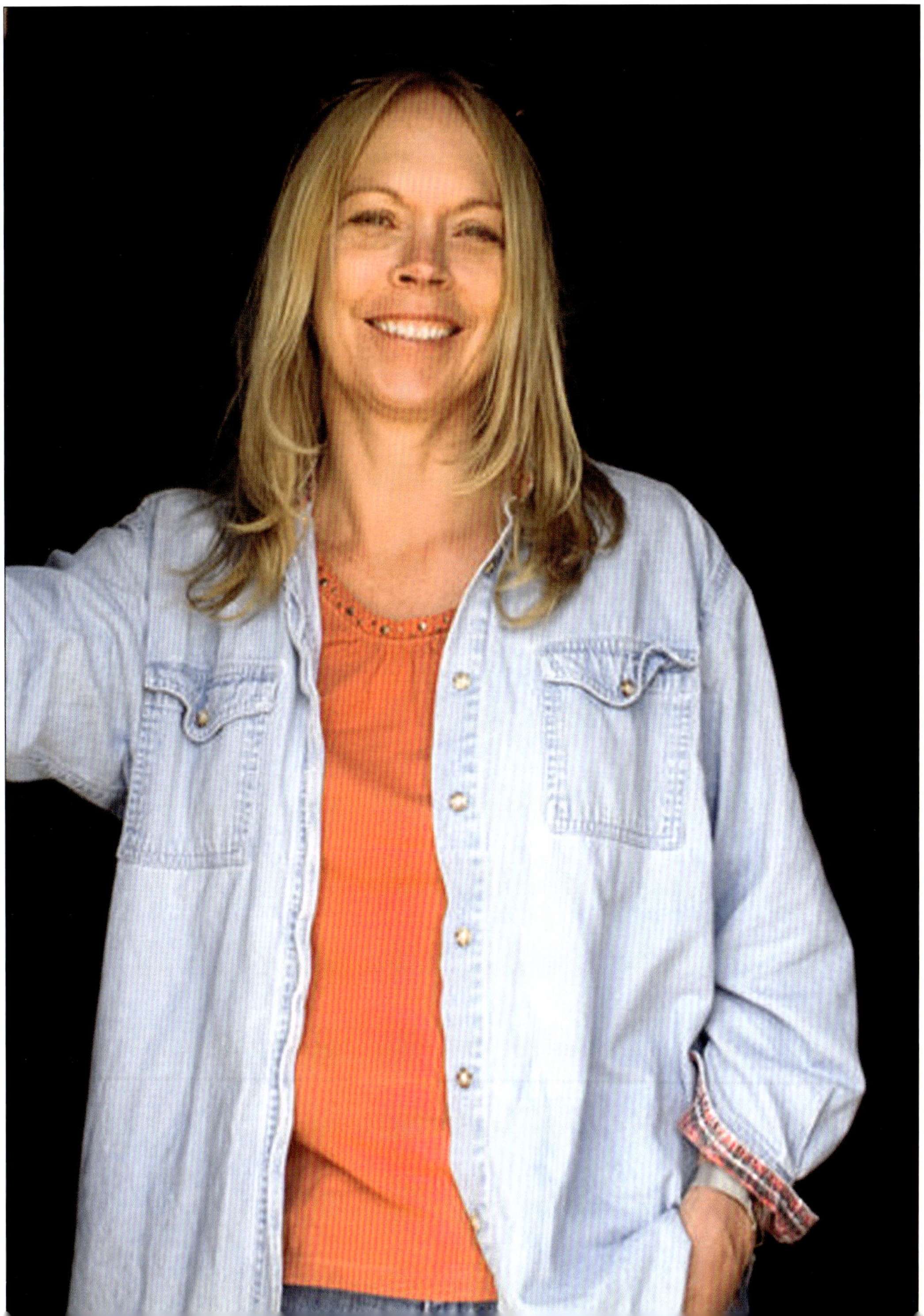

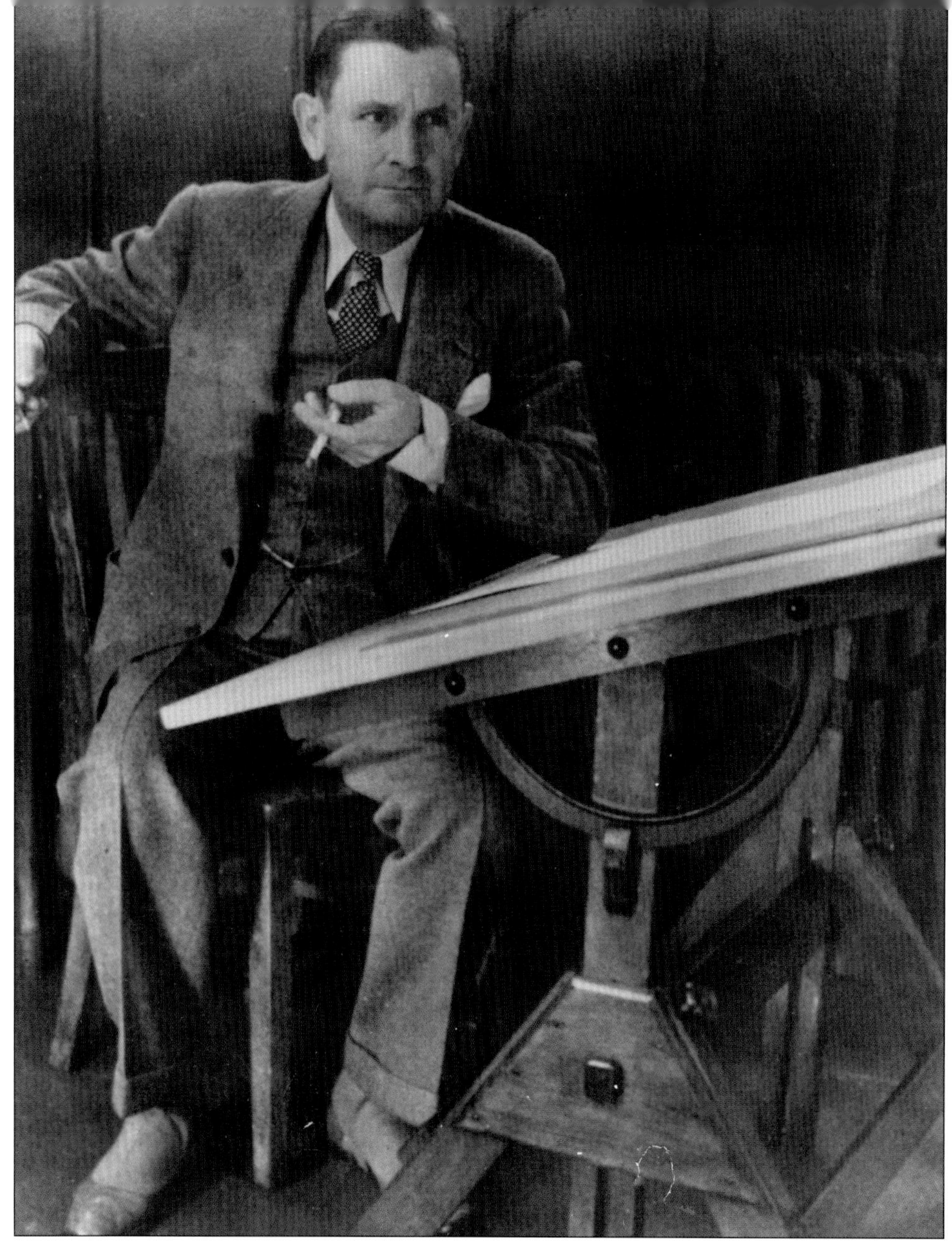

J.P. ALLEY

CARTOONIST

Pen and ink. Crosshatching. A drawing table worn smooth with work and scorched by cigarettes at rest when an idea sprang forth. These are just a few of the ingredients that came into play when J.P. Alley sat down to complete an editorial cartoon. But there were also copious amounts of wit, political and personal perspective, and a firm grasp of right and wrong.

James Pinckney Alley was editorial cartoonist for *The Commercial Appeal* from 1916 to 1934, helping the newspaper to win its first Pulitzer Prize in 1923 with his scathing representations of the Ku Klux Klan.

He was a self-taught illustrator who moved to Memphis in 1908 to work for the Bluff City Engraving Company, a company within *The Commercial Appeal* building, and came to know the paper's editor, C.P.J. Mooney, there.

After a period of freelancing for the newspaper, Mooney persuaded Alley to come on board full-time and was enlisted in the editorial battles against machine politics and E.H. "Boss" Crump, and commented on World War I which was raging at the time.

Alley is widely remembered for the nationally syndicated daily, single-panel cartoon, "Hambone's Meditations," featuring a wise African-American character who often poked fun with his down-home colloquialisms at the establishment, the times and the white man.

Alley died in 1934 and his obituary stated, "He had a fine sense of its [WWI] tragedies. Patriotism and idealism spoke through his pen." Alongside was a single panel cartoon of Hambone grieving at the drawing table of his creator.

Photograph courtesy the Alley family • **Story** by Richard Alley

SID EVANS

EDITOR

Born and raised in Memphis, Sid Evans attended Connecticut College and spent a year teaching high school English at the American School in Switzerland before heading to New York in 1993 to begin a career in magazine publishing. He worked as an editor at several national magazines, including *Sports Afield*, *GQ*, and *Men's Journal*. As the editor in chief of *Field & Stream*, he earned the magazine an unprecedented nine National Magazine Award nominations, including one for General Excellence.

In 2007, Evans left New York for an office eight hundred miles from the lights of Broadway. He went to work for a then-little-known magazine called *Garden & Gun*, based in Charleston, South Carolina, described on its website as "an idea about how to live—how to live a life that is more engaged with the land, the literature, the music, the arts, the traditions, the food, and the authenticity that shape the Southern way of life."

Just before departing for his homeland, Evans told *The New York Times*, "I sort of had the most ironic job in New York, editing the biggest outdoor magazine from an office in the middle of the most indoors city. In a way, it's about wanting to have physical space, mental space. It's about wanting to run a new magazine before running the one I'm running starts to become routine."

Garden & Gun has quickly grown into a mainstay for aficionados of all things Southern and has published work by some of the best in Southern literature, including Roy Blount Jr., Lee Smith, Clyde Edgerton, and Rick Bragg. Under Evans' leadership, in 2011 *Garden & Gun* won the National Magazine Award for General Excellence and a James Beard Foundation Award in the Food, Culture and Travel category.

Evans is now group editor for Time Inc.'s Lifestyle Division in Birmingham, Alabama, where he oversees five magazines: *Southern Living*, *Coastal Living*, *Cooking Light*, *Sunset*, and *This Old House*. He proved himself in a world far away from that of iced tea, bird dogs, Faulkner, and drawls, but this hometown boy recrossed the Mason-Dixon to make us even prouder, and to spread the Gospel of the South far and wide.

Photograph by Squire Fox • **Story** by Richard Alley

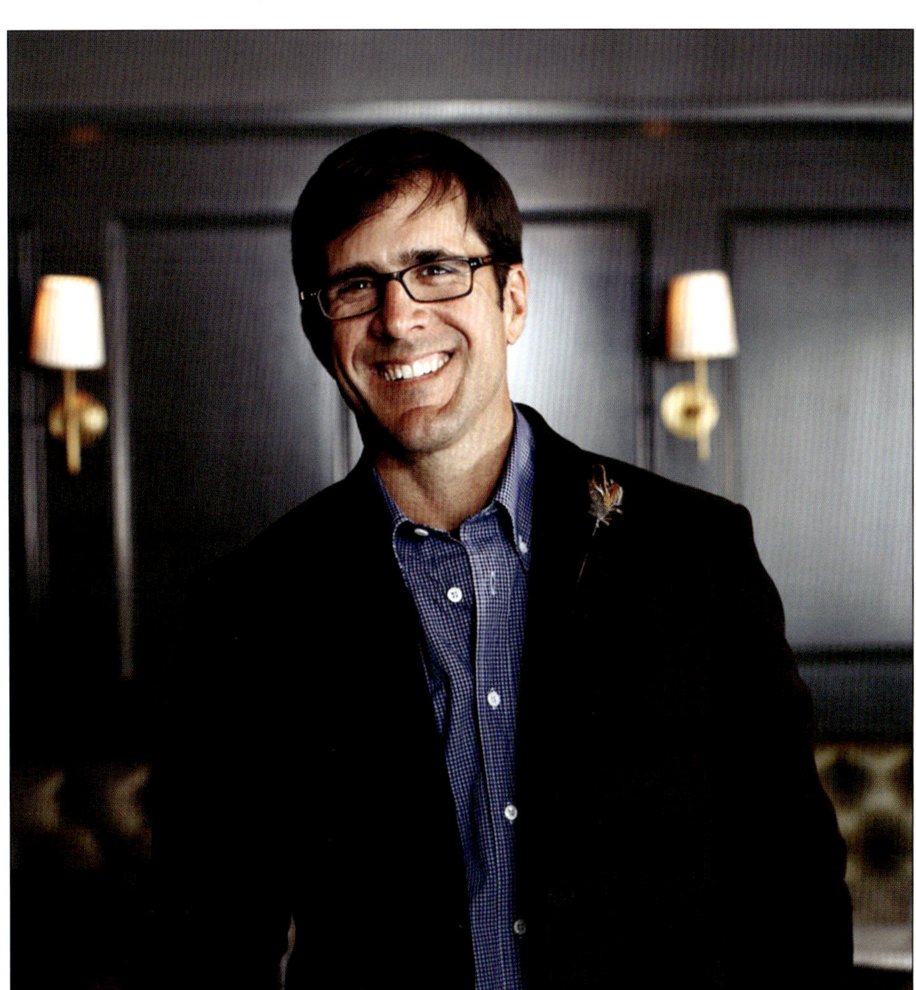

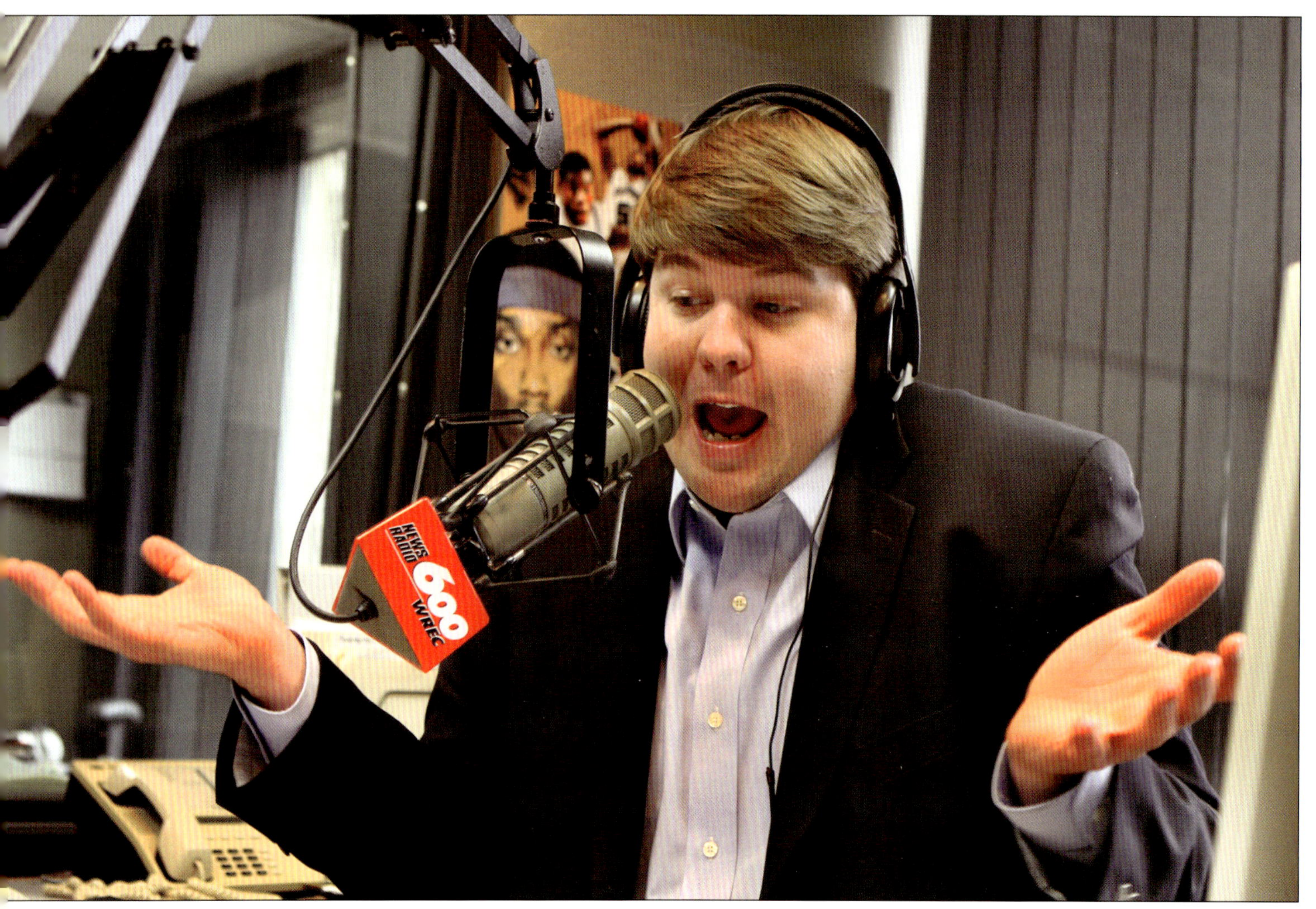

BEN FERGUSON

RADIO PERSONALITY

This Wunderkind of the Radio Right has been hard at it for some thirteen years now, which might make some people an old pro, but for Ben Ferguson, well, he's still a Wunderkind. When you start your broadcasting career at the age of 13, it takes a while to rid yourself of the "youngster" moniker. And when you look like you should still be hanging in the halls of high school . . . you get the picture. He fell in love with radio at an early age, and from the age of 13, Ferguson has been telling it like he sees it. That's when he grabbed his first radio slot. It didn't take him long to go from local to national. He's been a guest on local, regional and national TV and radio programs, and even addressed the 2004 Republican Convention. His book, *It's My America, Too: A Leading Young Conservative Shares His Views on Politics and Other Matters of Importance*, hit the stands in 2004.

Ferguson has been blasting the left and trumpeting the right for years now on the air-waves, and the future looks bright. He's now the head of his own network, ICON radio.

Photograph by Commercial Appeal • **Story** by David Tankersley

WOODROW WILSON "WOODY" PAIGE

SPORTS JOURNALIST

A native of Memphis, Woody Paige attended the University of Tennessee before staking his claim as a sportswriter. He started at *The Whitehaven Press* and later moved to *The Commercial Appeal*. He went on to co-host *Cold Pizza* and *1st and 10* for ESPN. Now a widely read, and prolific, columnist for *The Denver Post*, Paige is a regular panelist on ESPN's *Around the Horn*.

Photograph by Getty Images

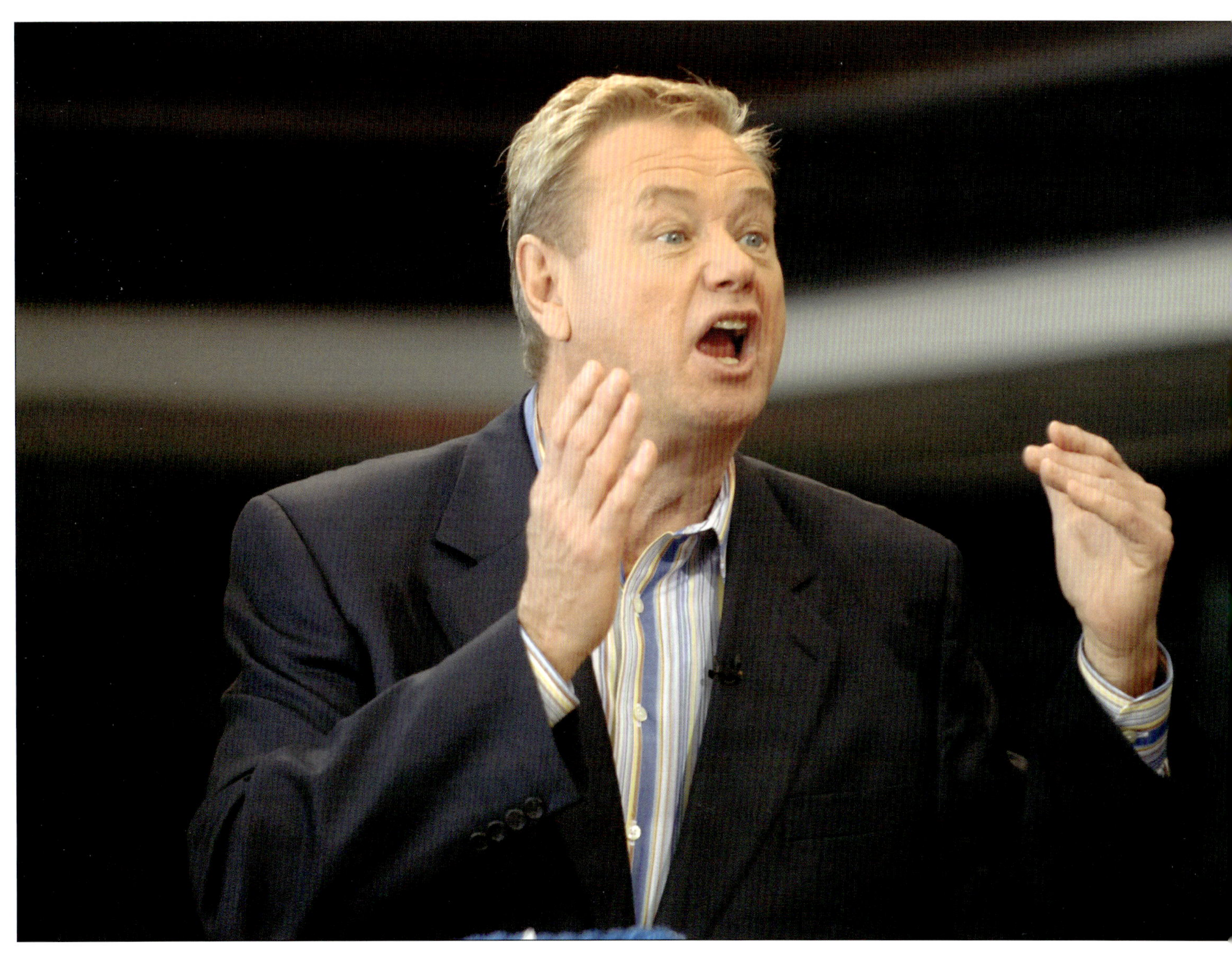

Law & Politics

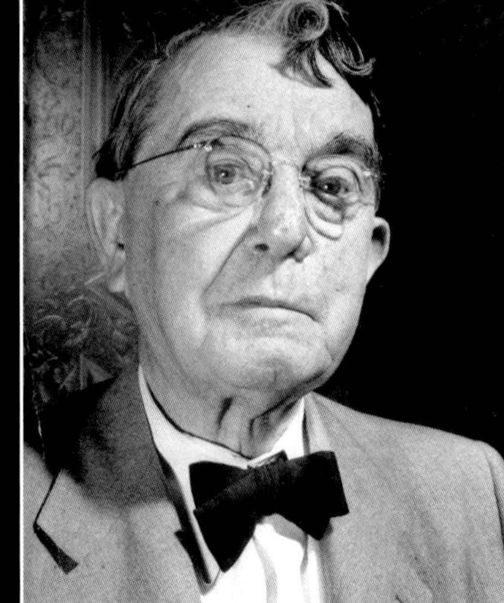

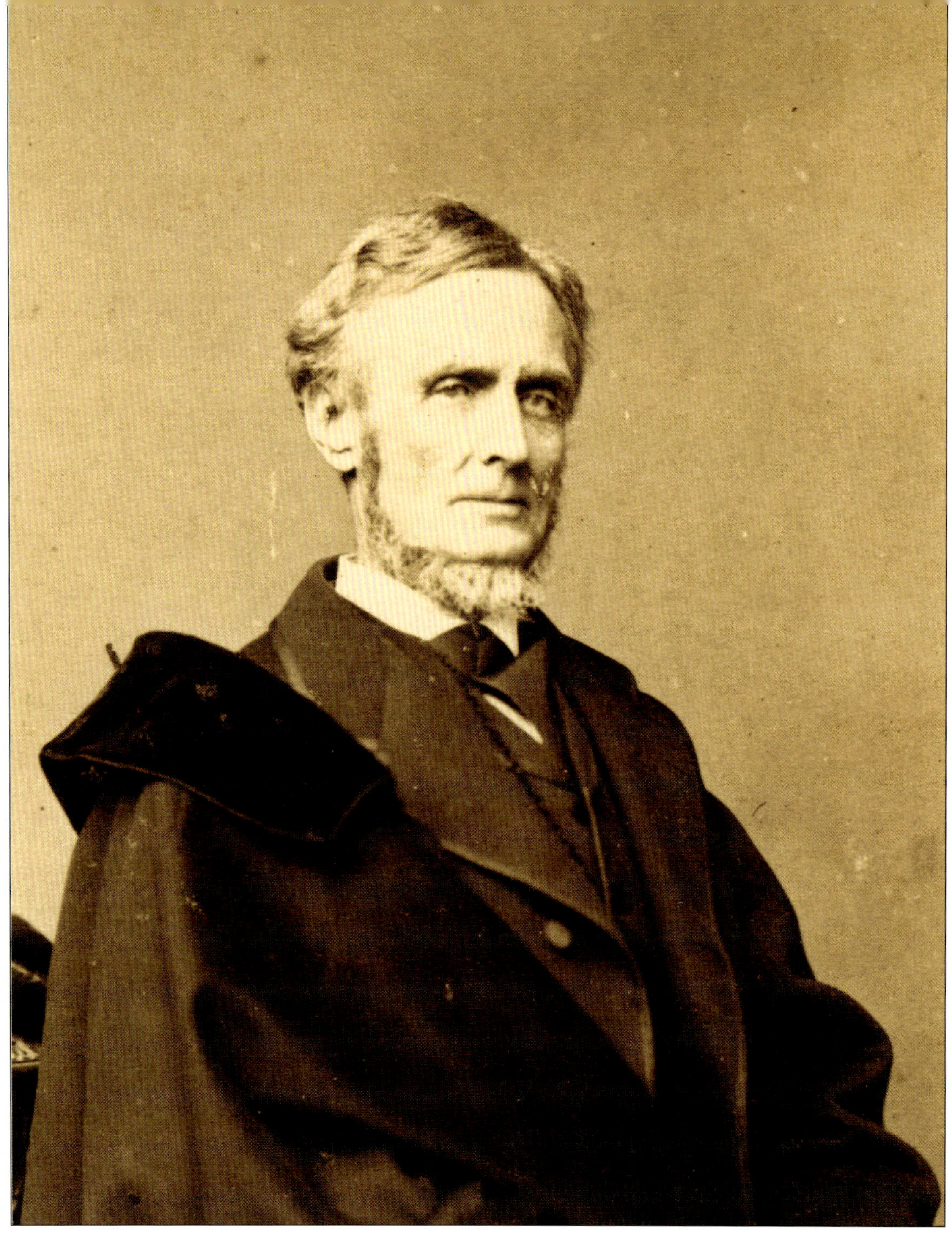

JEFFERSON DAVIS

STATESMAN

After he ended his political career that included serving as a representative, senator, US Secretary of War, and President of the Confederate States of America, Jefferson Davis chose Memphis as the place to settle down. In 1869, he became the president of the Carolina Life Insurance Company, located in Memphis. He wrote two books, *The Rise and Fall of the Confederate Government* (1881) and *A Short History of the Confederate States of America* (1889). Despite having served time in prison for treason, Davis' reputation in the South was boosted by his books and his Southern sympathies. In his final years, he encouraged Southerners to stay loyal to the Union, saying, "United you are now, and if the Union is ever to be broken, let the other side break it."

Photograph by Hutton Archive/Netterville Briggs

ABE FORTAS

SUPREME COURT JUSTICE

Born and raised in Memphis, Abe Fortas graduated from Southwestern at Memphis in 1930. He went on to Yale Law School, and, in 1933, graduated second in his class (interestingly, the first in that class was another Memphian, Luke Finlay). He co-founded the firm Arnold & Fortas in 1946 and was appointed to the Supreme Court by Lyndon B. Johnson in 1965. As a Supreme Court Justice, he was very concerned with children's rights, and was instrumental in extending the Fourteenth Amendment's guaranteed rights to certain juvenile proceedings. In 1969, he resigned from the Court and returned to private practice, where he remained until his death in 1982.

Photograph by Time & Life Pictures/Al Fenn

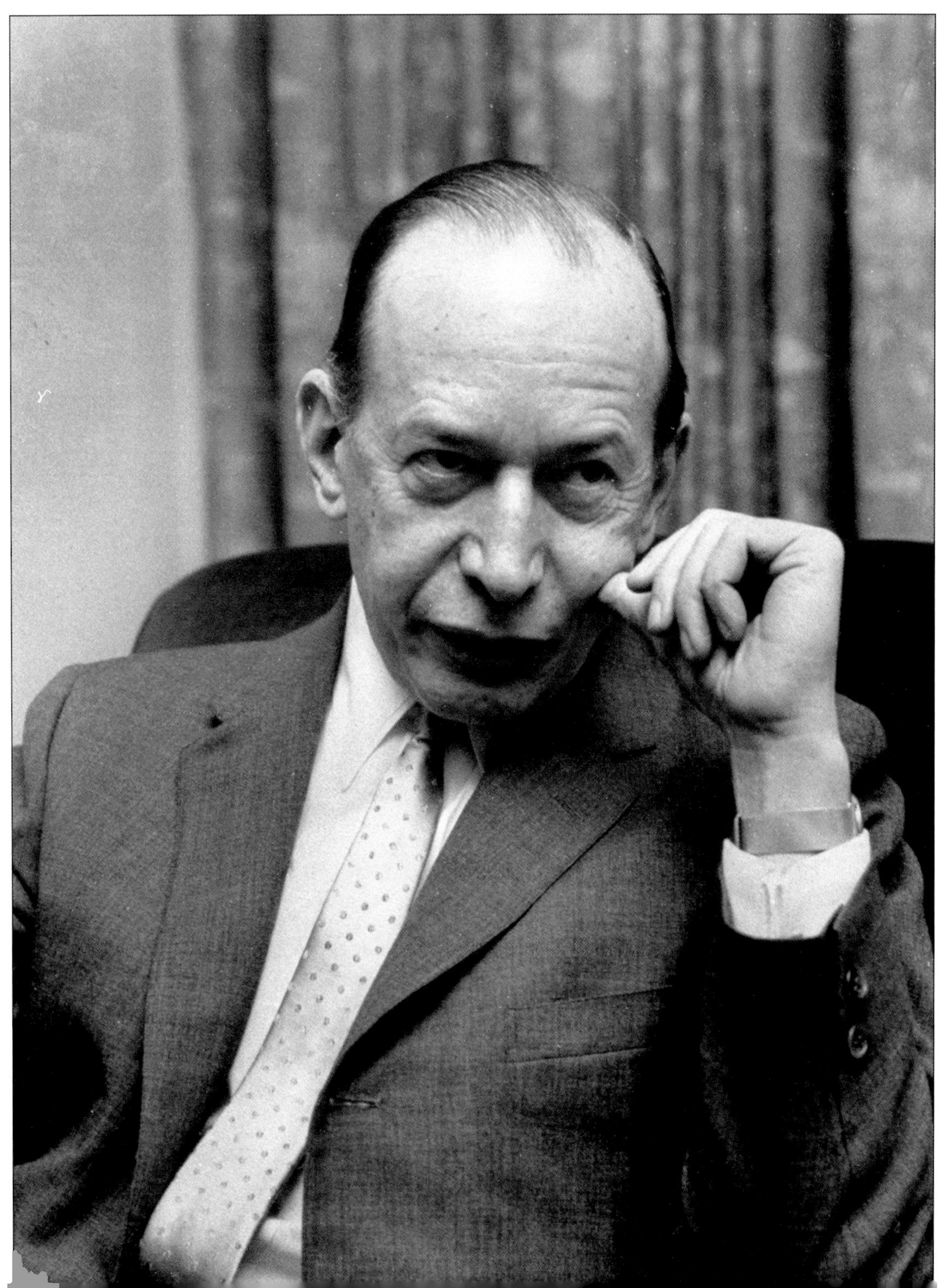

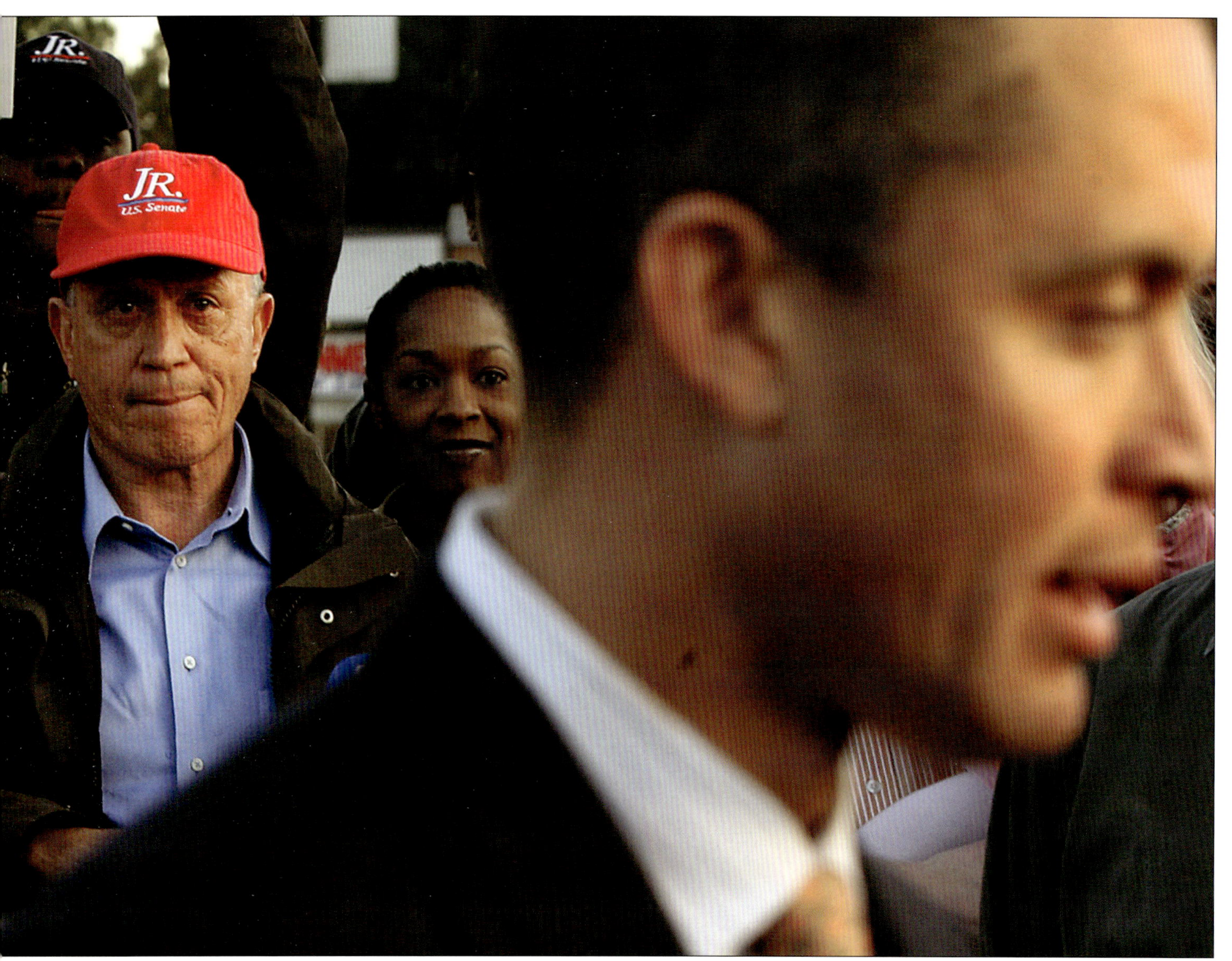

HAROLD FORD, SR.

POLITICIAN

Raised in Memphis and a graduate of Memphis' Geeter High School, Harold Ford was elected to the Tennessee House of Representatives in 1970, one of a very few African-Americans to have served in the Tennessee General Assembly at that time. In 1975, he was elected to represent the Memphis area in the U.S. House of Representatives. He was the first African-American to represent Tennessee in Congress. He served on several committees, including the Select Committee on Assassinations, which investigated the murder of Martin Luther King, Jr., among others. He also served as a delegate to the Democratic State Convention and to the quadrennial Democratic National Conventions, from 1972-1996. In 1997, he retired from Congress, after ten terms, and continues to be active in the Democratic Party.

Photograph by Commercial Appeal

KENNETH D. MCKELLAR

SENATOR

Kenneth McKellar moved to Memphis right after graduating law school in 1892. He was first elected as a US Representative in a special election to succeed George W. Gordon in 1911, and won his own seat in the election of 1912. He then joined the US Senate in 1917, and became the only Tennessee senator to have completed more than three full terms, serving until 1953, when he completed his sixth. He published the book *Tennessee Senators as Seen by One of Their Successors* in 1942, and passed away in 1957. Both Lake McKellar near Memphis and McKellar Airport in Jackson, Tenn., are named for him.

Photograph by Time/Life Archives

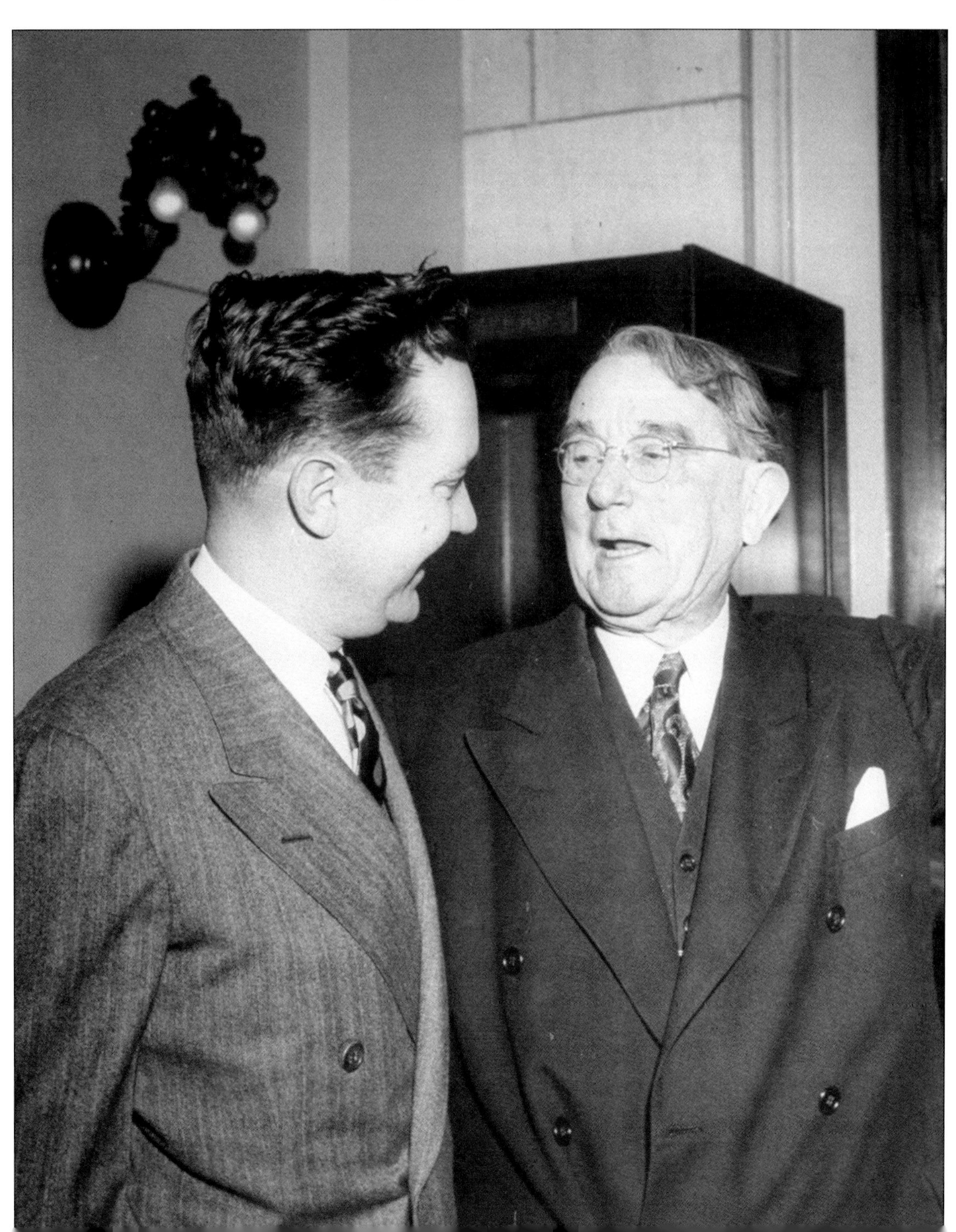

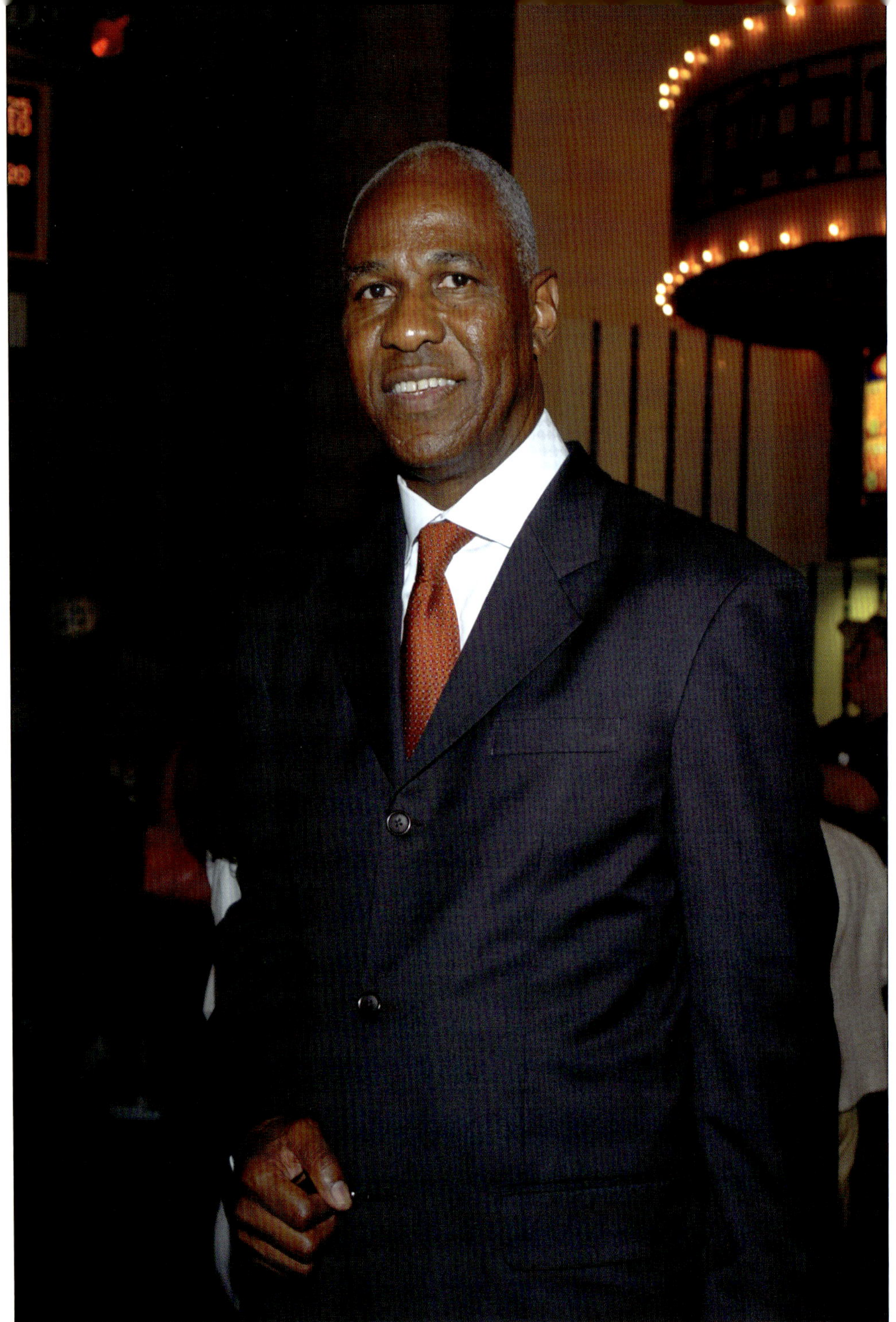

W.W. HERENTON

POLITICIAN

Willie Herenton, the first African-American to be elected Mayor of Memphis, is a graduate of LeMoyne-Owen College and the University of Memphis. He received his doctorate in education from Southern Illinois University, and has two honorary doctorates, from Rhodes College and Christian Brothers University. Before becoming mayor, he worked for twelve years as the superintendent of Memphis City Schools. First elected in 1991, he served five terms as mayor and resigned in 2009.

Photograph by Getty Images

A.C. WHARTON

ATTORNEY, PROFESSOR, POLITICIAN

When A. C. Wharton moved to Memphis in 1973 to work as executive director of Legal Services, he not only saved the organization from its financial struggles, but led the company to national recognition for its new ideas and programs. A graduate of Tennessee State University and the University of Mississippi Law School, he was the first African-American professor of law at Ole Miss. He was elected as mayor of Shelby County in both 2002 and 2006. In 2009, he ran in a special election to determine a replacement for Willie Herenton, and is currently serving as the mayor of Memphis.

Photograph by Commercial Appeal

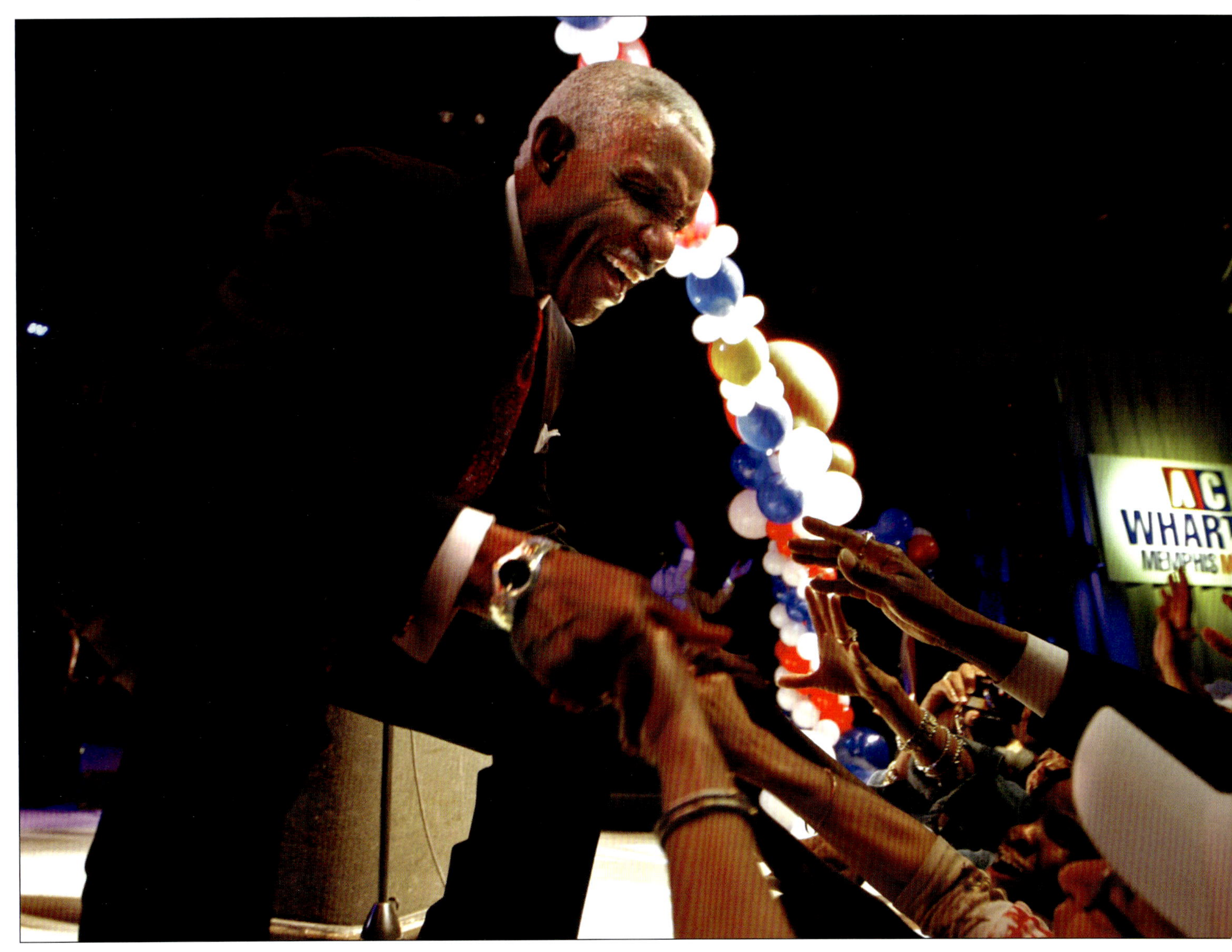

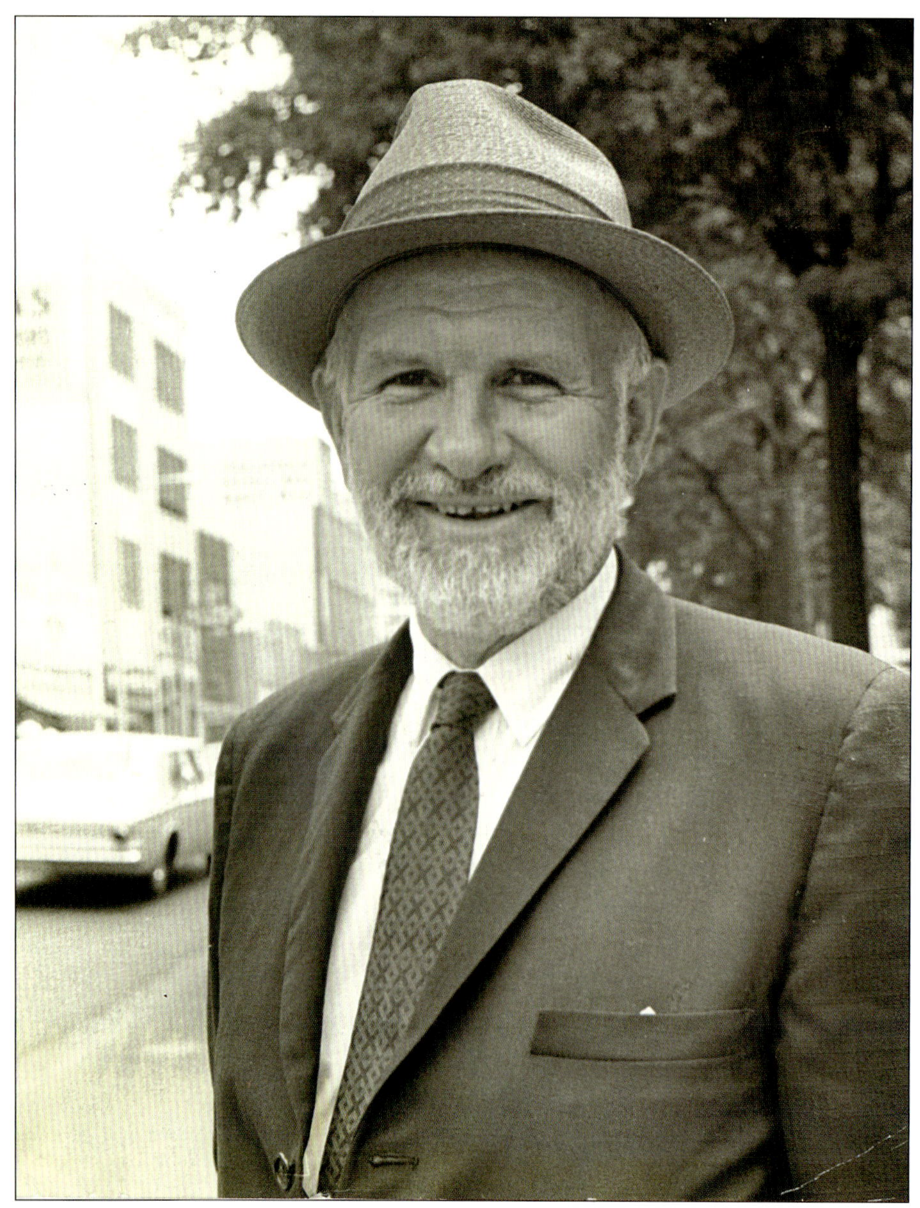

LUCIUS E. BURCH, JR.

ATTORNEY

As dogged as attorney Lucius Burch was in his search for adventure in the great outdoors, he was equally as tenacious in his pursuit of fairness and equality in the courtroom.

A descendant of presidents Andrew Jackson and James K. Polk, Burch was born in Nashville in 1912, the son of the dean of Vanderbilt Medical School. His grandfather was secretary of the United States Senate. Burch attended Vanderbilt before moving to Memphis to work in his uncle's law office, Burch, Minor and McKay. When his uncle and the other partners died within the next few years, Burch inherited the practice and brought on partners John Porter and Jesse Johnson.

Burch and partners represented Dr. Martin Luther King, Jr. in the successful attempt, on the day King was assassinated, to lift a restraining order on the 1968 march in support of the striking sanitation workers in Memphis.

The firm that bears his name has also logged many hours in the halting of the planned bisection of Overton Park by I-40, and in keeping Shelby Farms Park from being residentially and commercially developed.

As a result, the 728-acre natural area of wetlands, bald cypress-water tupelo swamps, bottomland hardwood forests, and open river channel habitat boasting hiking paths, biking trails and birdwatching in eastern Shelby County, is named for Burch.

The Lucius E. Burch, Jr. Natural Area has become just what the man would have wanted: a haven for everyone and anyone to experience the beauty of the world around them.

Story by Richard Alley

Little-Known Memphians

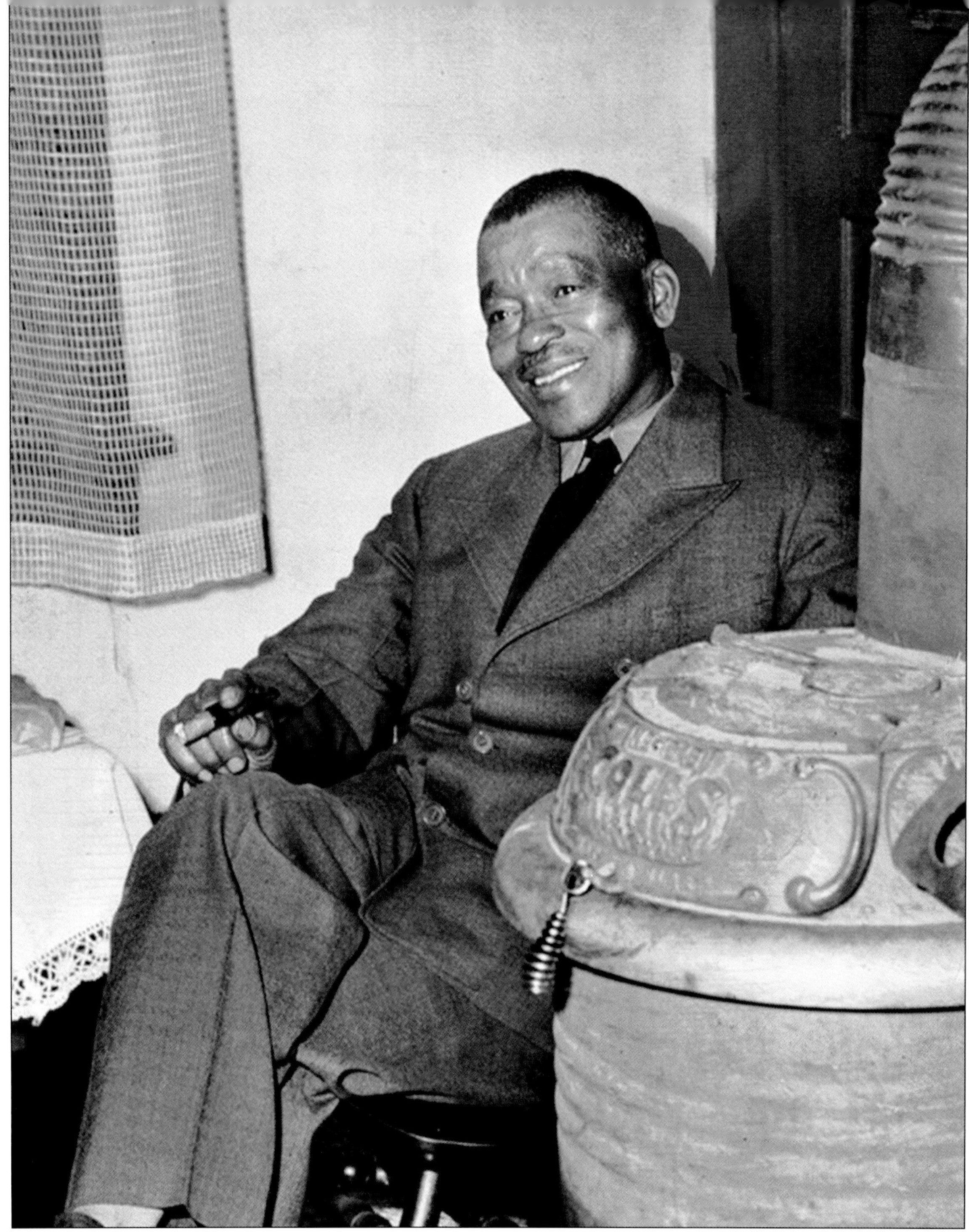

TOM LEE

HERO

Tom Lee was sailing on May 8, 1925, about 15 miles downriver from Memphis, when he saw a steamboat, the *M.E. Norman*, capsize. The boat was carrying members of the Engineers Club of Memphis and the American Society of Civil Engineers, along with their families. Even though he could not swim, Lee headed straight to the sinking boat and rescued 32 people, making 5 trips to shore. As thanks, the Engineers Club purchased a house for Tom and his wife. Lee passed away in 1952, but his legacy lives on. In 1954, Tom Lee Park was named for him, and in 2006, a bronze sculpture was erected to commemorate Memphis' "greatest hero."

Photograph by Commercial Appeal

EMIL WILLIAM HENRY

FCC CHAIRMAN

How did Emil William Henry end up as the youngest chairman ever of the Federal Communications Commission? Well…because he asked for the job. Born and raised in Memphis, Henry moved to Washington, D.C. to work on John F. Kennedy's presidential campaign. In 1963, after the FCC's chairman left, 34-year-old Henry asked Robert Kennedy if he could have the job. And he got it. Now, Henry lives in Memphis, and recently published *Triumph and Tragedy: The Life of Edward Whymper*. He is currently working on a book about Jimmy Hoffa.

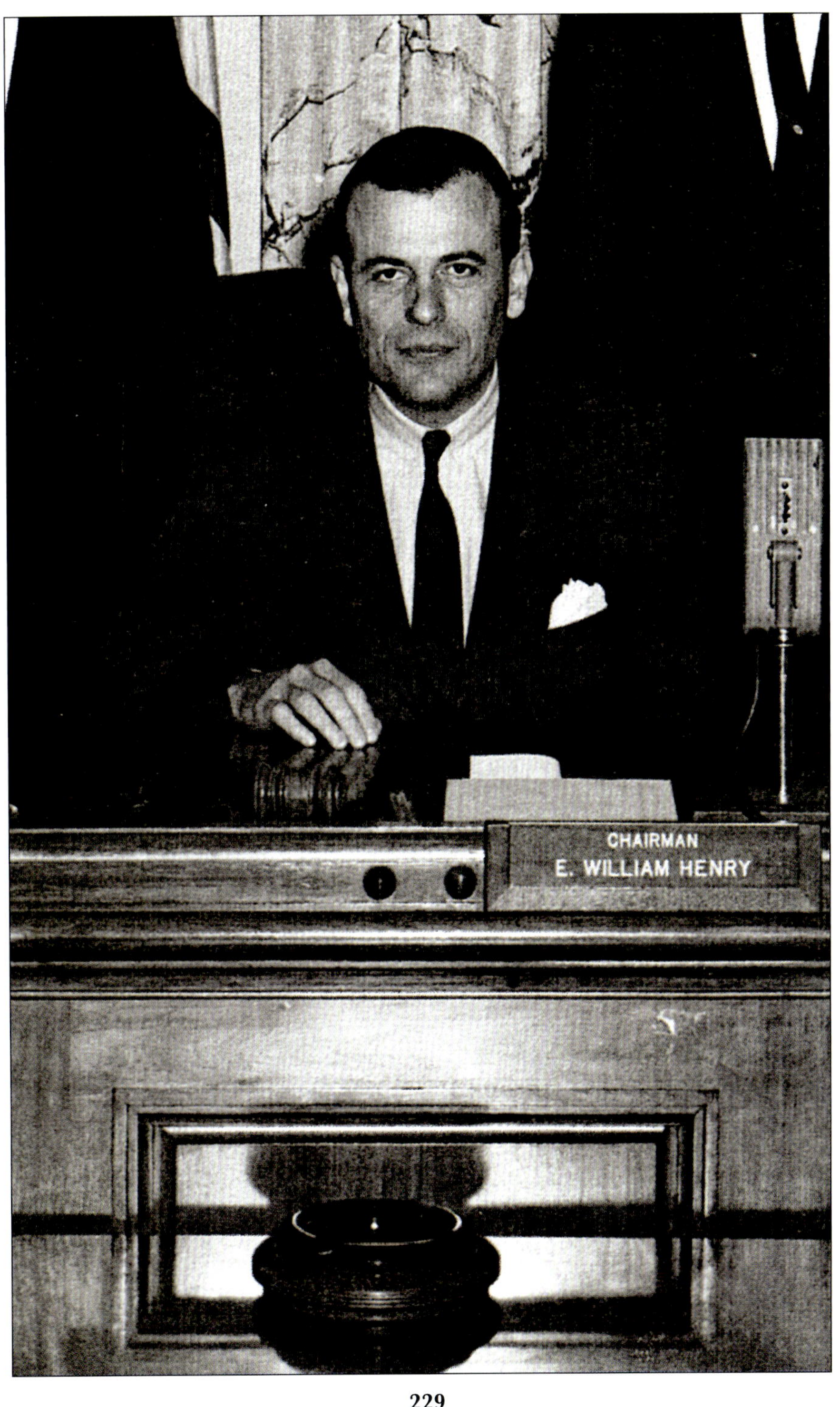

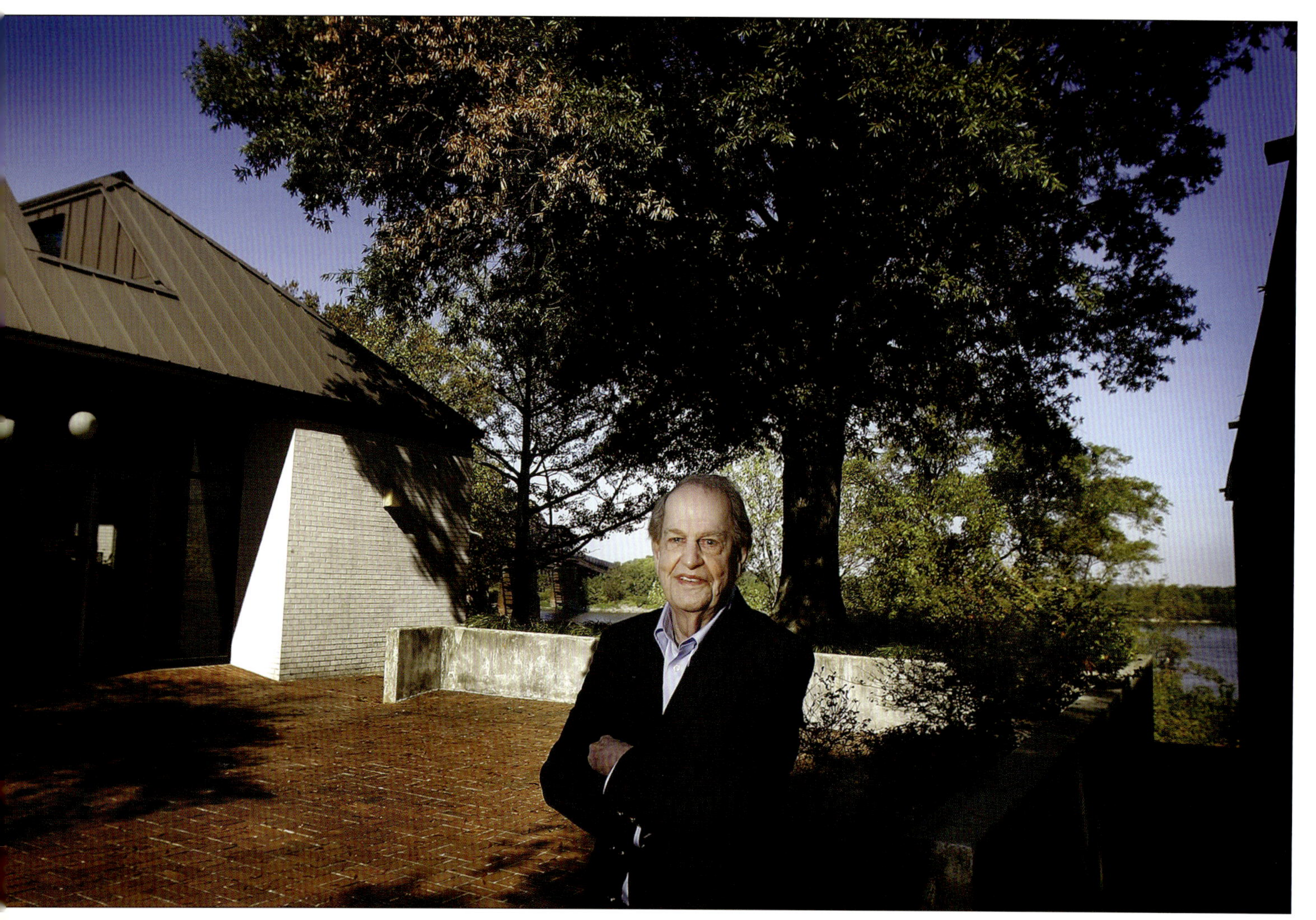

ROY HARROVER

ARCHITECT

Roy Harrover is a Memphis treasure, and so are many of the buildings he designed. With an architectural degree from Yale and a longing to return to the South, Harrover took a job with an architectural firm in Memphis. However, when he wanted to enter the contest for the new Memphis Academy of Art and Performing Arts Center, he was told by his firm not to do it. So he simply started his own. With Bill Mann and Lee Williams, their enterprise won the contest, and the completed building ended up on the cover of *Progressive Architecture*. In 1958, after traveling around the world to discover the future direction of air travel, Harrover and Mann landed the job for designing the new Memphis airport…before they had produced a drawing! Mann passed away before the final design was complete, and Harrover forged on alone. He later designed the popular location, Mud Island.

Photograph by Commercial Appeal

LEO THE LION

HOLLYWOOD ICON

Live in Memphis long enough and you hear the apocryphal tale of how the MGM lion came from the Memphis Zoo. As with many legends there is some truth to it, but it's a murky story and the truth is a little disappointing. The first lion, Leo, came from Africa, via the trapper/hunter, Volney Phifer, in 1913. Slats, the second logo lion, came from the Dublin zoo, again via Phifer. Phifer trained him to growl on command. Slats toured the states for MGM, but under the name Leo. In his later years, Slats was sold to the Memphis Zoo in 1942, and here renamed Volney. The lion most people connect to MGM is Leo II, who took over roaring mascot duties in 1957.

Photograph by MGM

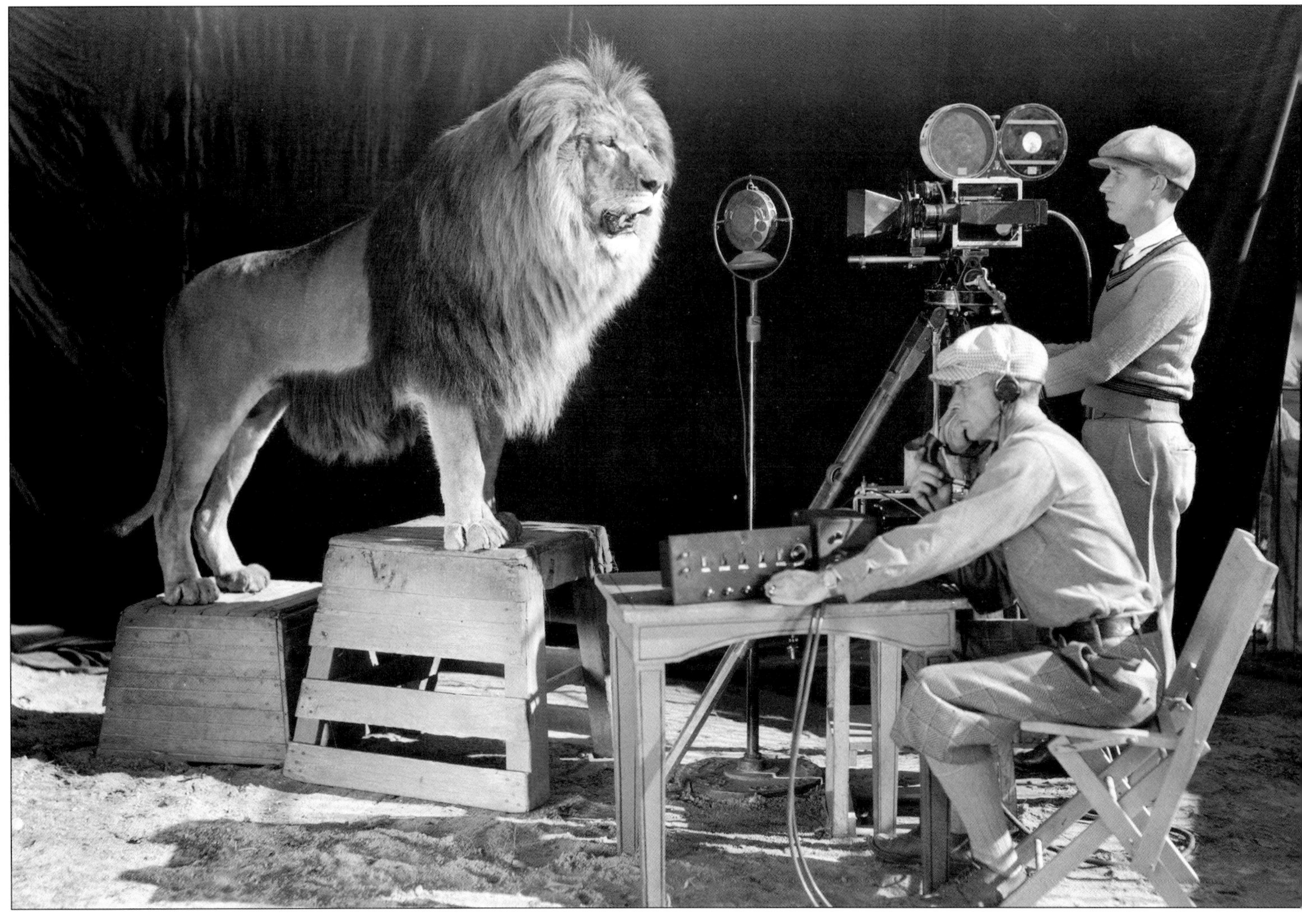

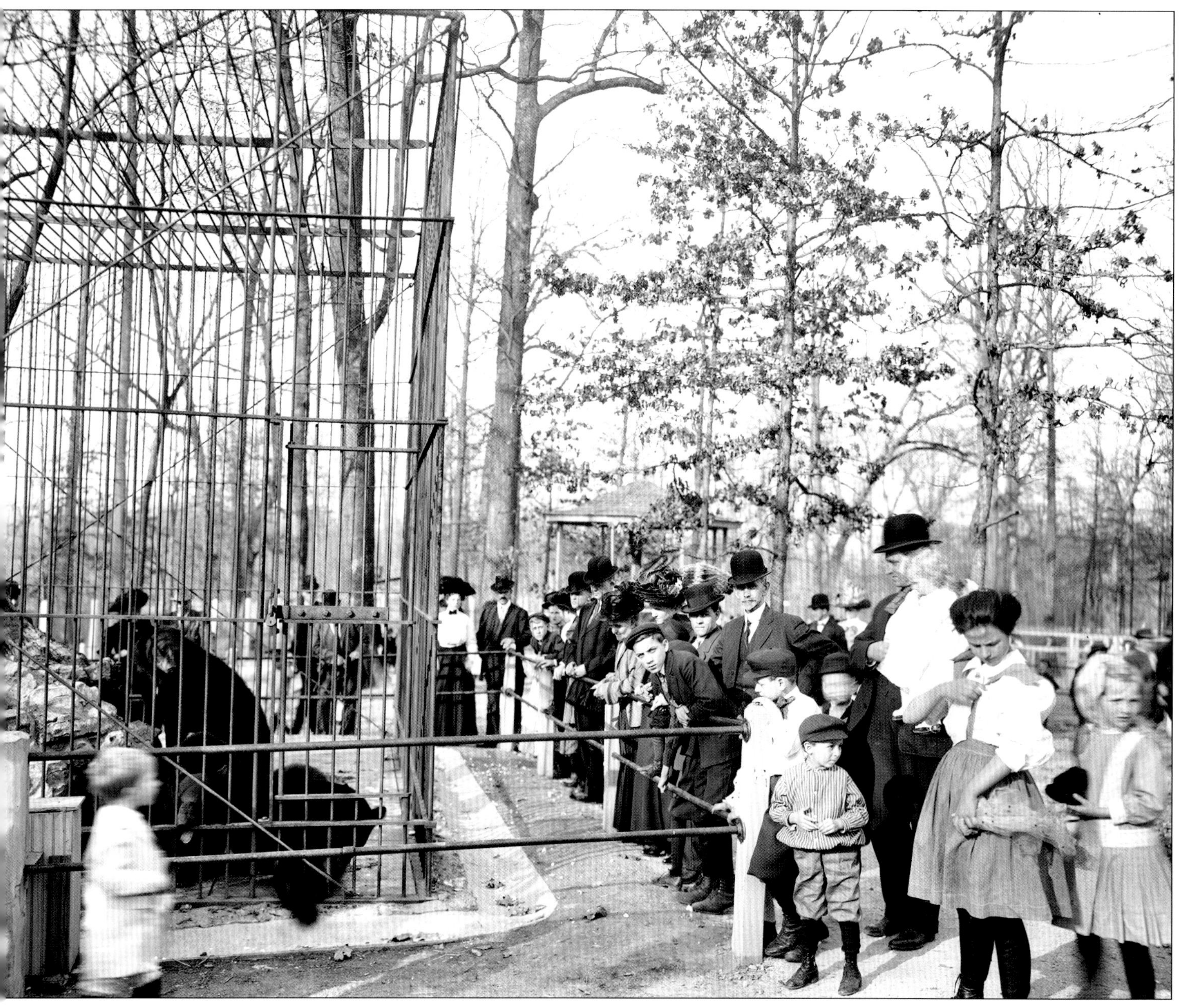

NATCH THE BEAR

AN INSPIRATION

In 1904, Natch the Bear was the mascot of the Memphis Turtles baseball team. With no home, he was kept chained to a tree in Overton Park. Colonel Robert Galloway, who was caring for the bear, starting looking for funds to build Natch a home. After a few other abandoned wild animals ended up in Galloway's care, he decided to build a zoo for them. Finally, in 1906, the Memphis Park Commission allotted $1200 to create a Memphis Zoo. Today, a plaque marks the spot where Natch was once chained, to commemorate the Zoo's first animal.

PETE GRAY

ONE-ARMED BALLPLAYER

In 1921, the smart money was that Pete Gray's baseball dreams were over when the six-year-old lost his arm in the spokes of a farmer's wagon. Gray liked the long odds. He learned to bat and field one handed with such skill that he made it to the majors. It was something to see, Gray catching the ball in his glove, which he then removed, transferring the ball back to his hand to throw in one fluid motion. Gray was the 1944 Southern League's Most Valuable Player when he was with the Memphis Chicks.

In 1945 Gray moved to the majors with the St. Louis Browns. The show was short-lived though, and with the return of many of baseball's greats from the front, Gray returned to the minors. Still, he became something of a hero to returning servicemen who had been disabled in the war. He passed away in 2002.

Photograph by Sports Illustrated

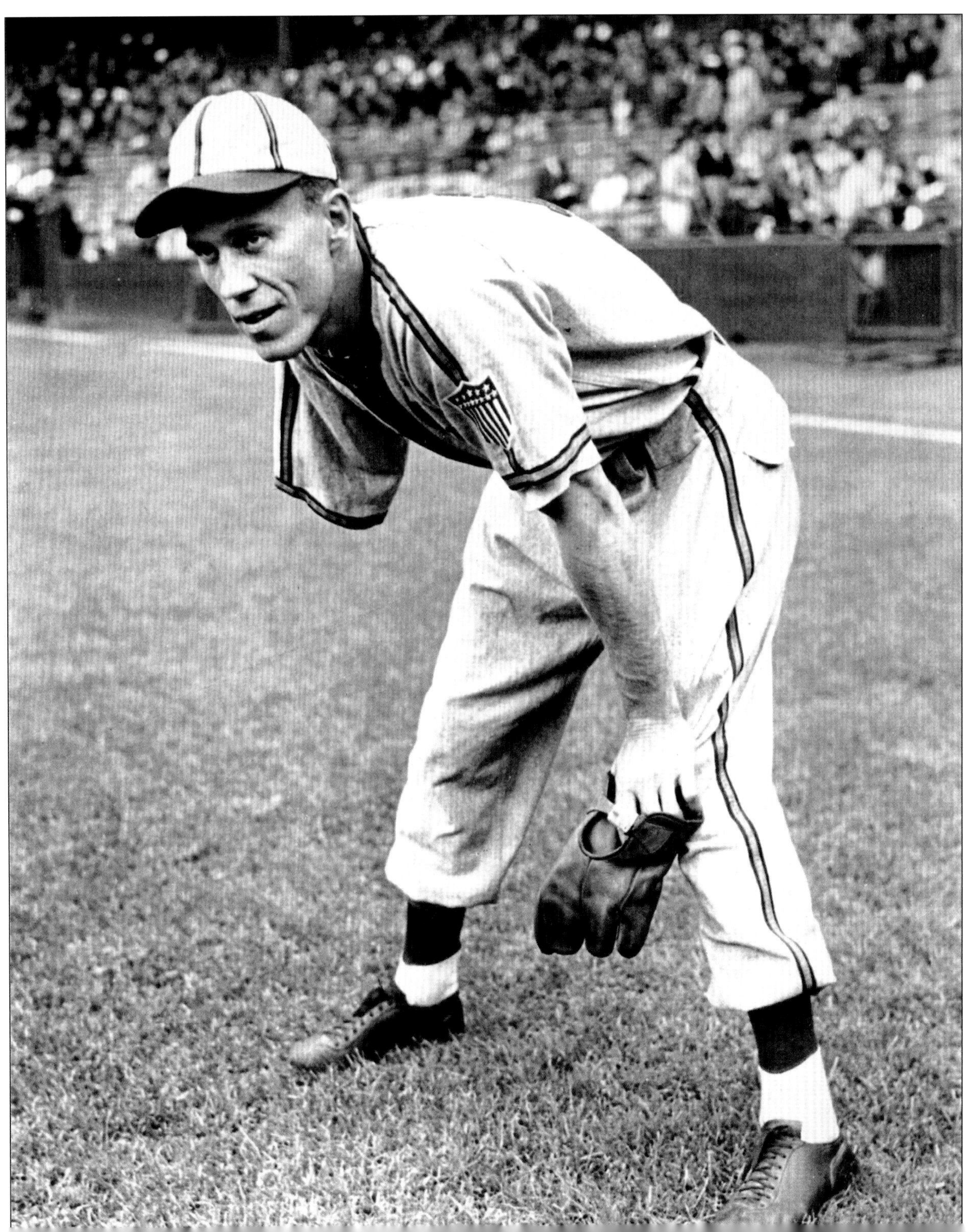

Law & Politics

Little-Known Memphians

Colorful Characters

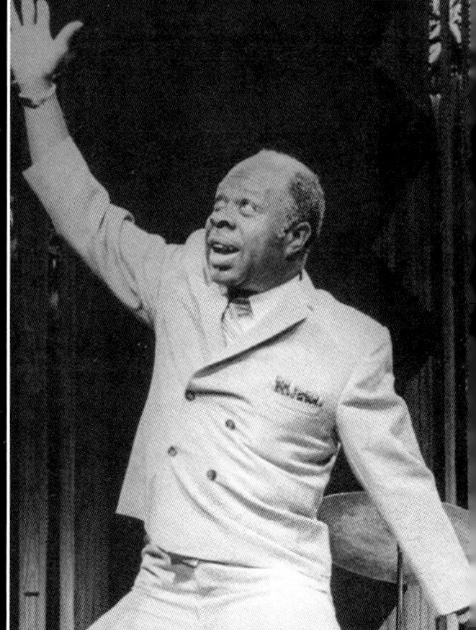

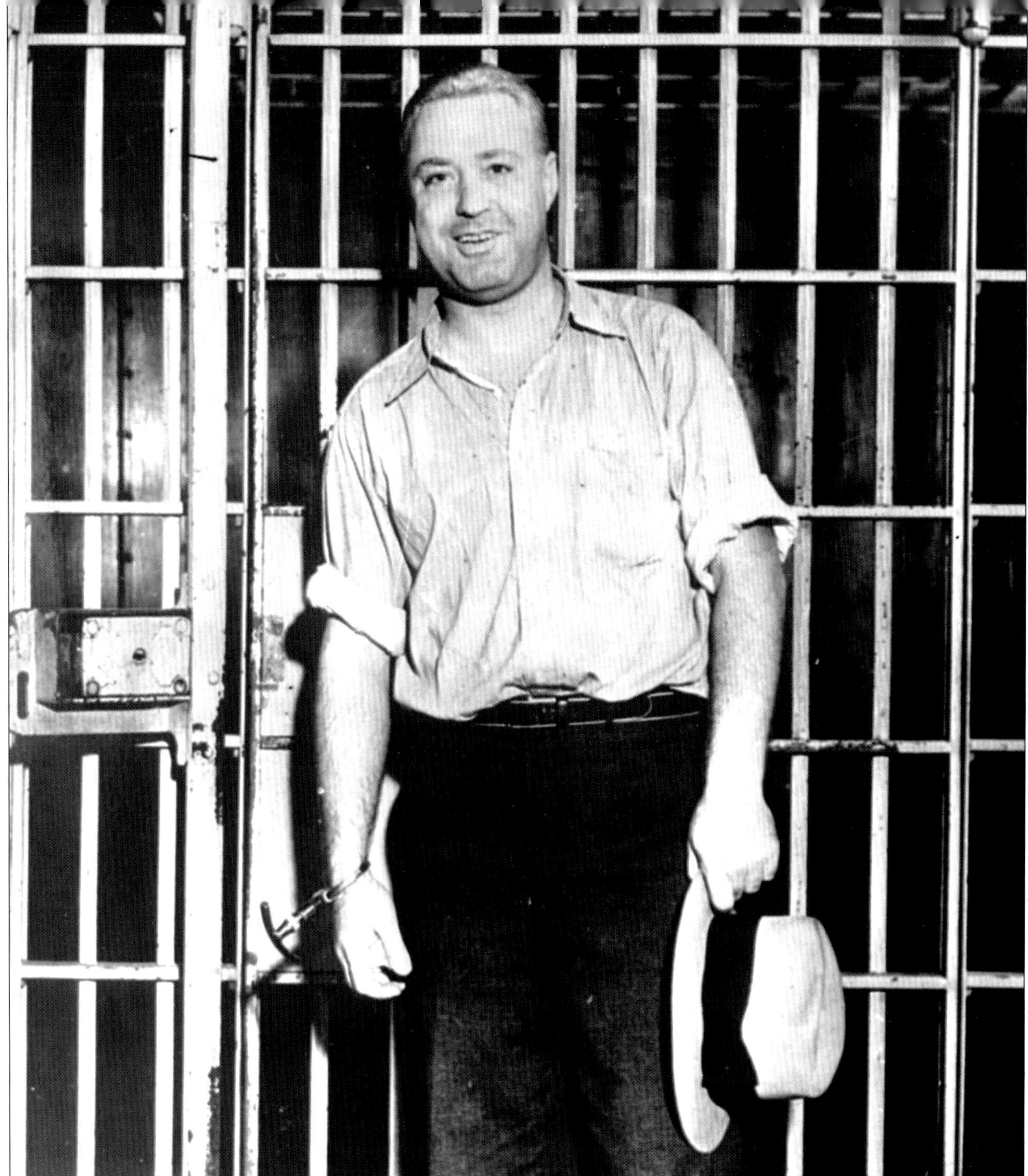

"MACHINE GUN" KELLY

OUTLAW

Choosing his own name from his favorite weapon, George "Machine Gun" Kelly was born George Kelly Barnes in Memphis in 1895. Living during Prohibition, he made a career of bootlegging and armed robbery, until, after a few encounters with Memphis police, he decided to head out of town. Barnes changed his name to George R. Kelly, and married Katherine Thorne, who bought him his first Thompson submachine gun. In 1933, Kelly and his gang kidnapped businessman Charles Urschel, demanding (and ultimately receiving) $200,000 ransom. Since Urschel made a point of leaving behind fingerprints and paying attention to everything from numbers of footsteps and background noises everywhere he was taken, Kelly was eventually identified and captured. The FBI found and arrested him, along with his wife, at their Memphis hideout on September 26, 1933.

Photograph by Getty Archive

JERRY LAWLER

WRESTLER

Born in Memphis, Jerry Lawler debuted as a professional wrestler in 1970. He won his first championship in 1971, and his career was on its way. Originally working as a "heel" (a villain character in wrestling storylines), he eventually became a "face" (fan favorite, often portrayed as the good guy or hero). In 1982, he began his notorious feud with Andy Kaufman, which resulted in a wrestling match between the two, right here in Memphis. (Lawler later appeared in the Kaufman biopic *Man on the Moon* as himself, revealing that the feud had been planned, and his relationship with Kaufman friendly.) With a career total of 164 championships, Lawler continues to work as a wrestling commentator, and was inducted into the WWE Hall of Fame in 2007.

Photograph by Getty Images

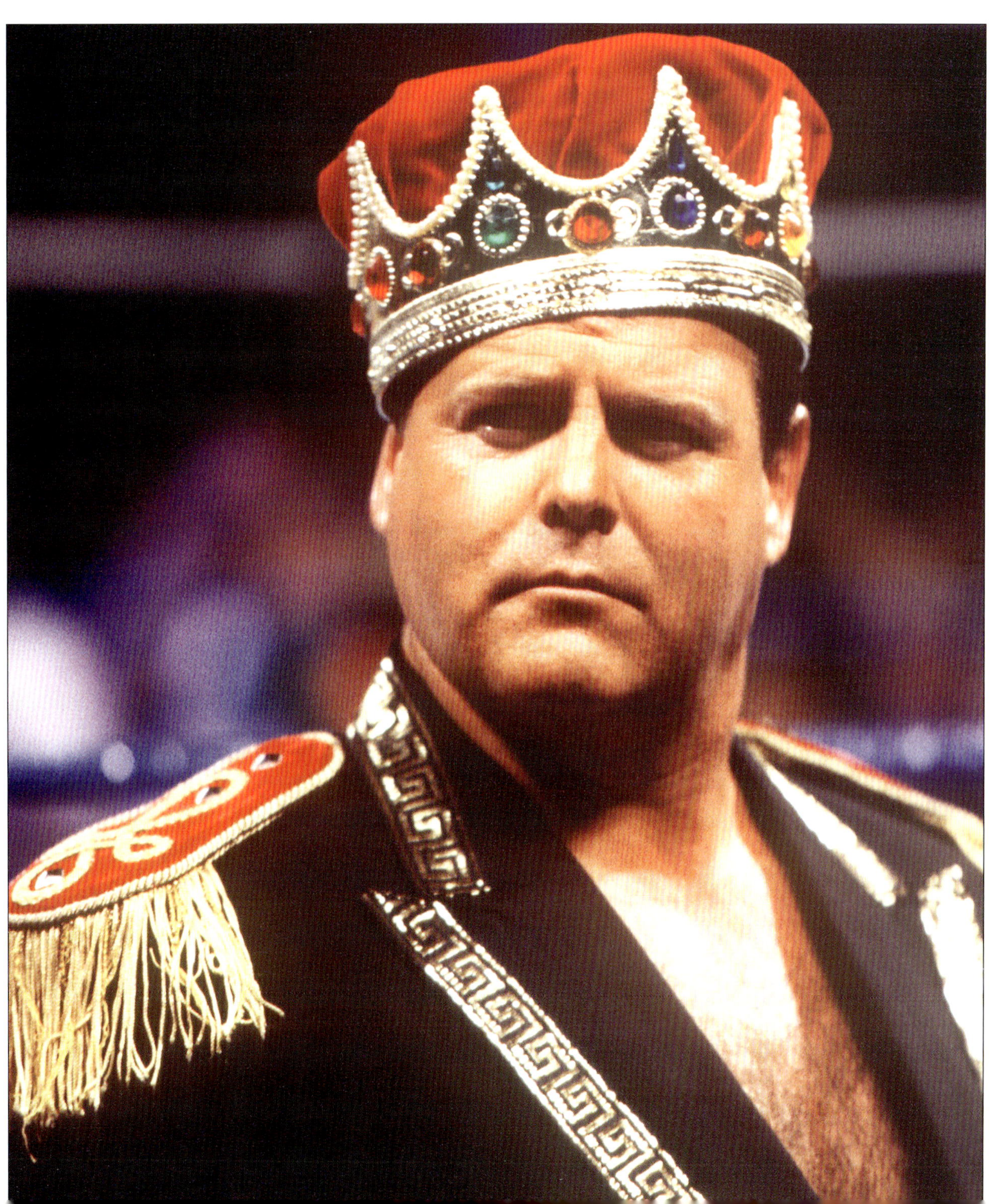

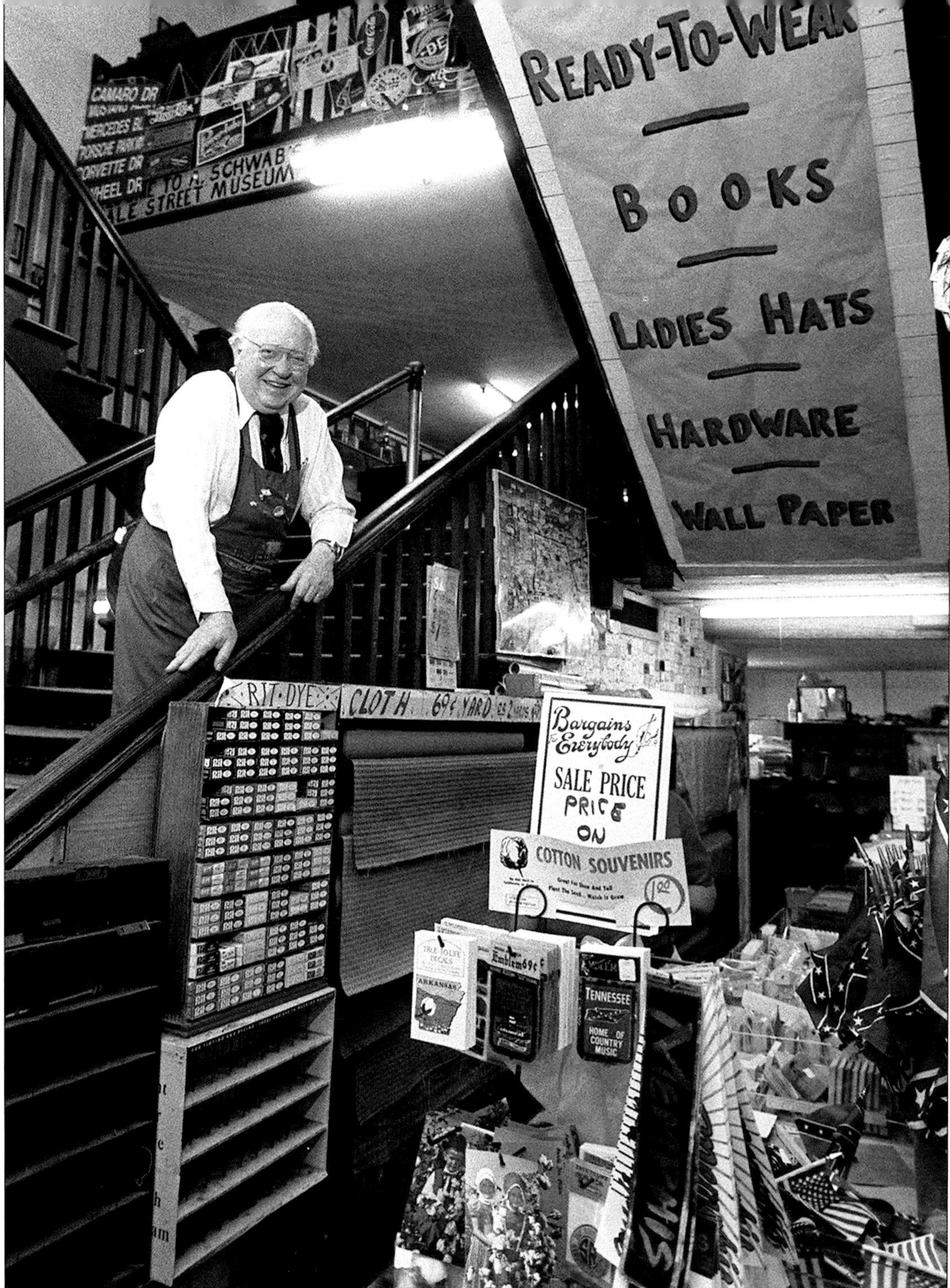

ABE SCHWAB

RETAILER

Abe Schwab took over the historic A. Schwab's Dry Goods store on Beale Street in 1978. Part retailer, part showman, he oversaw an empire that went from a men's clothing store to selling everything from books, overalls, candy, swords, lye soap, white cotton underwear, hoodoo items, viking helmets, tasers and kitchen utensils. While Schwab died in 2002, the store still sells hats . . . and switchblades.

Photograph by Commercial Appeal

RUFUS THOMAS

ENTERTAINER

The son of a sharecropper, Rufus Thomas loved performing at an early age, playing a frog in a school play at the age of six and becoming a tap dancer by the age of ten. After graduating from Memphis' Booker T. Washington High School, Thomas joined the Rabbit Foot Minstrels in 1936. As a singer, he recorded with both Sun Records and Stax Records, with a few hit songs, including "Walking the Dog." As a personality and self-dubbed "World's Oldest Teenager," he worked with WDIA radio, hosted a radio show called "Hoot and Holler," and hosted a live amateur show at the Memphis Palace Theater (where he, it is said, discovered B.B. King). Always a promoter of Memphis music, he was inducted into the Blues Hall of Fame in 2001, just a few months before his death.

Photograph by Hutton Archive

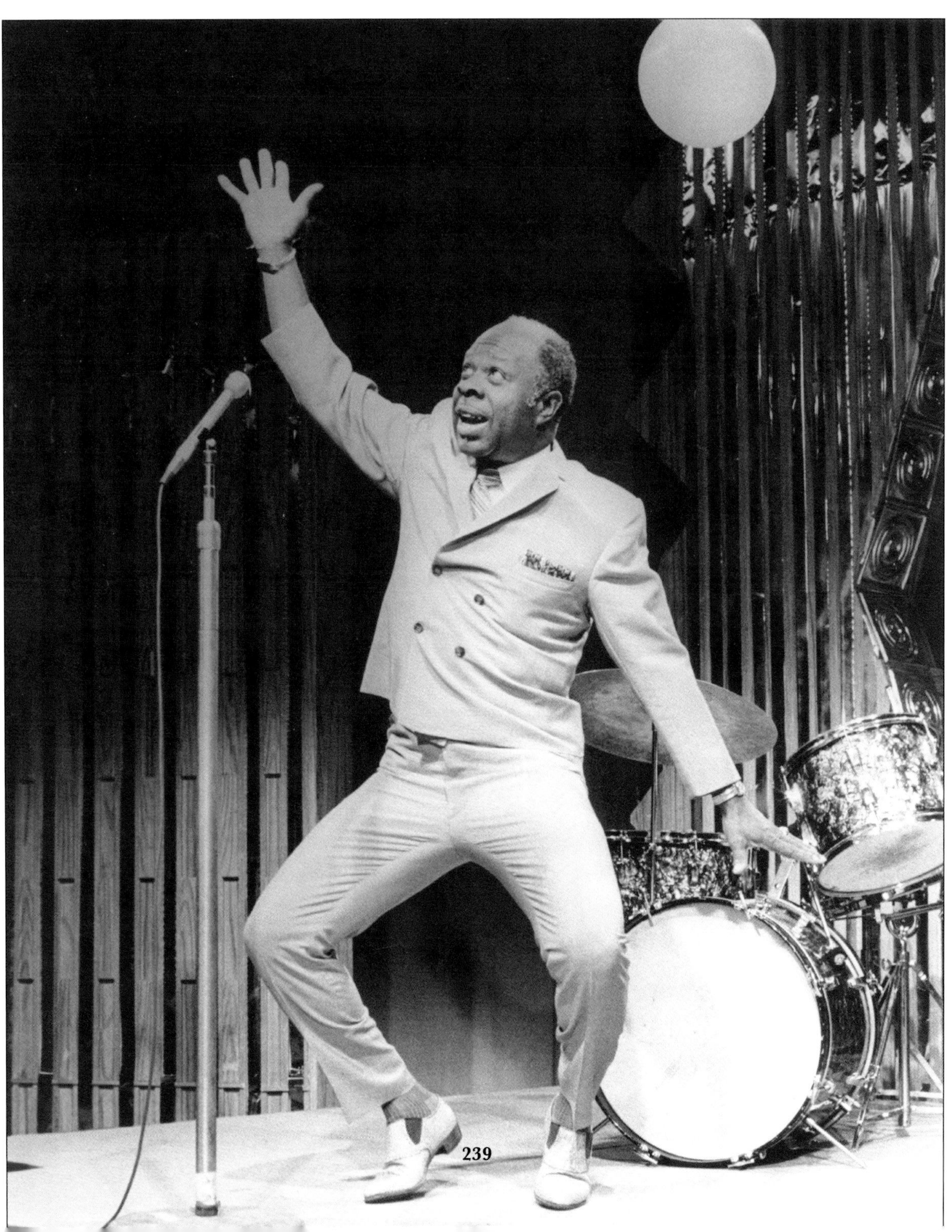

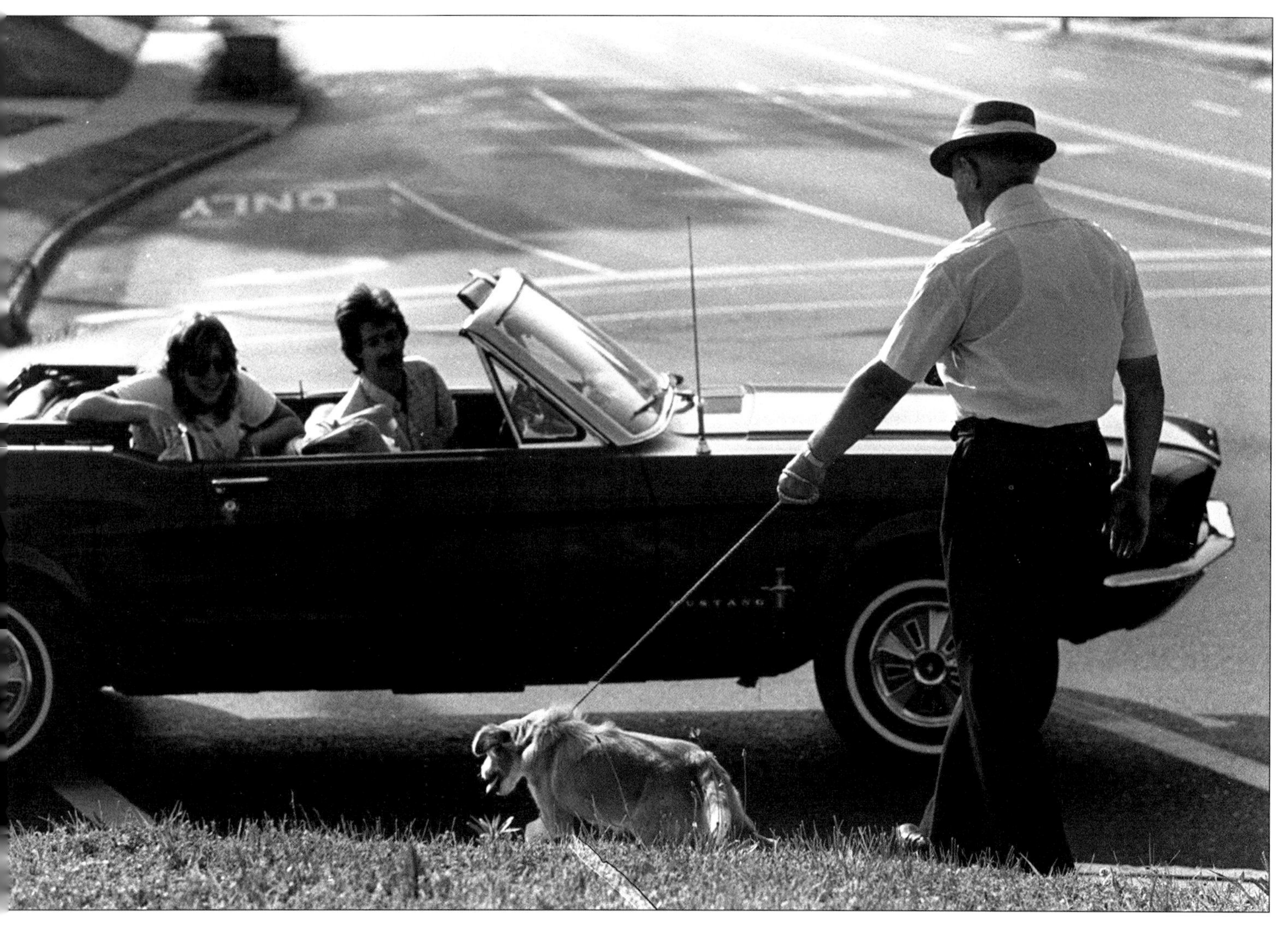

JOHN MARTIN

WAVER

Anyone with a morning commute that passed Poplar and Holmes in the eighties and nineties remembers the friendly wave of John Martin and his dog. A retired railroad man, he thought he should bring a little happiness to commuters every morning.

Photograph by Commercil Appeal

LAFAYETTE DRAPER

LEGENDARY BARTENDER

"I've made a lot of friends."
Lafayette Draper

Lafayette Draper has made a drink for about half the people in this book and nearly everyone reading it. He first started bartending at age 15 at the Elk's Club, standing in for his ill father who warned young Lafayette, "You're gonna hear things you don't want to hear, and see things you don't want to see."

He joined the Navy in 1955 and lived in Pearl Harbor and Japan. Returning to Memphis in '58 to finish high school, Layfayette worked his way up at the Crosstown Sears, still making drinks at the Knights Club and the Memphis Country Club. He's worked privately since 1976, and has made drinks for President George Bush, Sr., Baroness Rothschild, Armand Hammer, Trent Lott, Charlton Heston and two generations of Memphians. He's had two bars, Lafayette's Music Room and Lafayette's Corner, named in his honor.

Photograph courtesy Draper family • **Story** by Richard Murff

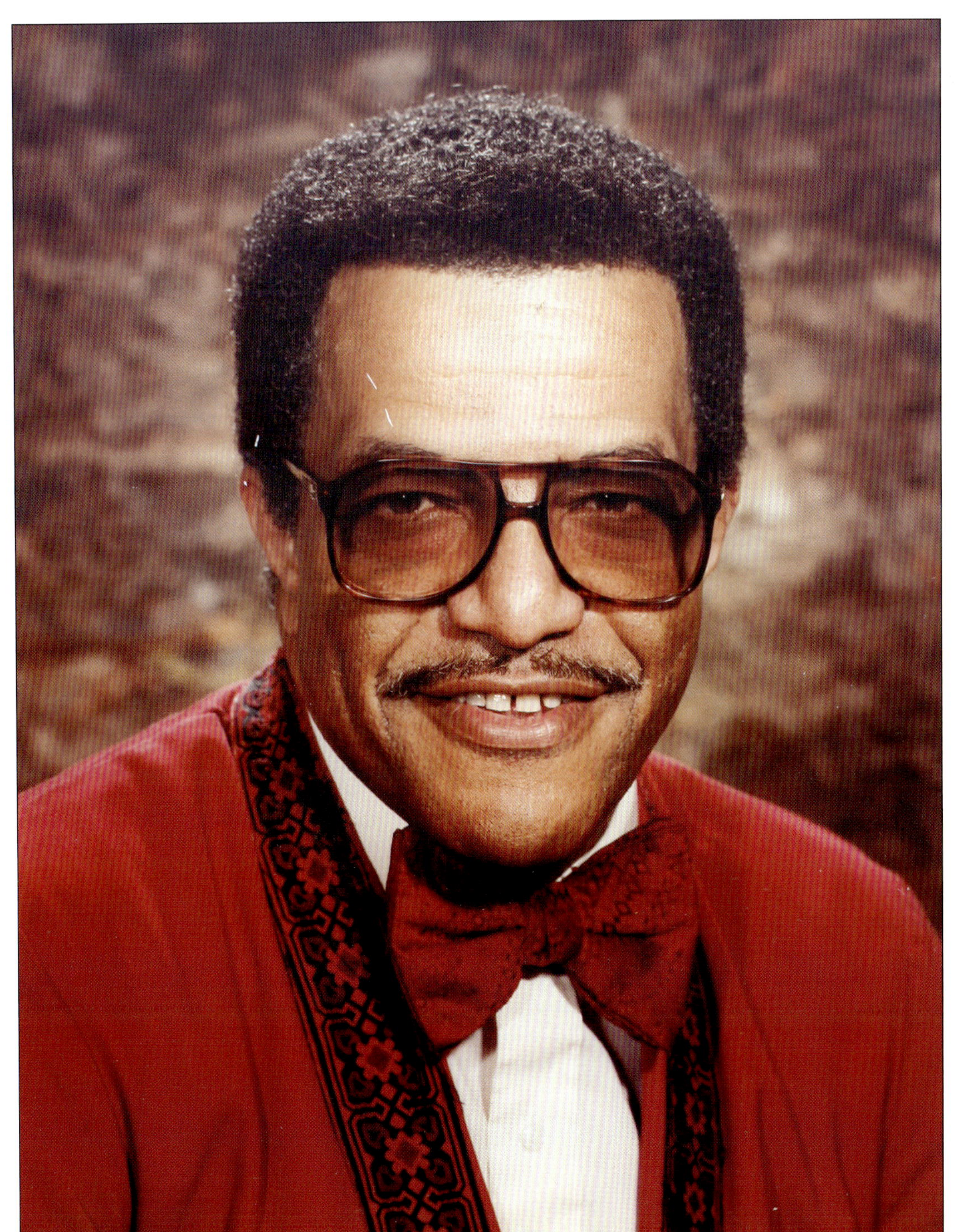

mphians

aracters

Beauties

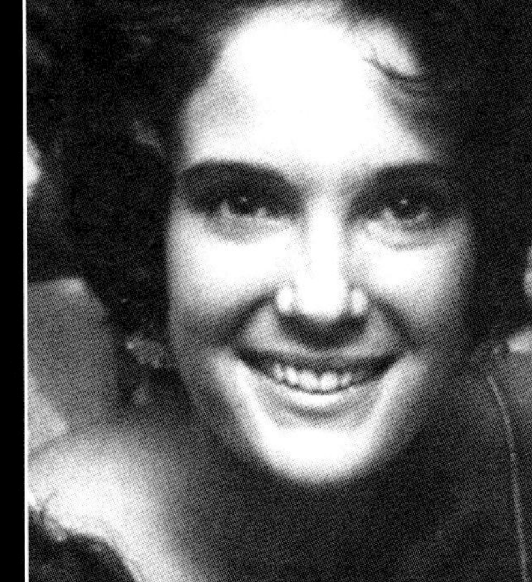

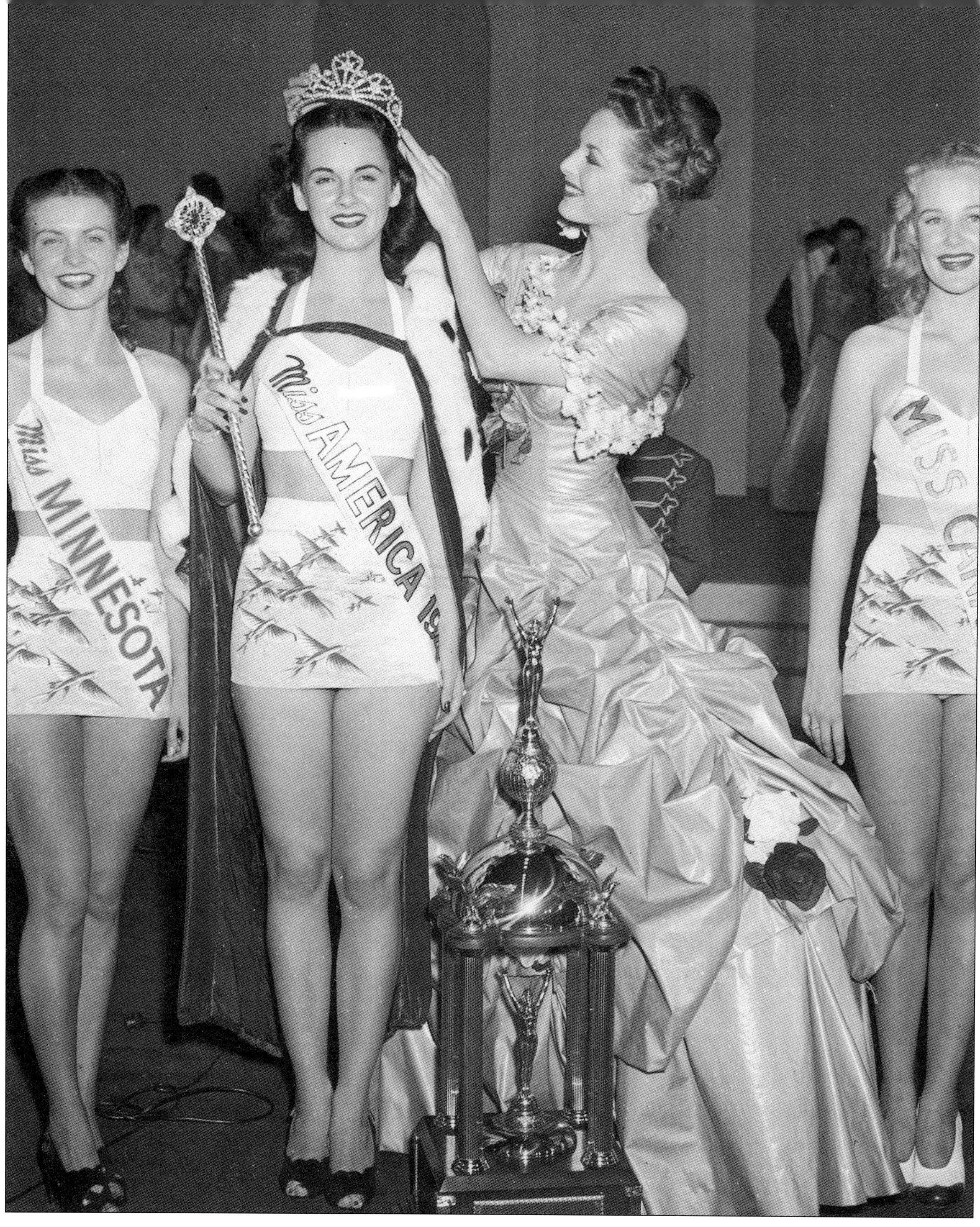

BARBARA JO WALKER

MISS AMERICA 1947

Photograph: Miss America 1946 Marilyn Buferd crowns the new Miss America 1947, Barbara Jo Walker, of Memphis, Tennessee. Walker was the last winner to represent a city (Miss Memphis) and the last to be crowned in a swimsuit. Hulton Archive/Getty Images

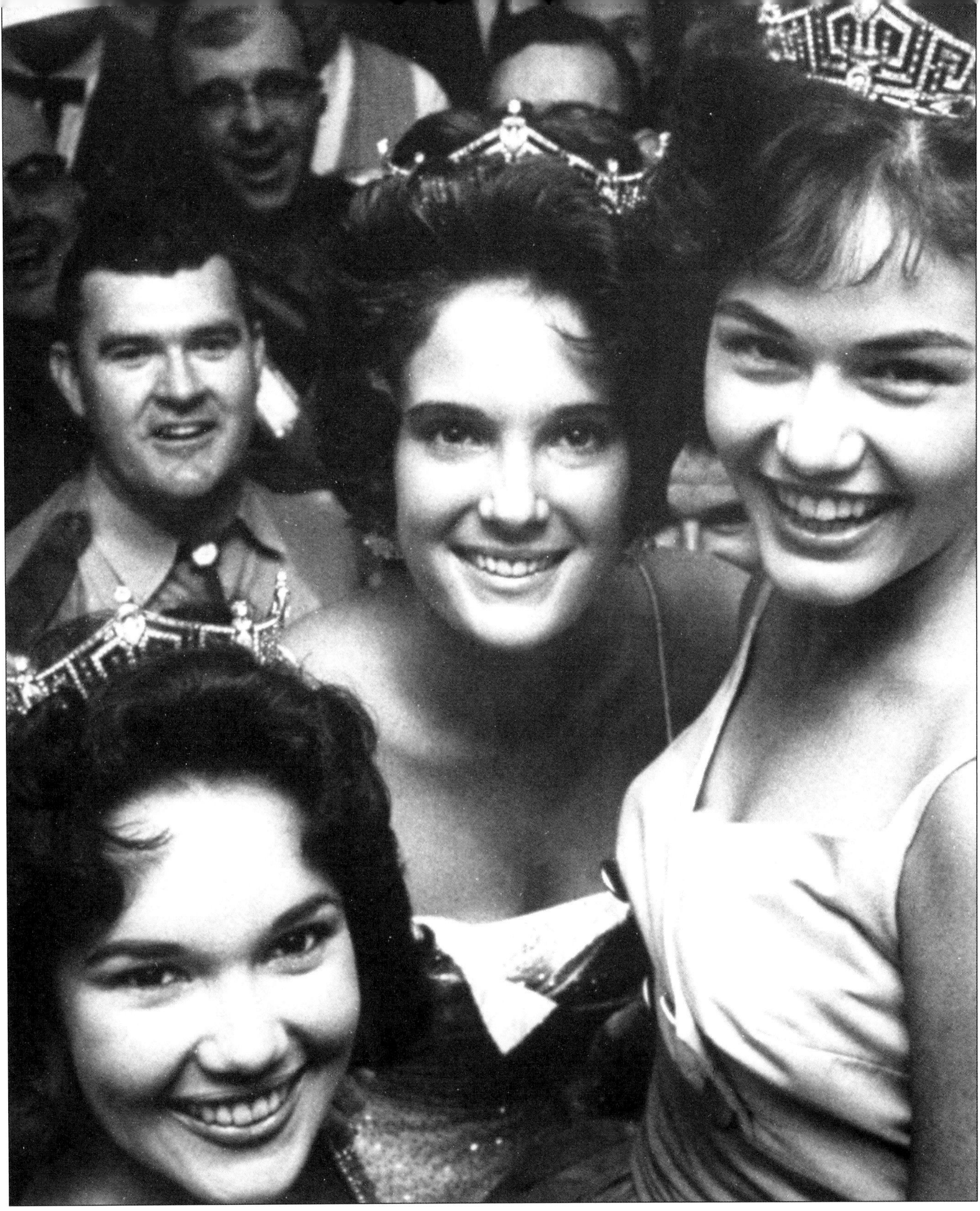

LYNDA LEE MEAD SHEA

MISS AMERICA 1960

Photograph: Miss America 1960 Lynda Lee Mead (center) attending a Chamber of Commerce convention with former Miss Americas Mary Ann Mobley (left) and Nancy Anne Fleming (right). Time Life Pictures/Getty Images

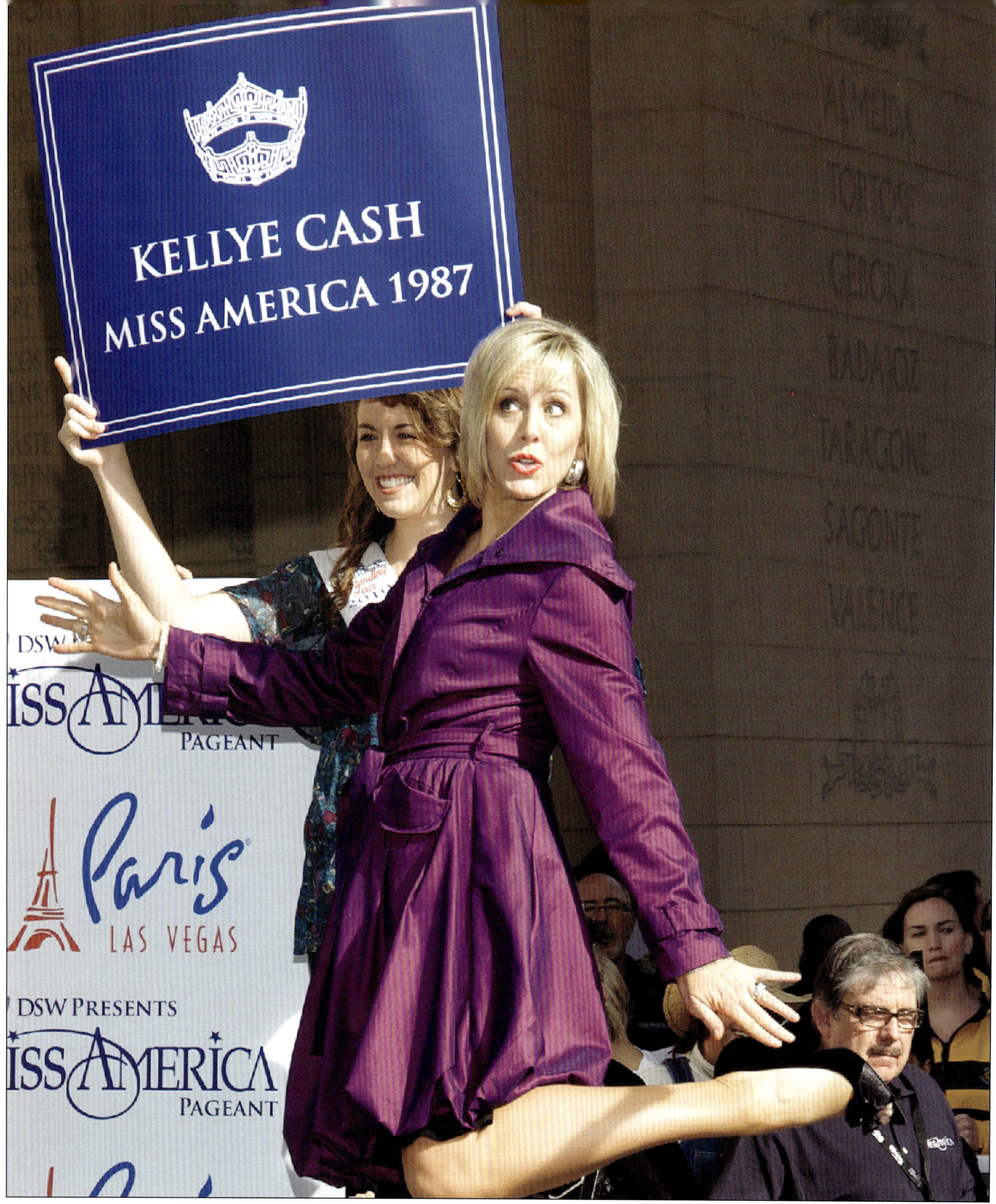

KELLYE CASH

MISS AMERICA 1987

Photograph: Miss America 1987 Kellye Cash attends the 2011 Miss America's 'Show Us Your Shoes' Parade at Paris Las Vegas. Photo by Mindy Small/FilmMagic

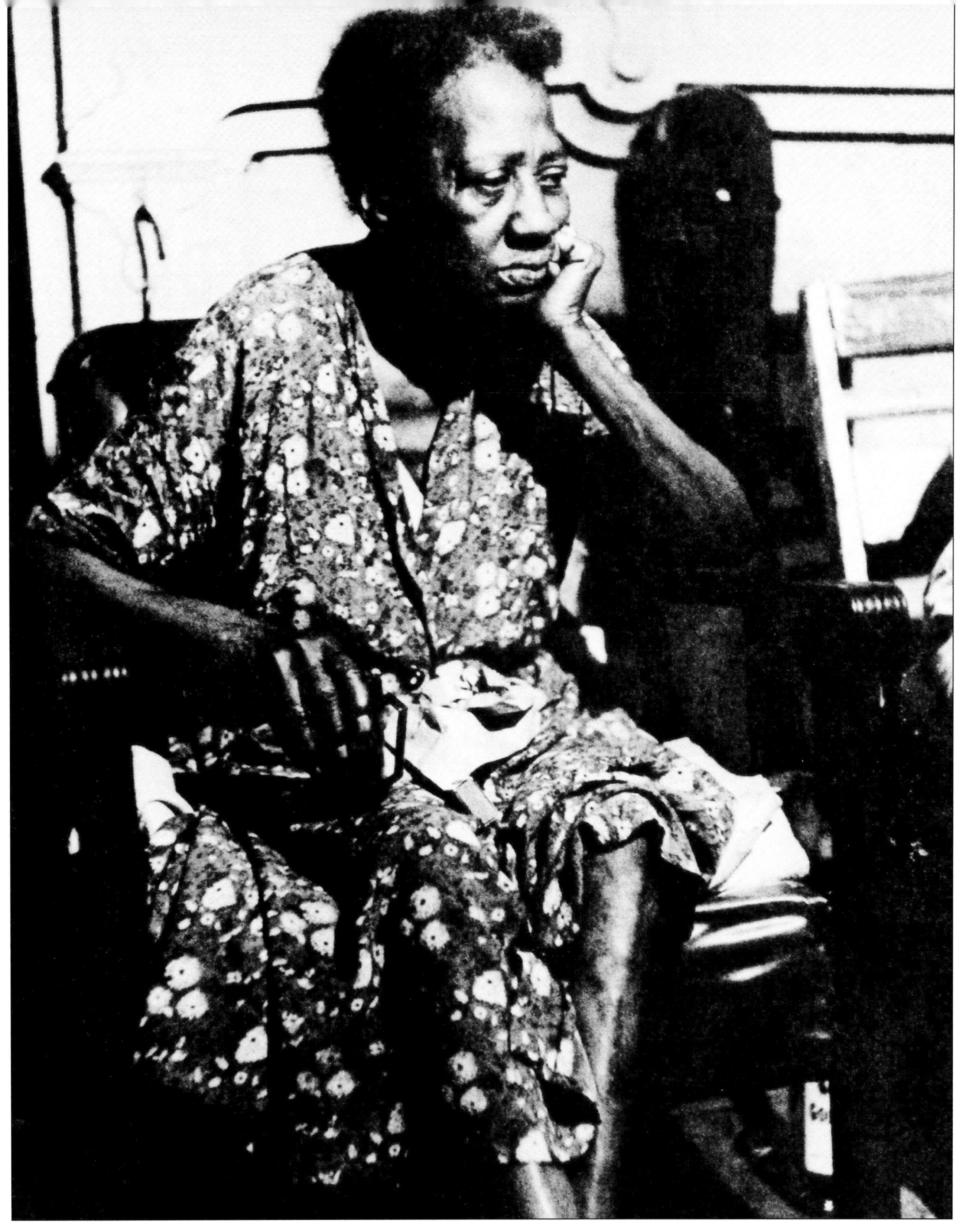

JENNIE SHADE

BEALE STREET BEAUTY

Photograph: Jennie Shade, said to be the most beautiful woman on Beale Street, was won over by a young Will Shade (see page 108) in the 1920s. Photograph (circa 1969) by Dick Waterman